Deer Hunting

Deer Hunting

4TH EDITION

Richard P. Smith

STACKPOLE
BOOKS

Copyright © 2011 by Stackpole Books

Published by
STACKPOLE BOOKS
5067 Ritter Road
Mechanicsburg, PA 17055
www.stackpolebooks.com

Printed in the United States of America

10 9 8 7 6 5 4 3

First edition

Cover design by Wendy A. Reynolds

Library of Congress Cataloging-in-Publication Data

Library of Congress Cataloging-in-Publication Data

Smith, Richard P., 1949–
  Deer hunting / Richard P. Smith. — 4th ed.
      p. cm.
  ISBN 978-0-8117-0597-4
  1. Deer hunting—North America. I. Title.
  SK301.S66 2011
  799.2'765—dc22

CONTENTS

ACKNOWLEDGMENTS

I would like to take this opportunity to thank all of my friends and relatives who have let me be a part of their deer hunts. Every experience made me a better and richer hunter. I also want to extend a sincere thank you to the many, many deer hunters who have shared their experiences with me over the years so I could write about them and share photographs of their success. What I have learned from all of you has made me a better hunter and I've tried my best to pass it on.

I'm glad my dad was a hunter. He passed that heritage and tradition on to me and my brother Bruce. Little did any of us realize where that would lead. Uncle George Smith deserves special appreciation for the introduction to deer hunting and for playing a major role in helping me become the hunter I am today. George made many deer hunts possible for my brother and me. I now share deer hunts with George's son Craig and his son Derek.

Uncle Leonard Yelle took me on the hunt during which I shot my first deer. My brother Bruce was on that hunt and many more since then. Bruce has always been willing to help drag when a deer was down, assist with photography, and provide support in so many other ways. Thanks, Bruce!

I want to thank Bill Jordan for allowing me to be a part of some of his deer hunts; Tony Knight for the hunts we have shared; Robbie and Marshall Digh for the continuing Canadian adventures; Brian and Shelly MacDonald for making me feel at home in their home, and their booking agent George Brainard; Buddy Chudy for making Manitoba hunts possible; Rob Keck, Hayward Simmons, and the gang at Trout Run for more valuable deer hunting experiences; Jimmy Dean, Greg Simons, Charles Dixon, John Weiss, Julian and Anita Toney, Mick and Gail Manson, Bob Eastman, and Lennie Rezmer for including me on some of their hunts; and Rudy Rudibaugh and Dick Rintamaki for helping me learn about mule deer.

I also want to thank Ted Nugent for allowing me to be a part of some of his hunts and being the upfront kind of guy he is as one of hunting's biggest promoters; Dick Johnson, Doug Leitch, Dan Vander Sys, and the guides I shared hunts with at The Wildlife Place; Dave Tuxbury, Penny Sigsby, and the guides at Deer Tracks Ranch; Dean Hulce along with the owners and staff at Smoky Lake Wilderness; Al Hofacker and Jack Brauer for allowing me to be a part of *Deer & Deer Hunting Magazine* for so many years as well as sharing their knowledge about deer hunting with me; many fine magazine ediors I have been privileged to work with; state and provincial wildlife biologists and researchers who have been so helpful in answering my many questions about deer and their management over the years; and Daryl Demoskoff and Karen Hill with Tourism Saskatchewan and other tourism personnel for assistance with hunts in their respective territories.

A special thanks to Buck LeVasseur who has allowed me to tag along while he gathered stories about deer hunting for his television show and who shared story ideas with me. Dan Bertalan has been kind enough to share his knowledge about shooting video so I, too, could begin videotaping deer and deer hunts. Thanks, Dan! I also want to thank Mike Avery for airing some of my deer hunting video on his television show. Many other people have helped me in some way with photographing deer. They include Mark Eby, Bill Mattson, Esther and Clyde Flink, Joan Saari, George and Ellen Planck, Justin Blain, Bucky O'Neil, and Randall Rogers. Richard Buquoi, Doug Blanchard, Bob Easterbrook Jr., Phil Henry, and Patti Charlier provided photos for use in this book. I also want to thank Betty Sodders for her continued support in promoting my books.

I want to thank the Lac La Belle Lodge crew, too, for allowing me to be a part of their tent camp experience and putting up with me. They are Troy Westcott, Dave Menominee (excellent camp cook), Bill and Matt Westerbrink, Bud Koljonen, and Bob Polly. Both Bob and Dave have been generous in allowing me to hunt from their blinds!

Jim Haveman has been a good friend and has also done some of my taxidermy work. Some other friends and relatives whose help I would like to acknowledge include Dan Schmidt, Jake Edson, Jim Butler, Larry Weishuhn, Gary Clancy, Greg Miller, Beryl Jensen, Ed Lindstrom, Mike Hogan, Fred and Tom DeRocher, Dave Raikko, Bruce Dupras, Ann and Dick Retaskie, Rick and Ricky Smith, George Gardner, Ken Lowe, Dave Richey, Tom Huggler, Jim Curtis, Rich and Bonnie Ryberg, Tira and Tom O'Brien, Terry Kemp, and many, many more. Thanks to every one who has been supportive, which includes my mother, brothers-in-law, mother-in-law, sisters-in-law and my two sisters, Kathy and Linda.

And I've reserved the biggest thanks of all for my wife Lucy. I couldn't have done many of the things that I've done or gone to the places I have without her help. And that's only the beginning. She's helped me and my career in many other ways, including making me a better person. Thanks, dear!

INTRODUCTION

One of the biggest rewards of being a book author is knowing that your work is read and appreciated. Over the years, I've received numerous compliments about previous editions of this book as well as other books I've written. One of the most memorable compliments I received about *Deer Hunting* was from a boy who called my home and left a message on my answering machine.

"I just wanted to tell you how much I've enjoyed reading your book *Deer Hunting,*" the boy said. "Thank you for writing it." Obviously nervous about making the call, he ended with, "I guess that's all I wanted to say."

He didn't leave his name or phone number, nor did he call back, but it was great to hear those words from a young man who was enthused and excited about deer hunting. I hope the book helped him become a better deer hunter and to enjoy deer hunting as much as I have. My hope is the same for everyone who reads this edition of the book as well as those who have read each of the previous editions.

Another compliment, which I received more recently and in person from an adult while autographing books at a hunting show, was perceptive, made me feel good, and has also stuck with me. "I've read a lot of the stuff you've written," the man said, "and it's obvious to me you are a hunter who happens to be a writer. Most of the other stuff I read is written by writers who want to be hunters."

I hope the contents of this edition of the book lives up to those compliments as well as many others I've received over the years. Each edition of the book contains as much new material as possible. Five new chapters have been added to this one and new information has been incorporated into each of the previously existing chapters.

Many new photos have also been added, and this time they are all in color instead of black and white, which should really improve the visual appeal of this edition.

The new chapters in this book are about how and where I got my best whitetail ("Best Buck at 50"), a controversial form of stand hunting that shouldn't be so controversial ("Facts About Baiting"), information about which does hunters should take for management purposes ("Doe Decisions"), what we can learn from penned deer ("Learning From Penned Deer"), and the importance of passing on the deer hunting tradition to future generations (Passing It On).

In some cases, chapters that were in previous editions of the book, such as the one on tracking, were entirely rewritten. Large sections of new material were added to others, such as the one on cameras. I didn't start hunting deer with a video camera until 2003 and that's also when I started filming deer hunts. The benefits of hunting and filming with a video camera that I've learned since then have been added to that chapter, as has information about digital still cameras.

In addition, the latest information about the spread of Chronic Wasting Disease (CWD) and tuberculosis (TB) among deer is in the chapter on diseases. Information about how to prepare your own European mount from bucks you bag has also been added to the chapter on antlers. And if you want help in choosing a crossbow to hunt deer with, that's been added, too, along with much, much more.

If you haven't read a previous edition of this book, all of its contents will be new to you, of course. There's more information than ever before between the covers of this book, all of which is designed to help you get the most out of deer hunting. I hope it accomplishes that goal.

About the Quarry

If you took whitetail bucks with the same size 8-point antlers from Minnesota, Virginia, South Dakota, Idaho, and Texas and put them next to one another, most hunters would not be able to tell where each animal came from. The bucks would look similar since they belong to the same species. The same thing would be true if you put mule deer from Colorado, California, and New Mexico side by side. Since they belong to the same species, they would all exhibit the same major features.

There are differences, however, between whitetails and mule deer from each of the states mentioned above that scientists have identified, and these differences have been used to divide species into subspecies. In most cases, the differences that separate subspecies are subtle, making them difficult to detect visually, but in some cases the differences are obvious. No less than seventeen subspecies of whitetails and eight subspecies of mule deer have been identified in North America. Another twenty-one subspecies of whitetails are found south of the US border. Three additional subspecies of mule deer have been identified in Mexico, two of which are restricted to islands.

Geographic isolation of a species of deer on islands often results in the animals evolving differently from those on the mainland as they adapt to their environment, contributing to eventual subspecies designation. A number of subspecies of whitetails are also restricted to certain islands. The geography and climates of the various regions where deer live on the mainland in the United States and Canada have also contributed to the evolution of subspecies designations.

Whitetails and mule deer represent the two major species of deer in North America. Columbian and sitka blacktails are considered subspecies of mule deer. Blacktails are examples of subspecies that are easy to identify because of their differences in appearance from other mule deer (those differences will be covered later). Whitetails are the most widespread and adaptable species of deer on the continent. One or

1

A mature Northern Woodland Whitetail buck that would weigh around 250 pounds. Bucks from this subspecies have weighed between 400 and 500 pounds. This is the most widely distributed subspecies of whitetail in North America.

more subspecies are found in every state in the lower forty-eight as well as in the southern tier of Canadian provinces. The range of the whitetail barely creeps into California, Nevada, and Utah, but the animals are still found within the borders of these states.

Where subspecies overlap, they frequently interbreed. Some states and provinces have more than one subspecies of whitetail, and the same is true for mule deer. Following is a breakdown of the seventeen subspecies of whitetails that inhabit North America and the states and provinces where they are normally found.

Subspecies of Whitetails

The northern woodland whitetail is the largest and most widespread of the subspecies. Two 402-pound (dressed weight) members of this variety are the heaviest known whitetail specimens. They were shot in Minnesota and had estimated live weights around 500 pounds. Whitetails of this subspecies with live weights in excess of 400 pounds have been recorded in Maine, Michigan, Wisconsin, and Iowa.

Michigan's heaviest whitetail was a huge buck that tipped the scales at 416 pounds in the round. Northville resident Gavrill Fermanis bagged the 12-pointer with bow and arrow in Oakland County on November 11, 1993. The story about how Fermanis connected on that exceptional whitetail can be found in book 4 of *Great Michigan Deer Tales,* one of a series of books I wrote about the biggest bucks bagged by hunters in that state.

Northern woodland whitetails are found in seventeen states and five Canadian provinces: Michigan, Minnesota, Wisconsin, New York, New Jersey, Massachusetts, New Hampshire, Maryland, Pennsylvania, Ohio, Delaware, Indiana, Illinois, Connecticut, Rhode Island, Maine, Vermont, Ontario, Quebec, Manitoba, New Brunswick, and Nova Scotia.

Virginia whitetails are found in Virginia, West Virginia, the Carolinas, Kentucky, Georgia, Mississippi, Tennessee, and Alabama.

Dakota whitetails inhabit the Dakotas, Kansas, Wyoming, Nebraska, Montana, Manitoba, Saskatchewan, and Alberta. This is also a large subspecies, with live

Coues whitetails like this buck in southern Arizona are one of the smallest subspecies that are hunted. They are also found in southwest New Mexico and Mexico.

weights of 300 to 400 pounds not unusual, especially in Canada. These deer grow big antlers, too.

The northwest variety calls the states of Oregon, Idaho, Montana (western), Washington, Nevada (northwestern), California (northeastern), and Utah (northeastern) home. They also reside in eastern British Columbia and western Alberta.

There are two distinct populations of Columbian whitetails that live in specific regions of Washington and Oregon. One population lives along the Columbia River, which the subspecies is named after, in Washington's Wahkiakum, and Cowlitz Counties and Oregon's Clatsop, Columbia, and Multnomah Counties. The second population is in southwest Oregon's Douglas County in the Umpqua River Basin.

Both populations were considered endangered and listed under the Endangered Species Act at one time. The Douglas County population of Columbians has recovered to the point that they are now hunted. The population along the Columbia River is still in the recovery stage.

Columbian whitetails were placed on the federal endangered species list in 1968. At that time, there were only estimated to be two thousand of the deer along the Umpqua River in Douglas County. There are now more than six thousand in that county. The Oregon Department of Fish and Wildlife delisted the species in 1996 and the federal listing was changed in 2003, opening the door for the establishment of a hunting season.

Coues or fantail whitetails inhabit desert regions of southern Arizona and southwest New Mexico, with far more of their range extending southward into Mexico. A few coues whitetails inhabit southeastern California bordering Arizona.

The Texas whitetail is found across the western two-thirds of the state it is named for, as well as in eastern New Mexico, western Kansas and Oklahoma, southeastern Colorado, and northern Mexico where it borders Texas.

A Kansas strain lives in its home state plus Oklahoma, Nebraska, Arkansas, eastern Texas, Missouri, Iowa, and Louisiana. This strain of whitetail grows large, both in body and antlers.

Three subspecies of whitetails live in Florida. The most widespread subpecies is appropriately referred to as the Florida whitetail. It is distributed over most of the state and into southeast Georgia. The Coastal Florida subspecies is distributed in the state's panhandle, southern Alabama, and Mississippi. The smallest subspecies is restricted to the Florida Keys and is called the Key deer.

Key deer are listed as an endangered species and can't be hunted, but their numbers have increased during recent years. There were only eighty Key deer on the National Key Deer Refuge near Key West when the refuge was formed in 1957. A recent census came up with as many as nine hundred of the deer on the refuge. The highest numbers of Key deer live on Big Pine Key.

Six subspecies of whitetails in the U.S. besides Key and Columbian whitetails in the northwest have very limited distribution, as indicated by their names: Carmen Mountains whitetails (Texas); Avery Island whitetails (Texas and Louisiana coasts); Bull's Island, Hunting Island, and Hilton Head Island whitetails (all in South Carolina); and Blackbeard Island whitetails (Georgia).

Some subspecies of whitetails have been introduced into areas where they wouldn't otherwise be found, which may account for some variations in the distributions listed above.

Mule Deer

There are eight subspecies of mule deer in North America. Mule deer are primarily western animals, confined to roughly the western third of the continent. They are found from the southeastern portion of Alaska to northern Mexico. Their extreme eastern range includes southwestern Manitoba and western portions of the Dakotas, Nebraska, Oklahoma, and Texas.

The Rocky Mountain variety of mule deer is the most widely distributed. In addition to the eastern boundary of their range mentioned above, they are found from northern portions of British Columbia and Alberta southward into northern Arizona and New Mexico.

Rocky Mountain mule deer are also the largest subspecies. The heaviest bucks on record came from Colorado. One had an actual dressed weight of 360 pounds and an estimated live weight of approximately 450 pounds. The largest weighed 410 pounds dressed and had an estimated live weight around 520 pounds.

Desert mule deer inhabit southern Arizona and New Mexico and western Texas. Their range extends southward into Mexico.

A total of six subspecies of mule deer are found within the borders of California, with the ranges of two of those limited to that state. The Inyo mulie is named for the county it primarily occupies on the east side of the state, but some of these animals are found in neighboring counties as well. California mulies reside in a band of habitat that extends east to west across the state north of the Inyo's range and then southward along the coast to Los Angeles. Southern mule deer are limited to an area from Los Angeles southward into Mexico along the coast.

Another subspecies of mule deer that inhabits the southeastern corner of California is referred to as the Burro deer. These mulies are also found in southwestern Arizona and Mexico. Rocky Mountain mulies inhabit northeastern California, and the final subspecies that lives in the state is the Columbian blacktail. The range of Columbian blacktails includes the coast and coastal mountains of the northern one-third of California northward through the southern half of British Columbia, including Vancouver Island and other islands along the coast.

Sitka blacktails are the smallest subspecies of mule deer and are found on islands along the coast of northern British Columbia and southeast Alaska.

As with some of the subspecies of whitetails, mule deer are not hunted in every state or province where they are found. Low densities in the extreme limits of their range prevent hunting of some populations.

The differences between subspecies of whitetail and mule deer are mostly variations of size, coat color, tail markings, geographic location, and other habitat adaptations. As mentioned earlier, most whitetails look alike. To the untrained observer, it can be difficult to tell many of the subspecies apart.

The differences between mule deer subspecies are more apparent. Mule deer are so named because of their large ears, which resemble those of mules. Six of the eight subspecies of mulies have narrow, ropelike tails. The undersides of mule deer tails are hairless. When running, this deer holds its tail clamped against its distinctive white rump. As the

Top: Rocky Mountain mule deer are the most widely distributed subspecies. They are also the largest. This buck is browsing and has 4 x 4 bifurcated antlers typical of mulies. Bottom: A Columbian blacktail deer with the characteristic black tail, photographed in Washington State. This buck is just starting to grow his new set of antlers. Blacktail deer are a subspecies of mule deer.

name implies, blacktail tails are black; the tails of the two subspecies of blacktails are much wider than those of other mule deer, but not as wide or long as those of whitetails.

Whitetails get their name from the distinctive white undersides of their tails, which they raise and flash as a warning signal as they run when alarmed. Many deer

Top: Different colored tails of a pair of whitetail bucks bagged in Manitoba. Their coat color was also different. Bottom: Mule deer have a prominent white rump, with a white, ropelike tail that has a black tip.

hunters may not realize that the tops of whitetail tails can be brown, gray or black or a combination of those colors. I've seen twin fawns born to the same whitetail doe, one with a black tail and the other with a brown tail. I took a photo of a pair of bucks bagged from the same area in Manitoba, one of which had a black tail. The tail on the second buck was mostly brown, but had some black near the tip. The coat colors of both bucks were different, too.

Telling Whitetails and Mulies Apart

There is also usually an obvious difference between the normal antler structure of adult whitetails and that of mature mule deer bucks. Typical whitetail racks exhibit unbranched tines rising from main beams. Points beyond the brow tine on mule deer antlers typically fork. Blacktail antlers are generally smaller than those of their mule deer relatives.

Another feature that usually varies between mulies and whitetails is ear size. Mulies typically have much larger ears than whitetails. Coues whitetails have larger

Top: Mule deer are so named because of their large, mule-like ears like the ones on this doe in Utah. Mule deer ears are much larger than those of whitetails. Bottom: Metatarsal gland (white hair) of a whitetail deer. These glands are much longer on mule deer.

ears than normal for the species, which is thought to be an adaptation to their desert environment.

A less obvious external difference between whitetail and mule deer is the size of their metatarsal glands. Metatarsals are located on the outside of the lower hind legs of deer. A patch of white hair marks the location of each metatarsal. Metatarsals are about an inch long on whitetails, more than two inches long on blacktails, and about five inches long on other mule deer.

Whitetails and mulies have four additional glands. The largest and most noticable to hunters are the tarsals. Tarsal glands are on the inside of the hind legs at the knee joint. The hair covering these glands is often stained dark during the rut.

Interdigital glands are found between the toes on each foot and deposit scent everywhere a deer steps. Does locate their fawns by following the scent from their interdigital glands and fawns can, likewise, trail their mothers in the same way. Bucks also rely on scent from interdigital glands to follow does during the rut. Whitetail deer that are alarmed sometimes stomp their feet before running off. When

Interdigital glands are between the toes on the hooves of deer. Each hoof has two toes.

they do this, more than the normal amount of interdigital scent is deposited. Other deer that encounter such scent may become alerted.

Preorbital glands are at the front corners of the eyes near tear ducts. Whitetail bucks often rub these glands on branches above scrapes during the rut as well as on saplings that they have scarred with their antlers.

Deer also have forehead glands. These glands are most active during the fall breeding season. When I've observed bucks throughout the year, I've watched the hair on the tops of their heads change color due to the increased activity of these glands. Scent from forehead glands is frequently applied to trees and saplings that bucks rub their antlers on.

When running, North America's two species of deer can be differentiated by their gait. Mule deer employ a stiff-legged bounce called stotting. Whitetails run in typical headlong fashion, but also make lengthy leaps or bounds. Deer may cover as much as thirty feet in a forward leap or bound. Whitetails have been known to scale barriers eight and one-half feet high.

Top speed for mule deer has been clocked at from 25 to 30 miles an hour. Whitetails are capable of speeds from 35 to 40 miles per hour, but are probably moving at closer to 20 or 25 miles per hour in hunting conditions.

Heights and Weights

Most deer hunters overestimate the size, both in height and weight, of deer. Mule deer typically measure from 36 to 42 inches high at the shoulder. The smaller blacktails stand a maximum of 38 inches at the shoulder, with most blacktails standing three feet high. Most whitetails that are hunted range between 32 and 42 inches in height. Big whitetail bucks will measure 40 to 42 inches high. The smallest whitetails (Keys deer) stand only 24 to 26 inches high at the shoulder.

Average field-dressed weights for adult bucks of the largest subspecies fall in a range from 150 to 200 pounds. Dressed weights of blacktails and southern whitetails range from 80 to 150 pounds.

Generally, deer will lose one-fifth of their weight during field dressing. A rough determination of a whitetail's or mule deer's live weight can be made by dividing the dressed weight by four, then adding the resulting number to the dressed weight. The weights listed below (dressed weight first, followed by live weight) should be accurate in most cases: 80, 105; 90, 115; 100, 130; 110, 140; 120,155; 130, 165; 140, 180; 150, 190; 160, 205; 170, 215; 180, 230; 190, 240; 200, 255.

Bucks may lose as much as 20 percent of their weight during the breeding season (rut), which occurs in the fall.

Senses

To be a successful hunter, you must learn how to overcome a deer's senses by reducing your chances of being seen, heard, and smelled.

For many years, it was thought that deer are color-blind. Recent research indicates they see some colors well, such as blue, green, and yellow, but they do not have color receptors in their eyes that enable them to see red and orange like we do. Consequently, reds and blaze orange don't stand out in the natural environment to deer like they do to people. Deer may, in fact, see color in much the same way as people who are color-blind.

So hunters who wear blaze orange, which is required during firearms seasons in many states and provinces for safety, need not worry about the color alone alerting deer to their presence. In situations where a full outer suit of orange is worn for hunting, it is better if the clothing has a broken pattern rather than being solid orange. The broken pattern will help hunters blend into their surroundings just like normal camouflage patterns do. The broken pattern of camo clothes that utilize various shades of green, brown, black, and gray is effective at reducing the visibility of hunters to deer as long as movements are kept to a minimum.

Movement, or the lack of it, on the part of hunters is far more important than the color of their clothing when it comes to avoiding detection by deer. Movement attracts the attention of deer. Hunters who remain motionless usually go undetected. Those that are spotted are often a source of curiosity rather than alarm. Whitetail and mule deer's sight is better to the sides than straight ahead because of the position of their eyes, but they frequently move their heads to get the best view possible of objects that catch their attention. Animals that live in open country tend to depend on their vision more than those in heavily wooded terrain.

It isn't unusual to have deer cautiously approach an immobile person they can't smell. They recognize the object as an addition to the landscape, but are unsure of what it is, so they are curious. Sometimes they nervously stamp a front foot or bob their heads up and down if they suspect danger. I have frequently seen deer do this while I was bowhunting or trying to photograph them. Occasionally, a wise doe will whirl as if to run off, but then will stop quickly and look back in an apparent attempt to catch me in the act of moving.

The sense of hearing is well developed in deer. Only sounds that are not normal in their environment, such as human voices, metallic sounds, fabric rubbing against brush, or noisy human feet, unduly alarm them. Hunters who try to mimic the sounds of a walking deer or other animal while traveling through the woods are least likely to alert nearby whitetails or mule deer. A deer's hearing is one of the easiest senses to overcome, simply by being quiet when they are close.

Deer rely heavily on their sense of smell. It is probably their strongest defense against hunters and other predators. If the wind is wrong from a hunter's perspective, deer often smell hunters and change directions before exposing themselves. Animals that "wind" hunters sometimes make a noise by blowing through their nostrils to warn other deer of danger. This sound is often referred to as a snort, but I call it blowing. Both bucks and does make this sound. The noise they make sounds like a train whistle or someone blowing on an empty rifle cartridge. Chapter 12 covers how to best avoid being smelled by deer when hunting.

Vocalizations

Whitetails and mulies make more sounds with their mouths than most hunters realize, and a variety of calls that duplicate these sounds are available on the market. Calls will be discussed in more detail in chapter 11. The most common vocalizations are between does and fawns when the offspring are young, between bucks and does during the rut, and from deer that are distressed. Hunters who spend enough time afield will eventually hear some of these sounds.

Even though does and their fawns are most vocal when fawns are young, they continue to use calls to locate one another when separated during fall months, too. So it's not unusual to hear a fawn that loses track of its mother during hunting season making periodic bleating calls as it tries to reconnect with the doe. If the rut is underway when you hear a fawn calling for its mother, she may be with a buck nearby.

On a number of occasions while hunting I have heard bucks grunting as they followed does during the rut. I have heard penned bucks make similar noises. Most of the buck grunts I have heard have consisted of a single note, but one time when hunting in Georgia I heard and then saw a spike buck that was making grunts that consisted of two notes as he followed a doe. So, just like with most sounds made by wildlife, the same calls can vary between animals.

When in heat, does make an estrus call to announce their readiness to breed to bucks within earshot. I was treated to a display of this call by a doe in Michigan one November while dragging a buck I bagged earlier in the day. There was snow on the ground at the time and I was in a stand of open hardwood trees when the doe came trotting by, calling steadily as she traveled. She smelled the buck I was dragging when downwind about 40 yards away, then stopped and stood there calling, apparently trying to attract the dead buck's attention. The doe must have also smelled and seen me, but she ignored me until it was obvious her calls were in vain and she eventually moved on.

Another vocalization that whitetail bucks make in association with the rut is what have been referred to as growls. These sounds are most often made by bucks in a heightened state of arousal when competing with at least one other buck for a doe in heat. These sounds are also sometimes made by a buck when a doe in heat does not allow him to breed her, ignoring his advances.

The snort-wheeze is an aggressive warning sound made by both bucks and does that essentially communicates "stay away" or "back off" to another deer that is approaching. It starts with a short snort, followed by a drawn-out expelling of air through the mouth and/or nose. This sound is often heard during the rut when one buck does a snort-wheeze at a competing buck, but I've also heard and seen both bucks and does do snort-wheezes during the summer in response to approaching deer. One time during the rut I observed an adult buck that was so worked up that he made an exceptionally long, drawn-out snort-wheeze that resulted in him blowing bubbles out of his mouth.

While deer are being handled by biologists during live trapping and marking operations, they sometimes blat loudly. Deer probably make similar noises when attacked by predators. I've seen black bears catch and kill whitetail fawns on two occasions. In each case, the fawns made high-pitched cries from the time they were caught until they were dead.

Habitat and Home Range

Deer, especially whitetails, are adaptable. There aren't many types of habitat they don't occupy. As a general rule, however, both whitetails and blacktails inhabit thick, brushy terrain. Blacktail habitat rivals whitetail country for denseness and short sight distances in many cases. The larger varieties of mule deer are usually found in more open terrain than either black- or whitetails, but they can be found in stands of timber, too.

Mule deer are generally considered a migratory species; whitetails usually spend their entire lives in a limited home range of two square miles, and in many cases, less. The truth of the matter is that both species exhibit these traits from time to time.

Most mule deer have distinct summer and winter ranges. Summers are often

Both whitetails and mule deer are migratory, depending upon the terrain, habitat, and winter weather conditions where they live. This group of whitetails in upper Michigan is traveling toward a winter yard on a migration trail.

spent at higher elevations than winters. There is a downhill migration in the fall to escape heavy snows. As the snow melts in the spring or early summer the deer move uphill. Whitetails that live in mountainous or hilly terrain do the same. In South Dakota's Black Hills, for example, whitetails migrate between their low winter range and high summer range twice a year. The distance they travel can be as great as twenty miles.

Some whitetail deer in northern climates migrate to wintering areas called yards, which are primarily lowland swampy areas. Deer yards vary in size from a few square miles to hundreds of square miles. To reach yarding areas, many deer move south, toward an area where snow depths are less. Most of the time there is little or no elevation change between yards and summer range.

Deer that make seasonal movements, regardless of species, often use the same routes year after year, unless habitat change requires an adjustment.

Most whitetail deer spend their lives in a limited home range. Some blacktails and mule deer have adapted similarly where the climate permits. Whitetail bucks mark territory during the breeding season, primarily to announce their availability to does, but also to let competing males know about their presence. Mule deer are generally not territorial, roaming at will during the summer and fall. Mulies spooked by hunters may travel miles to a new area. Whitetails seldom roam far. If pushed out of their territories, they usually return.

Longevity

In the wild, most bucks don't live past three or four years, but older ones occur in remote or lightly hunted areas. Does tend to live longer than bucks because they aren't as sought after by hunters and they don't undergo as much stress as bucks do during breeding seasons. The oldest whitetails and mule deer normally occur in captivity, but some wild deer have attained ripe old ages, too.

The oldest mule deer on record, for example, is a blacktail doe that lived on Gambier Island, British Columbia, according to Leonard Le Rue III in his book *The Deer of North America.* The doe was born in the wild, but she became tame after being fed on a farm for years. She was estimated to be at least 22 years old when she died.

The oldest whitetail doe I have a record of was 24 years and 6 months old when she died in captivity at the Deer Ranch in St. Ignace, Michigan on January 27, 2002. She may be the oldest whitetail on record for North America. This doe, which was named Elizabeth, had thirty-eight fawns during her lifetime, including twins that were born in 2001. She was carrying her thirty-ninth fawn at the time of her death. The old doe was born on June 3, 1977 at the Deer Ranch and she spent her entire life there.

A captive whitetail buck in Clearfield County, Pennsylvania, that was raised by Ben Lingle of Linglewood Lodge is probably the oldest on record. That deer lived to be 20 years, 10 months old. Interestingly, that buck grew its largest set of antlers when it was $15^1/2$, but that deer didn't undergo the stresses wild deer do and it had access to the best food and care possible.

Ten-year-old deer are not common in the wild, but they do occur. A pair of whitetail does taken by hunters in Alabama were over twenty years old. One was twenty-one and the other was twenty-three. Michigan's oldest hunter-killed doe was $19^1/2$ when she was shot during November of 1967 in the Upper Peninsula. Her age was verified by cross-sectioning a tooth. A number of bucks that were between $10^1/2$ and $12^1/2$ years old have been documented in the Upper Peninsula over the years. The ages of the old Michigan deer were verified by counting rings (annuli) in cross sections of the animals' teeth.

The most common method of determining the age of deer is by examining their cheek teeth. Fawns generally have four cheek teeth on each of the upper and lower jaws. Three are premolars and one is a molar. Yearlings typically have two more molars, although one is usually not showing completely. By age $2^1/2$ all molars are completely visible and the three premolars, which were temporary, have been replaced by permanent premolars. After that point the amount of tooth wear is a primary age indicator. Criteria for determining age by tooth wear vary slightly between species of deer and even among members of the same species found in different regions.

A buck's age is seldom reflected by the number of tines on his antlers. Antler beam circumference is more closely related to age. In Nebraska, for instance, if the beam circumference one inch above the burr is greater than $3^5/16$ inches on whitetails, the buck is usually $2^1/2$ years or older. Mule deer of the same age will have a circumference greater than $3^1/16$ inches.

Breeding and Fawn Production

Bucks are polygamous, meaning they normally mate with a number of does. Bucks are capable of impregnating about twenty does, but this is seldom necessary in the wild unless there is an extremely lopsided sex ratio. The rut usually takes place from late October to December, but may be as late as February and March in some parts of the south. Peak breeding occurs during January in parts of Alabama and Texas.

Most of the does are bred during November in my home state of Michigan, with peak breeding being close to when firearms season begins on November 15. I managed to film and photograph a mature 8-pointer breeding a doe on November 13 one year. For the first time in my career, I was able to capture quality images on film and tape of a buck breeding a doe.

I had seen the behavior before a few times, but I either didn't have cameras with me or was in a poor position to photograph the action. One evening a number of years ago while bowhunting from a tree stand the week before firearms season, I watched a trophy 8-pointer breed a doe and then walk into a perfect opening for a bow shot. Unfortunately, my arrow hit a branch and was deflected.

I was preparing for the upcoming firearms deer season when I happened to be in the right place at the right time to photograph a buck breeding a doe on November 13th. I saw a doe that was acting strange. She was flicking her tail in a way I hadn't observed a doe do before. The fact that she was in heat was responsible for her actions.

She was soon joined by a nice 8-pointer and it didn't take long to figure out what was going on. The antlered whitetail followed every move the doe made. I've seen bucks courting does plenty of times before, but the pair most often wanders out of sight before anything happens.

Not this time. I had both my Canon video and still cameras with me. The video camera was on a tripod and I had the still camera fitted with a telephoto lens in my hands, ready, just in case something exciting happened. I framed the deer in the video camera and let it roll so I could also make some still photos. Seconds before the buck mounted the doe, I anticipated what was about to happen and focused on the stationary doe.

I started tripping the shutter as soon as the buck mounted the doe. The camera was in manual mode, so I had to cock it by hand for each frame. After years of experience, it doesn't take me long to advance the film on my cameras. That was before I started using a digital still camera.

There was only time to expose three images before it was all over. In those few seconds, I was able to capture the behavior that drives the whitetail rut and is responsible for so many of North America's successful deer hunts each year.

Under optimum conditions, where winters are usually mild, a percentage of young-of-the-year does will produce fawns. In poor habitat does may not be productive until they are $2^{1}/_{2}$ years old or older. Does must breed within a 24 to 30-hour period when in heat. If they don't, they will come into breeding con-

An eight-point whitetail buck breeding a doe in a matter of seconds.

dition again at 28-day intervals. Most adult does give birth to one or two fawns, but triplets aren't unusual.

Fertile Does

Some of the most fertile whitetail does have been carrying as many as seven developing fawns when they died. A doe that was killed near Madison, Wisconsin, as part of a culling operation to reduce chronic wasting disease (CWD) had seven developing fawns in her womb. Another Wisconsin doe that ended up as road kill was carrying six fawns. A less extreme example of how productive some whitetails can be is a doe killed on a highway near Ann Arbor, Michigan, that had four fawns inside her. Had the does carrying six and seven fawns survived to give birth, it is not likely all of their fawns would have survived.

The gestation period for deer is seven months. At birth, fawns usually weigh from five to eight pounds, but some males born to healthy does have weighed over ten pounds. The number of bucks born is usually slightly higher than the number of does.

Young deer rely on their spotted coats to camouflage them against predators. If fawns are scentless at birth, the condition lasts for a short time. When one to three weeks old, deer are able to run well. Milk is the primary source of nourishment for deer during their first two or three months of life, but they begin foraging on grass when they are between two and three weeks old. When a month old, fawns often eat solid foods. They are usually weaned by three months of age, but may continue nursing longer.

Fawns lose their spotted coats when they are between three and four months old, which is usually in September over most of North America. In the southern United States, where peak breeding occurs in December and January, spotted fawns can still be seen later in the year. Adults go through two coat changes a year. A reddish-colored summer coat replaces the winter pelage in late spring or early summer. The heavier, darker winter hair takes its place in the fall. Adult bucks over much of North America begin developing their fall coats during late August into September.

Velvet Shedding

Not long after adult bucks grow their fall coats of hair, they shed the velvet from their antlers as hormone levels start increasing in preparation for another breeding season. Most bucks shed the velvet from their antlers during the first weeks of September. The oldest bucks normally lose the velvet covering their antlers first, followed by younger animals, with yearling bucks that are $1^1/2$ years old being the last to develop hardened antlers.

The timing of the growth of fall coats and velvet shedding are not necessarily linked, however, as I recently discovered. I was watching a pair of whitetail bucks in the hopes of filming the velvet shedding process. One of the bucks was $3^1/2$ and had 8-point antlers. The second whitetail was $4^1/2$ and had a much larger set of antlers with 9-points.

The younger buck developed his fall coat a good week ahead of the 9-point. Consequently, I guessed he would shed his velvet first, but I was wrong. The older

The three-year-old 8-point whitetail on the left developed his fall/winter coat before the four-year-old 9-point on the right, but the older buck shed the velvet from his antlers at least a week before the 8-point.

buck lost his velvet on September 2 and I missed it. Figuring the 8-point would shed his velvet soon afterward, I spent as much time as possible watching him over the next several days. That buck didn't end up losing his velvet until a week later than the 9-point, at a time when I was out of town, so I missed that episode, too.

I have been fortunate enough to photograph the velvet shedding of a couple of bucks over the years, but have learned that the exact timing of when it will occur is difficult to predict. Many bucks I've been following have shed their velvet after dark. When it happens, it does not often take long for bucks to remove the velvet from their antlers.

Abnormalities

Some deer exhibit abnormalities in coat color. Whitetails and mule deer that have more white hair than normal in their coats (piebald deer) are the most common abnormality, and are legal for hunters to shoot in most states and provinces. These mutants exhibit varying amounts of white, but don't have the pink eyes of true albinos. The genetics that cause piebald coloration can be passed on from one generation to another. One winter I photographed a trio of piebald whitetails in the same herd that had similar patterns of extra white in their coats.

The amount of white some piebalds have can vary from one year to the next. I photographed a piebald doe on Michigan's Drummond Island one winter that had more white in its coat that year than the year before, according to the people who were feeding her.

There are probably hundreds of piebald whitetails bagged by hunters across North America every year. Fourteen-year-old Meghan Westcott from Lac La Belle, Michigan is among them. She bagged an unusual piebald buck on opening day of

A trio of piebald whitetails with similar markings from the same herd. The piebald characteristics were passed on genetically.

the 2009 firearms season while hunting with her father, Troy. The deer had three white hooves and "socks" on its lower legs.

Due to its unique markings, the Westcotts knew some of the whitetail's history. They recognized the buck as one they passed up the year before. Meghan and her dad are not the only ones who saw the buck and passed it up as a yearling during 2008. Meghan's older brother, Zach, and mother, Cathy, also saw the buck, but decided not to shoot it.

At 1^1/2 years old, the young buck had a white blaze on his forehead in addition to the white hooves and socks. The deer was small, estimated to weigh 80 or 90 pounds. The buck's antlers were spikes that grew backwards rather than upward.

When the Westcotts saw the piebald spikehorn, and they saw it frequently, it normally raced into view and aggressively chased any other deer that were in the area.

The following winter, the Westcotts spotted the antlerless buck in a winter yard about 15 miles from where they saw it the previous fall. It was easy to identify due to its markings. The next time they saw it was opening day of the 2009 gun season, at the same location it had frequented the year before.

With age, the buck had become more cautious. Instead of running in to feed with reckless abandon, it approached slowly, circling to test for potential danger. The whitetail's body was much bigger than it had been the year before. His antlers had grown, too, but they only had four points, two per side, less than most 2^1/2-year-old whitetails. The beams were long enough to have six points, but there were no brow tines. That's a genetic characteristic exhibited by some bucks in that area. Since Meghan knew the buck was 2^1/2 years old and she would have limited time to hunt, she decided to take the buck.

Head and hooves of the piebald buck that Meghan Westcott shot in Michigan the second year she saw it. The buck had three white hooves and "socks" both years, but lost a white blaze on his head from one year to the next.

A melanistic whitetail fawn with its normally colored sibling and mother that Richard Buquoi photographed in Austin, Texas. © R. M. BUQUOI PHOTOGRAPHICS

The buck no longer had a white blaze on his forehead like the year before, but had the same three white socks and hooves. In a year's time, the buck had more than doubled his weight. He had a dressed weight of 170 pounds.

Melanistics

Melanistic deer (black-colored) are not as common as albinos; in fact, they are very rare. Despite their rarity, Dick Giles from Milford, Michigan, bagged two melanistic bucks from the same location in the state. He got an eight-pointer in 1977 and a spike in 1981. Genetics of the local deer obviously favored that coat-color mutation.

I've heard more reports of melanistic deer from the state of Texas than anywhere else. Richard Buquoi from Georgetown, Texas, photographed a melanistic whitetail fawn born to a normally colored doe in the city of Austin. The doe had twins and the second fawn was normally colored. An overproduction of melanin is responsible for melanistic coat-color mutations like this. Albinos have a lack of melanin or skin color.

Albinos

I have been fortunate enough to have photographed a number of true albino white-tails, including the only set of twin albino bucks that I know of. I photographed the twin white bucks from when they were fawns until they developed their first sets of antlers. I was also able to photograph one of the pair during his second antler growth cycle.

The first albino whitetail I photographed was a doe. She was a strange sight. Her eyes, ears, and nose were pink; otherwise, she was all white except for the tarsal glands on her back legs. There were plenty of normal deer in the area that seemed to accept her presence. She was spookier than the other animals though.

Most of the albino whitetails I've seen have been born to normally colored does, including the twin bucks. But some albino does do produce albino offspring. I've seen and photographed two that did. I also photographed an albino doe that gave

Twin albino bucks comparing antlers at 1¹/₂ years old. The buck on the left has already shed the velvet from his antlers.

An adult albino doe with a pair of normal fawns she gave birth to. Many of the fawns born to albino does do not survive.

birth to twins that were normally colored. Some albino does may be sterile, but in most cases when adult albino does don't have fawns, it's because their offspring did not survive.

It is legal for hunters to shoot albino deer in most states and provinces, but they are protected in some such as Wisconsin. Michigan protected albino deer from 1990 through 2007 and removed protection starting in 2008. The protection was removed for albinos because it doesn't make sense biologically, the regulation is unenforceable, and it protects exotic all-white deer that escape from enclosures.

The reason Michigan's law was unenforceable is that most albinos are not totally white. That first albino doe I photographed had stained tarsal glands that were brown in color. Adult albino bucks develop stained scalps from their forehead glands and from rubbing trees as well as stained tarsal glands.

According to former Michigan DNR Director Rebecca Humphries, it is not good deer management to protect albinos. In a letter to a hunter she wrote, "There is no compelling scientific reason to protect these deer as albinism represents a mutation that is not desirable in a deer herd."

The bottom line is that a law protecting albino deer has little impact on the number of white deer present. This mutation is rare whether or not albinos are protected. Michigan had a small number of albino whitetails prior to 1990, when they were legal for hunters to shoot, and the numbers remained low even when they were protected. The state will continue to have occasional albinos even though they are legal game animals again.

A population of all-white whitetails that are not albinos live on the Seneca Army Depot in New York. The eye color on these white deer is the same as that in normally colored whitetails and their noses are gray.

Blonde button buck next to a normally colored whitetail that I photographed one winter in upper Michigan. His coat color was different from any that of other whitetail I've seen.

One year during late winter in upper Michigan, I photographed a button buck with an unusual blonde coat color that was much different than that of any other whitetail I've seen. The animal hung out with a group of normal colored deer in a feeding area and the young buck really stood out due to his coat color.

Antlered Does

Additional abnormalities occur with varying frequency in deer herds. Does with antlers are not uncommon. Some have antlers in velvet. Antler growth among does is caused by abnormal amounts of male hormones. Nonetheless, some of these does breed normally. I photographed one antlered doe that had velvet-covered buttons on her head throughout her life. She produced fawns every year. Does with polished antlers are some times hermaphroditic, that is, they have both male and female sex organs, and are often sterile.

Larry Ridley from Lansing, Michigan, bagged an antlered doe that may have had the largest set of antlers grown by such a deer. The 15-point nontypical antlers grossed 181^3/$_8$ and netted 165^2/$_8$. The fact that she was 3^1/$_2$ years old, had a dressed weight of 207 pounds, and was not seen with a fawn indicates she was probably sterile. For the story behind the hunt on which Ridley shot that trophy doe refer to Book 5 of *Great Michigan Deer Tales.*

Odd Antler Growth

Occasionally, bucks will grow three antlers. There is a record of a Canadian buck that sprouted a third antler on its nose. I shot a 10-pointer in Saskatchewan one year that had a third antler (a tine) growing from the center of its head between two normal beams. Taxidermist Jim Haveman from Traverse City, Michigan, mounted the head of that buck for me. When examining the skull of the deer, he determined it had received a head injury when younger that may have been responsible for the tine that grew in the odd location.

I approach a Saskatchewan 10-pointer that has a tine growing from the center of its head between two normal beams. The buck had suffered a head injury when he was younger, resulting in the abnormal antler growth.

A Montana buck developed an extra antler below its right eye. Castrated bucks or those with a hormonal imbalance may grow oddball antlers, fail to shed their velvet, or not develop antlers at all.

Mark Eby from St. Ignace, Michigan, bagged an unusual buck with bow and arrow on December 17 one year. The animal didn't have any testicles. Its odd-shaped antlers were still covered in velvet due to a hormonal imbalance. The antlers had spikes growing out of the center of a knobby cluster of shorter tines. The deer was obviously older than $1^1/2$ years old because it had a dressed weight of 165 pounds.

Patti Charlier from Wilson, Michigan, bagged a trophy 15-point buck that still had his antlers in velvet with bow and arrow one October. The reason why it hadn't shed the velvet is it didn't have testicles, resulting in reduced testosterone levels. Increasing levels of this hormone during early fall cause velvet shedding as well as other physiological changes among normal bucks.

I photographed a live adult whitetail buck one winter that might have had a similar defect. The deer had two large, dark lumps on his head in place of antlers.

Goofy Spikehorn

A yearling whitetail buck that Michigan conservation officer Mike McDonnell from Negaunee shot on the last day of firearms season (November 30) one year in north Marquette County had the strangest set of antlers Mike had ever seen. Both antlers grew forward and downward, with the tips ending up near the sides of the buck's mouth.

"At first, I took it for a doe," McDonnell said. "It was about 100 yards away then. When it got closer, I saw one antler, then the second antler. I thought, 'nobody's going to believe this.'"

The odd-antlered spike was with a 6-pointer.

"I knew the 6-pointer was going to have better antlers the following year, so I passed him up," Mike continued. "If the weird antlers on the spike was a genetic trait, I didn't want it to pass it on, so I decided to take him."

Patti Charlier from Wilson, Michigan, with the trophy 15-point buck she shot with bow and arrow in October one year; the deer still had his antlers in velvet because he lacked testicles and the hormones they produce. PHOTO COURTESY OF PATTI CHARLIER

"A friend of mine who was hunting about three-quarters-of-a-mile from where I shot the spike thinks he saw the deer on opening day. He watched it breed a doe, but he couldn't see any antlers on its head. He had a rear view of the deer and you couldn't see its antlers from that direction."

McDonnell may have done the buck a favor. If the whitetail had survived and grown a larger set of antlers the following year, the bone could have affected its ability to feed. The buck's pedicles were angled forward, causing the antlers to grow the way they did.

The deformity apparently developed naturally. Taxidermist Skip Van Buren

Michigan Conservation Officer Mike McDonnell with a goofy-antlered spikehorn he shot on the last day of firearms season one year.

mounted the deer's head for Mike and he can't recall seeing any sign of damage or injury to the spike's skull.

No Tail
Don Allen from Shelby, North Carolina shot a unique trophy 12-point whitetail buck on the first morning of a November 2009 hunt in Saskatchewan that had little or no tail. The deer could have been born that way, but it most likely lost its tail to a predator such a coyote or wolf that tried to grab it from the rear when it was younger. I was in the camp where Don got the buck and saw the deer, but its antlers were so impressive, having a gross score of 150, I didn't notice the missing tail.

Other Abnormalities
Undershot jaws are seen on some deer. This mutation doesn't affect a deer's ability to feed. My brother shot a short-jawed doe that was eight or ten years old and in good health. Jim Strelec bagged a yearling buck in Georgia that had a short lower jaw, too.

Warts or tumors called papillomas or fibromas are also found on deer. In bad cases they give the animals an unappealing appearance. These tumors are usually not malignant, nor do they affect the edibility of venison from a whitetail or mule deer that has them. Warts are commonly on the head, but they may occur elsewhere on the body. Jim Shope from Rapid River, Michigan, encountered a doe one fall that had so many growths on her head that she was blinded. Such severe cases result in the death of the animal.

Mortality Factors
Parasite infestations can result in deer losses. Significant mortality has occurred among Alabama's herd, for one, as a result of lungworm. Screwworms used to cause many deer losses in the south, too, until a successful eradication program directed at the adult flies was undertaken during the late 1950s and early 1960s. Other internal parasites that sometimes cause problems include brainworm, liver flukes, and nasal botfly larvae.

If you see a deer frantically pawing at its nose with a hind hoof as it violently blows its nose, you are observing a whitetail or mulie trying to get rid of a botfly that just flew up its nose. I've observed this behavior numerous times after seeing a fly hovering around a deer's head.

On one occasion, I was close enough to actually see the strategy a botfly used to enter a whitetail doe's nose. The fly hovered under the doe's chin as she ate food on the ground. When the doe raised her head to look around, the fly dropped to the ground among the food. When the deer put her head back down to continue feeding, the fly entered her nose.

Many whitetails in eastern and central North America carry brainworm, but the parasites are spreading further west with the spread of whitetails, which are their primary host. Whitetails don't suffer any ill effects from these parasites; however, brainworms can kill mule deer, moose, elk, and caribou that they infect. Snails and slugs are the parasite's intermediate host. They eat brainworm eggs passed in drop-

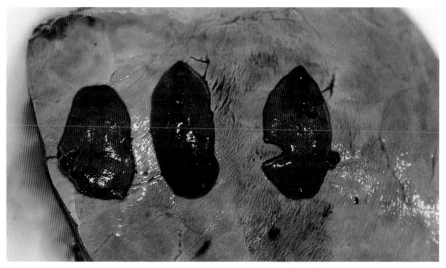

Liver flukes like these that were removed from the liver they are resting on are common in adult deer. Livers that contain flukes usually have external scarring from the parasites.

pings from whitetails. When feeding in wetlands, mulies, moose, elk, and caribou sometimes eat these snails with vegetation they consume.

External parasites include lice and ticks. Parasites, both internal and external, are common among deer, but their incidence is low in healthy whitetail and mule deer herds. A total of sixty-six internal parasites have been found in whitetails, and forty-five external parasites have been identified on them. Problems from parasites usually arise in populations on poor range or when herds overpopulate an area.

Extremes in weather such as prolonged cold winters, floods, and hurricanes take further tolls on deer. Here again, healthy deer herds are least susceptible to these conditions. Hundreds of thousands of whitetails and mulies also die on highways yearly as a result of being struck by automobiles. Many of these accidents could be avoided if drivers slowed down immediately upon seeing a deer along a road, even if the deer they saw has already crossed. Fawns are

Larval botfly in the nostrils of a Texas whitetail buck that was noticed when the head was being caped.

Many deer like this whitetail buck are killed on roads each year, resulting in millions of dollars in damage to vehicles as well as injuries and deaths of motorists.

often killed as they try to follow their mothers across a highway, and during the rut, bucks are frequently killed as they blindly race after does that crossed ahead of them. Less significant accidents, including getting stuck in fences and trees, and falls, account for more deer deaths.

One winter I photographed three whitetails that died in upper Michigan after getting stuck in trees. Amazingly, two of them were mature bucks that had already shed their antlers; they died together when a front leg of each animal lodged in the crotch between two maple trees. They had been standing on their hind legs facing each other in a boxing match with front feet when they became stuck. The left front leg of the larger buck was on top of the right front leg of the smaller animal. The only way they could have become stuck in this fashion is when their front quarters dropped toward the ground the bigger buck pushed the smaller one's front foot into the tree crotch with enough force to wedge them there.

The third deer was an adult doe that had her head in a tree cavity where it became stuck. The doe may have stuck her head in the cavity to get a morsel of food. All three deer died of exposure.

Deer are sometimes hit and killed by lightning, too. I once photographed the carcasses of three or four whiteails in a field that were killed at the same time when they were sruck by lightning. Since then I've heard and read about similar instances.

Deer also break through thin ice covering rivers and lakes and they either die of exposure or drown. Some of these aniamls are rescued, if they are seen in time, but most of them perish. I saw a whitetail doe that fell through thin ice covering the cold waters of Lake Superior one winter. I went to a nearby home where the resident had a boat in an effort to enlist his help to try to save the deer, but she was dead before we could get the boat in the water.

Predation is probably the most common mortality factor among deer herds. Mountain lions, wolves, black and grizzly bears, bobcats, and coyotes all take their

Pair of adult bucks that died in a freak accident when their front legs became lodged between two trees. They must have been standing on their hind legs and striking at each other with their front feet before this happened.

toll, and so do domestic dogs in some areas. One study documented predation on a whitetail fawn by a bald eagle, and golden eagles probably take some fawns, too, as do badgers and foxes. But humans are the most important deer predator today. Planned predation through hunting is the best means of maintaining healthy deer populations. The reproductive capacity of whitetails and mule deer is geared toward annual production of surplus animals in response to the many mortality factors they are subject to. If the surplus isn't removed through predation, population compensation will occur through disease, extremes in weather, road kills, and other factors.

Former Michigan DNR Wildlife Biologist Jim Hammill examines two of three deer killed by lightning in a field. Note the lines on the deers' bodies caused by the lightning strike.

Predation is responsible for some natural deer mortality. Deer are important prey species for wolves like this one in areas where these predators are increasing and expanding their range.

Losses to disease, weather, and accidents are less desirable than predation as a means of controlling deer populations. Adequate annual harvest through hunting will keep deer mortality from other causes at a minimum. For more information on deer management, refer to chapters 20 through 23.

Locked Antlers
One of the normal behaviors among bucks during the fall, sparring and fighting, sometimes results in the deaths of whitetails and mulies. In most cases, there's no problem when a pair of bucks bang their antlers together. Occasionally, however,

Locked antlers from a whitetail and mule deer at an Alberta taxidermy shop ready to be mounted. Michael Nichols shot the whitetail and the mulie was already dead. This is the only case where the two species of deer are known to have locked antlers.

the animals' antlers become hopelessly locked. Both deer usually die of exposure and exhaustion, unless they're found by hunters.

On October 20 one fall Gary Yancey of Lincoln Park, Michigan, and partner Dave Papas of Howell, Michigan, were bird hunting when they encountered a pair of bucks with locked antlers. Bow deer season was open and they both had unfilled tags, so they exchanged shotguns for bows and arrows as quickly as they could. Yancey filled his tag with the bigger of the two bucks, which had an eight-point rack, and Papas arrowed the six-pointer.

Brothers Eric and Dave Norden of Rock, Michigan, bagged with firearms a pair of trophy bucks that got their antlers locked in late November. Eric encountered the bucks first and returned to the scene with his brother and father. The buck Eric shot had a twelve-point rack and Dave's trophy sported eleven points.

Michael Nichols from Castor, Alberta documented the first known case of mule deer and whitetail bucks with locked antlers. When he pulled the trigger on his .270 during November of 1997, he thought he was shooting a whitetail with a nontypical rack. The rack was nontypical alright, but primarily because it was intertwined with the 4 x 4 antlers of a dead mule deer.

It wasn't easy to tell two bucks of different species had locked antlers at the 250 to 300 yards at which Nichols shot the whitetail because there wasn't much left of the mulie. He said all that remained of the mulie were two front legs, one back leg and the head. The rest had been eaten by coyotes. The whitetail had broken the mulie's neck after their antlers became tangled, enabling the coyotes to eat the carcass.

It was coyotes that attracted Nichols' attention to the locked bucks. He had stopped to shoot a trio of coyotes he spotted. When he put his scope on one of the predators, he saw something disappear over a hill. He went to see what it was and spotted the whitetail with the "weird set of antlers."

Nichols said the whitetail was in a weakened condition when he shot it. He did the deer a favor by finishing it because he didn't think it would have lived much longer. The meat from the buck was not salvageable. Consequently, the tag he used on the buck was replaced by the Ministry of Natural Resources.

The whitetail was a 12-pointer, including a pair of sticker points. A nontypical tine off of the antler base on the right side was largely responsible for holding the antlers of both bucks together. If that tine hadn't been there, the pair probably would have gone their separate ways after fighting.

Dianne and Peter Egge of Buffalo Taxidermy in Sherwood Park, Alberta completed a head mount of the locked bucks. Peter said there are some deer that are hybrid mule deer/whitetail crosses in the vicinity where Nichols got the locked bucks. Egge shot one of them himself a number of years ago.

He shot what he thought was a whitetail. The head, ears and antlers were those of a whitetail. When he went to field dress the carcass, however, he discovered it had a mule deer tail. Mule deer expert Dr. Valerius Geist said most mule/whitetail hybrids are produced by mule deer does.

"Even though mule deer does normally ignore the advances of whitetail bucks, in areas where there's hunting, big mulies are normally shot and mule deer does go into cover where mature whitetail bucks live," he said. "The mulie does don't have a chance to avoid being bred by whitetails under those circumstances."

"Female whitetails love mule deer bucks, but mulie bucks are not interested," Geist continued. "Students have observed whitetail does going through mating displays for mulie bucks and being ignored."

A buck will sometimes kill a rival during the course of a fight over breeding rights. Death is usually caused by stab wounds from sharp antler tines. One buck killed in a fight was stabbed in the heart.

On November 16 one year, Mike Ferguson from Sagola, Michigan found a trophy 8-pointer that he's sure was killed by another buck. A flock of ravens attracted him to the dead deer. Earlier in the day, Mike had heard a racket in the area where he found the carcass, which was probably a pair of bucks fighting.

"His head was mush," Ferguson said. "His whole forehead was broken into little pieces of bone. The skull was broken so badly I was able to cut his horns off the head with my knife."

Crystal Falls, Michigan resident Jim Vickerman found an 11-pointer that had been killed in a fight with another buck. The dead deer's tongue had been severed near the back of the mouth and there was a lot of blood in its throat, leading Vickerman to believe the whitetail choked to death. The dead deer also had a broken tine imbedded in its skull, but it didn't appear as though the tine penetrated the skull enough to hit the brain.

Serious fights between bucks more often result in broken antlers and superficial injuries than in the death of either deer.

Yearling dispersal

Fawns normally stay with their mothers through the winter and into the next spring. Does chase their offspring from the previous year away before giving birth. If the pregnant doe loses her fawns, however, her young from the year before may rejoin her soon afterward. I've observed instances where this has happened. Dispersing yearlings sometimes travel long distances before settling into a home range of their own. Most, however, probably disperse less than five miles from the area where they were raised.

Nebraska and South Dakota have some interesting findings on dispersal of young whitetails and mule deer. In South Dakota ten male mule deer tagged as fawns moved an average of 36.7 miles from that time to when they were killed as yearlings or adults. Some whitetails also disperse over long distances. Twenty-three members of this species moved an average of 38 miles in Nebraska. A pair of whitetails traveled 125 and 137 miles from points where they were tagged to points of recovery in that state.

Bucks frequently seek the company of other male deer during summer months. From my experiences, mule deer males seem to be more gregarious than whitetail bucks, but males of both species form bachelor groups during the summer and early fall. On September 30th one year I photographed a bachelor group of six adult mule deer bucks in North Dakota's Theodore Roosevelt

Whitetails like this one are ear-tagged or fitted with radio collars to track their movements and dispersal.

Bachelor group of mule deer bucks photographed in North Dakota on September 30 one year.

National Park. They all had respectable antlers, but a couple of them had great racks. I also observed bachelor groups of mulies in Colorado's Rocky Mountains, some of them containing even more bucks, during late August and early September.

Before breeding begins, the same group of bucks may fight or sparr among themselves to determine a pecking order. The bucks at the top of the pecking order will have most of the breeding rights. In these duels for dominance, the stronger of the two deer usually wins without any injury to either contestant.

Swimming

Whitetails and mule deer are good swimmers. Reports of them swimming for miles are common. When chased by dogs or predators, deer sometimes head for water to escape. Animals may also go in water to escape biting insects during the summer or to rid themselves of parasites such as ticks. Some deer feed on aquatic vegetation in the summer, too.

One spring a cousin and a friend of mine were trolling for trout and salmon from a boat on Lake Superior about 300 yards from shore when they encountered a white-tail doe that was swimming farther out into the lake with no apparent destination. No islands were in sight and the water was extremely cold. Concerned that the deer might die of exposure, they used the boat to turn the doe back toward shore and herded her in that direction. After reaching dry ground, the whitetail shook herself, paused for a short time, and then disappeared into the woods.

Foods and Digestion

Basically, whitetail and mule deer are browsers, but they also graze on grasses and other vegetation when they are available. Additionally, deer are fond of a variety of agricultural crops. Leaves from trees and plants make up a large part of their diet in the summer and a lesser part in the fall. However, deer frequently eat freshly fallen leaves during the fall and I've seen them eat dried leaves from branches and the

The stomachs of deer have four chambers to aid in digestion of food. Acorns and vegetation are visible in this Kentucky whitetail's stomach. Hunters can learn more about the foods deer eat in their area by examining stomach contents of deer they shoot.

ground during winter months, too. Mushrooms make up an important part of a deer's diet during spring, summer, and fall, too, when and where they are available.

Deer do most of their browsing in late fall and winter. Woody material such as the buds and tender tips of saplings and shrubs from sagebrush, mountain mahogany, dogwood, willow, maple, and oak are preferred. Evergreen leaves from yew, cedar, juniper, hemlock, and some pines are also favored. Acorns, beechnuts, and apples are prime fall and winter deer foods, when available. It is not uncommon for deer to stand on their hind legs to reach morsels of food on trees, especially in the winter when rations are sometimes in short supply.

Deer break or pull woody material that they ingest. Since only the lower jaw has front teeth, a deer can't bite through stems. For this reason, the ends of limbs or stems that deer feed on will be ragged. Farther back in the mouth, deer have teeth on both the top and bottom jaws which are used for chewing.

Ingested food is chewed when taken in, but is later chewed again. Deer have four cavities in their stomachs: the rumen, reticulum, omasum, and abomasum. When first swallowed, food goes in the rumen. Bacteria mix with the material here to help break it down. The strain of bacteria in the rumen depends on what type of food is being consumed, so the bacteria may vary during different seasons of the year. Cuds of food are regurgitated from the rumen and then rechewed. The digestion process is completed in the other three cavities of the stomach.

Whitetails and mule deer require a daily average of five to ten pounds of food per one hundred pounds of weight. Food requirements are greatest during periods of cold weather.

An interesting biological discovery about deer in areas where winters are typically severe is that they go into a physiological state similar to hibernation during the height of the cold season. The animals don't go to sleep, but their metabolism slows down. It seems to be an adaptation for conserving energy reserves necessary to carry them through the critical period.

Diseases

As I predicted when I wrote the third edition of this book, Chronic Wasting Disease (CWD) has continued to spread across North America, primarily in the United States. The transport of captive animals continues to contribute to the spread of the disease. In states where free-ranging deer populations are infected, CWD is transmitted within those herds, sometimes crossing state lines, but not at the rate that was previously predicted.

The disease had been detected in nine states and two Canadian provinces in 2003. By 2010, the number of provinces where CWD has been found remains the same (Saskatchewan and Alberta), but the number of states has grown to seventeen. Missouri, North Dakota, and Virginia are the newest additions to the list. A captive deer in Linn County, Missouri tested positive for the disease in early 2010. Deer bagged by hunters during the fall of 2009 in Virginia and North Dakota were found to have CWD by January and March of 2010. The infected whitetail in Frederick County, Virginia, wasn't a surprise because it was killed near the border with West Virginia, where sixty-two wild whitetails have tested positive for the disease since 2005. The mule deer buck from Sioux County, North Dakota, that had the disease was a surprise because it's the first case for that state and there's 200 miles between where that deer lived and areas where any other cases of the disease had been confirmed.

The first free-ranging whitetail in Minnesota with CWD was shot during the 2010 hunting season and was not identified until early 2011. Until that discovery, the disease was thought to be limited to a captive elk herd in that state. Due to problems with the fencing around that captive elk herd, it's thought that the infected deer represents a spillover of the disease from the fenced facility into the wild. More deer have been culled from that area for testing to determine how widespread the disease is.

Michigan had its first and only case of CWD, so far, in 2008, that of a captive whitetail in Kent County near Grand Rapids. Extensive testing of wild deer for three years in the county where the infected animal was located, as well as the rest of the state, have failed to find any other whitetails positive for CWD, which is a good thing.

The states where CWD-infected deer have been detected, besides those already mentioned, are Wisconsin, Illinois, New York, South Dakota, Kansas, Nebraska, Montana, Colorado, Wyoming, Utah, and New Mexico. So far CWD has only been found among captive elk in Montana, not deer. The disease was detected in two captive deer herds and two free ranging deer in New York during 2005, but no cases of CWD have been found in that state since then, so hunters and wildlife officials there are hopeful CWD has been eradicated from the state.

Outbreaks of Chronic Wasting Disease (CWD) in mule deer and whitetails and Bovine Tuberculosis (TB) in whitetails have brought new attention to deer diseases in recent years. For the first time ever, the presence of disease in deer herds is starting to have a major impact on deer hunting and deer management nationally rather than regionally. The last time there was an outbreak of a serious disease in deer was during the 1940s and 50s when Epizootic Hemorrhagic Disease (EHD) started killing whitetails in the southeast. That disease was a mystery when it was first recognized, but researchers eventually figured out what was behind it. Prior to the appearance of EHD, mule deer in California developed hoof and mouth disease way back in 1923 and 1924. Fortunately, that disease was eradicated as quickly as possible.

Efforts to accomplish the same thing with CWD and TB are underway, but the process is being hampered by a lack of solid information about the diseases and how they are spread. Far more is known about TB than CWD and, for that reason, major strides have been made to control TB, but unanswered questions remain that hinder even better control of the disease in deer. TB is far from a new disease, and it is not as serious an ailment as CWD because it seldom results in the death of its host, but what is new is that it has managed to sustain itself in a population of wild whitetails in Michigan, Manitoba, and Minnesota. CWD is relatively new as far as diseases go, and because CWD is always fatal to deer that contract it, because it has spread to a number of states and provinces due to poor control of the transport of captive animals, and because little is known about how deer develop this disease, the process of controlling it is more difficult.

Deer are subject to a variety of diseases besides CWD and TB, many of which have been around as long as deer have; a couple of them have proven to be more deadly than CWD. However, due to the current emphasis on CWD and TB, let's look at these diseases first and then discuss others that have been around longer.

One point I want to make clear early on is that although CWD and TB are reasons for concern among deer hunters and managers, there is no reason to panic or to quit deer hunting. Some deer hunters may be inconvenienced and be forced to endure low deer numbers in the short term, but in the end, the tradition of deer hunting will survive. I'm confident that the mysteries surrounding these diseases will eventually be solved, enabling better control, if not elimination, of them in deer populations. Better and quicker testing practices that will make it possible to identify diseased deer taken by hunters should help eliminate worry about eating infected animals. Venison from whitetails and mule deer remains some of the best-quality and healthiest meat for human consumption available today. I plan on continuing to eat my share in the future and I hope you do, too.

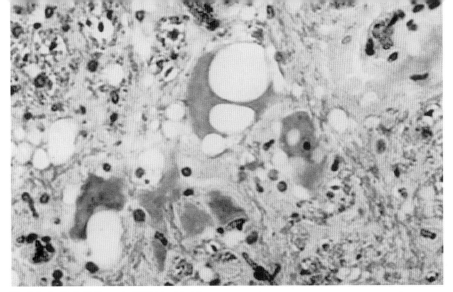

The late Dr. Beth Williams in 1978 identified the sponge-like holes in the brains of deer infected with what has become known as Chronic Wasting Disease (CWD). PHOTO COURTESY OF COLORADO DIVISION OF WILDLIFE

CWD

CWD was first detected at the Colorado Department of Fish and Game's Foothills Wildlife Research Facility near Fort Collins in 1967, but what was responsible for the disease wasn't identified until more than a decade later. Diseased mule deer exhibited excessive thirst, urinated frequently, had saliva dripping from their mouths, and grew increasingly thin until they died. The animals basically wasted away. In the later stages of the disease, deer often appeared to be in a stupor, walking aimlessly or standing with their heads down and their ears drooping.

In 1967, mule deer at Colorado's Foothills Wildlife Research Station near Fort Collins developed a mysterious illness that started killing deer. In the later stages of the disease, they drooled like this antlerless mule deer buck, urinated frequently, and wasted away. It was eleven years before the disease was recognized as a brain disorder. PHOTO COURTESY OF COLORADO DIVISION OF WILDLIFE

Eleven years after the malady was first observed, what was causing the deaths of affected deer was recognized. The late Dr. Beth Williams, who was a veterinarian, discovered during 1978 that the brains of infected deer had holes in them, giving them a spongelike appearance. The affliction resembled scrapies in sheep, a disease that had been known about for years. These diseases, as well as mad cow disease (bovine spongiform encephalitis), are grouped under the name transmissable spongiform encephalophathies (TSEs).

Most diseases are caused by bacteria or viruses. Current thinking is that TSEs are different. Mutated prions (pronounced "pree-ons") cause the holes in the brains of animals affected by TSEs. Prions are proteins that are a normal part of the brains of mammals. What causes prions to mutate remains a mystery. More on that later.

CWD was officially identified and named in 1980. It's interesting to note that mad cow disease did not surface in the United Kingdom until 1985. The cause of that disease was reported to be additives in cattle feed consisting of animal protein products—ground up remains from slaughterhouses. It's speculated that some of the animal protein products fed to cattle in Great Britain may have been from sheep that had scrapies. Whether or not that was the case, the fact that animal protein products are not part of the normal diet of cattle is important. A diet with steady doses of any animal protein products may have been enough to cause changes in prions.

Before CWD was identified, it was spread from the research facility in Colorado to another research station in Wyoming near Wheatland (Sybille Canyon) through transfer of infected deer. The disease appeared at the Wyoming compound during 1977. Deer from Colorado's Foothills Research Station were also routinely released into the wild. Captive deer were the first to be diagnosed with CWD, but wild deer and elk with the disease eventually started showing up in the vicinity of the research facilities. It is possible that wild deer that lived outside the fences at the research stations were infected by captive animals through the single fence, but more likely captive deer that were released took the disease with them. Double fencing has since been added at the research pens to eliminate the possibility of contact between captive and free ranging deer.

Gene Schoonveld was a Colorado State University graduate student who did deer research at the Foothills facility when CWD first appeared there; he worked as a biologist with the state Division of Wildlife for a number of years until he retired. He said the mule deer that were his research subjects had close contact with sheep for a long period of time at the installation. It is suspected that the sheep had scrapies and passed the disease on to the deer.

Once CWD turned up in wild deer and elk, testing for the disease was expanded within Colorado and Wyoming through examination of hunter kills, and new locations with CWD were identified. CWD was not found outside of Colorado and Wyoming until 1996, almost 30 years after the disease was first noticed. A captive elk on a farm in the Canadian province of Saskatchewan tested positive for the disease. Captive elk in South Dakota were diagnosed with CWD in 1997.

For years, the only way to determine whether deer or elk had CWD was to test the brain or brain stem of animals after they died. It now appears that a biopsy of a live deer's tonsils can be used to determine if the animal has CWD because the aberrant prions that cause CWD show up there during the early stages of the disease. However, this has not yet been found to be the case in elk. Deer don't normally show symptoms of CWD until they are at least 18 months old, and the incubation period can be as long as five years.

After 1996, testing for CWD began in other states and provinces and new cases began cropping up regularly. Both deer and elk were infected. Most of the animals that had CWD were captive, but some of them were free ranging. It's unknown whether the disease began in the wild and spread to captive animals or vice versa.

CWD was diagnosed in Wisconsin whitetails during February of 2002. Three bucks taken by hunters in the southern part of the state near Mt. Horeb during the 2001 season tested positive for the disease. The illegal release of captive deer from Colorado on private land in Wisconsin is thought to be one way the disease reached the state. PHOTO BY MIKE MILLER, COLORADO DIVISION OF WILDLIFE

That's not as important as learning more about what causes the disease and how it spreads so it can be controlled and then eliminated.

It was thought that CWD was confined to western North America until February of 2002. That's when three wild whitetails taken by hunters in southern Wisconsin tested positive for the disease. CWD didn't get to Wisconsin on its own. Infected deer were transported there by people in the same way the disease was spread from Colorado to Wyoming and to many other states and provinces where CWD now exists.

Some deer hunters from Wisconsin reportedly purchased captive whitetail bucks that had large antlers from Colorado and released them in the wild on their property, which is illegal. The intent of the release was to eventually increase the antler size of resident bucks as the transplanted whitetails bred resident does. One or more of the relocated bucks was apparently infected with CWD.

Since the discovery of CWD in Wisconsin, the disease has turned up in free-ranging whitetails in Illinois just across the border from Wisconsin as well as all of the states further east mentioned near the beginning of this chapter.

What Causes CWD

Steve Basl from Mio, Michigan thinks he's solved the mystery about what causes CWD, and his theory makes a lot of sense. Basl operates the 365-acre Big Creek Shooting Preserve, where he's been raising whitetails for a number of years. While experimenting with the best diet to produce healthy deer, he tried some commercial pellets made by Purina. Despite assurances that the pellets were great for whitetails,

Animal protein products in commercial deer and elk foods, a common additive until 2000, may cause CWD in some deer. A captive whitetail herd owned by Steve Basl lost weight when they were fed that type of food. Mad Cow Disease in Great Britain, which is similar to CWD, was caused when the remains of livestock from slaughter houses were added to the diets of cattle.

Steve noticed his animals were hesitant to eat the food. However, they eventually got used to the pellets and were consuming them on a regular basis.

After the pellets were established as a regular part of the diet of Basl's herd, he noticed his deer lost an average of 50 pounds in weight and antler development among bucks declined. Around that time, Mad Cow Disease appeared in the United Kingdom and it was determined that the illness was caused by feeding cattle the remains of livestock mixed with their normal food. Steve checked the ingredients of the pellets he was feeding his deer and discovered the same animal byproducts that were added to cattle feed were a part of the deer feed.

That explained the reluctance of his deer to eat the pellets initially. Whitetails instinctively know what's best for them and they generally only eat the most nutritious foods, if given a choice. However, captive animals that don't have much choice in what's available to them are forced to eat what they are given.

Steve stopped using the Purina pellets once he realized they contained animal protein. After all, whitetails are herbivores, not carnivores. They seldom, if ever, feed on the remains of animals. But deer and elk that are or have been fed such rations on a regular basis could develop CWD. Basl's deer herd might have developed CWD if he had kept feeding them the Purina pellets. We already know that CWD is related to mad cow disease and cattle that developed mad cow disease in the UK were infected by eating the remains of livestock, which probably included brains and/or spinal chords, mixed with their normal food. It makes sense then that deer and elk that were fed animal protein products would or could develop CWD.

Steve said animal protein products were used in commercial deer food until 2000. The additives were removed due to concerns about CWD.

Commercial deer pellets are and have been available to individuals who supplementally feed wild deer and elk in addition to the owners of captive deer and elk herds. Captive herds are more often fed commercial pellets, but the owners of private property in southern Wisconsin who subscribe to Quality Deer Management reportedly fed wild deer food containing bone meal supplements. That can explain how some wild whitetails like those in Wisconsin and fenced herds anywhere could become infected with CWD other than through the transfer of infected animals. During severe winters when natural foods are scarce and deer might have been fed a steady diet of pellets laced with animal protein, the odds of whitetails becoming diseased would have increased.

I predict that a link between CWD and food to which animal protein products have been added will be proven when and if researchers get around to studying this aspect. Biologists and researchers I questioned about this topic said no research had been done along those lines because they didn't think contaminated food was responsible for CWD. It's a good thing scientists studying Mad Cow Disease in Great Britain didn't have the same mindset.

More than one factor may be responsible for deer developing CWD. An excellent case can be made for scrapies in sheep at the Foothills Wildlife Research Station in Colorado being responsible for the outbreak of CWD among deer that shared the compound. There's speculation that interaction with sheep with scrapies has infected wild deer with CWD, too. Sheep are routinely pastured on public land in mule deer country where CWD has appeared.

Ingestion of pesticides along with animal protein products in their diet is suspected of having something to do with development of mad cow disease in British cattle. Organophosphates could play a role in deer becoming infected with CWD as well.

Tulane University Professor of Pathology Frank Bastian thinks that spiroplasma bacteria may be responsible for CWD. When the bacteria are injected into mice, the rodents develop a disease of the brain similar to CWD. Bastian theorizes that the bacteria enter prions, causing them to mutate and allowing the bacteria to avoid detection. Insects can infect rodents with spiroplasma bacteria and they may be able to do the same to deer. Another deer disease that will be discussed later is known to be spread by biting insects, so this form of transmission is plausible.

Copper deficiencies in deer are thought to be another possible cause of CWD. Healthy prions contain copper, but if an animal's diet has little to no copper, this ingredient may be removed from prions, causing them to change. A study of penned elk found that those that got adequate amounts of copper in their diets did not develop CWD. As high as 7.5 percent of elk in the study that got low doses of copper developed CWD. As high as 55 percent of the elk that did not receive copper supplements became infected with CWD.

One way the disease may be transmitted from deer to deer is through feces or droppings, according to Colorado Division of Wildlife employee David Clarkson. He said mule deer fawns have a habit of eating feces. If altered prions are shed in droppings, some deer could become infected at a young age. Mutated prions may also be shed in urine from infected animals and healthy animals that come in contact with that urine could become infected.

Controlling CWD

One of the most important things that can be done to help control the spread of CWD and other diseases is to establish better controls on the captive deer and elk industry. The disease has obviously spread as far as it has because of how common a practice it has become to transport deer from one fenced property to another. This is most often done within the same state or province, but interstate and provincial transfers are still common.

Rules that were previously in place to prevent the spread of disease were obviously inadequate and frequently circumvented. The fact that CWD may not show up in an infected animal for five years and the lack of an easy way to detect the disease in live wild animals compound the problem. Financial incentives have also caused some people to knowingly break the law. The Wisconsin hunters who released big bucks from captivity into the wild is a prime example. That's probably not the only place where this has happened.

And wild deer have also been caught illegally to augment captive herds. One case involved the live trapping of wild whitetails in Ontario that were then sold to a number of captive facilities. This practice has probably been more common than most people realize.

The only way to prevent the further spread of CWD among captive animals is to require that transfers be restricted to deer from herds that have been certified disease-free for five years. Properties with captive herds where disease is known to exist should be required to have double fencing. This would go a long way toward eliminating the potential for disease transmission to captive from wild deer and vice versa. I would think owners of property with captive deer that are disease-free would

One of the best ways to control the spread of CWD and other diseases is to more carefully regulate the trade of captive deer and elk. Captive herds should be enclosed by a double fence to eliminate contact with wild deer like the one shown outside this fence, and to reduce the chances that captive animals will escape.

want to protect their investment in this way. They risk losing all of their animals if even one becomes infected with CWD.

A CWD-positive deer showed up at a Wisconsin deer farm in Walworth County, near Troy, during 2002 and the place was immediately quarantined. To make matters worse, a yearling buck that escaped from that enclosure during March of 2002 and was shot by state wardens on October 22, also had CWD. If the farm had been double fenced, the odds of that deer escaping would have been reduced. No wild deer with CWD have turned up in Walworth County yet, but it may only be a matter of time before they do. If they do, it will complicate Wisconsin's efforts to control the disease.

Eliminating diseased animals, as well those that are thought to have been exposed to the disease, is the best known course of action for controlling CWD. Since CWD is transmissable, if the disease shows up in captive herds, all of the animals are destroyed. Accomplishing this goal is not as easy in wild deer populations.

"Hot Spot Culling" was used as a means of trying to control the disease among free ranging mule deer in Colorado between 2001 and 2005. Through testing, deer managers determined where disease prevalence was the highest. They established a perimeter that included most, if not all, of the deer with CWD and then reduced the herd as much as possible. Deer in those areas were monitored to keep track of the disease prevalence and further culling was undertaken when necessary.

By 2006, Colorado wildlife officials halted culling operations because the herd reductions did not appear to be reducing prevalence rates of the disease where culls had taken place. Only a small number of deer removed during culling operations had CWD. And concerns arose that removing healthy deer from these areas, some of which may have developed natural immunity to CWD, would be counterproductive.

Other states and provinces also tried culling deer herds to reduce or eliminate CWD. Those efforts appear to have been successful in New York, but the jury is still out on the effectiveness of herd reductions in other areas.

Special early and late hunting seasons have been set in some cases to allow hunters to play a role in controlling the disease. However, these are not normal "hunting" seasons as the term is normally applied. The purpose is to kill as many deer as possible to reduce disease transmission. State and federal agency personnel do the culling in many situations. Ranchers and farmers who are willing to do some culling on their property have also been issued permits to do so.

Nebraska Game and Parks Commission personnel, for instance, culled 104 mule deer from an area where an animal tested positive for CWD in 2000. That sample included one more mulie with the disease. The state agency culled 113 more wild deer from terrain surrounding a game farm where CWD was found and nine of those animals had the disease.

The toll of deer from disease control efforts was far greater in Wisconsin than western states where whitetail densities are much higher than those of mule deer. The Wisconsin Department of Natural Resources (DNR) originally established a deer eradication zone encompassing 411 square miles in parts of Dane, Iowa, and Saulk Counties, which was later expanded, from which they optimistically hoped to remove 25,000 whitetails. Thousands of whitetails were killed in an effort to control CWD in Wisconsin with negligible results.

Deer certainly were not eradicated. Nor was the disease. In fact, by 2010 prevalence of CWD had risen in some areas over what it was in 2003. During the same time period, the state DNR lost a lot of public trust and support over their aggressive approach to reducing deer numbers.

By 2010, 111,173 whitetails had been tested for CWD in southern Wisconsin's eradication zone and 1,354 deer were found to be infected. What isn't known is how many of the deer that were culled were immune to the disease. By eliminating a significant number of animals that were least likely to become infected with CWD along with their ability to spread that immunity through the population, herd reduction could be contributing to an increase in the prevalence rate of the disease.

The Wisconsin DNR banned the use of bait for deer hunting during the regular 2002 seasons and all deer feeding statewide due to concerns that these practices could contribute to the spread of CWD. Those regulations have since been modified to allow baiting and feeding deer in northern Wisconsin where CWD does not exist. Baiting and feeding deer is banned in twenty-one southern counties where CWD is present as well as surrounding counties to serve as a buffer against spread of the disease. No more than two gallons of bait or feed can be put out at one time.

Wisconsin has not been the only state to restrict deer feeding in response to CWD. Virtually all of the states where the disease has surfaced have done the same thing. Most states and povinces have also put restrictions on the transport of captive deer and elk. We can only hope that those restrictions are not too little, too late. Some states have even established restrictions for import of deer and elk harvested by hunters from other states and provinces to eliminate the potential of an infected carcass being discarded within their borders. These states and some provinces limit hunters to bringing deboned meat, hides, and antlers on clean skull caps across their borders.

The province of Manitoba requires that the skull cap attached to the antlers of any member of the deer family be treated with chlorine before transport across its borders. Capes must be sealed in a waterproof container (plastic bag or bucket). It is also illegal for hunters to possess products "that contain urine, feces, saliva or scent glands" of a deer, elk, or moose due to concerns about disease transmission. That elminates the use of popular deer scents for hunting in this province!

The question of whether the remains (head, brain, organs, and spinal chord) of deer that had CWD can contaminate the site where they are left or discarded, resulting in the infection of other animals, should be addressed through research as soon as possible. There is concern that this might be the case and that's why Colorado regulations require hunters to leave those items at kill sites, when possible. It is illegal to transport an entire carcass outside an area where CWD is known to exist.

Precautions For Hunters

Since the altered prions that cause CWD are concentrated in the nervous system and lymph nodes, the meat from deer that have the disease can be eaten safely. However, it's not recommended. How do you know if a deer you shoot has CWD?

If you are hunting an area where the disease has not been detected, you don't need to be concerned. Nonetheless, it's wise to avoid shooting mule deer and whitetails that act sick or behave strangely, especially in regions where CWD occurs.

Even deer that look and act healthy can have the disease, so if you are hunting in a CWD zone or nearby, submit the head from your deer for testing. This is required in some locations.

Even where testing is voluntary, it's worth submitting the head from your deer for testing if you are the least bit concerned. All states where the disease has been found have testing programs. Call the nearest DNR or Fish and Game office to find out how and where to submit samples for testing and if there is any charge. This information can also be found on websites for state agencies. There's normally no charge for testing in areas where doing so is mandatory.

Hunters who drop deer heads off for CWD testing are often assigned a number. They can check a website or dial an 800 number to get the results. Hunters who shoot deer that test positive for CWD are usually contacted directly as soon as possible.

To be on the safe side, hunters who bag deer that they are confident do not have CWD should wear rubber or latex gloves when field dressing, skinning, and butchering the carcass. The head, lymph nodes, organs, and skeleton should be discarded. If it's a buck and the antlers are cut from the skull with a saw, remove and discard any portions of the brain attached to the skull cap. That saw should not be used to butcher the carcass. In fact, it's recommended not to use a saw at all when butchering deer.

The meat should be removed from bones with a knife. An explanation of how to do this can be found in chapter 18. Deboning venison before it's frozen makes it easier to cut the meat into meal-size portions for your family, and it will take up less freezer space.

If you bag a deer in a state or province where CWD has been found and you will be transporting the meat across the border, the meat should be deboned for transport. The antlers should also be removed from the head and the skull cap cleaned. When shooting a deer in an area known to have CWD, deboning the meat and removing the antlers on the spot is recommended. Hunters who are concerned that the deer they shot might be diseased should turn the head in for testing.

The fact that the deer hunting tradition continues strong in Colorado, where CWD has existed the longest, is testimony that the disease is not devastating to either deer or deer hunters. The state continues to sell plenty of deer hunting licenses. If CWD can't be licked, at least hunters can learn how to deal with it. That's something more of us will probably have to do in the future.

Bovine TB

Bovine TB is a strain of the disease that originated in cattle and has been spread to wild deer in a number of instances. In most cases in which the disease was detected in deer, it eventually disappeared. For years, Michigan was considered the lone exception where TB persists in free ranging deer. But both deer and elk in the vicinity of Manitoba's Riding Mountain Provincial Park have been infected with TB for more than 20 years. And an outbreak of TB among wild whitetails in northwestern Minnesota was detected in 2005.

Due to aggressive efforts to eliminate TB from Minnesota whitetails, the disease could be short lived there, like it has been in other cases. Time will tell. Deer with the disease have surfaced in parts of four counties in the state: Rosseau, Lake of the Woods, Marshall, and Beltrami. As of 2010, testing of harvested deer had turned up twenty-seven that had the disease. Continued testing will determine if any diseased deer remain. If the situation was addressed soon enough, TB should not get the foothold in Minnesota that it has in Michigan.

The fact that a new outbreak of TB in free ranging deer surfaced so recently is evidence that monitoring deer—and the livestock they can potentially mingle with—for disease is, or at least should be, an important part of modern deer management. A total of eleven herds of cattle in northwest Minnesota tested positive for TB. And captive deer with TB have recently been detected in three more states: Indiana, Nebraska, and New York.

The disease was discovered in three captive deer facilities in Indiana. One captive deer in Columbia County, New York tested positive for TB. Captive fallow deer and elk had the disease in Nebraska.

In Manitoba, by October 2010, a total of forty-three elk and eleven whitetail deer had tested positive for TB since 1991, according to Rick Davis of the wildlife and ecological protection branch of the Manitoba Ministry of Natural Resources. Over the same time frame, Davis said, ten cattle herds in the area had tested positive for the disease and those herds were all eliminated. Nine of the herds of cows tested positive for TB before 2003. Then a single cow from a herd in 2008 also tested positive. The last deer that was confirmed to have TB was also identified in 2008. Davis said they are hopeful that the disease is on the decline in the area. Since the disease remains in free ranging animals after so many years, however, and since the incidence of the disease was high among local cows, the problem may be worse than the numbers indicate. The low numbers of deer and elk that have been tested for the disease have probably not been enough to assess the extent of the problem either. Davis said about seven hundred deer and two hundred to four hundred elk are tested for TB annually.

Michigan's experience with TB in deer is a prime example of why the problem may be more widespread in Manitoba than expected. In Michigan, wild deer are known to have been infected with TB longer than anywhere else. Some whitetails in the northeastern Lower Peninsula are known to have been infected with TB since at least the 1970s. The fact that the scope of the problem was not identified until 20 years later is one of the reasons why the disease lingers in that area. Extremely high deer densities in that portion of Michigan, encouraged through massive supplemental feeding programs on private land and inadequate antlerless harvests, allowed TB to be maintained and spread.

Five wild elk from Michigan have tested positive for TB, too. The range of the state's elk herd overlaps the region where infected deer live. However, it appears as though the disease may no longer exist in Michigan's elk herd. No infected elk have turned up since 2006. Fortunately, the prevalence rate of TB in elk did not reach the level it has in deer. Over the years, 2,483 elk have been tested for the disease and there were only the five positives.

Besides wild deer, TB was confirmed in a captive herd of whitetails in Michigan. The captive herd originated from wild stock where the disease was present when a large area was fenced. So the herd was most likely infected from the beginning. The captive herd was totally eliminated to prevent spread of the disease from that source.

TB is caused by a bacteria that usually enters through nasal passages and infects the lungs, but transmission can also occur by eating or drinking food or milk contaminated with the bacteria. Before the days of milk pasteurization, people frequently became infected with TB by drinking milk that contained the bacteria because cows with the disease shed the bacteria in their milk. The bacteria is also shed in urine and feces from infected animals. TB bacteria can become airborne when an infected animal coughs or sneezes.

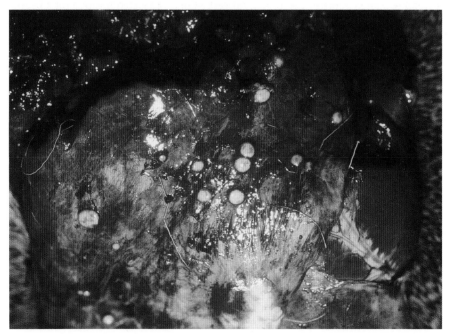

Lungs from a deer infected with TB. Note the light-colored nodules or lesions on the surface of the organ. Photo courtesy of the Michigan DNR.

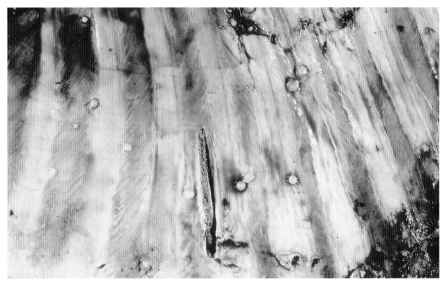

Internal chest cavity of a whitetail that has TB. Light-colored nodules or lesions are symptomatic of the disease. PHOTO COURTESY OF MICHIGAN DNR

Only one whitetail in Michigan is known to have died directly from TB. It was an old doe that died during the winter. Deer with TB don't normally exhibit any obvious symptoms, but in advanced cases, animals may cough reguarly. Unless the animal has an advanced case of the disease, hunters can't even tell if they've harvested an infected deer. The only way it can be determined if most deer have TB is through examination of lymph nodes in their heads by experts. In obvious cases of TB, pea-sized nodules (lesions) that are whitish, tan, or yellow in color are visible on the inside walls of the chest cavities of infected deer and on the lungs.

Historically, TB was common in cattle across North America. The disease was more prevalent in Michigan cattle herds during the 1940s and 50s than anywhere else in the U.S. Thirty percent of the cattle testing positive for the disease in the country during that era were in Michigan.

A bovine TB eradication program was subsequently begun and the state's cattle were classified as free of the disease by 1979. In spite of the TB-free classification, there is good reason to believe that the eradication effort in cattle was not totally successful. We have learned more recently that the disease can remain dormant in an animal for years until some form of stress causes it to surface. Dr. Earl Fairbanks from Rogers City, Michigan, was a veterinarian with the Department of Agriculture for twenty-five years, involved in testing cows for TB, and he doesn't think the disease was eliminated.

"It is my supposition that TB was never eradicated from the area," Fairbanks said. "The way the state was accredited TB free was not a test of all cattle over a 5-year period. They relied on meat inspection over a 5-year period. Some cows could have carried the disease and not shown any visible signs of it."

That has been proven to be true. With the high historic prevalence rate of TB among Michigan cattle, it is no surprise that the disease was spread to whitetails.

TB was common in North American cattle during the 1940s and 50s, with a higher prevalence rate among cows in Michigan. Even though Michigan cattle were declared TB-free in 1979, they weren't, and the same thing was probably true in other states and provinces such as Minnesota and Manitoba. The disease eventually spread to deer.

The same thing happened in New York and Ontario and domestic livestock transmitted the disease to mule deer in Montana (one animal) and Alberta (two animals). A total of three whitetails infected with bovine TB were recorded in New York prior to the more recent case of a captive deer in 2008. A pair of 3-year-old bucks with the disease turned up in 1933 and in 1961 TB was confirmed in a $5^1/_2$-year-old doe.

A $2^1/_2$-year-old deer with TB was identified in Ontario during 1958. The New York deer had contact with cattle herds carrying the disease. The source of the infection for the Ontario whitetail is unknown, but was most likely through contact with infected cattle, too. These historical reports of wild deer infected with TB in Ontario, New York, Montana, and Alberta were isolated cases, with the disease disappearing afterward.

The first whitetail in Michigan known to have TB turned up in November of 1975 in Alcona County. It was a 9.5-year-old doe. The diseased deer was considered to be an isolated case like the others, but, based on what is known today, that assumption was not accurate.

The finding of a second whitetail infected with TB during 1994, about eight miles from where the diseased doe had been in 1975, set the stage for testing more animals from the area and a better understanding of the extent of the problem. The TB-positive deer that was identified in 1994 was a $4^1/_2$-year-old buck that was shot during the firearms season in Alpena County.

Most of the TB-positive deer in Michigan have been in a contiguous eight-county region, with the majority of the diseased deer coming from Alpena and Alcona Counties. There have been a few isolated cases from other counties miles away, but, for the most part, the disease is restricted to the northeastern Lower

Peninsula. A total of 88,566 Michigan deer were examined for TB between 1995 and 2001 and 398 of those animals tested positive. Between 2003 and 2009, another 78,058 deer were tested for the disease and 212 were positive. Deer management unit (DMU) 452 has the highest prevalence of TB.

TB in Michigan Deer

YEAR	DEER EXAMINED FOR TB	NUMBER HAVING TB
1995	403	18
1996	4,966	56
1997	3,720	73
1998	9,057	78
1999	19,496	58
2000	25,858	53
2001	24,278	61
2002	18,100	51
2003	17,302	32
2004	15,131	28
2005	7,364	16
2006	7,914	41
2007	8,316	27
2008	16,309	37
2009	5,722	31

How TB Is Spread

How did whitetails get TB from cattle? Probably as a result of close contact during the winter and/or spring. Natural food supplies for deer are at their lowest during those seasons and that's when whitetails would have been drawn to feed lots to try to take advantage of food provided to cattle, especially during severe winters. The stress associated with tough winters would increase the vulnerability of deer to diseases such as TB when coming in close contact with cattle.

In the same way that cattle can transmit TB to whitetails, deer that have the disease can infect cows and other deer through repeated close contact. Widespread supplemental feeding of whitetails during the winter on large hunting clubs in the northeastern Lower Peninsula is thought to have played a major role in spreading the disease among the deer herd in that area. Deer populations were allowed to expand far beyond the natural carrying capacity of the habitat, compounding the problem. The more whitetails are present, the greater the potential for spreading the disease.

Research done at the National Animal Disease Center at Ames, Iowa, in research pens that are totally enclosed and have ventilation systems, confirmed that infected

Mule deer raiding cattle food in Wyoming during the winter. A similar situation in Michigan in which where cows and whitetails shared a feed lot is probably how deer got TB.

whitetails can infect other deer and cattle that they have close contact with. However, transmission seemed to be primarily through the air rather than through contaminated food. A summary of the results of the study involving diseased deer that infected healthy whitetails stated, "Lesion distribution in exposed deer suggests aerosol transmission as a likely means of infection."

TB was so common years ago because cows were—and often still are—housed in barns under crowded conditions. Conditions were perfect for disease transmission, just as they are in enclosed research pens occupied by infected animals. The large winter supplemental deer feeding sites that existed in northeastern Michigan were also ideal for disease transmission because they brought hundreds of deer into close contact. Since baiting was unregulated for many years and large quantities of food were also used for that purpose, the practice probably played a role in the transmission of TB as well. There was actually little, if any, difference between baiting and supplemental feeding at the time, and feeding went on year-round.

Once the TB problem was identified, all deer feeding was banned in the affected area and regulations were established for baiting. All baiting in DMU 452 was eventually banned, too, even though there was a controversy about whether regulated baiting contributed to the spread of TB. The role regulated baiting plays in controlling TB is now much clearer. More on that later.

What is known about transmission of TB through food is that calves can become infected from their mother's milk. Dianna Whipple, who is lead scientist at the Disease Lab in Iowa, said she thinks whitetail does infected with TB also shed the bacteria in their milk, but she hasn't come up with a way to test that hypothesis experimentally. She said one of the deer infected with TB from a captive herd in Presque Isle County was a fawn that had been bottle fed from the time it was a couple of days old. The only way that fawn could have become infected is through its mother's milk or before it was born.

Researchers at Ames, Iowa, accidentally confirmed that does with TB can infect their fawns while they are developing in the uterus, according to researcher Mitch Palmer. He said a group of does that were thought not to be pregnant were infected with TB. As it turned out, a pair of the does were indeed pregnant and their fawns had the disease before they were born. Those deer got a larger dose of bacteria than planned, however, and that might be responsible for transmission to the unborn fawns.

The passing of TB from does to fawns may, in fact, be the major means of transmission among whitetails. This doesn't mean that all fawns born to does that have TB become infected, but a portion of them do. The opportunity for transmission of TB to fawns from does is much greater than any other means. If fawns do not become infected before they are born or while nursing, they can breathe the bacteria in during close nose-to-nose contact with their mothers. Does and fawns do a lot of mutual grooming by licking each other, including touching noses.

Michigan DNR Veterinarian Dr. Steve Schmitt said he believes the biggest risk of does transmitting TB to their fawns is through close contact. He said, "There is a tremendous amount of nose-to-nose contact between does and fawns."

There appears to be a correlation between the prevalence rate of TB in adult does and yearlings in DMU 452, which adds credibility to the premise that infected does are passing the disease along to some of their offspring. Between 1996 and 1997, for example, the prevalence rate in adult does went up to 4.7 percent from 3.4. During those same years, the prevalence rate in yearlings jumped to 1.5 percent from 1.

There was a significant drop in the prevalence rate among does from 1997 to 1998, from 4.7 to 1.8 percent. The rate also went down among yearlings, but only slightly—from 1.5 to 1.4 percent—probably because there were still a significant number of infected offspring in the population carried over from 1997. The low rate of infected does during 1998 is really reflected in the reduced number of diseased

The primary way TB is now spread among whitetails in Michigan and elsewhere is from infected does to their fawns. If fawns aren't born with the disease, they can become infected from their mothers' milk or through repeated nose-to-nose contact.

yearlings in the harvest for 1999, at 0.6 percent.

The prevalence rate among does increased again during 1999, although not by much; it went up from 1.8 to 2.1 percent and it remained the same for 2000. The increased disease rate among adult does for 1999 and 2000 showed up in yearlings during 2001, with a prevalence rate of 0.7 percent.

The theory that adult does spread TB to their fawns is reinforced by research done at Michigan State University by Dr. Ken Scribner. He and his students have compared the DNA of infected deer and concluded deer with TB are often more closely related than other deer. Their hypothesis is that this is because related deer are more likely to interact and infect one another.

Julie Blanchong, who was a graduate student at the time, presented the DNA findings at a TB conference in Lansing,

A whitetail doe urinating. Does that have TB may also be responsible for passing the disease to bucks during the rut through their urine. Research has confirmed that deer with the disease pass the bacteria in their urine. Bucks routinely smell a doe's urine to determine if she is ready to breed.

Michigan, during March of 2001. Regulated baiting was banned at the time in counties where deer infected with TB had been identified.

"We used the genealogical results to develop a model of the prevalence and distribution of TB in deer over time," she said. "Preliminary results indicate that current management practices will result in a decrease, but not elimination of TB-positive deer over time."

Adult does also have close contact with adult bucks during the breeding season, so it's possible does that have TB can spread the disease to their mates, too. Actually, does with TB are most likely to infect bucks with the disease through their urine and they can spread the disease to a number of bucks in this way, not just those that they mate with. Research has shown that does with TB shed the bacteria in their urine. Since bucks repeatedly smell and taste the urine of does to determine if they are ready to breed, the bacteria can gain access to their nasal passages in that way.

According to veteran whitetail researcher John Ozoga, who studied deer as an employee of the Michigan DNR for forty years, bucks determine if does are ready to breed by taking in urine through their mouth by licking the liquid, which goes into the vomeronasal organ on the roof of the mouth. This repeated close contact with the urine from does is bound to increase the chances of developing TB among bucks that interact with infected does.

The prevalence rate for TB has been consistently higher among adult bucks that are at least $2^1/2$ years old than in any other segment of the deer population of DMU 452, according to DNR data. It's assumed that the larger territories of these deer and the resulting stress during the rut make them more susceptible to the disease. But

Whitetail bucks commonly exhibit a lip curl like this one is doing to test a doe's urine. They may inhale some urine along with TB bacteria when they do this. Since bucks breed with more than one doe they have an increased chance of exposure.

what makes them even more vulnerable to TB is the close contact they have with does and their urine during the courting and mating process, some of which could be infected with the disease. Adult bucks breed with multiple does, increasing their chances of exposure.

Once again, there's a correlation between the prevalence rate of TB among adult bucks and does from DMU 452. During 1996, the prevalence rate was similar for adult does (3.4 percent) and bucks (3.6). The proportions of diseased deer among both sexes went up in 1997. For does, the prevalence rate was 4.7 percent and it was a whopping 9.3 percent for adult bucks, although that's to be expected because more than one buck can be infected by the same doe.

The number of infected does underwent a significant decline in 1998 to 1.8 percent. The rate of infected adult bucks also went down (to 7.8), but not by as much, probably because the number included diseased animals from the year before. Adult bucks are often the toughest for hunters to get. The decline in the infection rate among does really started to show up in adult bucks during 1999, when it dropped to 4.1 percent.

The slight increase in the prevalence rate among adult does for 1999 appears to have shown up in bucks during 2000. However, with overall lower deer numbers in DMU 452 and a very low prevalence rate of the disease, the odds of does transmitting TB to bucks have gone down. Most bucks are also more healthy as a result of a smaller herd, making them less susceptible to getting the disease.

It's worth noting that adult bucks can spread the disease among themselves through mutual grooming in the same way that does infect their fawns. Bucks form bachelor groups during the summer months and they routinely groom each other. This form of nose-to-nose contact is more direct, with a higher risk of disease transmission than at bait sites.

To determine if animals could contract TB by eating food contaminated with the bacteria, a study was conducted at the Iowa disease research lab. Calves were fed corn and hay contaminated with high levels of TB (doses of 100,000 bacteria) and half of them did not contract the disease. This experiment proves that although

Bucks may transmit TB to one another through mutual grooming as shown here or through nose-to-nose contact. Bachelor groups of bucks routinely engage in mutual grooming.

animals can get the disease from contaminated food, it is not an efficient way of spreading the disease. The calves were fed hay and corn spiked with TB bacteria every day for five days. After five days of exposure to TB, the calves were kept alive for five months to give the disease a chance to develop. After that time, they were killed and examined for symptoms.

Dianna Whipple commented that some animals may have immunity to the disease. She added that the bacteria are also more likely to be killed or rendered ineffective in the gastrointestinal tract than if they are inhaled. Whipple also said that the rate of infection in the study might have been higher if the calves had been allowed to live longer.

What's even more important than the fact that not all deer that ingest large quantities of TB bacteria become infected is that the odds of whitetails eating viable bacteria with their food in the wild is extremely low because exposure to sunlight kills TB bacteria. Consequently, the organisms have a short life span in the outdoors. That is probably the major reason why researchers have been unable to culture TB bacteria from food, soil and water samples in the natural environment, even where the disease has been most prevalent.

Proof that the bacteria does not survive well in the outdoors was verified on a 1,500-acre fenced ranch in Presque Isle County that had deer infected with TB. The prevalence rate for this captive herd was 12 percent, almost three times as high as the highest prevalence rate for free ranging deer in DMU 452. Food, soil and water samples were taken from this ranch at and near feeding sites and there was no success in culturing the bacteria from these samples.

The supplemental feeding sites that were tested were where large quantities of food had been placed and high numbers of deer visited. If the bacteria can not be cultured at supplemental feeding locations where the prevalence rate of TB among deer is three times higher than in unfenced habitat, it stands to reason the bacteria would be impossible to detect at bait sites where smaller quantities of food are scattered.

Regardless of how deer get TB, symptoms of the disease develop slowly in many cases, so an animal that has TB may not show any visible signs of having it, yet is capable of spreading it. The good news is that the prevalence rate of the disease among all deer has slowly but steadily been declining, as the table below shows. Since 2003, however, the prevalence rate for all deer has been relatively constant even though baiting has been banned, which reflects continued direct transmission between deer that are related or interacting during the rut.

Prevalence Rate Of TB-Infected Deer In DMU 452

YEAR	ALL DEER	ADULT BUCKS	ADULT DOES	YEARLINGS
1996	2.3	3.6	3.4	1.0
1997	4.4	9.3	4.7	1.5
1998	2.5	7.8	1.8	1.4
1999	2.2	4.1	2.1	0.6
2000	2.5	4.9	2.1	0.6
2001	2.3	3.8	1.6	0.7
2002	2.8	7.17	1.2	1.4
2003	1.7	4.2	1.2	0.3
2004	1.7	3.6	1.5	0.0
2005	1.2	2.2	1.4	0.2
2006	2.3	5.7	0.8	1.3
2007	1.4	2.9	0.8	0.4
2008	1.8	3.7	1.2	0.6
2009	1.9	2.8	2.2	0.4

The only way to reduce these numbers further is through increased deer harvests in DMU 452, especially among antlered bucks. Amazingly, the Michigan Natural Resources Commission, which is responsible for setting hunting regulations, adopted rules for the 2010 season that will do the opposite. The commission approved more stringent antler restrictions for that part of the state like those that have been in effect for the Upper Peninsula since 2008.

Hunters who buy combination deer licenses, which include two buck tags, are now limited to shooting one buck with at least three antler points on a side and one with a minimum of four points on a side. Until 2010, one buck tag on combo licenses was valid for a buck with at least three-inch spikes in the entire Lower Peninsula. The change will protect some yearling bucks, allowing them to live another year and increasing their chances of getting TB.

Deer hunters in the TB zone who buy single gun or bow licenses will be able to shoot a buck with at least three-inch spikes, but they will be limited to shooting one buck a year instead of two. This will also reduce the buck harvest in that area. The new rules, in fact, will further reduce the total deer harvest in that management unit because some hunters who have been hunting there will choose to hunt elsewhere where the regulations are more liberal. The end result will probably be an increase in the prevalence rate of TB in the future.

Regulated Baiting & TB

Deer baiting regulations began in Michigan's TB Zone during 1998 as a means of reducing the spread of the disease. Quantity limits of five gallons of bait per day were set and the practice was limited to the months of September through December. Prior to that time, deer baiting was unrestricted, meaning it was legal year-round in any amount that hunters chose. There's no question the change was necessary and it played an important role in getting a handle on the potential of the practice for disease transmission.

The year before the baiting restrictions were put in place, a Michigan State University study was begun in the TB Zone to assess close contact between deer at bait sites in an effort to determine the potential for the spread of disease at these locations. Whitetails were observed feeding at baits consisting of more than five gallons and quantities of five gallons dumped in piles, in lines, and scattered. The number of times deer had nose-to-nose contact and times their noses came within three feet of one another were counted.

It was determined that deer feeding at baits had more close contact at piles consisting of five gallons than those of larger quantities. Contact was reduced, but still significant, when five gallons of bait was spread out in lines. However, when a limited quantity of bait was scattered, close contact between deer was practically eliminated at baits.

A report on the findings stated that it was almost impossible for deer to make contact with one another when corn was spread thinly. Even with nearly one hundred deer feeding on bait scattered in that manner, there was only one instance of whitetails having nose-to-nose contact, and the noses of deer came within three feet of each other only five times.

Something else of extreme importance that was noticed with baits limited to five gallons is that the quantity limit increased daytime visitation by whitetails. When large quantities of bait were used, many deer fed at baits after dark. Due to increased competition for the limited food at bait sites when quantities of food were restricted, hunters were more likely to see deer during legal shooting hours, increasing the value of baiting as a management tool.

Due to information gathered about baiting during the study, it was recommended in 1998 that hunters who use bait scatter the food to reduce close contact between deer. The opportunity to transmit TB would be eliminated by doing that, and at the same time the odds of filling tags were increased. And the best way to control and then eliminate TB was for hunters to harvest as many infected whitetails as possible, so it was a win-win situation.

Although some critical information was gathered about deer baiting during the Michigan State University study, there was a major omission in data collection that would have been valuable in determining the potential of spreading TB among deer at bait sites. There was no effort made to identify related does and fawns and the

Studies done in Michigan found that when bait such as corn was spread, it eliminated nose-to-nose contact between unrelated deer along with the potential of spreading diseases like TB.

close contact between them versus that between unrelated deer. As already discussed, does and their fawns have frequent nose-to-nose contact even if they don't visit bait sites, increasing the potential for infected does to pass the disease on to their offspring. Consequently, I suspect most, if not all, of the close contacts at baits observed during the study were between related deer.

I feel very strongly that this is the case, as I have conducted my share of observations of deer at baits over the years, both while photographing and hunting, and I've discussed this issue with other hunters who use bait. My conclusion is that close contact, either nose-to-nose or within three feet, between unrelated deer is rare to nonexistent at baits. Adult does will not tolerate the close proximity of unrelated deer while they are feeding at baits. Unrelated deer that approach are chased away. Antlered bucks are given plenty of room at baits, too. Antlerless deer either leave when bucks approach or move out of their way.

If I'm right, regulated baiting in which quantities of food are limited and scattered does not contribute to the spread of TB. At the same time, the practice can increase the potential for hunters to harvest infected deer, thereby reducing the prevalence of the disease. There's more information that follows to verify that.

The Michigan DNR's policy-setting body, the Natural Resources Commission (NRC), decided to allow baiting for deer hunting in management unit 452 during 1999 in quantities of no more than five gallons per day, so the hunting method could continue its role as a management tool. The type of bait was to be restricted to individual grain seeds like corn and pelletized food. However, after that decision was made, the DNR and NRC received a letter from the U. S. Department of Agriculture (USDA) stating a ban on baiting in that unit was necessary.

"The United States Department of Agriculture is requiring a ban on the use of bait in the Bovine TB Management Unit," the letter said. "This non-negotiable condition is required for granting tuberculosis zoning for Michigan within the National TB Eradication Program."

To comply with the USDA directive, the NRC voted at their next monthly meeting to make baiting illegal in DMU 452 during 1999. By that time, there had already been plenty of publicity that regulated baiting would be legal in the TB Zone. The on-again, off-again way the issue was handled did not foster support among many hunters in the area, especially private land owners. Many hunters also did not like the fact that baiting and feeding of captive deer was legal in DMU 452 under Michigan Department of Agriculture rules, but was illegal on unfenced property in that same unit in response to USDA mandate. The inconsistencies generated resistance. DNR TB Eradication Field Coordinator Elaine Carlson reported that there was 60 percent noncompliance with the ban on baiting in DMU 452 during 1999. There was still more than 50 percent noncompliance with the ban on baiting in DMU 452 during 2000, according to DNR Law Division Chief Richard Asher.

As regulated baiting was legal in DMU 452 during 1998 and continued at a fairly high rate during 1999 and 2000, and the prevalence rate for TB declined during both 1998 and 1999 and has remained low since then, it is clear that regulated baiting does not contribute to the spread of TB. The technique can better enable hunters to help eliminate the disease by maximizing deer harvest. The ban on baiting resulted in the harvest of fewer deer. Forty percent of the hunters who tried their luck in DMU 452 during 1999, many of whom were bowhunters, did comply with the baiting ban. A survey done by the DNR to gather data on what impacts a ban on baiting had in DMU 452 during 1999 clearly shows a significant drop in success among bowhunters. During the early archery season in that management unit, the bow harvest was down by 35 percent even though more archers hunted there during 1999 than in 1998. And the harvest during firearms season declined by 11 percent in spite of an 18 percent increase in hunter numbers. Overall hunting success also declined in DMU 452 during 2000.

Even though a significant number of hunters chose to ignore baiting regulations in DMU 452 during 1999 and 2000,

When regulated baiting was resumed in Michigan's TB Zone during 2001, it attracted more hunters to the area and those who used bait had a higher rate of success than those who didn't, increasing the chances of harvesting diseased deer. The fact that prevalence of TB did not increase with the use of bait confirms the practice is not responsible for spreading the disease.

60   DEER HUNTING

many more chose to hunt in other regions where baiting remained legal. Quantity restrictions on baiting were established statewide outside DMU 452 during 1999 and baiting was limited to dates that coincided with deer season. By 2001, the NRC realized that if progress was going to be made in further conrolling TB in DMU 452 an incentive would be necessary to increase hunter numbers in that unit along with the deer harvest. So they legalized baiting in that management unit for 2001 in quantities of one gallon of grain per day.

As expected, DNR survey results from 2001 seasons in DMU 452 show that hunters using bait had a much higher rate of success than other hunters. Bowhunters using bait had a 41 percent rate of success compared to only 13 percent for non-baiters. Among firearms hunters, those who used bait had a 51 percent success rate versus 39 percent among hunters who used other methods. Since survey results confirm that hunters using bait can be more successful than those who don't and the prevalence rate of TB among deer is not increasing with the use of bait, it appears this hunting method can play an important role in reducing TB-infected deer in the state.

Survey results among hunters who hunted in DMU 452 during 2001 also showed that the previous ban on baiting resulted in 51 percent of bowhunters spending less time hunting that area; 21 percent avoided hunting DMU 452 altogether. Among gun hunters, 12 percent chose to hunt elsewhere when the ban was in effect and 31 percent spent less time hunting in DMU 452. The best way for hunters to harvest enough deer to significanty reduce TB is obviously to encourage them to hunt in DMU 452, not to discourage them.

Unfortunately, baiting was once again banned in DMU 452 in 2002 in spite of favorable results, due to political pressure and inaccurate interpretation of scientific data.

Estimates of Number of Hunters, Harvest, and Hunting Success in DMU 452 in 2001

SEASON	HUNTERS		HARVEST		PERCENT SUCCESS	
	Baiters	Nonbaiters	Baiters	Nonbaiters	Baiters	Nonbaiters
Archery	2,856	3,278	1,185	422	41	13
Firearm	4,593	9,721	2,337	3,603	51	37

From a 2002 survey on deer baiting.

Controlling TB

A number of factors are responsible for the decline of TB-infected deer in Michigan's core area. Outlawing winter feeding of deer and elk along with the increased harvest of antlerless whitetails are the two most important measures. Placing controls on deer baiting (not banning it) has also helped.

Antlerless permits have been unlimited in number for the TB Zone as an incentive for hunters to take as many deer as possible. Disease control permits have also been issued to farmers and other landowners. Both early- and late-season firearms hunts for antlerless deer only have been held in the management unit to increase the harvest, too.

Expanded hunting seasons and bag limits in DMU 452 have resulted in approximately a 35 percent reduction in deer numbers in that zone. That's good news, but the remaining does are healthier and therefore more productive. Recent mild winters have also contributed to the difficulty of controlling the deer population and TB infection rate. More deer survive during mild winters and because does come through the winter in good shape, they are more likely to produce more fawns. Most adult does have twins and some give birth to triplets. Excellent fawn production and survival can easily offset high harvests.

Consequently, it is important to maintain the cooperation of hunters to achieve as high a deer harvest as possible every year to further reduce TB prevalence rates. Incentives that will draw new hunters to DMU 452 as well as keep those who have traditionally hunted there would be helpful.

Double fencing of captive deer facilities in DMU 452 to prevent the transmission of TB either way through single fences is just as important as in areas with CWD. Double fencing reduces the chances of captive deer escaping or wild animals entering through a damaged fence, too. The owner of the 1,500-deer ranch in Presque Isle County who lost his entire herd to TB, released healthy

Liberal antlerless harvests and special seasons in the TB Zone have enabled hunters to reduce the herd closer to an acceptable level while eliminating diseased animals. Unlimited antlerless permits and disease control permits have been issued for that unit. Additional incentives to attract hunters, such as resumption of regulated baiting, as was done in 2001, are needed to further reduce prevalence of the disease.

animals in the enclosure a year later. He voluntarily put up a double fence to make sure his healthy stock wasn't infected by wild deer.

Precautions For Hunters

The same precautions for handling harvested deer outlined above in the discussion about CWD also apply when hunting in areas where TB-infected deer are found. Use rubber or latex gloves when gutting, skinning, and butcherng carcasses. Since TB bacteria infect internal organs, you don't have to be concerned about cutting through the spine or skull with a saw. However, if you do use a saw to butcher a deer, make sure it is thoroughly cleaned and disinfected to remove any bacteria that may have gotten on the blade. Knives used to field dress, skin, and butcher deer should be thoroughly cleaned as well after each process.

The meat of deer that are infected with TB is perfectly safe to eat, but the decision to do so is a personal choice. TB bacteria are killed through cooking. Venison from a deer that had TB or could have had the disease should be cooked to an interal temperature of 165 degrees for 15 seconds to kill any bacteria. The Michigan DNR does test deer for TB at no charge. Testing is voluntary.

EHD/Blue Tongue

Two viral disease that are similar are transmitted to deer by tiny biting insects called no-see-ums. They are Epizootic Hemorrhagic Disease (EHD) and Blue Tongue. Humans are thought to be immune to both viruses.

EHD has taken a greater toll on deer in North America than CWD, yet many deer hunters have probably not heard of it. Ninety percent of the deer exposed to the virus usually die, sometimes within a matter of a few days. Diseased animals develop a fever, lose their appetite, have difficulty breathing, and become disoriented. The fever causes sick deer to go to water to drink or cool off. Consequently, animals that die of EHD are often found in or near rivers, creeks, ponds and lakes.

Before death, deer go into a state of shock. The disease destroys blood vessel walls, causing hemorrhaging in organs such as the lungs, liver, heart, and spleen as well as the digestive tract. Tongues swell and develop sores that may also appear on the roof of the mouth. Lower jaws are often swollen, too. EHD outbreaks occur in the summer and early fall during hot weather. Incidence of the disease ceases after a frost because the tiny gnats or midges responsible for causing it are usually killed.

EHD was a mystery disease in the southeastern U.S. during the 1940s and 50s, like CWD now is, when large numbers of whitetails started dying from it. Through research, scientists eventually figured out that no-see-ums were transmitting the disease by sucking blood from infected deer and passing the virus on to other deer they subsequently fed on. Besides southeastern states, EHD has occurred in Nebraska, Oklahoma, Kansas, Montana, Wyoming, Alberta, Idaho, Iowa, Indiana, North and South Dakota, Wisconsin, Michigan, Ohio, Pennsylvania, West Virginia, and New Jersey.

Hundreds of deer died of EHD in Ohio during 2002 and there was another outbreak of the disease in that state during 2007. In fact, there was a major outbreak of EHD during 2007 that affected more than thirty states. According to estimates of the disease's impact, it claimed more than 65,000 deer that year alone. The disease was documented for the first time in Pennsylvania during 2002. Seventy whitetail are known to have died there, fifty in Greene County and twenty in Washington County. West Viginia deer also died of EHD during 2002.

An especially severe outbreak of EHD occurred in Kansas, Wyoming, Nebraska and New Jersey during 1976. Thousands of deer died of the disease in each state. It was estimated that 30 to 40 percent of Nebraska's deer population died of EHD that year. Smaller groups of deer are normally killed when the disease surfaces. Eighteen whitetails that were found dead in Wisconsin's Iowa County near Arena during 2002, for example, were claimed by EHD. Due to the recent occurrence of CWD in that county, it was originally thought that was what they died of.

When EHD first started claiming large numbers of deer in the southeast years ago, what was causing the deaths of numerous whitetails was a mystery. That mystery was soon solved. Hopefully, researchers will also be able to solve the mystery surrounding CWD. Meanwhile, outbreaks of EHD are occurring in new areas and claiming more deer than CWD.

Deer that develop EHD are often found dead in or near water.

Confirmed outbreaks of EHD were documented in Michigan during 1955 and 1972. Dead deer were found in ten counties across the center of the Lower Peninsula during the episode in 1955. Fishermen started finding sick and dead whitetails along rivers and streams on September 3. The highest deer losses to the disease occurred during September, but dead deer turned up into November. EHD killed deer in different parts of Michigan in 2006 and 2008, too.

Blue Tongue is more common among domestic livestock such as sheep and cattle than deer, and this disease does not result in the death of infected animals as often as EHD does. The disease is so named because the tongues and lips of infected animals often swell and turn blue or purple from a lack of oxygen in the blood.

Anthrax

Anthrax is a bacterial disease like TB, but unlike TB, this one normally kills whitetails and mule deer that become infected with it. Deer get it by eating or drinking contaminated food and water. Symptoms include abnormal behavior brought on by a fever and difficulty breathing.

This disease usually occurs in areas with alkaline soils during droughts following heavy rain. Anthrax spores can live in the ground for a long time and these conditions tend to bring them to the surface where they can infect deer.

Texas has experienced serious deer losses to anthrax. The disease hit during the summer of 2001 in the western part of the state and it has infected both deer and livestock in that region periodically in the past. One land owner reportedly lost 70 percent of the deer population on his property to anthrax.

Carcasses from deer that die of anthrax contaminate the soil as they break down. The remaining bacteria can then infect other animals in the future when the right conditions develop.

Anthrax is transmissable to people. If precautions such as wearing gloves and masks aren't taken, hunters can become contaminated with the bacteria while handling infected carcasses. It is not recommended to eat deer that have anthrax. However, since this disease kills deer quickly, if hunters avoid shooting aimals that act sick the opportunity to eat infected venison should not present itself.

Lyme Disease

Lyme Disease isn't known as a problem for deer, but it is for people, and deer are indirectly responsible for spreading it to people and their pets (dogs). Small external parasites known as deer ticks can transmit Lyme Disease to humans, and whitetails are one of the ticks' hosts. The more deer there are, the more ticks there are, and the greater the risk of becoming infected with the disease is for individuals who spend a lot of time in the outdoors, like hunters.

Deer ticks go through a couple of larval stages in their development. Small mammals like white-footed deer mice are one of the primary hosts of larval deer ticks. The ticks become infected with the agent that causes Lyme Disease from mice. When infected ticks attach to humans, they can transmit the disease to them if the parasites are not detected and removed within a period of hours.

When scouting or hunting in areas known to harbor deer ticks, it's important to check your clothing, body, and hair for ticks at the end of the day, if possible, to find and remove any you may have picked up. Use a mirror to check your back or enlist the help of a spouse or family member. My wife Lucy does not like ticks and she insists on performing tick checks when I get home to make sure none of the parasites avoid detection. Besides her dislike for ticks, she realizes that if I have been bitten, early detection is the best defense against the disease. One time when I returned home from several days of turkey hunting out of town, Lucy noticed the characteristic bullseye rash from a deer tick bite on my back. The red rash had a white center. This rash is common from deer tick bites, but it does not appear in all cases.

I did develop Lyme disease, but I saw my doctor right away and he put me on antibiotics that quickly cured it. Feeling more tired than normal, sleeping more than normal, headaches, a fever, and having aching joints are symptoms of Lyme Disease. Much more serious effects to the heart and nervous system can develop if the disease is not detected early. Tests are available to detect Lyme Disease, but the results are not always accurate.

Dogs that are exposed to the outdoors where deer ticks are found should be examined for parasites, too, because they can also contract Lyme Disease.

Tucking pant legs inside socks, when possible, will prevent ticks from crawling up legs. The parasites are easier to see and remove when on the outside of pant legs, too, espcially when you wear light colored clothes, but that's not normally possible when hunting. Repellents can be sprayed on pant legs to discourage ticks from hitching a ride, but that doesn't eliminate the need for tick checks. Strong-smelling repellents are not recommended while hunting because deer can detect such odors better than we can.

A record number of cases of Lyme Disease were reported in the U.S. during 2009, exceeding 30,000 for the first time, according to the Center for Disease Control. It is most common in eastern states. The disease was first identified in Connecticut, which in 2009 ranked fifth for the number of cases reported (with 4,156 cases), behind Pennsylvania (5,722 cases), New York (5,651), Massachusetts (5,256), and New Jersey (4,973). Other states where the disease is common are Rhode Island, Maryland, Delaware, Wisconsin, and Minnesota, but it occurs in many others, including Michigan. It can develop anywhere deer ticks are found.

We have a tall plastic garbage can that's light in color in our house known as the tick bucket. Clothes that are worn outside and that could have ticks clinging to them go in that bucket until they are washed. Even though clothes are examined for ticks before they go in the bucket or the wash, it's easy to miss them.

Since ticks normally climb upward, I sometimes find the ones I missed on the top rim of the bucket. To get rid of ticks when I find them, I throw them in a fire, if one is handy, cut them in half with a knife, or flush them down the toilet. Since ticks are flat, they are impossible to squash. After handling ticks, I wash my hands thoroughly and clean my knife, if it was used.

Ticks may be on deer carcasses taken by hunters, especially those killed during early seasons, and the parasites tend to drop off the carcasses as they cool. Hunters who are concerned about contaminating their vehicle, yard, garage, or basement with ticks should put a piece of plastic or paper under a deer to collect ticks. The accumulated parasites then can be rolled up in the plastic or paper and disposed of.

If precautions aren't taken, the ticks could end up on people, pets, or small mammals. Parasites that succeed in getting a blood meal from another host could lay eggs, resulting in an increase of ticks in the area.

A way to reduce the possibility of transporting ticks on a deer carcass from the area where it was shot is to hang the whitetail in the woods as long as possible before taking it to camp or home. Then most ticks will drop off where they won't be a concern. However, this method will not get rid of all ticks, as I found out on a whitetail I shot opening day of Michigan's gun season (November 15) in Menominee County one year.

The buck I tagged was hung near where I shot it for two days and it snowed on the second day, so I figured it was cold enough to kill any ticks that remained on the carcass. But when I skinned the deer on the evening of the 17th, I found two ticks that were very much alive. I sealed the hide in a plastic bag to make sure any remaining ticks would be contained.

Ticks can transmit at least two other diseases to people that hunters should be aware of—ehrlichiosis and Rocky Mountain spotted fever. Spotted fever can occur in many western states. Ehrlichiosis has been reported in east Texas and may occur in neighboring states.

Conclusion

Although these are the major diseases associated with deer, they certainly are not the only ones and new maladies can crop up at any time. Livestock worldwide are known to carry at least three hundred different diseases. Due to the small world we now live in, it would not be a surprise if a disease common in another country suddenly appeared in North American deer with the assistance of humans. So be careful out there!

3

Where to Hunt

Sometimes deer hunting can be easy, especially if you choose your hunting spot wisely. That's what it was like for me to fill a tag with a mature buck the first time I hunted whitetails in Michigan's Keweenaw County during firearms season. This northernmost county in the state has a reputation for having few deer. However, the key to success, regardless of where you hunt, is being in the right place at the right time and that's what happened for me in the land of few deer.

I decided to hunt Keweenaw County because I got an invitation from Troy West-cott of Lac La Belle to hunt out of a tent camp with him and his friends. Troy owns and operates Lac La Belle Lodge with his wife Cathy. I had bear hunted out of the lodge and got to know Troy and his deer hunting buddies. We got along well and I liked the rugged country, so I took him up on the offer, but it would be the evening of November 17 before I could get there (the season opened on the 15th).

I met Troy at the lodge the evening of the 17th and we left for the tent camp at daylight the next morning. We reached camp around 9:30 A.M. I had hunted bear near the camp earlier in the fall, so I knew a little bit about the terrain and had a spot in mind to hunt.

I got in a position where I expected to see deer at 10:15 A.M. on November 18. An hour later, a $3^{1}/_{2}$-year-old buck came walking in front of me and I shot him. I thought the buck had an eight-point rack when I dropped the deer, but the antlers actually only had seven points, since he didn't have any brow tines. If the antlers had had brow tines, he would have been a nine-pointer.

The buck had a dressed weight of 160 pounds, so he would have weighed around 190 on the hoof. Not bad for my first Keweenaw County buck after an hour of hunting!

So how did I do so well in a county with so few deer? My more than forty years of deer hunting experience obviously played a role. So did some timely preseason

Left: I pose with the 3½-year-old 7-pointer I shot during my first hunt in Keweenaw County after only posting for an hour. Right: I examine the scrape I found under a leaning cedar tree during October that prompted me to hunt nearby during the November firearms season. By then, there were more scrapes and numerous antler-rubbed trees along the base of an oak ridge.

scouting, along with the fact that there was an excellent acorn crop in the Keweenaw that year.

Both bear and deer like acorns. During the latter part of my bear hunt in October, I spent some time on an oak ridge near the deer camp looking for bear. I didn't see any bear, but I did see a couple of deer. I also found a fresh scrape under a cedar tree along the base of the oak ridge.

Bucks make scrapes to advertise their presence to local does prior to the breeding season. Older bucks are usually the first to make scrapes. Since the scrape I saw while bear hunting was made during late October, I knew it was made by an adult buck. Besides being at the base of an oak ridge, the buck sign was also along the edge of a thick swamp, which would be a perfect place for a buck to cruise for does during daylight hours.

When Troy invited me back to hunt deer, I couldn't get that scrape out of my mind. I knew it would be a perfect place to ambush a buck. That's why I went there right after arriving in camp. I was hoping the scrape was still active and it was.

Not only had the original scrape been enlarged, there were at least two other scrapes that had been made under limbs on the opposite side of the leaning cedar tree. Besides the scrapes, bucks had rubbed a total of seven nearby saplings with their antlers. Based on the amount of sign, I figured it had been made by more than one buck.

Prior to November 15, while preparing for the hunt, one of the camp members had seen a big buck with a rack that had at least ten points not far from where that scrape was. That sighting was ample evidence of the presence of at least one trophy whitetail in the area.

The spot looked so good, I knew I had an excellent chance of taking a buck there. I simply picked a spot to stand on the side of the ridge where I had a good view of the buck sign and waited. And I didn't have long to wait.

I heard the buck coming from right to left along the edge of the swamp and he was in my sights as soon as he stepped in the open. A neck shot dropped him instantly. Shooting the buck was not only easy, getting the buck back to camp was also a snap. Bill Westerbrink was able to drive his four-wheeler next to where the buck fell. He and Dave Menominee then loaded the deer on the ATV for transport to camp.

One of the first steps on the way to a satisfying deer hunt is to make a good choice about where to hunt. Doing so often takes time and effort, but the consideration this phase of the hunt gets can prove to be well worth it. The process of picking the best location possible increases anticipation of the upcoming season and adds an important touch of confidence to a trip, which can make the difference between success and failure.

Planning where to go on a deer hunt should be done as far in advance of the season as possible. However, it is still important to be flexible, so that you can change locations based on key information that might come in at the last minute. Most of the work involved in deciding where to go can be done from home. This stage of deer hunting fills the gap between one season and the next. It is homework deer hunters shouldn't mind doing.

Preseason selection of an area for deer season is important on any deer hunt, but it is vital in some states. These states require hunters to specify a region or management unit in which they wish to hunt. That area is marked on their licenses and restricts them to hunting within that area. This requirement will probably become more prevalent in the future.

Planning where to go is just as important for deer hunters who hunt in their home region or state as it is for those who travel to another state or province. Typically, deer hunters who confine their hunting to home territory know little about deer densities a county or two away, and so miss out on what might be better deer hunting. These hunters hunt the same locations year after year and often accept the hunting available in their spots as representative of what is available throughout the region or state. In many cases this is far from the truth.

Varying Deer Densities

My home region, the Upper Peninsula of Michigan, will serve as a perfect illustration of how deer densities can vary regionally. Some of the best and some of the worst deer hunting in the state, in terms of the average number of deer per square mile, can be found in this fifteen-county area. Northern counties that border Lake

Superior such as Keweenaw, have a high percentage of mature forests and long, cold winters, resulting in low deer numbers. Farming is common in southern counties of the region, younger forests are also found there, and winters aren't as severe as farther north. Those circumstances are responsible for high deer densities and some of the best deer hunting in the state. A drive of 50 to 100 miles south in upper Michigan can take hunters from poor to excellent deer hunting.

Other Factors

Deer density is one of the most important considerations in deciding where to hunt, but other factors must be considered, too. These include hunter density, availability of public land to hunt, and antler growth. Many times where there are the most deer, there will also be the most hunters. I don't like to hunt deer where the odds favor seeing more hunters than whitetails or mule deer. If little or no public land is available in an area of high deer density, permission to hunt private property must be obtained. When that isn't possible, an alternate location must be found. And deer hunters interested in trophy heads won't often find them in areas of high deer concentrations, unless the spot is lightly hunted.

When interested in hunting a different state or province than the one where you live, a number of additional factors should be considered. They include season dates, bag limits, availability of licenses, license fees, and hunter success ratios. Sometimes season dates and differing hunter success are considerations from area to area within one state or province, too.

Gathering Informaton

Most of the necessary information on deer densities, harvest figures, hunter success, seasons, licenses, antler growth, and availability of public land can be obtained from state/provincial fish and game agencies or departments of natural resources. All states and provinces publish an annual hunting digest that contains pertinent information on licenses and seasons. Much of this information is now available on the internet at sites maintained by each state and provincial agency. *Deer & Deer Hunting* magazine publishes an annual *Deer Hunters' Almanac* that has postal service and internet addresses as well as telephone numbers for every state and Canadian province. The almanacs are available on magazine racks in stores, or can be ordered with a credit card online through www.deeranddeerhunting.com. Some other magazines also publish contact information for states and provinces, in hunting annuals or their fall issues.

Most game departments also compile data on deer harvests, populations, or other indices that reflect the general abundance of deer by county, management unit, district, or region. The largest harvests normally occur where deer numbers are greatest. Hunt digests and harvest figures will often be available upon written request to the state agency's main office, if they are not posted on the internet. A regional or district office would be a better source of information if you are interested in only a portion of a state or province.

Various maps are always valuable references for determining where to hunt, whether you refer to them at home or in the field.

Wildlife biologists are usually the best contacts for queries on deer densities, antler growth, and hunter success. A phone call or personal visit is generally the best way to reach biologists for information. Try to write questions down on paper before calling or stopping in, to prevent forgetting what you want to ask. If you plan a personal visit, call ahead to make an appointment because biologists aren't always in the office and when they are, they often have to attend meetings and take care of other duties.

Maps that show public and private lands should be available from state or provincial offices, too. There is usually a charge for these. If maps aren't available from state offices, try other sources, including online ones. Aerial and topogaphic maps can be obtained from Maptech (www.maptech.com). County map books that are now available for many states are valuable references. The Delorme Company publishes books of state maps (800-561-5105). Plat books can be obtained from individual counties, and U.S. Forest Service offices usually have maps of any areas in their jurisdiction.

Maps are not only good references for determining land ownership, but they can also be used to determine where roadless tracts of land are located. Areas without roads that are at least a square mile in size are prime locations for getting away from large numbers of deer hunters. Few hunters penetrate far into tracts that aren't easily accessible.

Big-game record books are great references for learning where most of the big-antlered bucks are taken in individual states and provinces. Many states and provinces now have organizations that maintain big-game records within their boundaries. The Boone and Crockett and Pope and Young Clubs are national big-game record keepers who maintain deer records for North America. Pope and Young only accepts bow kills while Boone and Crockett accepts all legally taken trophies that meet their restrictive minimums.

If you are looking for a trophy set of antlers, state, provincial, and national record books will give you an idea of which states or provinces, or what parts of a specific state or province, big racks come from. Additional large-racked bucks are likely to be found in regions where others were bagged. Characteristics of the habitat in these parts of North America plus the genetics of the herd are often conducive to producing outstanding antlers on bucks. Hunting seasons and pressure also play important roles in consistent production of trophy bucks.

States that yield the highest number of world-class bucks year after year, for instance, often have short firearms deer seasons or limits on the number of nonresident hunting licenses available. Light hunting pressure contributes to an abundance of trophy bucks in most Canadian provinces.

When planning a deer hunt, try to dig up as much information as possible that will be helpful in determining which state or province and which region within it is most likely to provide the deer hunt you want.

Choosing An Area To Hunt

To illustrate how to go about choosing an area such as a county or management unit to hunt deer, let's look at a couple of examples. For convenience we will assume that the hunters in these examples want to hunt somewhere in the Upper Peninsula of Michigan.

The first group of hunters we'll consider just want to see deer. They will be satisfied with any legal whitetail—other hunters in the area won't bother them.

Michigan's Department of Natural Resources and Environment (DNRE) compiles a yearly list of the number of deer seen by its field personnel for each county. The number of hours involved in the sightings is also noted. This information is used to determine the average number of deer seen for every one hundred hours DNRE employees are in the field. The figures for each county represent an index of the general abundance of deer there. It is easy to determine which county has the highest density of deer by comparing the number of animals seen per hundred hours in each one.

Menominee County stands out as the number-one choice for this group of hunters. For July through August one year, an average of 165 deer were seen for every hundred hours in deer country. The next highest count was 52.5, which was for Dickinson County.

A check of the deer harvest for that year by counties would show there were an average of more than two bucks per square mile taken by hunters in Menominee County. Further checking would show there were from seven to twelve hunters per square mile in Menominee County during gun season, which is about medium pressure. Part of the reason for the lower-than-expected hunting pressure is private ownership of much of the county's land.

A look at a county map would show that since there is enough public land to choose from, there wouldn't be any problem finding a place to hunt if permission

Canoes and boats on rivers and lakes can be the ticket to reaching areas that are lightly hunted or not hunted at all.

couldn't be obtained to hunt on private property. Heavy hunting pressure isn't always the rule in areas with limited public hunting land and lots of deer. I have hunted for days at a time in locations in both Menominee and Dickinson counties (hunter density is supposed to be as high as twenty per square mile in Dickinson) without seeing any hunters who didn't belong to our group. Few hunters make the effort to reach out-of-the-way locations, and one area we frequent is surrounded by a marshy bog. We wear chest waders to get across the marsh, then put boots on when we reach dry ground.

Boats and canoes can also be used to reach remote hunting spots where hunting pressure is light to nonexistent on lakes and rivers. Horses provide a convenient

Horses provide the best means of accessing some of the most remote deer hunting country in the west for mule deer. They also come in handy for packing out game.

means of transportation to get away from crowds of hunters when hunting mule deer in western states and provinces. Some hunters use lamas as pack animals to aid in hunting remote locations.

A group of hunters interested in trying for trophy bucks in upper Michigan would find that 92 bucks from the Upper Peninusla had antlers large enough to meet Boone and Crockett minimums for all-time listing (170 for typicals and 195 for non-typicals) by looking at the current edition of Michigan Big Game Records. Thirteen booners have been taken in Iron County over the years and ten each have been recorded for Baraga and Delta Counties. Chippewa and Alger Counties are credited with eight and seven world-class bucks, respectively. Michigan Big Game Records is published by Commemorative Bucks of Michigan (CBM), the state's record-keeping organization. Copies of the latest edition of this book can be obtained through the organization's web site: www.buckfax.com.

For those who want to compete with as few hunters as possible and who are trying to decide between the three counties of Alger, Baraga, and Iron, Alger or Baraga county would be the best selection. Hunting pressure data shows there were 7 to 12 hunters per square mile in Iron County. Alger had 4.6 to 7 hunters per square mile, and Baraga had fewer than 4.5.

Knowledge of deer densities in these counties would make the choice among them fairly easy. An average of 22.3 deer were seen per hundred hours in Alger, but only 3.6 in Baraga. An average of 31.4 deer were seen for every hundred hours spent in Iron County.

Public hunting land is abundant in all of those three counties.

The same sort of information used in these examples can be employed to help determine where best to hunt in any region, state, or province. When hunting outside of your home state or province, such factors as the number of licenses available to nonresidents must also be considered. Some states and provinces sell their quotas of mule deer or whitetail tags, at least those for preferred areas, well in advance of season openings.

Getting More Specific

After a general hunting location such as a county or management unit has been determined, hunters should concern themselves with finding the best huntable-size chunks of terrain available. We have already seen that deer densities are not the same throughout a state or province. By the same token, their distribution is not equal throughout a square mile of cover. There can be ten whitetails or mulies utilizing an area a fraction of that size and only a few throughout the rest of the region. Some portions of deer habitat are simply more attractive to the animals than others.

Sources of large quantities of high-quality food are great for attracting concentrations of deer. Agricultural crops are favored by whitetails and mule deer. A good crop of acorns will attract a lot of local deer, too, and that food source is what helped me score on that seven-pointer during my first deer hunt in Keweenaw County. If you've got both white and red acorns in your area, deer prefer nuts from white oaks over reds. A good beechnut crop will attract lots of deer, too. Other favored deer haunts are areas that have been burned or logged in recent years. Young vegetation that mulies and whitetails thrive on grows profusely in either type of opening.

In hilly or mountainous terrain the biggest bucks are usually found at the highest elevations. Islands in lakes or large rivers also can be hotspots for deer hunting. Whitetails and mulies that reside on some islands aren't hunted often. The same is true of any piece of deer habitat that is exceptionally thick or difficult to reach.

Some of these locations can be pinpointed on maps. Talking with wildlife biologists, conservation officers or game wardens, sport shop owners, and other deer hunters in the area you plan to hunt is a good idea, too. From that point on, the final decision of where to hunt should be made after spending time in

Finding areas where foods that deer prefer, such as acorns, are abundant can be the key to a hunting hot spot.

the field scouting the area to look for deer sign like I did when deciding on a spot to hunt in Keweenaw County.

There is one more consideration that can play a decisive role for some hunters in determining where to hunt deer. That factor is familiarity. Hunters who have spent a season or two or maybe a dozen in one area are bound to become familiar with the terrain, its deer, and the deer's behavior. The more familiar a hunter is with an area and its deer, the better his or her chances are of scoring there. For this reason, some hunters may prefer to hunt locations with low densities of deer over those that have more animals, especially if they don't have time to check out distant spots. Many deer hunters simply don't have as much time to devote to deer hunting as they would like.

Tradition has a lot to do with return trips to familiar deer hunting grounds, too. Over the years the list of fond memories associated with a location grows. Each season then becomes an opportunity to recall past experiences as much as it is an opportunity to have new ones.

4

Preseason Scouting

The preseason scouting I did in Michigan's Keweenaw County the first year I hunted whitetails there played a critical role in me being able to bag a $3^1/2$-year-old buck in one hour's time, as mentioned at the beginning of the last chapter. That example illustrates the importance of preseason scouting. Preseason scouting is, in fact, one of the most important parts of any deer hunt, whether you are hunting an area you've frequented for years or trying a location for the first time. Granted, preseason checks of familiar hunting grounds need not take as much time as looking over new territory. Nonetheless, doing it or not doing it can play a significant role in determining the number of whitetails or mulies that end up on the game pole by the end of the season.

Look For Changes

It is not unusual for centers of deer activity to shift from year to year for a variety of reasons. Hunters who fail to detect a change in movement or use patterns before the season opens can lose the most valuable day of hunting of the season: opening day.

One year an uncle of mine found what proved to be a hot spot for bucks on state land. On the first day of the season he missed a whitetail with a six- or eight-point rack. A spikehorn he saw the next day wasn't as lucky.

The next season he was all set to go back to the same spot, but routinely went to check it out before the season began. It was a good thing he did. A road had been opened in the area and a large field created right where his stand had been. Since there were still a few days before opening day, he had a chance to locate an alternate position.

Dramatic changes can also occur from one year to the next on private land you may have access to hunt. Houses have been built on some land where I used to hunt

Preseason scouting is valuable for determining if there have been any major changes where you normally hunt, especially if it's on public land. If there has been a large clearcut like this one, you may have to find a new spot to hunt.

Any number of things can happen from one year to the next that can influence your chances of success. A forest fire could alter the habitat as well as deer movements, for example.

whitetails, for example, and commercial development has overtaken other former hunting grounds. Even when private land isn't developed, ownership sometimes changes, and when that happens, it's necessary to seek permission to hunt from the new landowner.

Changes that can affect both public and private lands include forest fires, logging, weather, food availability, and maturing of the habitat. Each of these factors, as well as others, can cause shifts in deer abundance and activity in certain locations.

Exceptionally dry weather one year affected the success of a hunter I spoke to at a deer show. He was hunting a funnel area between two wet swamps, an area that had produced consistent deer sightings for many years; the spot was so reliable, he had been hunting it since 1953. Last fall, he wasn't seeing deer there like he normally does. He took the time to check out the swamps before going home and discovered they were dry instead of full of water as usual. He said deer were staying in the swamps instead of skirting them like they normally did due to the absence of water. If this hunter had determined the swamps were dry during preseason scouting, as he should have, he would have been able to take advantage of the change by shifting positions.

Something I try to do when scouting territory hunted year after year is to explore patches of cover I haven't been in before or am not familiar with. This often results in the discovery of new deer hiding places. I often don't get into some of these deer hangouts because they are out-of-the-way or extremely thick. Deer easily find safety in such spots.

Make A Change

Some hunters who hunt the same territory every fall get in the habit of using the same stands, making the same drives, or still-hunting the same course all the time. There is nothing wrong with this, but it often leads to overlooking areas that are worth trying. In addition, deer that live in the vicinity are quick to catch on to the routine and may avoid spots where they have encountered hunters. A change of pace may be the ticket to some easy venison.

A New Location

When visiting deer country that you will be hunting for the first time, try to scout as much terrain as possible. At the same time as you are familiarizing yourself with the deer situation, you are guarding against getting lost. This is a second advantage of preseason scouting in an unfamiliar area.

Along the same lines, features of the terrain such as boulders or stumps that might be mistaken for deer can be checked out while scouting. Then hunting time won't be wasted looking at these deerlike objects. This also makes out-of-place shapes that may be deer more noticeable.

Hunt While Scouting

One more benefit of visiting hunt locations ahead of deer season is the possibility of combining scouting missions with other forms of hunting. I was bear hunting in Keweenaw County, for instance, when I found the fresh scrape that helped me decide to hunt the spot where I shot my first buck in the county. In many states and provinces, archery or muzzleloader deer hunts end the day before firearms seasons begin. In those situations, what is learned during early seasons can contribute to success during later seasons.

Small game hunting can be combined with scouting, too. Such small game as squirrels, rabbits, grouse, and other game birds provide action in many states right

This deer hunter combined ruffed grouse hunting with scouting for the upcoming season. With grouse in hand, he's pausing to examine an antler-rubbed tree. Any type of small game hunting can be combined with scouting, as long as the season is open and you have the proper license.

up to the time some deer seasons begin. Some states or provinces may prohibit carrying a gun in the field the week before deer season, however, so be sure it is legal before planning on hunting other game when scouting for deer.

My brother and an uncle collected three Canada geese and a pair of ruffed grouse during a preseason check for deer sign one fall. They bagged more game that day than they often do when intentionally hunting small game or waterfowl. Our luck isn't always that good on scouting trips, but the results of that day are indicative of what can be one of the peripheral benefits of preseason reconnaissance.

The week before deer season opens is usually the best time to scout an area. Starting sooner is a good idea if the location isn't far from where you live and you will be hunting it for the first time. When hunting another state or province, scouting must often be restricted to the two or three days before the season, but anything is better than starting cold at the crack of dawn on opening day. That is, unless a relative or friend has set up a spot for you or you've hired a guide who has done preseason preparation for you.

What To Look For

What do you look for when scouting an area for deer hunting? Feeding and bedding grounds, regularly used trails, signs of buck activity, and deer themselves are the primary things to watch for. Water holes should be considered in terrain where water is in short supply. I spend most of my time checking remote locations or those near heavy cover when visiting a new area. This type of terrain invariably gets the heaviest use by good bucks throughout the year, and especially once the shooting starts.

While scouting the territory I also try to anticipate where other hunters might be. I prefer not to hunt too near other people, but sometimes it is unavoidable. If I find someone's blind, I go elsewhere in search of a place to hunt.

In open country it is often possible to look over a lot of territory from elevated observation points with the aid of binoculars or spotting scopes. Under these cir-

In open terrain such as this agricultural area in Montana, hunters can use binoculars and spotting scopes to scout deer movements from distant vantage points, as Jimmy Dean is doing here. He's using a fence post to both break his outline and steady a spotting scope to study deer in distant fields. A herd of deer is visible in a field to his right.

cumstances deer movements can be observed and it's usually possible to determine where specific bucks enter and leave feeding areas. Based on those observations, you can determine where the best places are to ambush them. Animals that aren't disturbed will generally follow the same movement patterns once deer season opens.

One fall Dave Raikko and I were hunting mule deer from a drop camp in the Colorado Rockies. We got to our camp a couple of days ahead of the season to look the area over and adjust to the altitude. The first morning out we located a group of bucks using a patch of willows above timber line. They were still there opening day. We both dropped our deer there on the first day of our hunt.

Read The Signs

Centers of deer activity in wooded terrain can be determined by reading the signs. Trails or runways used regularly will normally be well worn. The course of a runway through grass or weeds is marked by a narrow lane of trampled vegetation. Trails through heavily wooded areas will be marked by a line of leaves that have been scuffed by whitetail or mule deer hooves. Good runways will sometimes be worn right down to the soil in certain spots and tracks can be seen there. Trails are most obvious in sandy areas or when snow is on the ground.

Most regularly traveled trails used by deer are routes they take from bedding to feeding areas and back again. Sometimes animals use different runways going each way. Where water is scarce, trails leading to watering areas are also common. Many times the same network of trails will be used as escape routes. Once a good trail is discovered, feeding and bedding areas can be located by following it both ways. Or, if a feeding area is located, runways leading from it will go to bedding grounds, and vice versa if a bedding area is found.

Deer feeding grounds are often open areas. For the most part they are agricultural or woodland fields, burned or logged-over areas, or fruit trees or orchards. Whitetails and mule deer also feed in locations where there is a lot of low brush and

in groves of nut-bearing trees. Groups of deer droppings are common in feeding areas that get regular use.

Deer often bed down in heavy cover or where they have a good view, such as on the sides or tops of hills. Beds are oval-shaped areas where the vegetation has been flattened under the weight of the animals. In sand or snow, beds will appear as shallow depressions. Beds can be found next to tree trunks, among rocks, under evergreen boughs, under brush piles or windfalls, in open bogs, and in other locations. A number of beds of varying ages will be present in locations used regularly.

Whitetails and mulies generally move from higher to lower elevation or from heavy cover toward open areas when feeding, and vice versa when retiring. Since deer adapt to their habitats, which vary from state to state and province to province, this isn't always true. I have encountered situations hunting both species of deer in which bedding and feeding locations were the same. Some animals also feed uphill and others travel different trails on a day-to-day basis.

Scouting provides a perfect opportunity to locate well-used deer trails like this one at a fence crossing. Drawing a rough map of deer trails in a new area can help determine where to hunt.

There have been countless times I've watched mulie bucks feed and then lie down in the same patch of cover. It doesn't take brush that is very high to conceal bedded deer. Animals frequently feed for a period of time then lie down out of sight for a couple of hours, then get up and eat some more. They may do this all day and cover very little ground while browsing.

Some of the bigger bucks are the least predictable. They often travel routes no other deer use and many times don't move during daylight hours, when they are vulnerable to hunters. Their normal cautiousness is usually lost during the rut. During this time they frequent areas where does are and travel with them.

Scrapes and Rubs

Mature whitetail bucks leave telltale signs along the runways they use during the rut. They paw patches of ground that attract does, which are called scrapes. I believe these scrapes also serve as territorial markers for the benefit of other bucks. Scrapes are often checked at regular intervals by the bucks that made them.

Bucks also rub their antlers on trees along trails they use during the rut. A series of rubs or a rub line often develops along a route regularly used by one particular

Most hunters would be elated to find this type of sign in an area they plan on hunting during a scouting trip. A tree this size ripped up so badly has to be the work of a trophy buck. And there's a huge scrape next to the ravaged tree. Most travel routes used by bucks are marked by rubs and scrapes, but smaller than these, as it gets close to the rut.

buck or a number of bucks. If all of the saplings or trees that are rubbed are rubbed on the same side, the buck or bucks are generally traveling in the same direction each time. When rubs are made on opposing sides of some trees, buck travel is usually in both directions. Picking a spot to wait downwind of a rub line can be a great way to ambush a buck.

Any size buck can rub its antlers on saplings, but when you see rubs on full-fledged trees, there's an excellent chance the sign was left by a mature buck with a big rack. Concentrations of rubs tend to develop at or near feeding and bedding areas.

I have seen rubs and scrapes in mulie country, too. Since mule deer are not territorial, however, there is no evidence that they return to check scrapes as do whitetail bucks.

Monitoring Deer Activity

Once you locate trails or areas that are being used regularly by deer, try to spend a day or two determining when deer are using them. Deer use some runways only at night; hunting these during the day is a waste of time. Watching promising locations from a distance during the hours you will be hunting is the best way to determine whether deer will be there and what their sex is. Try not to alert or alarm deer during this time; it could upset their routine.

Trail cameras have revolutionized preseason scouting for deer hunters. It is no longer necessary to watch trails, scrapes, and feeding or watering areas in person to

Bill Westerbrink checks a trail camera. Scouting cameras that are set up to monitor deer trails, feeding areas, or scrapes may produce photos of big bucks that you might not have known about otherwise. However, don't expect to capture all of the bucks in your location on film. Capturing a buck's image with a set camera and then getting him once the season opens is not guaranteed either, but knowing he is there is a benefit.

determine which deer travel on or to them at various times. These cameras do all the work with a minimum of disturbance. They capture pictures or video of any deer that triggers their sensors along with the time photos were taken. This technology enables hunters to scout a number of locations at the same time.

Before trail cameras came along, one of the ways that multiple trails were checked for deer activity, in the absence of snow cover, was by stretching thread across them. If the thread was broken during the course of a day, you knew deer were traveling that trail, but you didn't know how many deer there were, when they were there, or their size and sex. When snow is on the ground, the number and size of the deer using a trail can be determined by looking at tracks. To determine if deer are using a trail between visits when snow cover is present or there's bare soil, brush out old deer tracks with a branch or stamp them out with your feet. Any fresh tracks that were made in your absence will be easy to see when you return.

Continue Scouting During Season

Preseason scouting increases the chances of hunters collecting their deer the first couple of days of the season, if done properly but it is no guarantee. Time and time again when I think I know exactly where to intercept a buck or doe something happens and I draw a blank. Whitetails and mulies simply are not always predictable. With this in mind, try not to forget about scouting once the season opens and even after it closes.

If I have failed to score after several days of sitting at a promising stand, I often combine still-hunting or tracking with a reconnaissance of my surroundings. Sometimes I roam around a little during late morning or early afternoon of each day. This practice has paid off more than once when hunting both whitetails and mule deer. In cases where I have scored and others in my party haven't, scouting during the season has been beneficial in locating more promising territory for them to try.

Tracking deer when snow is on the ground is a surprisingly good way to find animals. Pursued deer often lead trackers to areas where other mulies or whitetails are or have been. After tracking a buck in the snow, hunters may be able to better determine where to ambush that animal from a stand in the future.

That's exactly what Richard Brandt from Metamora, Michigan, did one year. He followed the tracks of a buck through the snow most of one day without catching a glimpse of the animal. However, the next day he waited on a ridge where he thought he would have a good chance of seeing the whitetail, based on the knowledge he gained while tracking the animal, and his hunch proved correct. The buck only had one antler with four points. The second beam was broken off, but the deer was a trophy to Brandt nonetheless because of the effort he put into getting it. Since that day, he's taken other bucks the same way.

One fall when I had scored early in the season, a light covering of snow fell. I started tracking deer in an effort to keep them moving, which would increase the chances of my partners getting shooting. The freshest tracks I located one morning were of a doe and her youngster. I tailed them for several hours and they led me to a patch of high ground surrounded by thick lowland swamp. There was a lot of buck sign there. We didn't get a chance to hunt there that year, but we did in following seasons. Between my brother and me we took six bucks and missed a couple of others on that isolated patch of high ground over a period of years. One of them was a trophy whitetail.

Another cold, snowy day, I took a walk to a partner's stand at noon to warm up. I hadn't seen a thing. My partner saw one deer at a distance and was unable to tell if it was a buck or doe. I tracked the animal for a while and it led me through an area with a heavily used runway. Three of us posted in that vicinity the next morning. An eight-point buck walked by me shortly after daylight. I missed it, but he made the mistake of running past my brother. Bruce downed him.

Trail Camera Booner

Bill Rushford from Newberry, Michigan has five deer blinds, but he's only able to hunt from one of them at a time. So he keeps trail cameras at the blinds he isn't hunting to monitor what deer are in the vicinity. During the 2008 firearms season, one of his cameras captured a photo of a huge buck at one of his blinds that he wasn't hunting, but the photo prompted him to quickly change spots.

The picture was taken on November 23, during the second week of the state's gun hunt. Rushford didn't see the picture until the twenty-fourth.

"I had four days off work around Thanksgiving and I planned on hunting every day to try to get him," Rushford said.

As it turned out, he didn't have to hunt too long to get a shot at the whitetail. Rushford was in a box blind covered with camo netting when the buck appeared on the evening of the twenty-sixth.

"The wind was from the northwest that day," Bill said, "but it would swirl somewhat, so I only had the front window on the blind open."

Due to the swirling wind, Rushford was concerned about deer winding him even though he wears Scent-Lok clothes. He certainly did not want to risk having the big

Bill Rushford from Newberry, Michigan, with a Boone and Crockett nontypical he switched blinds to hunt after one of his trail cameras photographed it during the second week of gun season. The buck's antlers netted 197³/₈.

buck smell him. Bill said if the wind had been calm, he would have had more windows in the blind open.

Four deer, all antlerless, were feeding on food Bill had placed within 20 yards of the front of his blind when he suddenly noticed a huge set of antlers out the window off his right shoulder. The thought that flashed through his mind was, "There he is!"

"That trail camera picture saved me a few minutes of thinking about how big he was," Bill said. "There was no doubt in my mind that was the buck I was waiting for."

Even though Bill saw the buck first, the big fella had come in behind a doe. With the buck so close, he didn't dare try to open the window for a shot. He decided to take a shot through the plexiglass window.

Before doing that, he had to stand up, turn around and squat down to get the buck in the 3x-9x Leupold scope that was mounted on his Remington Model 700 in 7mm magnum. He feels the camo netting over the blind enabled him to make the necessary movements without spooking the deer at the bait or the buck and doe that were approaching.

"I decided to take the shot because he was looking right at me and he was five steps from possibly winding me," Rushford said. "He was on the east side of the blind, heading south, and would soon be downwind of me."

When the crosshairs were behind the buck's shoulder, Bill pulled the trigger and the deer took off running.

"I thought I possibly missed him because of shooting through the plexiglass. I went out the door and the doe the buck had been with was standing 50 yards away. She took off and went in the swamp near the blind. I couldn't remember if I bolted a fresh round in the chamber, so I opened the bolt to check and saw that I had worked the bolt automatically."

Bill didn't have to go far to find blood—lots of blood—confirming that his bullet had connected. He followed the blood trail 80 yards and found his trophy buck with its antlers lodged among some trees where it fell. The monster 14-point nontypical antlers had an official gross score of $199^7/8$ and the final net score came to $197^3/8$, qualifying for a place in all-time Boone and Crockett Records.

Post Season

Post-season scouting can be valuable preparation for hunting in the same area the next year. During the course of a hunting season deer frequently change their travel patterns as well as their bedding and feeding grounds. Whitetails and mule deer generally react to hunting pressure the same way each season. Learning which trails animals in your area use most once the shooting starts can help determine how to connect quickly the next fall.

It is difficult to do too much scouting for deer. Often, you learn something new about whitetail or mulie behavior each trip. The more you know about deer in the area you hunt, the better your chances are of collecting one there consistently. That is what scouting is all about.

Stand Hunting

During November of 2009, I hunted from a blind in Saskatchewan for ten days straight, from daylight to dark, before finally shooting a buck to put my tag on. After approximately one hundred hours of stand hunting, I shot a nice 12-pointer that gross scored about 130. On that hunt, I saw bucks every day and could have shot one sooner, including four that would have scored in the 140s, but I was being selective. I was hoping to shoot one that would score at least in the 150s, but when time was running out and it was clear that wasn't likely, I "settled" for the smaller buck that I was still very pleased with.

On other hunts closer to home, I have hunted from stands at least as long, and sometimes longer, for a chance at any legal buck.

Patience is one of the most difficult, but important attributes for a deer hunter to develop. It can make the difference between success and failure in most whitetail or mule deer hunting methods.

Patience is especially rewarding for the stand hunter. Hours or days may pass before a legal buck, or one you are interested in shooting, is sighted. But determined vigilance on a stand often pays off; in fact, stand hunting probably accounts for more downed deer in the fall than any other method.

The reasons for this success are easy to understand. Virtually anyone, from the youngest to the oldest, can hunt deer from a stand. And stand hunting may be the only technique available to handicapped hunters. Two of the other options for hunting methods available to solitary hunters, stillhunting and tracking, match pursuer and pursued on a one-on-one basis. The average deer hunter's senses and stealth in the field are simply no match for those of the quarry.

Hunting from a properly chosen stand places all the advantages in the hunter's favor. In a stationary position the sitter's strongest senses, sight and hearing, can be utilized to the fullest. At the same time, the effectiveness of a deer's faculties in detecting a hunter will be impaired.

The 130-class 12-point whitetail I shot while stand hunting in Saskatchewan during November of 2009 after passing up four larger bucks during 100 hours of hunting. When being selective, you run the risk of ending up with a deer that is smaller than others you've seen or not shooting anything at all.

If you are downwind of where animals are expected to appear or wearing scent-absorbing clothing, your scent will often go undetected. The use of natural cover or a properly constructed blind to conceal yourself, combined with minimal movements, will reduce your visibility to a deer. With little or no movement, unnatural sounds are avoided and a deer is not likely to hear you. Hunting from a stand can be productive most hours of the day and under most weather conditions. This is another factor in the technique's favor. The circumstance in which a stand hunter would be least likely to see game is during stormy weather when both deer and hunter activity are at a minimum, except during the rut. During the rut, deer are active in most weather conditions.

On most days during the fall, animals will travel to and from feeding areas or their reproductive drive will keep them on the move. Where hunting pressure is heavy, the vulnerability of deer to stand hunters is increased. Plenty of hunters in the

Hunters have all of the advantages in their favor when occupying a properly chosen blind like this one I shot a buck from in Saskatchewan during November of 2009. Hunters can use their strongest senses while reducing the chances of being detected by deer.

woods are bound to keep the deer stirred up and increase the likelihood of trail watchers seeing game.

Basically, stand hunting can be broken down into a sequence of four steps: selecting sites, preparing them for the hunt, hunter preparation, and procedure once in position.

Preseason work and scouting are important for successful stand hunting. Three of the four points mentioned above should be attended to before opening day. Far too many hunters waste opening day by not having any idea where they want to be once shooting time begins, or spend the first few critical hours fixing up a stand selected the night before. The bulk of the nation's deer harvest occurs the first few days of the season, especially in heavily hunted whitetail country. A hunter who doesn't take advantage of every minute of the first few days is drastically reducing his or her chances of success.

Selecting Stand Sites

Ideally, scouting activity should be concentrated one to two weeks before deer season begins. That way a hunter will get a handle on current conditions. Deer concentrations and movements can vary greatly from one month to the next. A shift in habits will often accompany a weather change. For example, deer will use different travel routes when snow is on the ground and when it is bare.

Without snow covering the landscape, whitetails and mulies blend into their surroundings fairly well, even in relatively open terrain. With a white backdrop of snow in open to semi-open country, deer stand out in stark contrast to their surroundings. They seem to sense their increased visibility to hunters and other predators under these circumstances and have a tendency to move into timber, swamps, or brush.

There is a swampy swale in Michigan where either my brother or I have taken a whitetail buck during the first couple days of firearms season for a number of years. Tag alders grow thick in the swale along with tall marsh grass, which provides plenty of concealment for whitetails. There was never snow on the ground when we met with success in that spot.

One year we had an early snowfall, and the ground was snow-covered the first week of the season. My brother sat in that swale for two days without seeing a single deer. Because of the snow, visibility was about three times greater than normal. The alders didn't look as dense as they did without snow, and the marsh grass was matted down. Whitetails that normally traveled through that swale were probably using an alternate route through evergreens where they would be less conspicuous.

Sometimes the available cover itself will undergo a change, which will cause deer to adjust their travel patterns. A prime example is leaf fall from deciduous trees such as maple, beech, birch, oak, and aspen. One fall when I was hunting mule deer in Colorado a heavy rain combined with strong wind practically defoliated all of the quaking aspens in my area overnight. Before that time my party had been seeing mulies in the quakies on a regular basis. After the leaves fell most of the deer moved into the surrounding timber.

If you aren't able to visit the hunt area a week or two ahead, it is advisable to set up camp at least two days before the season opens. An early arrival has other advantages in addition to allowing time for scouting; you can also set up camp or arrange motel accommodations at a leisurely pace. Last-minute arrivals and the corresponding hassles that often arise can overtax your system and reduce productivity during the hunt.

If preseason scouting isn't possible, secure a guide who will do it for you. A guide who knows the habits of the deer in the area can give you a distinct advantage. Guides will be discussed in greater detail in chapter 17.

The most important procedure in successful stand hunting is selecting a spot to wait for deer to show. Not only must the hunter consider the animals' normal movement patterns, but he or she must also try to anticipate how the deer will react to hunting pressure, unless he or she is on private property with light hunting pressure or in a remote location where few other deer hunters tread. Otherwise, the number of competing hunters and access points are prime concerns.

The Search Is On

Step number one in selecting a stand site is to become familiar with the locality that will be hunted by learning the lay of the land. County and topographic maps come in handy for deciding on an area that might be suitable for hunting. Try to isolate one chunk of terrain at a time. One square mile, or less, of country is plenty to work with. In many cases a 40-acre plot is enough. Territory completely surrounded by roads is easily defined. In many cases, however, a fence, river or creek, lake, ridge, or transition zone from one type of cover to another will have to be chosen as a boundary.

Once you get a feeling for the lay of the land from maps, get out there on foot with a compass. Some hunters carry Global Positioning System (GPS) units to navigate with and these can come in handy, but you should always carry a compass, too, because the battery-operated units can malfunction or fail when batteries weaken or

Always take a compass with you when scouting and deer hunting. This hunter is using a model that can be worn on the wrist. A GPS unit can also come in handy for navigation, as long as the batteries last and the canopy doesn't interfere with the signal.

die. GPS units are sometimes useless when under a thick canopy of trees and leaves, too, because the canopy can block the satellite signals that the units navigate by. Walk as much of the location that you've chosen as possible to familiarize yourself with the various cover types present and the basic features of the terrain. By becoming familiar with the tract, you will also be guarding against getting lost. While familiarizing yourself with the terrain, keep an eye out for deer. Any sign of them, such as feeding and bedding areas, trails, tracks, antler rubs, and scrapes are worthy of note.

If, after scouting an area, you aren't satisfied with what you found—not many deer signs, too many roads, evidence of other hunters, or some other displeasing factor—pick out another locality. Keep it up until you find an area you will be happy with. This is the advantage of beginning preparations well in advance of the season opening. If you don't allot enough time for scouting, you might end up hunting in a location with which you aren't completely satisfied.

Incidentally, a high density of deer isn't necessary in an area to be able to score from a stand. It's just a matter of being able to intercept one animal. Proper scouting is the key to accomplishing this.

In the northern counties of the Upper Peninsula of Michigan, which border Lake Superior, winters are long and severe and winter deer range is poor. As you would expect, deer densities are low. Nonetheless, my brother, an uncle, and I managed to collect at least one whitetail buck a year (one season we got two) among us from a spot within sight of the big lake for a number of consecutive years.

The location we hunted was a series of rugged hills that dropped off to lowland swamps on two sides. On preseason scouting trips the first year we hunted there we learned what runways whitetails used to get into the hills from the lowlands. When other hunters moved the deer out of the swamps on opening day at least one of us would drop a buck.

Once the lay of the land and areas of heaviest deer use have been pinpointed, choosing specific stands should be a simple matter. As a general rule, it is better to situate yourself closer to bedding areas than to feeding grounds. (There are exceptions to this that I will get to shortly.) The odds of seeing animals in these localities are best during daylight hours. Whitetails and mule deer often reach resting areas after daylight and leave before dark.

In addition, bedding grounds are usually in heavy cover or higher in elevation than feeding areas. Deer disturbed during any hour of the day by moving hunters commonly seek thick cover or gain altitude to escape, so they are likely to move your way.

During firearms seasons, deer often use the same escape routes year after year, trails that lead to exceptionally heavy cover or relatively inaccessible country. If you know where such a trail is from experience in your territory, posting along it could be productive.

Hunting Food Sources

Early in the fall, primarily during bow or muzzleloader seasons, choosing a stand near feeding areas may be better than locating close to bedding grounds, at least for hunting in the evenings. Deer often start feeding before it gets dark at this time of year. Mast-producing stands

Posting within view of feeding areas such as this apple tree can be productive during bow season, but getting closer to bedding areas is usually more productive when gun season is on.

of oak or beech trees are excellent deer feeding areas throughout North America. So are agricultural fields. Apple orchards, feral apple trees, and trees that produce other types of soft mast can also be preferred feeding areas. Where it is legal, some hunters bait deer with foods such as apples, corn, potatoes, sugar beets, and cabbage.

Bucks Feeding Early

Rural Michigan resident Jim Butler encountered a couple of bucks that were feeding exceptionally early in a farm field during a recent fall and he used a unique trick to be able to arrow one of them. Butler spotted the pair of 8-pointers already feeding in a field at three o'clock in the afternoon on October 8, 2009, as he was on his way to begin bowhunting. He made a mental note to be in that field the next afternoon to see where the bucks entered it. One of the bucks was already in the field when he arrived the next afternoon, but it was close enough to the edge of the woods that he had a good idea where it entered the field.

Jim Butler with the 3^1/$_2$-year-old 8-point he spooked from a field with his truck, then shot from his tree stand when it returned. PHOTO COURTESY OF JIM BUTLER

The next morning, he put a tree stand where he hoped to ambush one of the bucks, then returned at two-thirty to get in position. An 8-pointer was already 20 yards from his tree stand. The wind was in Butler's favor, so he started to stalk the deer. Halfway into the stalk, Jim decided the stalk wouldn't work and came up with another plan.

He left his bow and arrows where they were, went back to his truck, and drove it into the field, spooking the buck back into the woods. He knew that farmland deer are used to seeing vehicles and farm machinery, so wouldn't go far after it was in the woods. As an experienced farmer, he knew the buck would most likely return to the field before long.

After accomplishing what he wanted to with his truck, he parked it out of the way, grabbed his bow and arrows, and climbed into the tree stand on the edge of the field. An hour later, the buck returned to the field and Butler nailed the 3^1/$_2$-year-old whitetail. If this plan hadn't worked, Jim was planning on being in position much earlier the following day.

Go Remote

If you are looking for a buck with a nice rack or if there is expected to be a high density of hunters in your area, it may be advisable to head for the remotest parcel of land within your scouted acreage. The harder a location is to reach, the better the chances mature bucks will be there. A large influx of hunters will usually push additional deer into remote sections as well.

Big bucks are easier to locate once the rut has started. Moss-horned mulies will leave elevated haunts and go to lower areas in search of does. And whitetail bucks leave evidence of their presence on saplings and trees they've rubbed with their antlers in addition to ground scrapes. Both species of bucks are also more active during daylight hours when they are looking for does.

Scrape Hunting

Antlered whitetails mark their breeding territories with scrapes. These are patches of ground from one foot to four feet across that have been pawed clear of leaves and other debris. Scrapes are most often underneath overhanging branches, which bucks mouth and damage with their antlers. Bucks frequently urinate in scrapes.

Antler rubbings are trees varying in size that have been rubbed free of bark on one side by bucks exercising their neck muscles and depositing scent. These rubs serve both as visual and scent markers. Antlered whitetails leave scent from their forehead glands on trees so other deer will be able to identify which animal was there.

Keep your eyes open for buck sign while scouting. Bucks periodically check their network of pawings, and being located along a trail marked with scrapes can put you on the way to success. Here again, pick a spot in or near heavy cover. There is more of a chance a buck will cruise that stretch during daylight hours. Scrapes in open areas will, most likely, be saved for after dark.

Through research with the use of trail cameras, it has been determined that whitetail bucks most often visit scrapes under the cover of darkness in heavily hunted areas. Bucks don't have to go directly to scrapes to check them, however. Many scrapes are checked from some distance downwind, where bucks are out of view of cameras, but would be visible to hunters properly positioned nearby. Posting downwind of scrapes to intercept bucks that scent-check them, while still being able to see scrapes, is the ticket to success.

Trophy 8-point I shot while scrape hunting a prime breeding area marked by a number of scrapes, one of which is in front of the buck and me, along the edge of the snow. This is the third adult buck I shot in the same area while watching scrapes from a stand.

I've had excellent luck hunting scrapes. I look for exceptionally large ones, a concentration of them in a small area, or a scrape line consisting of numerous pawings along a hot trail. Antler rubs are freqeuntly found in the same areas. I shot a pair of 8-points and a trophy 11-pointer over a period of years from one particularly productive breeding area marked by numerous scrapes. I've shot bucks that were checking scrapes early and late in the day, but more of my tags have probably gone on bucks during the middle of the day while scrape hunting. So hunters who only hunt scrapes early and late in the day often miss seeing bucks that check them.

For information about using mock scrapes, refer to chapter 12, "Fooling A Deer's Nose."

Late Season

Search out migration trails for a late-season stand. Once snow flies, mule deer head from mountains to valleys; whitetails, in some locations, move toward yarding areas, which are often expansive lowland swamps. The animals generally follow the same trails to winter quarters every year. Trails leading to feeding areas or feeding grounds themselves can also be focal points for excellent late-season stand sites. Areas that are being logged can be late-season hot spots because the tops of felled trees provide plenty of browse for hungry deer. Locations with acorns, beechnuts, and apples are great late-season feeding areas, too, as are agricultural fields or food plots.

Wind Considerations

Consider prevailing wind currents when selecting specific sites for stands. You want to be downwind of where deer will appear, if possible. When in hilly country, remember that air currents rise in the morning and flow downhill in the evening. It may be advisable to watch a runway from up the slope early in the day and move to a vantage point below the trail later in the day.

Wind direction varies from day to day, and it is a good practice to have alternate stands to cover a hot trail. Going one step farther, a wise hunter will select one or two backup spots for stands before the season, separated by a quarter mile or more, in the event his or her first choice doesn't pan out. This way there is no great loss of valuable time in relocating.

When selecting a stand location, it is rare to be able to situate yourself where you can keep an eye on everything, so it's best not to try. By trying to watch too much, you make it tough to properly cover what may be the best spots, thereby reducing your chances of success. Being able to see one well-used travel route, the junction of two runways, the hottest scrape, or the preferred feeding area is normally plenty. That way you can concentrate your attention on the locations where deer are most likely to appear.

Also, stay within a reasonable shooting distance of the areas where you expect to see whitetails or mule deer. This distance will vary, depending upon the terrain and whether you are hunting with a handgun, shotgun, muzzleloader, centerfire rifle, or bow and arrow. In brushy country it may be only 20 to 30 yards with both bow and

Selecting a stand overlooking one well-used trail like this one or the intersection of two trails is a good strategy. Trying to cover too large an area from a stand can be a problem.

Blinds made from natural materials, like the one my brother Bruce is shown occupying here, blend in well with their surroundings and are less likely to be noticed by deer. A hunter's hearing and vision are also not impaired by an open blind like this.

gun, while in open areas it may be 20 yards for archers, 50 yards for handgun and shotgun users, and 100 to 150 yards for those carrying rifles.

Natural Cover

Once you've decided on one to several spots for stands, some cover will be necessary to break your outline while on stand. There are four options available: using natural cover, building a blind, erecting a portable blind, or using an elevated stand. Natural cover is preferable whenever it is available. On many occasions, I've simply used the trunks of large standing trees to break my outline while sitting or standing in front of them, but movement has to be kept to a minimum under those circumstances. More cover on the sides and in front of you allows more freedom of movement without the worry of being seen by deer.

Clumps of brush or brushpiles, fallen trees, large rocks, and low-hanging boughs of evergreen trees usually do the job. However, don't restrict freedom of movement and your line of sight for concealment. It will do little good to be so well hidden from a buck or doe that a good shot is impossible. Many times hunters are so screened they can't see the deer until it is too late.

When you are building blinds, try to use materials available nearby, such as fallen trees and limbs or pine boughs. As an alternative to using natural materials, camouflage netting or fabric can be used to fashion a ground blind quickly and easily. One way to use netting or fabric is to wrap it around two or three trees that are close together. Tacks are great for securing fabric to trees. Sticks, stakes, brush, or bushes can also serve as a framework to attach the material to around the chosen stand site. Here again, try not to construct a covering that obscures sight, sound, or maneuverability.

When stand hunting in agricultural areas or overgrown homesteads, consider using buildings, vehicles, or equipment that have been abandoned in some of these areas as makeshift blinds. Local deer accept them as part of the natural environment. The same thing applies to hay bales.

Blinds

Box blinds made of plywood or similar material are popular for deer hunting because they provide excellent concealment and the structures make it possible for hunters to remain comfortable for longer periods of time while they wait for deer to appear. It's possible to stay dry in them during wet weather and it's also warmer in them than in blinds made of natural material because the structures help block the wind. Portable heaters can be added to make box blinds comfortable on the coldest days. Blinds of this type should be put in place at least a week before the season opens so local animals will grow accustomed to them. A blind erected the day before the season may make deer wary of your position. This applies to blinds made of natural materials, too, if the setting is disturbed enough that local deer will notice.

One disadvantage of box blinds is they are not legal on many public hunting lands. Plenty of lightweight portable blinds made of camouflaged material are now available on the market for deer hunters as alternatives to box blinds. These portable blinds are not only legal on public property, they are excellent choices for private land as well since they can be put up and taken down quickly and they offer many of the comforts of box blinds. Regulations in some states require owners of portable blinds to have their name and address visible on the outside when the blinds are placed on public land.

Whether you are using natural cover or a blind, a backrest and comfortable seat will make the vigil more bearable, which is necessary for you to be able to stay in place for any length of time. Stumps or tree trunks serve well as backrests and can be used in conjunction with a log, boat cushion, or collapsible stool. A folding lawn chair is best of all if carrying it in isn't a problem. Placing it in position before the season can be an advantage.

My cousin Craig Smith with an 8-point whitetail he shot from the portable blind in the background. Portable blinds are great for both public and private property. Those on public land often have to be labeled with the owner's name and address.

A variation of the ground blind that isn't used by many deer hunters, but is effective, involves digging a pit, either circular or rectangular. The best position for a pit blind is on the slope or crest of a hill. When such a blind is dug on level ground, brush and small mounds easily obstruct a hunter's view. A hatchet and shovel will be necessary to dig a satisfactory hole because roots are often encountered during the excavation.

Circular pit blinds resemble a Thermos bottle cap, stopper down, from the side. The upper portion of the hole should be about six feet across and three feet deep. It should be deep enough for all but a hunter's head to be out of sight when he or she is sitting in it. Another, smaller hole about three feet wide is then dug in the center of the first one to make a space for feet and legs. With this design a hunter can sit facing any direction.

Box blinds, shacks, or shooting houses like this one are popular blinds because they are roomy and comfortable. Hunters can remain warmer and dryer in them than in open blinds and can also get away with more movement.

Squared-off pit blinds are also constructed with two levels so that it is possible to sit comfortably in them. The sides of the pit serve as a backrest. This type can be constructed to allow sitting at one or both ends of the pit. They can be six feet long and half as wide.

Dirt removed from holes can be distributed around the outside edge and should be covered with leaves or brush after the job is completed. Pine boughs can be used to cover a portion of the pit, leaving just enough room to sit. This helps protect fox-hole hunters from cold. The side of the pit hunters will be leaning against can be covered to keep their backs dry. Cushions can be added to pit blinds to sit on.

Check to make sure this practice is permissible whether you are hunting on private or public land. Digging pit blinds is generally prohibited on public property.

Elevated Stands

Elevated stands (where legal) are popular for deer hunting in wooded locations. With their use, hunters can get above their quarry's normal line of sight and often escape detection. Most whitetails and mulies do not expect danger from above and seldom look up, unless alerted by an out-of-place noise. However, deer that have detected a number of hunters in tree stands do adapt to looking for danger from above. Another advantage of hunting from trees is deer are less likely to wind a hunter in an elevated position.

While trying for a mule deer one fall in Wyoming with bow and arrow, I began the day from a ground stand. Wind currents were finicky that day. For a time the wind would be blowing one direction; then it would shift for fifteen minutes before changing again. Since it was morning, the general flow of air was uphill, so I chose a position on the uphill side of where I expected deer to show.

Several groups of does passed by at a distance; then a buck began working toward me. He was feeding uphill and the wind was in my favor. When that mulie buck was 20 yards away and I was about to draw, the wind shifted. He scented me and wasted little time getting out of there.

After that episode I found a tree with sturdy limbs to stand on about 15 feet off the ground and continued my vigil. Within a half hour another buck showed and came within 25 yards, where I arrowed him. Switching wind notwithstanding, that buck didn't know I was there.

Permanent tree stands made of wood are not legal on public lands, nor are they recommended for deer hunting on private property because the wood eventually rots and weakens and can fail when least expected, resulting in hunters falling and injuring themselves. Hunters who use permanent tree stands made of wood must check them on an annual basis for any damage and make repairs to prevent falls. Another disadvantage of permanent tree stands is that the trees they are attached to are damaged by the installation.

Portable tree stands are the way to go for deer hunting. There's a wide selection of commercially manufactured models to choose from that are safe, durable, and reasonably priced. All tree stands made by members of the Treestand Manufacturers Assocation (TMA) go through a rigorous safety testing program before they are approved for sale. All stands made by TMA companies should have stickers on them stating they are TMA approved.

The three major types of portable tree stands available on the market are hang-ons, climbers, and ladders. Hang-on stands usually consist of a platform and seat that are attached to a tree trunk with a chain or cable. Hunters frequently use screw-in steps (prohibited in some areas), climbing sticks, or ladders to put these stands in place. Tree steps that clamp onto tree trunks and don't damage trees are becoming more popular as scew-in steps are outlawed in more states. A safety harness or belt should always be used when putting up and taking down these stands to prevent falls. A harness is definitely the better of the two fall restraint devices, and they often come with climbing belts.

Climbing tree stands normally come with a platform and climber, both of which are designed to fit around the trunk of a tree at ground level and allow hunters to climb a tree to the desired height. This is the type of stand I use most frequently because they are quick and easy to put up and take down and they are extremely safe since you are on the platform at all times. To insure the utmost safety, hunters should wear a safety belt or harness when climbing up or down a tree as well as while hunting from any type of tree stand.

Ladder stands consist of a seat and ladder that are secured to tree trunks with chains, cables, or straps. I like these stands even more than climbing stands because they are quick and easy to get in and out of once they are in place. Although a single hunter can install a ladder stand, it's safer and easier if at least two do the task. One person can hold the ladder while the other secures it in place.

A hunter ascends an aspen tree with a Summit climbing tree stand. With his feet strapped to the platform, he does a pullup with a climbing bar to raise the platform. Some climbers are designed to be used while in a sitting position. Climbing stands allow hunters to change positions quickly if the wind shifts.

Slings, which are harnesses designed to sit in, offer another alternative for hunting from trees. I've interviewed a pair of very successful bow hunters who use tree slings, or saddles, exclusively. Slings are lighter and more portable than any other

Left: A hunter takes aim from a ladder stand. Tree stands like this one are popular among hunters to increase the chances of going undetected by whitetails and mule deer. This type of tree stand is safe and is easy to get in and out of. Right: Tree slings like the one worn by Jimmy Dean in this photograph are the lightest, most portable tree stands available.

type of tree stand and are safe when used properly. Self-supporting elevated stands that can be used in fields or areas with few, if any, trees are also available commercially. They are called tripod stands. The simplest tripods have a seat atop the three legs, with a ladder to climb into position. More elaborate tripod stands have roomy blinds on top of them.

I've shot some deer from trees by simply perching on a large limb and that option is a possibility, but be extremely careful if you try this because it could be dangerous. Some hunters have been seriously injured or killed when the limb they were standing on broke under their weight. A safety belt or harness is recommended whenever hunting above ground level, whether on a stand or tree limb.

When hunting from an elevated position, I seldom climb higher than 15 feet, but some hunters get as high as 20 to 30 feet. The chances of being detected by mule deer and whitetails are reduced the higher you go and visibility can often be better from greater heights, though not always.

A tree stand should be located on the side of a tree opposite a deer trail, unless there is plenty of cover on the side of the tree facing the trail. In this position there is less likelihood a deer will see the hunter. This is an especially useful tip for bowhunters. The movement an archer makes when drawing his or her bow sometimes attracts a deer's attention. When you are on the opposite side of a tree trunk from the deer, there is less chance of this happening.

Whether using a gun or bow from a tree stand, use a rope to raise and lower it from the platform. Archers should have all broadheads in a covered quiver. Centerfire rifles, shotguns, and handguns should not have a shell in the chamber when raised or lowered from a tree. Ignition sources such as caps, discs, or primers should be absent from muzzleloaders. You don't have to worry about a firearm discharging accidentally if there's no way for it to go off.

Site Preparation

The next step in readying a stand is to clear away all forest litter within several feet of where you will be positioned if you are on the ground. A nervous foot crunching dead leaves won't do much for keeping your presence a secret. This is also a precaution in case you have to stand up to stretch cramped muscles or try to get a better look at a deer.

Similarly, branches and twigs that may restrict your view or bump your

When hunting from a tree stand without much cover, it can be a good idea to be on the opposite side of the trunk from where you expect to see deer, so you can be in position to shoot after they walk by. I'm in a climbing stand made by Summit in this photo.

weapon when you raise or swing it should be removed from around where you will be sitting or standing. Check all quadrants—front, sides, and back—by shouldering or drawing and swinging your weapon. Trimming limbs to create shooting lanes is also a good idea once a tree stand is in position, but don't get carried away. Bucks tend to shy away from spots that have been altered too much since they were there last.

A pole saw can come in handy to reach some limbs that are in the way. When possible, having a partner do the trimming while you are in your stand is a great way to clear shooting lanes.

Limbs that are trimmed should be cut flush with tree trunks rather than leaving stubs that are several inches long. Stubs of limbs will eventually die and fall off, which reduces the quality of the tree for lumber. When the stubs fall off they will leave holes in the wood.

A hunting companion of mine didn't get a shot at what he guessed was a 10-point whitetail buck one year because he failed to remove twigs on all sides that might be in his way. He was sitting with his back against a stump when he heard something walking behind him. It was making so much noise he thought it had to be another hunter. When my partner peeked around the stump he saw the big buck. He slowly brought his rifle around and up to take a shot. When the gun was halfway to his shoulder, the barrel hit a twig and the twig snapped off. That buck was gone in less time than it takes to tell about it.

Once interfering brush and limbs are removed, a bowhunter should consider determining the distance from the stand to various points where shots at deer can be expected. Range finders are great for accomplishing this. These gadgets allow hunters to be prepared for shots at known distances quickly and easily. It's far better than pacing the distance to various objects and contaminating the area with your scent before getting in your blind or tree stand.

There is one more step in preparing a stand for the hunt. Since you want to be seated before first light, if possible, and stay until shooting light has faded, be sure you will be able to find your way to and from your post by flashlight. If you can do it with no aids, all the better. Consider marking some sort of a trail if you can't find your stand unaided.

Left: Once a tree stand or ground blind is set, it may be necessary to cut some limbs that might interfere with a clear shot. A pole saw like the one shown here can be helpful for reaching some limbs. Try not to remove too much. Bucks will detour around spots that are too open. Right: A range finder like the one this bowhunter is using can come in handy for determining distances to various landmarks after you get in position. Then when a deer shows up, you will have a good idea of how far away it is.

Fluorescent tape is handy for marking trees. In some cases blaze marks can also be used. Light-reflecting tacks or tape are also good. Don't designate your route from where you leave your vehicle all the way to your stand, however, unless you are hunting private land. Only use guideposts where necessary. Otherwise, you may have a number of curious hunters visiting during the day.

The Hunt

Proper mental attitude is important in preparing yourself for the hunt. Mentally, you have to convince yourself that your post is the best position available in your area. Be confident and tell yourself that by being patient you will eventually get a chance for a shot. Staying put for only a few hours usually isn't enough, unless, of course, you score quickly. A quick score can happen, but don't count on it. Plan on spending the entire day in your spot, if possible. If you can only handle a few hours at a time, spend the first few hours of the day, midday, and the last couple of hours in position. Most kills occur during those time periods.

During morning hunts, it's best to be in position before first light, so you will be ready to shoot if a deer you want comes along soon after it is light enough to see. I've known that for years, of course, but I relearned the lesson during a recent gun hunt while hunting out of a remote tent camp. I was scrape hunting where I knew a big whitetail was roaming, based on the numerous rubbed trees and scrapes I found.

I had been bowhunting in the area the week before firearms season opened and passed up a forkhorn a couple of times. I also heard, but never saw, another deer between eleven o'clock and noon that I suspected was the bigger buck checking his scrapes. I planned on changing positions for opening day of gun season. The day before, I put my Summit Climbing Stand on the tree I wanted to be in the next morning.

Once I arrived at the stand, I would simply climb to an acceptable height and be ready for action. I planned on being there before daylight to climb the tree, but I had a half-hour drive and another thirty-minute walk to get to the stand, and I ended up arriving late. It was getting light as I walked toward the stand. I didn't want to rush, to avoid working up a sweat and then getting chilled, so I took my time. I rationalized the slow pace, thinking I was most likely to see the buck I wanted during the middle of the day anyway.

I didn't waste any time getting in the tree when I got there. I tied a rope to my rifle before I climbed up so I could hoist it up to me after I was in position. Once I reached the desired height, I decided to screw a hook into the tree to hang the rifle from. As I was doing that, the buck I wanted came trotting off a ridge right toward me. Caught with my rifle on the ground, I immediately grabbed the haul rope and tried to start pulling the gun up.

The buck saw me move, trotted about 50 yards, and stopped, looking back at me. The whitetail had at least ten long tines and would have weighed in the 200- to 250-pound range—a true trophy big-woods buck. If my rifle had been in my hands, he would have been dead, but it wasn't, and I never saw that deer again.

Eating sunflower seeds that are in the shell like these can help hunters keep alert during all-day sits.

Going hand-in-hand with a proper mental attitude and getting in position before daylight is a good night's sleep. Don't stay up until all hours playing cards with the guys or drinking. A groggy mind can't be enthusiastic about anything.

The last point to consider is how to wait. Sounds simple enough, but there are a few points worth mentioning. Always be alert and ready to shoot. One way to stay alert during all-day sits is to eat sunflower seeds. Consuming these tiny morsels helps break up the boredom when deer activity is slow. Some hunters stay alert by reading when stand hunting.

Listen for sounds and look for movements. Keep your gun, bow, or camera on your lap or gripped in your hands, ready to shoulder, draw, or raise. When hunting from a tree stand for most of a day or all day, especially in cold weather, it's important to have a hook or limb to hang a gun or bow from periodically to take breaks and avoid fatigue. However, the weapon should be hung where it's handy in case a deer shows up.

If at all possible, don't wear standard earmuffs or a hood, since these will affect your ability to hear or see a deer approaching, but this may be unavoidable if the weather is cold and or windy. Some head phones are now on the market that actually improve your hearing and are designed for hunters who are hard of hearing. These earmuffs not only increase your chances of hearing deer that are coming, they muffle the loud report of gunshots, protecting your ears from further damage.

After a time, familiarity will develop for how everything looks and sounds in the immediate vicinity. More often than not, you will notice anything out of the ordinary immediately. Keep looking all around you, moving your head slowly from side to side.

Keep your personal noises to a minimum. Wrap food in material that isn't exceptionally noisy. Clear Saran Wrap is great for wrapping sandwiches, and aluminum foil isn't too bad either. Zip-Lock sandwich bags are also great. Shifting positions regularly to maintain comfort is unavoidable. Always stay alert while doing it.

As far as smoking is concerned, if you are situated downwind from where deer are going to be, they probably won't notice it. Whitetails and mule deer are apt to notice the movements associated with smoking, however, so it is best to smoke as little as possible.

There are plenty of things to keep your mind occupied while you wait. Observing birds and animals other than deer can be entertaining. Sometimes they will warn you of an approaching deer. Every time a jay squawks or a squirrel chatters, you should wonder why.

A nearby shot, the snap of a twig, or the rustling of leaves may mean a deer is coming your way. Look for and identify the source of every sound.

I collected a nice 10-point mule deer in Colorado one fall by paying attention to rifle shots in my area. When I heard a group of shots over a ridge from me I knew that hunters had jumped some game and, if the shooters didn't connect, the animals should come uphill and over the ridge. I kept my eyes glued on the skyline.

Within five minutes, not one, but seven bucks came over the top and into my lap. The ten-pointer I dropped was the biggest of the bunch. I've heard numerous stories from whitetail hunters about a nearby shot tipping them off to

Be sure to bring a lunch with you when stand hunting all day. Try to wrap sandwiches in quiet material such as Saran Wrap. Even when you are only planning on hunting for a short time, always bring snack foods with you in case you end up staying longer than expected.

the approach of a buck that was missed by some one else.

Once a whitetail or mule deer is sighted, get ready as quickly as possible. If you are sure a deer is approaching, get your weapon up. That's one less movement you'll have to make when it comes in sight. If deer catch you off guard and are visible before you hear them, don't move unless the animal you want is on the move and will be out of sight shortly. Take the first opportunity for a clean shot when the buck's head goes behind a tree or bush, when he puts his head down, or when he is looking the other way.

When that antlered deer goes down, you will be a confirmed stand hunter. Hunting in this fashion may take a lot of time, work, and patience, but it will be worth it when you walk over and inspect that buck.

For in-depth information about ambushing whitetails, refer to the book I've written titled *Stand Hunting For Whitetails.*

Facts About Baiting

Deer hunting over bait is a form of stand hunting that involves ambushing white-tails and mule deer at a food source. The food source or bait is provided by hunters, either placed on the ground or distributed from feeders. Even though the practice of hunting deer at other food sources such as agricultural fields, food plots, or fruit and nut trees, is universally accepted, baiting is controversial. However, it shouldn't be. The purpose of this chapter is to provide some insights and dispell some myths about this hunting method through the use of facts.

One year, when I was deer hunting in Alabama with Charles Dixon, he made a comment about baiting that I will never forget. He said, "Baiting is legal every-where. It just depends on how you define it." This still rings true today, and brings light to something many hunters fail to recognize.

Alabama pioneered the use of "green fields," now called food plots in many places, for deer hunting. Baiting, as it is usually defined (putting corn, apples, and other foods deer eat in a specific spot so the animals can be seen and shot), is illegal in Alabama. But planting foods that deer eat in a plot of any size to attract them so they can be seen and shot is legal. That's why green fields and food plots, many of which are too small to be considered fields, are so popular in Alabama and other states where "baiting" is illegal.

Food plots, some of which are smaller than the areas some hunters spread corn over in states that allow baiting, are legalized baiting. Many food plots serve the same purpose as baiting, the way the practice is normally defined, and that's why many of them are planted. The larger food plots are designed to keep deer fed and happy during times of the year when hunting isn't legal, too. But if it weren't for hunting and the desire to attract and keep deer on private properties, many food plots would not be planted.

Baiting is legal for deer in every state, it just depends upon how the practice is defined. In most states, food plots or green fields like the one this Alabama buck is feeding in are not defined as "bait" even though they serve the same purpose as foods placed by hunters to attract deer so they can be seen and shot.

The definition of baiting definitely benefits deer hunters who own or lease property and leaves hunters who rely on hunting public land out in the cold in states where baiting is illegal. Baiting, where legal according to the common definition, offers hunters who hunt on land open to the public the opportunity to attract deer to a specific location to see and possibly shoot one, just like private land owners who plant food plots, giving all hunters fairly equal access to a public resource. In most states, it is illegal for citizens to plant food plots on public land and many state agencies don't plant them either. When and where baiting is illegal, hunters who do not own land are put at a disadvantage when state agencies don't plant food plots on public land, since food plots on private property are not defined as baiting.

I'm not advocating that the definition of baiting be changed, that planting food plots so that deer can be shot over them be made illegal, or that baiting be made legal everywhere. What I do want to do in this chapter is provide some factual information about baiting and hunting deer over bait to counteract some of the shortsighted, emotionally driven, false information I've seen printed about the subject.

One of the things that prompted me to write this chapter is an article I read in a high-circulation national magazine by a writer who is opposed to hunting deer over bait even though he has obviously had little experience doing it. As a result, his opinion was poorly developed and much of the information he presented about the subject was false. The author had a holier-than-thou attitude that I've often heard from hunters opposed to baiting: "I don't hunt over bait and don't think it's necessary, so no one should."

The writer used the same tactic anti-hunters have mastered to portray many forms of hunting in a bad light: false information. And, unfortunately, many hunters who don't know any different believe what they've read. My position is that baiting, where legal, is a perfectly legitimate hunting method for hunters to consider using. If you don't like baiting and don't want to do it, that's fine. You don't have to. By the same token, if some one else decides to try the technique, please respect their decision.

There are enough anti-hunters criticizing hunters and trying to end all types of hunting without hunters themselves bad-mouthing legal hunting methods in an attempt to reduce the options hunters have available to them. I refer to these folks as anti-hunting hunters. There are far too many of them.

A photo of a massive pile of corn used with the anti-baiting magazine article was just as misleading as the text. The image did not represent a real-life baiting situation. In fact, that much corn in one place would have been illegal to hunt over in most, if not all, places where baiting is legal. Limits on the quantity of bait that can be used at one time are in place in most states and provinces where the practice is legal. In other words, where legal, baiting is usually regulated.

What's ironic about the photo of the huge pile of corn is that much larger quantities of corn are in every North American cornfield where whitetails routinely feed. And if the amount of deer food generated by many food plots were put in a pile, that pile would be larger than the exaggerated quantity of food in the photo.

In my home state of Michigan, for example, hunters are limited to using a maximum of two gallons of bait at one time and the bait must be spread over an area at least 100 square feet in size. Wisconsin hunters are limited to a maximum of two gallons of bait per 40 acres of land.

The following states currently allow baiting for deer statewide: Arizona, Kansas, Nevada, New Hampshire, Mississippi, New Jersey, North Carolina, Ohio, Oklahoma, Oregon, South Carolina, Utah, and Washington. Canadian provinces in which deer hunting over bait is legal are British Columbia, New

Where baiting (as it is commonly defined) is legal, the practice is regulated, as it should be, by limiting quantities and requiring that bait be spread to reduce the chances of close contact between deer. Feeders like this one being used in Texas spread corn and limit the quantity dispensed. Many hunters who use bait spread it around by hand.

Baiting remains legal in Saskatchewan's northern forests, even though deer infected with CWD have been diagnosed in the southern part of the province. The same thing is true in Wisconsin, where baiting is carefully regulated. But baiting remains legal statewide in Kansas, Oklahoma, and Utah even though the disease has been detected in those states.

Brunswick, Nova Scotia, Ontario, Quebec, and Saskatchewan. Only designated portions of the following states are open to baiting: Connecticut, Florida, Kentucky, Louisiana, Maryland, Michigan, Pennsylvania, Texas, and Wisconsin. I was surprised to find out baiting is only legal on private land in Texas. The same thing is true in Louisiana and perhaps some of the other states listed above.

As of 2010, the Upper Peninsula is the only region in Michigan where deer hunting over bait is legal, but that may change by 2011. A captive whitetail with chronic wasting disease (CWD) was found in the Lower Peninsula's Kent County during 2008, causing the state to ban baiting throughout the Lower Peninsula while testing of wild deer was conducted to determine if any of them were infected. No more deer with the disease have been detected after three years of testing. Since results from 2010 were also negative, baiting may resume.

Check local regulations for all states you plan to hunt for any possible changes and to determine what baiting restrictions are in place.

Many of the states in which CWD has infected free-ranging deer have banned baiting due to concerns the practice might contribute to the spread of the disease. That rationale has not been uniform, however. Deer with CWD have been found in Kansas, Oklahoma, and Utah, but baiting is still legal statewide in those states. Wisconsin has also had an outbreak of CWD, but baiting is still legal in counties many miles from where diseased deer have been identified, primarily in the northern part of the state. The same thing is true in Saskatchewan.

Regulating baiting is just as important as establishing controls or guidelines for other forms of hunting. Without rules, some hunters have gotten carried away and engaged in competitions to see who could put out the most bait.

Bob Polly admires four of the five adult bucks we got while hunting over bait in upper Michigan. A 7-pointer bagged by Dave Menominee had already been taken down to be butchered when this photo was taken.

Studies done in Michigan confirmed that when baiting was unregulated and large amounts of bait were used, many whitetails visited these food sources after dark. Further research found that when the quantity of bait was limited, as it is now and has been, bucks were more likely to be seen during shooting hours. In other words, smaller quantities of food bring better results when baiting.

I found out how effective baiting with limited quantities of food can be on adult bucks during a recent season while hunting out of a camp in Michigan's Upper Peninsula. There were six of us. Five of us got bucks while hunting over bait and they were all at least $2^1/_2$ years old. One was $3^1/_2$ (10 points) and one was 4 or 5 years old (12 Points).

I shot the 10-point on the morning of November 18 (the fourth day of gun season) around ten-thirty. He came in cautiously, following a hot doe. When he reached the bait, he ate some, and that distracted him enough that I was able to raise my rifle for a shot. Prior to reaching the bait, the buck was so alert that if I had made a move to raise my rifle, I think he would have seen or heard me and bolted. It was a quiet morning, so if I had made any noise, he and/or the doe certainly would have heard it. I was in a ground blind, but a large front window was open, increasing the chances of the deer seeing movement inside.

Baiting is also very effective on adult bucks in Saskatchewan, where baiting is the most common hunting method for nonresidents because they are limited to hunting from stands. I've seen as many as ten adult bucks per day visiting baits there. Without baiting, hunters in the province's big woods would see fewer deer. Bucks are most vulnerable to baiting where hunting pressure is light. Where hunting pressure is heavy, bucks adapt by visiting baits most often after dark. During the rut, however, adult bucks may follow does that are in heat to a bait, like the 10-pointer mentioned in the previous paragraph did.

Baiting can also be an important management tool by increasing the harvest of antlerless deer. Deer hunters using bait often have more opportunities to shoot antlerless animals when deer numbers are too high. In areas where diseases such as CWD and TB are present, regulated baiting can play an important role in reducing disease prevalence through the harvest of higher numbers of deer. That's why sharpshooters hired to cull deer rely on bait to accomplish their goal. Regulations that require limited quantities of bait to be spread rather than dumped in a pile reduce the chances of disease transmission.

Contrary to what you may have heard or read, a link between baiting and bovine tuberculosis has not been proven in Michigan. It started as a theory and remains speculation. The mantra that baiting spreads TB has been repeated so often by DNR personnel and the media, people think it's a fact. When feeding and baiting were unregulated and conducted year-round with large quantities of food to produce huge deer herds, it may have helped spread TB. But the

Baiting can play an important role in deer management by making it possible for hunters to harvest more antlerless deer like this one. The use of bait to allow hunters to harvest a maximum number of antlerless deer can also help reduce the prevalence of diseases such as TB. Hunting over bait also increases the opportunity for clean kills.

spread of the disease through regulated baiting with reduced deer herds is not likely. Attempts to isolate TB bacteria at deer feeding sites in enclosures where the prevalence rate was much higher than it is in the wild have failed. Exposure to sunlight kills the bacteria that causes TB.

The primary means of disease transmission among whitetails and mule deer is through direct contact between related deer such as siblings or does and their fawns, between bachelor groups of bucks, and between bucks and does during the rut. Whitetails are especially social animals and they routinely have nose-to-nose contact even where baiting is not practiced. Does and their fawns engage in mutual grooming on a daily basis. I've seen and photographed unrelated adult bucks in bachelor groups engage in mutual grooming, and four-year-old sibling bucks and does do the same thing. During the rut, bucks come in contact with the urine from multiple does by taking in small quantities of the liquid through their noses and mouths to determine if the females are ready to breed. Since the bacteria that causes TB and the prions that cause CWD are shed in the urine, adult bucks tend to have a higher prevalence rate of these diseases than does even where baiting is not practiced.

It's important to note that Minnesota, where baiting is not legal and has not been for a long time, has had an outbreak of TB in wild whitetails since 2005. TB also persists in the vicinity of Manitoba's Riding Mountain Provincial Park, where baiting has been illegal for many years. If baiting were an important link in spreading and maintaining the disease, the disease would have disappeared in deer in those locations by now.

The same is true in Michigan, where baiting has been banned for about ten years in the counties where the majority of free-roaming deer with TB live. Yet the disease persists at low prevalence rates. It's not because of baiting, but because of direct contact between deer that is impossible to eliminate. For more on deer disease and how it relates to baiting, please refer to chapter 2.

One of the criticisms of baiting is that it can cause lactic acidosis in deer, a condition that can develop from eating large quantities of grain. Limits on the quantity of bait eliminate the potential for lactic acidosis. Another criticism of baiting is that the activity can concentrate large numbers of deer in a small area. That problem can also be solved, and usually is, through limiting the quantity of bait.

Controls on baiting also reduce homesteading, or hunters claiming a parcel of public hunting land. Hunters who claim territories on public land as their own, however, occur even where baiting is not legal. The practice is not unique to baiting. Limits on quantities of bait that can be used also eliminates competition between hunters. When limits are in place and some hunters don't abide by the rules, they are often reported to law enforcement personnel by their neighbors.

Claims that the general public doesn't understand or accept baiting are false. In 1996, an attempt was made to ban bear hunting with bait and dogs in Michigan. The hunting methods were put on the statewide ballot as proposal D. After a major educational effort by sportsmen and women, 62 percent of the general public voted against a ban on these methods because they understood that they play an important role in bear management in the state. The general public will understand the role regulated baiting plays in deer management where it's legal when they are provided with the facts. False information about deer hunting with bait fans the anti-hunting flames against both deer and bear baiting and is a form of resorting to the same tactics anti-hunters use to try to accomplish their goals.

There are benefits of baiting for deer besides increasing the potential for antlerless harvest and population control: It increases the chances of seeing whitetails when they are at low numbers, which is satisfying to many hunters even if they don't shoot anything. Baiting increases the chances of clean kills, too, with both bow and gun, allowing hunters to shoot at known distances and wait for a good shot. Baiting also makes it possible for young, old, inexperienced, and handicapped hunters to participate in deer hunting. And the tactic makes it possible for hunters to be selective of the deer they shoot, passing up button bucks and other young bucks, where desired.

Having as many hunting methods to choose from as possible is a good thing for deer hunters. At the same time, it is never a good idea for one hunting technique to be relied upon exclusively. This makes it easier for deer to adapt by avoiding hunters and reduces hunting success. When it comes to baiting, it should be a personal choice whether to try it or not, where it's legal. The information presented in this chapter should help you make up your mind.

It's worth restating that one of the most important points that state agencies should consider regarding the legality and definition of baiting is equitable availability of public resources such as deer to all hunters. If baiting is illegal, food plots are not defined as baiting, and the state does not plant food plots on public ground, then private land owners and lease holders are given an advantage by default in their ability to harvest deer. The best way to offset lopsided access to the resource is to begin establishing food plots on public land, perhaps through cooperative agreements with sportsman's organizations who have the manpower, equipment, and incentive to get the job done. Drafting contracts with farmers, with some or all of the funding coming from hunters, is also an option. Another option where the previous two are not practical, of course, is legalizing regulated baiting.

7

Best Buck At 50

When Saskatchewan guide Ron Button from Swift Current dropped me off near my blind before daylight on the morning of Thursday, November 18, 1999, he said, "This is the day. You're going to get one today!"

"I hope so," I responded, appreciating his optimism, and headed uphill to the blind I had been occupying since Monday, following the light beam from the 4-wheeler. Although this would be my fourth day in that particular blind, it would be my tenth day of hunting from dawn to dark in the Canadian bush with Proudfoot Creek Outfitters. I had hunted two different spots the previous week, one from a ground blind and the other from a ladder stand, spending about ten hours per day waiting for the buck I wanted.

I had seen bucks every day, usually more than one, and enjoyed plenty of excitement. I watched bucks make rubs and scrapes, chase does, and respond to rattling. The biggest bucks I had shots at were, on average, 8-pointers. I was waiting for a whitetail that would score at least in the 140s.

I knew they were around. Other hunters had taken bucks scoring as high as the upper 160s during the time I was hunting. I had taken a pair of whoppers myself from the area the last time I hunted there in 1993. The bag limit was two bucks then, but had since been reduced to one deer.

In 1993 I put my first tag on a nontypical 12-point with a 9-inch drop tine during the muzzleloader season in late October that had a net score of $165^6/8$. I returned about a month later to fill my second with a wide-antlered 10-point that netted $147^2/8$. I passed up a number of bucks before getting the 10, so I was well aware of the value of patience. Each day during my hunt in 1999, I knew a trophy whitetail could appear at any second. He finally did on that tenth day, as Ron had predicted.

A doe was feeding in front of me at first light and I scanned the surrounding cover with my binoculars through the front window of the ground blind, looking for

The blind I shot my best whitetail from in Saskatchewan. I got the buck on the fourth day of hunting from the blind and my tenth day of hunting from dawn to dark. In this photo I'm looking inside the blind to see if I left anything behind.

other whitetails. About ten minutes later, the head of a buck emerged from the trees behind the doe. An inch or two of fresh snow was covering the ground, so his antlers stood out in sharp contrast to the white background. I counted five distinct tines on the right antler and two of them were long.

It didn't take long to realize this was the buck I had been waiting for. I quickly dropped my binoculars and grabbed my rifle where it was leaning in the corner of the blind, easing the barrel through the window to avoid making any noise. With the rut in full swing, I knew the buck could chase the doe out of sight any moment.

By the time I was looking at the buck through my scope, the doe was gone. I could only see the buck's head and neck. His body was blocked from view by a couple of trees. I took the time to make sure the deer's antlers had ten points, then concentrated on making the shot.

The whitetail soon took a couple of steps forward, revealing the front half of his body. When I shot, the buck jumped straight in the air before kicking out with his hind legs. "Heart shot," I said to myself.

The buck took off running to the left and out of sight when he hit the ground. Even though I was confident I had made a good shot, I didn't waste any time getting out of the blind to confirm that. The big deer only made it about 35 yards before crashing.

Patience and persistence had paid off once more, only the reward this time was much better than I realized. Once I confirmed the buck was dead, I relaxed and silently thanked the hunting gods for my success and admired the fallen whitetail.

I pose with my best typical whitetail where he fell in Saskatchewan on November 18. Notice the frost on the buck's neck and body. The whitetail's antlers proved to be larger than I thought they were.

The hair on his heavy neck and back was covered with frost, testimony to how cold it had been the night before and to the insulating qualities of the whitetail's coat.

The antlers were every bit as good as I thought they were and then some. The beams were wide and fairly heavy and there was excellent tine length. That whitetail definitely had a better typical rack than any other I had previously shot, but I quickly rejected the idea that they might score 170, the minimum for all-time listing in national records maintained by the Boone and Crockett Club. I figured the antlers might gross in the 160s and net in the 150s and let it go at that.

At the time, exactly what the antlers measured wasn't that important. I knew they would tape better than 140, so I had accomplished my goal. Like so many whitetail hunters, I often dreamed of bagging a buck with a Boone and Crockett qualifying rack, but I knew the odds were against it. Consequently, I had myself convinced it would probably never happen.

That mindset was so strong that when it happened, I had a hard time believing it was true. The fact that I got a buck of that caliber at the age of fifty makes the accomplishment extra special. However, it was months after I got the whitetail when I realized my age, along with the buck, were somewhat of a milestone.

It's somehow fitting that I got my highest scoring typical whitetail at fifty even though I never consciously strived for that goal. I had become a selective hunter at least ten years earlier. I seldom shot a buck unless it had at least an 8-point rack, and selected antlerless deer over young bucks when I wanted meat, for the sake of management purposes.

Having shot my share of whitetails, including young bucks, over the more than forty-five years I've been hunting them, and understanding the role hunters play as managers have contributed to my selectivity. Taking my best buck at fifty was ample reason to reflect back on how far I've come since I started hunting whitetails.

I shot my first buck in 1966 at the age of seventeen. It was a 3-pointer, but I didn't know it was a buck when I shot. I had an antlerless permit, which was valid for a whitetail of either sex, so I fired without getting a look at the deer's head. I was ecstatic upon discovering I had bagged my first buck, but I still would have been excited about taking a doe. My first deer, which I shot a year or two earlier, was a doe.

I looked forward to opening day of deer season more than anything else back then and that hasn't changed much. The only difference now is I'm usually fortunate enough to take part in more than one opening day every year. Excitement-induced sleepless nights prior to opening day were common in my younger days, largely due to anticipation of what might happen. Those sleepless nights are mostly a thing of the past, not because of lack of excitement, but because I more often know what likely lies ahead and recognize the value of a good night's sleep in getting the most out of opening day.

How I hunt hasn't changed much over the years. I learned early on how important it can be to scout thoroughly for a potential stand site and to stick it out all day to increase your chances of seeing deer. If you pick the right spot, they will come, eventually.

My attitude about shooting bucks has changed dramatically though. During the early years, I could not comprehend passing up a legal buck. That was because I seldom saw them and the animals were a mystery to me. I thought they had magical powers that allowed them to appear and disappear at will.

I remember reading magazine articles by hunters who claimed to have passed up bucks, bucks I could only dream about seeing. I could not understand how they could do it. I wondered if they were telling the truth.

During recent years, the mystery surrounding whitetail bucks for me has been replaced by respect. I now understand the animals more than ever before. However, the older, bigger bucks, most of them anyway, still remain elusive.

I now understand how hunters can pass up legal bucks, and I do it routinely myself. When I write about it, I'm sure that there are some young hunters out there who can't understand and may even doubt my words. Some day, hopefully, they will reach the stage I have.

While some whitetail hunters may consider cutting back on participation when they reach the age of fifty, that's the furthest thing from my mind. I will be at least sixty-two by the time you read this and I look forward to as many more years of deer hunting as possible. The fact that I accomplished something at the age of fifty that I thought might never happen is sort of an incentive to keep trying. But even if I had ended my Saskatchewan hunt without filling a tag, whitetail hunting would remain just as valuable to me. It always will.

My Saskatchewan 10-point from 1999 had a gross score of 170⁶/₈ the day after I shot him and netted 165⁶/₈. After the mandatory drying period, the antlers had an official gross score of 166⁵/₈ and netted 163⁷/₈, qualifying for honorable mention in Boone & Crockett Records during the twenty-fourth scoring period from 1998 through 2000. The minimum score of typical whitetail antlers to qualify for honorable mention is 160.

There were a total of 2⁶/₈ inches of deductions between the right and left antler. The greatest deduction was for a difference in length between the fourth tines on each beam. The one on the right side was 3⁷/₈ inches long and the left one was 2³/₈ inches in length. There was also a half-inch difference between the lengths of the third tines and a quarter-inch difference between the second tines. There were minor differences in the circumferences of the beams, too. Overall, however, the antlers were more symmetrical than most.

Although a minimum 60-day drying period is required before antlers can be officially measured to allow for shrinkage, the antlers from my deer dried for close to 90 days before they were scored and there obviously was some shrinkage. The inside spread of the antlers went down to 21³/₈ from 21⁶/₈, for example. Tine lengths

were also shorter and there was a reduction in mass. The second tines were the longest on the rack, measuring 12⁶/₈ inches when I got the deer. That tine on the right side measured 12²/₈ inches after drying and the one on the right side taped an even 12 inches. The circumference measurements at the base of the antlers went from 5⁵/₈ inches to 5³/₈ inches.

Some of the differences in measurements between the green and official scores have to do with how carefully they were taken as well as shrinkage. Measurements taken the day after I got the deer by my guide Ron Button from Swift Current were done quickly and with less precision than by Boone and Crockett measurer John Ohmer. For this reason, the beam lengths of the rack ended up being longer when measured officially than when I got the buck.

Taxidermist Rich Ryberg with Outdoor Ventures Taxidermy puts the finishing touches on the head mount of my Saskatchewan buck. Ryberg aged the buck at 7¹/₂.

To measure beams properly, it's important to follow the curvature of the bone along the middle of the beam. Most official measurers like Ohmer use a cable that they tape to the beams and then measure the cable. Ron simply used a tape measure to gauge the length of the beams. He came up with 22⁶/₈ inches for the right beam and 23 inches on the left beam. When John measured the beams, he ended up with final official lengths of 23⁵/₈ inches for each one.

A short nontypical point sticks up at the base of the fourth point on the right beam. When the rack was green scored, more than an inch was deducted from the net score for this sticker point, but the Boone and Crockett measurer did not count it as a scorable point because the base of the tine is wider than its length.

The antlers were also entered in the Buckmasters Whitetail Trophy Records with a score of 145²/₈. The right antler tallied 73⁴/₈ and the left antler measurements totaled 71⁶/₈ under this system. Unlike in the Boone and Crockett scoring system, there are no deductions for differences between the right and left antler in the Buckmasters method of scoring. The minimum for entry of firearms kills in that record-keeping system is 140. For more on measuring antlers, refer to chapter 19.

The buck was aged at 7¹/₂ based on tooth wear by Rich Ryberg of Outdoor Ventures Taxidermy, and the deer had a dressed weight of 213 pounds. I'm sure he had lost a lot of weight during the previous two to three weeks of rutting activity. Due to the deer's age, it's not likely his antlers would have gotten much bigger. And it's a safe bet the animal had plenty of opportunity to pass his genes on to lots of offspring.

8

Stillhunting and Stalking

One of Michigan's highest-scoring typical bucks claimed by a bowhunter was taken as a result of a stalk executed by brothers Rock and Scott Vore on November 6 one year. The weather wasn't the best for hunting that day (it was windy and raining), so the pair had watched a hunting video they rented from a local store. They were driving home after returning the video when Scott spotted a bedded buck with huge antlers on state land. They rushed home to put their hunting clothes on and get their bows and arrows, then returned to find the buck still bedded in the same place.

They started their stalk 300 yards downwind from where the whitetail was bedded in some cattails, approaching from the buck's rear to reduce the chances of being seen, heard, or smelled. The wind and rain increased their odds of sneaking within bow range of the deer undetected. After two hours of slow, painstaking crawling the brothers reached the 25-yard mark.

The pair drew their bows and released their arrows at the same time. Scott's arrow missed, but Rock's connected, and the buck only made it 20 yards before dying. The $5^{1}/_{2}$-year-old 11-pointer had a dressed weight of 203 pounds and the antlers netted $180^{2}/_{8}$.

Stillhunting and stalking are difficult to separate because the same basic skills are required for each. The major difference is that while stalking, a deer hunter already has the quarry in sight. A stillhunter is searching for deer, but he or she may become a stalker as soon as he or she spots a whitetail or mule deer that must be approached before a shot is possible.

Stillhunting requires more activity than stand hunting. The hunter is on the move, but not constantly. When he or she is moving, it is at a very slow pace. A stillhunter actually takes many stands during a hunt, but occupies each one for a brief period of time compared to the duration a dedicated stand hunter often remains in one spot.

Normally, a hunter using the stop-and-go technique only remains motionless for a matter of minutes, but on occasion he or she will stay in place for as long as half an hour. It depends on the circumstances.

Stalking is simply a matter of decreasing the distance between a hunter and the quarry without being detected. The acceptable range depends on the weapon a hunter is using and his or her shooting ability. A bowhunter, for instance, might want to get within 20 or 30 yards of the target like Scott and Rock Vore did; a black powder hunter or shotgunner might consider 100 yards the maximum range; and a rifle hunter using a .270 might feel confident of dropping a deer from 200 to 300 yards away.

Obviously, deer hunters who use primitive weapons or shotguns will have to be more skillful at stalking than hunters who use centerfire rifles. Where

Rock Vore with the Boone and Crockett 11-pointer he and his brother successfully stalked on a windy, rainy day after spotting the bedded whitetail from a road.

open country is common, as it is in many of the western states, stalking ability can be an important skill for rifle hunters, as well.

Stillhunting and stalking can be employed successfully in most covers and terrains and under varying conditions. The only cover where stalking is seldom necessary is where visibility is fifty yards or less. Vegetation in these locations is often so dense that deer that are encountered are usually already in range when spotted.

Stillhunting

Stop-and-go hunting can be practiced most effectively in territory a hunter is familiar with. Knowledge of prime bedding and feeding areas and preferred travel routes allow a stillhunter to make the most of wind, terrain, and his or her own ability. When planning on stillhunting unfamiliar country, try to scout the area as thoroughly as possible before the season opens.

Contrary to what some hunters may believe, stillhunting is not a technique that goes hand-in-hand with covering long distances and lots of terrain, especially in typical whitetail and blacktail habitat or when searching for mulies in timber. Covering

Master Stillhunter Gary Clancy moving slowly through deer country, using his eyes more than his feet in an effort to locate whitetails or mule deer. He takes a few steps at a time, doing so as quietly as possible while scanning every inch of his surroundings for any sign of a deer. At the same time, his ears are in tune with what's going on around him.

a distance of 100 yards can take an hour. Where visibility is a couple hundred yards or more, a stillhunter may travel farther than he or she would in denser cover—not a great deal more, however, because the hunter should spend correspondingly more time carefully looking over every place a deer might be.

Stillhunting is not a casual approach to collecting a deer, either. Practicing it properly takes a lot of concentration; at least it does for me. I have to remind myself at regular intervals to move slowly and search every inch of the area around me. If I start daydreaming and forget about what I'm supposed to be doing, my pace automatically quickens and my eyes start bouncing from one view to the next with casual glances rather than the thoroughness necessary for stillhunting properly.

Admittedly, I'm not the best stillhunter. Nonetheless, I've taken a number of deer while hunting this way and have seen many more that got away. One advantage stop-and-go hunting has over hunting from a stand is that you usually see more deer stillhunting. But many of them are no more than flashes or waving tails.

One of the best whitetail bucks I bagged while stillhunting was a big-bodied Saskatchewan 7-pointer. It had been an 8-point, but one of its brow tines had been broken off, probably while fighting. This was before regulations went into effect restricting nonresident hunters from roaming more than 100 yards from their stand without a guide. I had occupied a stand during the morning and was stillhunting the half-mile back to camp for lunch along a packed trail where it was quiet walking.

As I neared a spot where I had passed up a young buck on my first day of hunting, I heard a noise ahead of me coming from a dip in the trail. I proceeded at full alert. The buck saw me before I saw him and blew before starting to run off. I quickly recognized this whitetail as a much bigger one than I had seen previously and decided to take him. My variable scope was set on three power, giving me maximum field of view, and I found the deer in the scope as soon as my rifle was at my shoulder. I fired as soon as the crosshairs were on him, dropping him instantly with a 150-grain .30-06 bullet.

That whitetail's body was more impressive than his antlers. We never weighed him, but I would guess his dressed weight was close to 250 pounds. I later found out that the noise I heard that alerted me to the deer's presence was the buck rubbing his antlers on a tree.

The skills inherent in stillhunting can become second nature with practice. I've watched some stillhunters who are old hands at the technique and are regularly successful. Their movements are as instinctive and stealthy as the deer they hunt.

The late Beryl Jensen is a perfect example of a skillful stillhunter. One day while we were hunting together, we made arrangements to meet at my stand late in the morning. My post was in an old burn, and Beryl would have to cross an opening about 100 yards across to reach the spot.

I was watching for him as well as keeping an eye out for deer. When Beryl arrived, he appeared as suddenly as deer often do. He was a full 20 to 30 yards into the opening before I noticed him. I watched him closely as he approached.

A big-bodied 7-point I shot while stillhunting my way back to camp in Saskatchewan after an unsuccessful morning of stand hunting. A noise ahead of me tipped me off to his presence.

It looked as though he floated across the remaining distance. He would take several short steps then pause and look around. The movement of his legs was almost imperceptible. I'm sure he saw me as soon as he entered the opening, but he advanced at his normal stop-and-go hunting pace. If there had been any deer in the vicinity, his presence certainly wouldn't have spooked them.

There are no hard-and-fast rules designating the perfect stillhunting pace. The terrain, ground cover and condition, visibility, and weather will dictate, to some degree, how to proceed. Each hunter will probably develop his or her own variations in pace.

As a general rule, taking from three to five steps between pauses is about right. Each advance often brings a new area into view or gives the stillhunter a different perspective on a piece of cover looked at minutes before. Try to check each shadow and clump of trees, brush, or tall grass carefully with your eyes. Deer can blend in surprisingly well with their surroundings.

I stand over the 8-point whitetail that came along on the trail of a doe and fawn after I had already passed their tracks. If I hadn't been looking back behind me as I stillhunted, I would never have seen him.

Look In All Directions

Try to remember to look in all directions, behind as well as in front and to the sides. One year while I was stillhunting along a snow-covered logging road, a doe and fawn crossed the road ahead of me. I stopped where I was and waited for a half hour, hoping a buck was following them. When no other deer appeared, I continued forward. After passing where the doe and fawn had crossed, I kept looking back toward their tracks every time I paused. When I was about 50 yards beyond where the antlerless deer had appeared, I looked back in time to see an 8-point buck following their tracks. I was able to turn, aim and shoot before the buck could react, filling another tag while stillhunting.

When stillhunting, try to move your head not in quick, jerky movements, but in a slow, rotating motion. Also try to keep in mind the importance of focusing on the terrain as far ahead as possible. Don't expect deer to wait until you are almost on top of them. Their senses are keener than yours. To increase the chances of seeing them before they see, smell, or hear you, look as far ahead as possible.

Look For Parts Of A Deer

Don't expect to see an entire animal. Try to pick out the deer's ears, legs, antlers, or tail, or the horizontal lines along the back or belly. Subtle movements like a twitching ear or swishing tail can give a mule deer's or whitetail's position away, too. Once you home in on a part of an animal, the rest of its body will usually jump into focus, unless it is obscured.

If the deer you spot isn't the one you want, keep looking. There may be others with it, either to the sides or behind it. If you haven't been detected, try to remain motionless as long as possible, unless moving won't disturb the animal. Other deer will probably give themselves away eventually.

You should make an effort to get by deer that you aren't interested in without spooking them. An alarmed deer may alert others in the vicinity. If deer are on their feet, it's normally a good idea to stay put and let them move off on their own. In situations where deer are bedded, they may be there for a while, so you will either have to wait and watch them until they move or try to detour around them without tipping them off to your presence.

A Doe's Trail

When the rut is on and several does are encountered it can be worthwhile to watch them, or where they were, for at least a half hour, on the chance a buck might trail them. I blew what could have been a perfect chance at a whitetail buck one time by not waiting long enough after seeing a doe.

I had stopped and was checking the cover ahead of me when the doe walked into view from left to right about 60 yards away. When she went out of sight I got down in a sitting position with my rifle ready, on the chance a buck was following her. Nothing happened after several minutes, so I got up and slowly walked toward where the doe had been. When I reached her tracks, there was a snort off to my left as a buck whirled and hightailed it. There wasn't enough time for a shot. If I had waited even five minutes longer, I'm sure I would have gotten the drop on that buck instead of vice versa.

Howard Musick was on the way to a stand on opening morning of Michigan's firearms season one year when he saw a doe cross a logging road ahead of him. Since daylight had arrived before he reached his blind, he had taken advantage of the opportunity to stillhunt toward the blind. Upon seeing the doe, he decided to stop and wait for a while to see if a buck was following the doe.

That was one of the best deer hunting decisions he ever made. There was a buck following the doe that Musick saw and he managed to shoot it. The trophy 10-pointer had a gross score of 173^3/$_8$ and netted 170^3/$_8$, qualifying for a place in national records maintained by the Boone and Crockett Club as well as a high-ranking spot in state records.

Hearing is important to stillhunters, too, as I pointed out earlier in regard to the 7-pointer I got in Saskatchewan. If you hear a nearby noise you can't identify, you should pause until you determine its source. If the noise is in a location where it's

Howard Musick got this Boone and Crockett buck while stillhunting toward his stand one morning. He saw a doe cross a logging road ahead of him, so he stopped and waited to see if a buck was following her. One was and he got it. PHOTO COURTESY OF HOWARD MUSICK

impossible to determine its source from where you are, proceed cautiously to try to find out what made the noise.

The same advice applies for determining what's behind an unidentified movement. The disturbance may have been caused by a flitting bird or a nervous squirrel, but there is always a chance a deer was the source. Patience often provides the best means for a stillhunter to discover the source of what attracted his or her attention. A pair of binoculars can also come in handy for pinpointing what made a movement that caught your eye.

Cornfields

Uncut cornfields provide a unique opportunity for stillhunting with firearms or bow and arrow. Whitetails not only feed in cornfields, they often bed in them as well, and skilled stillhunters who have permission to hunt such fields can take advantage of that tendency. On windy days, corn stalks rattle in the wind and that noise helps

Judd Cooney stillhunts through a Minnesota cornfield. Stillhunting through cornfields for whitetails can be productive. Many deer spend all day in these fields. On windy days, the sound from corn stalks will cover any sounds hunters make.

cover any disturbance stillhunters might make. Rainy days are also great for stillhunting cornfields, or anywhere else for that matter. Concentrate stillhunting efforts in cornfields on times when deer are most likely to be bedded, such as late morning and early afternoon.

Walk into or across the wind, peeking down the rows ahead of you as you proceed. Once you spot a deer, plan an approach that will put you within range, if you aren't already, while keeping you out of the deer's sight and allowing for the wind direction. Keep in mind that other deer could be bedded near the one you saw and you want to avoid disturbing them, too, until you get a shot. When you spot deer you aren't interested in shooting, try to detour around them to avoid spooking them. If you spook one deer, it is likely to alert others to the presence of danger.

It's possible to spend lots of time stillhunting in a cornfield before seeing any deer, so try to stay alert and focused on moving as slowly and quietly as possible. Patience and persistence are usually rewarded.

Steve Williams from Vicksburg, Michigan, found out how much big bucks like cornfields when he was sixteen years old. Some friends who own

Sixteen-year-old Steve Williams with a world-class buck he got in a cornfield. The 16-point typical antlers had a net score of 179. PHOTO COURTESY OF STEVE WILLIAMS

land where he has permission to hunt shot at a huge buck that went into a cornfield. There was snow on the ground, so the hunters tracked the buck, hoping to get a shot at it in the corn or to chase it out to other hunters posted on the edge of the field. The buck circled ahead of them for a long time. Eventually, a big deer was seen leaving the corn and the group suspected it was the big buck, so they called it quits.

In the meantime, Steve's stepfather saw a small buck start to leave the cornfield then re-enter it. Steve decided to stillhunt through the corn to look for the smaller buck while his father posted on the edge of the field. As it turned out, the big buck hadn't left the field after all. Steve managed to shoot the bedded buck with his 16 gauge shotgun. The 16-pointer had a net score of 179.

Use A Call
Some of the deer a stillhunter sees will be running, having been spooked by the still-hunter's presence or by other hunters. These shots should be passed up, unless the animal's sex can be determined and there is an opportunity to put a bullet or slug in a vital area. If there's no opportunity for a shot and you're not sure whether the deer was a buck or doe, try blowing a deer call. By imitating the sound of a doe bleat or

buck grunt, you may get the animal to come back. Since other deer may be in the vicinity, be alert for deer to come from any direction, not just where you saw the animal disappear.

Calls can come in handy at other times while stillhunting, too. If you accidentally snap a twig or make some other type of disturbance while moving, you can fool any deer within earshot into thinking another deer was responsible for the noise by imitating a buck grunt or doe bleat with a call.

Avoid Being Winded

You should keep several things in mind while stillhunting that can increase the chances of getting standing shots. Scent, sight, and sound, or the lack of them, are the three major factors that will make a difference. It is best to stop-and-go hunt into the wind. This eliminates the possibility of any deer ahead of you smelling you. Wearing scent-absorbing hunting suits like those made by Scent-Lok further reduce the chances of being smelled by deer. A moderate to strong wind will also cover up some of the noise made by a stillhunter while walking.

Hunting across the wind is all right, too. Deer ahead of you still won't be able to wind you, nor will those on your upwind side. You should be able to spot any whitetails or mulies on the downwind side before they can scent a hunter traveling across the wind.

Going Unseen

A stillhunter's movement can be kept to a minimum if he or she takes short steps and swivels his or her head slowly. Visibility can be reduced by wearing camouflage clothes when possible. Additionally, stillhunters should avoid exposing their presence in the open by walking through fields or skylining themselves on ridges. Try to skirt the edges of fields and openings and take advantage of shade, where available, to reduce your visibility. When crossing a ridge, keep a low profile.

Stillhunting along a ridge can often be productive, since deer don't usually expect danger from above and elevation gives the hunter an excellent view of the surrounding terrain. It is better, however, to walk just below the ridge rather than directly on top.

Being Quiet

The amount of noise a stillhunter makes or doesn't make is a function of how light-footed he or she is, how thick the cover is, how moist the ground is, and the material the hunter's outer clothes are made of. The way you walk can be just as important as how much you walk. You should try to walk with most of your weight either on the toes or balls of your feet. Either portion of the foot should touch the ground first, then the rest of the foot can be lowered. This, in effect, reduces the surface area making initial contact with the ground, thereby reducing noise. Before shifting your weight to the leading foot, however, feel for twigs that may snap. If you detect one, try to avoid it. Stillhunters should also try to lift their feet clear of noisy ground cover rather than dragging their heels or shuffling their feet.

Outer garments of wool, fleece, and acrylic are the quietest clothes for deer hunting in cool or cold weather. Cotton is a quiet fabric, too, but since it isn't as warm as wool it is best suited for hunting in warmer weather. Many cotton-blend fabrics are as quiet as cotton.

Where you walk when stillhunting can have a bearing on how much noise you make, too. Try to stillhunt along packed trails whenever possible since these offer the quietest footing. Both manmade and game trails offer quiet footing.

Don Brugman from Marquette, Michigan, hunted sitka blacktails on an island in southeast Alaska during August one year and he was amazed to discover that the deer had worn trails along the tops of the huge trunks of fallen trees that were everywhere. Brugman followed the blacktails' example and stillhunted along the tops of fallen trees. He bagged a pair of small bucks that way.

However, it's not always possible or practical to stillhunt along trails. When you leave the trail, ground cover and conditions can have a significant impact on the effectiveness of stop-and-go hunting. The quietest ground conditions are moss, grass, sand, and solid rocks, ground after a soaking rain, or a forest floor blanketed with soft snow or pine needles. Stillhunting can be excellent under any of these conditions. The technique is also worth trying in a strong wind, regardless of the ground conditions. Disturbance created by gusty winds is often enough to mask noises a hunter might make.

One noise hazard stop-and-go hunters should always be mindful of is brittle twigs and sticks that are sometimes hidden under leaves or snow. Try to avoid snapping these when you walk, but don't spend so much time watching where your feet are going that any deer up ahead might go unseen. If a twig is broken it is a good idea to stop for a few minutes and then continue. Blowing a deer call or imitating the clucks or purrs of a turkey while pausing may calm any deer that were alarmed by the sound.

Dry leaves, crunchy snow, and loose rocks are the worst conditions to stillhunt in. Yet even in these noisiest of situations the stop-and-go method can be productive. Noise, in itself, doesn't alert deer, but the cadence or frequency does. Many hunters walk at a consistent pace. Animals pause frequently when traveling. Mulies and whitetails know the difference. When they hear a stop-and-go hunter approaching they are apt to be more curious than afraid. As a result, they are likely to stay put and offer a shot. Deer and hunters are at an equal

Wearing rubber boots or waders to sneak through water is a perfect way to stillhunt for deer to avoid otherwise noisy ground conditions.

Canoes provide the ultimate means of stillhunting silently along rivers with the current, as these bowhunters are doing. Concentrate on float hunting with either gun or bow along rivers where public land is abundant.

disadvantage when conditions are noisy since each can hear the other better than usual.

If you are deer hunting when crusted snow is present, pay attention to weather forecasts. On days when temperatures are supposed to go above freezing, softening or eliminating the crust, stillhunting will be more effective.

Stillhunters can reduce the amount of disturbance they make under noisy conditions by walking on logs, rocks, exposed tree roots, and pine needles.

One way for stillhunters to overcome noisy situations completely, turning them to their advantage, is to head for water. Shallow creeks, marshy areas, and rivers are perfect avenues to use to outwit whitetails and mule deer. Rubber boots are necessary for walking creeks or wet areas with water less than a foot deep. Hip boots or chest waders are a must for anything deeper. Hip waders are less cumbersome and noisy than the chest type.

A canoe offers the ultimate means of stillhunting rivers and streams. Gliding with the current in one of these streamlined crafts is much quieter than walking in water. Stillhunting from a canoe works best with two hunters: One steers and paddles while the other sits in the bow with rifle or bow ready. It is often possible to float within close range of bedded or feeding deer while in a canoe. Lone hunters can also float rivers in belly boats or inner tubes with seats.

Horseback

Hunting on horseback is another form of stillhunting. Horse travel in deer country is most common in the west for mulies. Horses aren't as quiet as canoes, but deer don't seem to mind. Approaching them to within rifle range on horseback is possible. If their riders don't talk, mule deer may mistake horses for elk.

One time when my brother Bruce and I were hunting mule deer in the Colorado Rockies with guide and outfitter Rudy Rudibaugh from Parlin, we rode up on a herd of deer that would have otherwise been difficult to approach. We were riding through willow brush above timberline when the group of five mulies, three of them bucks, got up from their beds about 150 yards away. They stood and watched us, seemingly more curious than alarmed.

Bruce dismounted and grabbed his rifle from its scabbard. Not wanting to take an offhand shot, my brother started crawling toward a pile of rocks where he could

Greg Simons uses a spotting scope from a high point to look for deer and then determine if a stalk is feasible once a decent buck is spotted.

steady the rifle. As he did, the deer got nervous and started to move off. Bruce quickly got into a sitting position and tried two shots, but both missed their mark, a buck with four points on one side and three on the other. Bruce was forced to shoot too quickly. If a rest had been handy where he dismounted, that buck would have been his.

Horses are most useful while stop-and-go hunting in mountainous terrain as a means of transportation from one observation point to another. A common and productive practice for locating mule deer and sometimes whitetails is to stop at high vantage points overlooking basins or valleys. Binoculars or spotting scopes are then used to scan the terrain for deer. Glassing properly can take several hours at each stop. Bedded animals are often difficult to spot, but they usually get up at regular intervals to feed and can be detected then. Sometimes a deer will appear suddenly in a location where nothing was visible minutes before.

Stalking

Once an animal a hunter wants to try for is spotted, a stalk is made. The cardinal rule for stalking in hilly terrain is to always approach from above. Deer seldom expect danger from above; consequently they spend most of their time looking downhill. If you spot a deer above you while glassing or stillhunting, you should continue out of sight and hearing of the animal and climb above it before beginning a stalk, if possible.

Wind direction, hunter movement, and noise are just as important in stalking as in stillhunting. Any one of them can make or break the endeavor. The stalking hunter has an advantage over the stillhunter, however, because he or she has located the quarry. The hunter's major task is choosing the best course that will put him or her in range of a deer without alerting it to his or her presence.

Determining Wind Direction

Always go into or across the wind to stalk a deer. If there is much wind, its direction can be determined easily. When it is light to gusty try dropping sand, snow, or light blades of grass to see which way it drifts. The cool side of a wetted finger is also a clue to wind direction. A piece of thread tied to a bow or firearm, the smoke from a lighted cigarette, or the exhaust from a running vehicle can aid hunters in determining air flow, too. When temperatures are below freezing, or close to it, a determination of air current direction can be made by exhaling and watching the vapor.

Even when great pains have been taken to stalk with the breeze in a hunter's favor the effort can be ruined by a change in wind direction, an unexplained gust, or a new current. Wearing an outer layer of scent-absorbing clothing can reduce the chances of a ruined stalk when the wind switches direction.

Try to be mindful of any change in wind patterns while stalking and, if necessary, make a change in course. If the only avenue of approach to a deer puts you upwind of the animal, don't go after it if using a bow, shotgun, handgun, or muzzleloader, unless you are wearing a scent-absorbing suit. Hunters using centerfire rifles that are prepared to make long shots might be able to get within range before they are winded even without scent protection. If there is a possibility that the animal will move to a position more favorable for a stalk or that the wind might change, it is best to wait.

If the breeze or air current is flowing downhill when you are above a buck, move down to the animal's elevation or slightly above, off to either side. When at an appropriate level, stalk across the slope at a downhill angle or on a line with him.

Timing Movements

Hunter movement isn't a problem in stalking if done under cover or at the right time. Try to plan a stalk to take advantage of such terrain features as gullies, river beds, valleys, hills, trees, brush, and rocks—and always consider the deer's behavior. Let's look at deer behavior first.

Any deer is easier to approach when it is lying down rather than feeding. When on their feet, whitetails and mule deer are more alert than when bedded. Don't get me wrong; deer don't throw

Stalking a bedded deer like this mulie is often better than trying to stalk one that's up and moving. I shot this one with a camera.

Paul Kintner with the huge nontypical he successfully stalked with bow and arrow. The buck's antlers netted 211 as a nontypical.

caution to the wind when they lie down, but they are more relaxed and less likely to detect a stalking hunter. An additional consideration for long stalks is that once bedded, deer usually remain in one place for at least an hour. A feeding deer can move surprisingly far during a long stalk, which increases the hunter's chances of losing track of it or spooking it.

In many situations it may be difficult or impossible to wait for a deer to bed down before trying a stalk. If time isn't a problem and a deer can be kept in sight without alarming it, try to wait until a deer beds before attempting a stalk. I've interviewed a pair of Michigan bowhunters who bagged Boone and Crockett bucks by stalking bedded animals, one of whom was mentioned at the beginning of this chapter. In both cases, the bucks were bedded when they were spotted.

Paul Kintner from Adrian, Michigan, arrowed a whitetail with a nontypical 19-point rack netting 211 on Halloween one year. It was a windy day and he was in the process of moving his tree stand during the middle of the day to a location where he had seen a lot of buck sign, when he spotted the outstanding whitetail bedded in tall weeds and grass on the edge of an uncut bean field. Since he wasn't hunting at the time, he didn't have his camo clothes or bow and arrow. It took him twenty-five minutes to get his hunting clothes and bow and arrow.

The buck was in the same place when Paul returned and started his stalk. When Kintner had closed the distance to 50 yards, the big buck got up and began walking toward the woods where Paul had seen the buck sign, which brought the deer closer to the hunter. He took his shot when the buck was 25 yards away.

If stalking a deer that is feeding where cover is sparse, try to restrict movements to the intervals when the animal's head is down. Keeping a low profile by crawling on hands and knees or belly is advisable in such a situation. Deer will raise their heads at regular intervals while feeding to look around. They often wag their tails before looking up. Be sure you are motionless when a buck or doe looks up.

When moving in on a feeding deer in a crouched or upright position, it is best to shuffle your feet or take short steps if you are on grass or other ground cover that isn't noisy. It is possible to be caught off balance, standing on one leg, when lifting your feet for long steps to close the distance on a deer.

The sun can be an advantage to a stalking hunter if you approach a deer with the sun at your back. If it is at the right angle, the strong backlighting can impair a deer's ability to spot you. The same principle can be applied while stillhunting. Wind direction should be considered before sun angle, however, whether you are stillhunting or stalking.

Hunter movement isn't as important when stalking a deer from above as it is in other situations. Countless times members of my party and I have stalked deer from above in plain sight. If the animals had looked up they would have seen us, but few of them do. The advantages of moving in on deer from above can't be overemphasized.

Whenever possible, plan a stalk so you will be out of a deer's sight throughout the approach. The best way to close the distance unseen is by heading down a valley or gulley or by aligning trees, brush, or rocks between you and the deer. If the screening cover isn't high enough to walk upright, crouch or crawl. Before starting out on such a stalk, be sure to pick out landmarks to use as reference points so you will know where to come out of a valley and where the deer is supposed to be. Prominent trees, fences, ridge lines, or rocks should be noted carefully.

Hand Signals

It may be possible to check on a deer periodically during a stalk. If not, be doubly sure you know where you are going or work out a system of hand signals with a partner who will be able to see the deer. Also, make sure he or she knows when you will want directions.

When I want directions in such a situation, I wave my hat. When my partner holds both arms up, it means the deer is still there. Just the right or left arm extended means the deer moved that way. A wave back is a sign that the animal spooked. Additional signals can be added to expand communication between a stalker and lookout. Just be sure you both understand what they are before starting a stalk.

Noise can be kept to a minimum in stalking by taking advantage of the same guidelines listed for stillhunting. Noise isn't usually critical until within 100 yards or less of a deer, depending on ground and weather conditions. Beyond that point, stalkers can move in as quickly as possible without much regard for disturbance from sounds they make.

Interference

Unexpected interference can sometimes ruin a stalk no matter how good a job a hunter does. A coyote abruptly ended my chances of taking a trophy mule deer buck with bow and arrow in Montana one fall. Other predators, unseen deer, and competing hunters can have the same impact.

I once spotted a group of four mulie bucks from a vantage point where my guide had seen the bucks a number of times in the past. It was September 28 and the bucks were feeding their way uphill. The wind was blowing downhill, so I moved across it toward the deer. I angled downhill, keeping some evergreen trees between me and them.

When I reached the same level as the bucks, I slowly closed the distance between us. I got to within 35 yards of one of the bigger mulies and considered taking the shot because he was standing broadside, with his head down. I could have come to full draw without him seeing me. The conditions were so favorable, I decided to get just a little bit closer before releasing an arrow. Bad decision.

I took two more carefully placed steps, then the deer suddenly took off running. I was puzzled about what happened until a coyote came trotting into view near where the bucks had been. It had obviously scared them.

Even though I didn't get the shot I was hoping for, the stalk was still exciting. It was also rewarding knowing that I got as close as I did to those muleys without being detected. If it hadn't been for the interference, I stood an excellent chance of putting my tag on one of those bucks.

Kodiak Island Blacktails

Before making a stalk on the biggest blacktail buck Dean Hulce has ever taken on Alaska's Kodiak Island, he had to wait for a brown bear to clear out of the area. The bear was chasing salmon on the beach when Dean and his companions landed in a floatplane on the inland lake. They had to wait for the bear to walk off before beaching the plane. Soon after getting out of the airplane, Dean spotted the big buck with binoculars.

"This buck was several hundred yards straight up the mountain," Hulce explained in an email. "Unfortunately, it was also straight above the patch of timber that the brown bear had just walked into and I refused to go in until he was out. A short time later, the bear topped out and went over the ridge above where the deer were.

"I started up the hill zig-zaging on a bear trail, which is the only place that you could put your feet. Even though we were only a few hundred feet above sea level I was struggling to keep going without stopping every five yards. When I finally arrived at the edge of the finger ridge where the good buck had been peering over he was nowhere to be seen.

"I could feel the wind blowing from my back into the alder patch that the buck had stepped into, so I assumed it would be just a matter of time until I saw him slip out the uphill side. It only took a few seconds and I saw him trotting up the other side of the alders."

Larry Godwin proudly poses with the sitka blacktail buck he stalked on Kodiak Island with his son.
PHOTO COURTESY DEAN HULCE

Dean's first shot missed, but his second one killed the blacktail instantly. His partner caught up to him soon after he shot the buck, so Dean stood guard while his partner retrieved the deer. Brown bears have been known to home in on the sound of shots to claim the remains of any deer that have been killed and they sometimes arrive while the hunters are still there. That's why deer hunters on the island usually hunt in pairs.

"The two of us brought the buck downhill to a point where we could see several hundred yards in each direction so that any bear that might approach would be spotted long before he was on top of us," Dean continued. "After taking photographs, we pulled the buck back to the lakeshore and butchered him.

"In Alaska you are required to bring out all usable meat. We were just finishing our butchering and bagging of meat when a young bear came running down the beach from a couple hundred yards away. It was running directly into the wind and had its nose in the air as it ran towards us. We had put most of our gear into the float plane, except for one rifle for protection. I grabbed the cape, antlers, and rifle and my partner grabbed the bag of meat and we ran the 50 yards to the plane. When we arrived, we yelled and screamed and the bear walked around us on the hillside for a while then melted into the alders."

Dean's blacktail had 4 x 5 antlers that scored 103, five inches shy of the minimum for Boone and Crockett Records.

Fortunately, all deer stalks on Kodiak don't involve bears. Larry Godwin from Menominee, Michigan, enjoyed such a hunt with his son. They were dropped off along the shoreline by boat a couple of hours after daylight and followed a stream uphill until about midday. Once at a vantage point, they glassed until they spotted a buck they were interested in, then completed a successful stalk.

Early in the season, blacktail bucks are usually above timberline, just like other mule deer. To get to them on Kodiak Island, you either fly in to an inland lake or hike uphill from the ocean. Either way, due to the presence of bears, it's important to have time to debone the meat and hike back to your starting point by dark.

"There are a lot of times when hunters had to pass on deer because they were afraid that they would not be able to get it taken care of and get out by dark," Dean Hulce said. "The fines for wasting meat in Alaska are very high and the cost of spending the night near a bloody deer in bear country is even higher. So with short days, you have to be prepared and move fast once a deer is on the ground."

Hunters who elect to camp in Kodiak Island's blacktail country for a number of days would be wise to install battery-operated electric fences around camp that are designed to keep brown bears away. Bowhunters after blacktails in grizzly country should carry pepper spray or handguns for protection from bears.

Blacktail hunting on Kodiak is most popular after the rut kicks in during November. Then the bigger bucks are often found along the island's beaches where they are more easily accessible to hunters operating from boats or airplanes.

You never know what's going to happen during a stalk, but most of the time, if you do your part to close the distance between you and the deer you want, you have an excellent chance of scoring.

Drives

My brother Bruce and I shot our first deer ever during drives on the same day. I was a stander when I dropped mine. Bruce's was collected while he was a driver.

There were five of us the day my brother and I scored. Besides ourselves, there was an uncle, Leonard Yelle, his son Randy, and Jim Rankin, Leonard's brother-in-law. Our group size was just right for small drives. Leonard put Bruce and me on stands 50 to 75 yards apart and instructed us to stay put until the drive was over. Jim also posted. Leonard and Randy made the push toward us.

It wasn't long before I heard something running toward me. A deer broke from cover, moving from right to left, about 30 yards away. It was a doe, but I had an antlerless permit. I shouldered my 12-gauge pump and fired. I was using rifled slugs.

The deer showed no immediate sign of a hit, continuing at a fast clip without faltering. I assumed I had missed, but before she went out of sight, she fell. I found out later my slug hit the deer in the heart. My excitement knew no bounds that day. I had become a deer hunter.

On the next drive our groups switched assignments. Randy and Leonard were standers; Bruce, Jim, and I moved through a piece of cover toward them. Moments into the drive there was a shot, and Bruce had his deer. The whitetail almost ran him down in an effort to get away from Jim. It tried to escape by going to the side rather than straight ahead.

At certain times of day and in certain types of cover neither stand hunting nor stillhunting is productive. Deer that don't move from their daytime resting areas until dark make sitting at a stand all day a waste of time. The same holds for a stillhunter: Many of the deer in the area may be too wary to get a shot at because they hole up in cover so thick that approaching them undetected is impossible.

When the two techniques are combined in a team effort, however, the chances of success improve and a third popular deer-hunting method emerges: the drive.

Some groups of hunters rely almost exclusively on this technique all season. Their success usually explains why. The story of the first whitetails my brother and I claimed illustrates how effective drives can be. As we found out on successive drives, both standers and drivers have a chance to connect, though the odds usually favor hunters waiting on post.

Drives can be broken down into three categories: quiet, noisy, and dog-pack. The intent of all three is the same: to push deer from areas where they are resting or feeding, which are usually locations where their vulnerability to hunters is minimal, to standers. This is the only way hunters get a crack at some whitetails and mule deer.

Bucks that make it past the first few days of the hunting season in heavily hunted areas often seek out the thickest patch of cover in their home range and stay there until the season is over. They travel only at night, unless they are forced to do otherwise. Some deer follow these habits year-round, due to their age or the habitat they live in. For these reasons drives can be productive any time during deer season if they are organized and carried out properly.

A group of hunters lined up ready to make a drive as soon as the signal is given to begin. Standers are posted somewhere ahead to intercept deer jumped by the drivers. Both noisy and quiet drives can be effective.

Group Size

Only two hunters are necessary to make a drive: one to post and the other to move the deer. Information about where deer are most likely to go when jumped is important to increase the chances of success when so few hunters are involved. Jimmy Dean had that knowledge about whitetail habits in Montana where he normally hunted and he used that experience to push bucks in front of me on two separate one-man drives while I was hunting with him in that state one year.

Only one driver and one stander are necessary for a successful drive. Jimmy Dean drove this Montana 9-pointer to me on a cold day in November. I failed to get a shot at the bigger 10-pointer he pushed by me on an earlier drive.

He pushed a dandy 10-pointer in front of me on the first drive, but I failed to get a shot at it because I had difficulty getting the safety of my rifle off in time. Jimmy pushed a smaller 9-point by me on the next drive and I made good on that opportunity.

A group numbering from five to ten people is much better for conducting drives. Upwards of twenty or more hunters can be effective when driving large areas. Some states limit the number of hunters who may take part in drives. The time required to organize a drive, as well as the chances of a foul-up, increases proportionately with the number of participants, and this reduces hunting time.

To work effectively as a unit, drivers and standers should know the area being hunted. When new hunters are involved, an explanation of the lay of the land with the aid of a map will help. An attribute at least as important as familiarity with an area is that participants be able to follow directions. Worthy of equal attention is that there be someone to give directions and assign duties—a hunt captain or leader.

The only difference between a quiet and a noisy drive, as the names imply, is the amount of disturbance made by drivers. On a noisy drive, for example, drivers sometimes blow whistles, beat on pans, shout, bark like dogs, and break branches in an effort to flush deer from hiding places and make them run toward standers waiting ahead. On a quiet drive, drivers move toward standers without making an unusual amount of noise. They may advance as if they were stillhunting or as if going for a casual stroll, but without trying to conceal their presence.

Quiet drives are usually more effective than loud drives. The noise made by drivers sometimes has an effect opposite its intent. Instead of scaring deer into panicking and running blindly toward standers, the animals may stay put, go out the ends, or run between the drivers. This is especially true of the wise bucks who have survived other drives. Deer are tipped off to the positions of drivers by the noise they make, and the animals use the information to their advantage.

Noisy Drives

One season I hunted from a stand that was in a narrow section of woods on public hunting land. That piece of cover proved to be a favored area for drives by a group of hunters I didn't know. It was obvious a drive was in progress when a line of men moved toward me shouting and barking like dogs.

I stayed put, hoping they would push a buck by me. They didn't. More to the point, however, was the fact that none of the drivers saw me, and they made the push three days in a row. I was wearing red and not as concealed as a deer would have been. Any deer in the area could have escaped detection as I did—by staying put. Most of them probably did.

The first two days the drive was conducted, there were no shots fired. I did see one deer, a fawn, that was a direct result of the drive. It came from where the drivers were after they had passed by! The youngster didn't want to go the way they wanted him to and slipped through the line.

On the third day the drivers pushed the cover there were shots fired, apparently by a stander. From the shouting that followed I assume a deer was bagged, so noisy drives do work once in a while.

In fact, I've participated in some noisy drives since then that were very effective, on Trout Run Development property near St. Marys, Pennsylvania. There is more than a 100-year tradition of drive hunts on this large chunk of private property. Drives are well organized and generally very effective. For safety reasons, drivers do not carry guns on Trout Run hunts. Safety is also the reason why noisy drives are conducted there.

Hunters who are posted know where drivers are by the noise they make and refrain from shooting toward them. Each driver also knows where his or her partners

Former National Wild Turkey Federation Executive Director Rob Keck holds the antler on a buck he shot during a Pennsylvania drive on Trout Run Property near St. Marys in December. The buck's antlers fell off after he shot the whitetail. Rob's father and a pair of drivers pose with the successful hunter.

are and can maintain the desired formation and spacing while moving ahead. I have to admit that it is an advantage for posted hunters to follow the progress of a drive by listening to drivers. The level of excitement and anticipation never fails to increase as the line of drivers approaches your position.

Deer are always seen on noisy drives conducted on Trout Run property, and whitetails are bagged on most hunts. It isn't unusual for a number of bucks to be tagged on some of the best drives.

Quiet Drives

The primary function of drivers—jumping and moving deer ahead of them—can sometimes be accomplished with more consistency on a quiet drive. Any deer in the drivers' paths will hear them as twigs snap or leaves rustle, but usually not enough to determine where they are at all times. This uncertainty is apt to make the deer nervous and cause them to move out.

Some deer may still hold tight or slip through the line, but the chances of it happening are reduced. Drivers on a quiet push should be looking carefully for deer as they go. They may spot one bedded or sneaking away from another driver. Noisy drives reduce the chances that drivers will get to shoot. I'm sure my brother's tag would have gone unfilled that year we both scored on successive drives if we had tried to push the deer by intentionally making noise.

Wisconsin deer hunter Randy Onsager shot a Boone and Crockett nontypical with a 21-point rack that netted 208⅞ on the afternoon of November 21 one year while making a quiet drive with two partners. There were also three standers. The party was hunting a 20-acre patch of cover that often harbors plenty of whitetails, including some big bucks.

Randy said the woodlot is the biggest patch of cover for a long distance, with a lot of large fields in the area. Hunting pressure in the surrounding terrain consistently pushes deer into the woodlot his party often drives. Onsager said he was moving through a creek bottom during the drive when he jumped the big buck.

Hunters are limited to the use of shotguns in the county he was hunting (Dane). Randy was carrying an Ithaca Model 37 12-gauge with a smoothbore slug barrel that he had taken plenty of whitetails with. He also had lots of experience shooting at fleeing bucks, so as soon as he saw the deer had a big rack, his instincts took over.

He got the buck's shoulder in his sights as quickly as possible at a distance of 50 yards and sent a slug on its way, dropping the whitetail instantly. As the deer struggled to get up, Randy got a much better look at the antlers. Realizing they were huge, he put a finishing shot in the buck's neck to ensure it wouldn't get up.

Other bucks were seen on the drive that Randy shot the nontypical, but none of them were bagged. Some of them circled back into the cover. Before the season was over, Onsager's party bagged three more mature bucks from that woodlot. Two were taken on the second day of the season and the final whitetail was collected on the last day of the season.

"They were three of the nicest bucks you've ever seen," Randy said. "One was a 10-point and there were two 8s. Their antlers were in the 20-inch range in terms of inside spread."

Cornfields are great places for drives when the corn is still standing during hunting season. A drive of sorts takes place when a field is cut and resident deer are forced to move to adjoining cover. Knowledgeable hunters can take advantage of the opportunity.

Randy added that drives like the ones his hunting party took those bucks on tend to be more successful when cornfields have been cut, like they were at the time. When cornfields remain standing during firearms season, deer use the grain fields for cover and are spread over a wider area. It only stands to reason that when whitetails are not concentrated and have more escape cover, they are harder to intercept on drives. Drives can still be successful then, but not as consistently as when the corn is cut.

In fact, cornfields themselves can be the focal point of drives because of the tendency of whitetails to hide in them. However, it's essential for hunters to get permission from land owners where uncut cornfields remain before conducting drives. A deer drive of sorts occurs when cornfields are cut, and hunters who know when this will happen can take advantage of that opportunity by posting in woods where displaced whitetails are most likely to go.

It isn't critical that standers be able to follow the progress of the drivers. Posted hunters should be alert from the time they get into position until the push is completed. On a quiet drive, drivers can signal standers if and when deer are jumped by shouting, "Here they come," or "Heads up," to make sure standers will be ready. Once the deer are moving, sound made by the driver that jumped them won't make much difference.

Drivers should be close enough together to see each other at intervals on the most effective pushes. When this isn't possible, they can whistle, hoot, or crow call once in a while to maintain contact. Well-spaced whistles, owl hoots, or crow calls may be accepted as natural sounds by deer and not associated with hunters. On the other hand, they may not be. It is best for drivers not to make any sounds at all if possible. Drivers familiar with an area and their partners' paces should be able to progress properly without auditory assistance.

Safety

More often than not, driven deer are far enough ahead of drivers that any shots fired by standers won't endanger drivers. To be on the safe side, however, drivers can move to the sides as they approach standers on the chance a deer may not show itself until the last possible moment. An alternative is for drivers to announce themselves by whistling or calling as they near standers. Drivers must be familiar with the driven area to use either technique.

Neither of these precautions should be necessary, in my opinion. It goes without saying that drivers and standers alike should never take a shot in a direction that might endanger a partner. And above all else, hunters should be sure of their targets before shooting, regardless of the hunting technique used, but especially on drives where hunters can be in close proximity to one another.

No whitetail or mule deer, no matter how big, is worth wounding or killing a fellow hunter for. If it is considered unsafe for both drivers and standers to carry firearms or bows, drivers should leave their weapons behind until taking their turns at posting. The usual procedure is for drivers and standers to alternate duties. Hunters who have filled their tags join the ranks of the drivers for the rest of the season in our group. The fellow who quits hunting after bagging his deer is seldom invited along again, unless he has a good reason for dropping out of the hunt.

Selecting Locations

Terrain that you and your hunting partners are most familiar with is the best to drive for deer. It is important to know where deer bed, feed, and travel in order to plan a drive effectively. This information should be readily available.

Woodlots like this one are ideal for drives. The trick is to get standers into position without spooking resident deer. Standers should always try to go to their posts as quietly and cautiously as possible and always be alert for deer.

The smaller the area that can be isolated for a drive, the better. A swamp, valley, ravine, thicket, or woodlot that is a quarter-mile or less on a side is ideal. Cover that is narrower than it is long is best of all for a drive.

Areas larger than a quarter-mile can and are driven successfully, but the deer's chances of escaping increase as the size of the area increases. More area means more cover for deer to hide in unnoticed and wider gaps in the line of drivers for deer to slip through. A quarter-mile is simply a guideline, not a hard-and-fast rule. I have had my best success on drives conducted in areas within that size range. Another general rule is that drives work well in the thickest cover around.

Any number of natural and man-made features can be used to isolate a driveable tract of land. Roads, rivers, lakes, ridges, power lines, railroad tracks, and changes in cover such as places where swamps change to hardwoods, hardwoods to fields, timber to meadows, or sagebrush to aspens are examples of convenient borders. Cover that is very long but narrow might best be driven in stages.

If you can't think of suitable areas to drive in terrain you frequent or if you want to discover new possibilities, checking out a map or aerial photographs is a good way to locate suitable spots. Topographical or quadrangle maps are best for this purpose. All features of the terrain are clearly marked on these maps.

Placing Standers

Once a location or two has been decided on for drives, selecting stands is the next step. This is where the chances of success for many drives disappear. The idea is not to choose stands where you want the deer to go, but where they want to go when jumped. Deer can seldom be forced to go where they don't want to, and few drives succeed in doing so. Hunters should use their knowledge of normal deer behavior and escape routes to determine where to place standers.

In the morning, deer generally move from feeding grounds to bedding areas. Many of them may already be bedded by daylight, especially after they have been hunted for several days. The trend reverses in the evening—deer move from bedding to feeding grounds. Deer will be bedded during a large part of the day.

Generally, drives should be made from feeding grounds toward bedding areas in the early morning. Pushes at other times of day will be through bedding grounds themselves. Bedded deer are the focal point of most drives I've been on.

For morning drives, if bedding and feeding areas are not far apart, say from a quarter-mile to half a mile, standers should be positioned far enough beyond bedding locations (100 to 200 yards) that they won't spook any deer that are there when getting in position. When distances close to a mile separate the two key locations, the area can be driven in stages.

Deer jumped on a drive in the evening will not head toward feeding grounds as they normally would, unless that direction offers the most security. Their first reaction is to get away from what disturbed them. Bedding areas are often in thick cover; consequently, they mean safety to deer. A deer's dinner table, on the other hand, is often in open country, which whitetails and mule deer try to avoid during daylight hours when being hunted. This explains why deer will go toward bedding areas on morning drives but aren't likely to head for chow when driven in the latter part of the day.

Bedded deer like this whitetail buck are the focal point of most drives. Drives are an excellent means of collecting deer toward the end of the season, when most of their movements are after dark.

Outside of early morning drives, then, standers should be located along escape routes. These routes normally lead from bedding areas toward the nearest patch of cover where deer hope to elude hunters. Escape routes may follow valleys and creek bottoms or narrow necks of woods, or go over ridges.

If you have jumped deer from bedding areas before, you should have an idea which way they are likely to go. If not, do your best to anticipate routes driven deer are apt to take. Take the wind into consideration when doing so. Deer most often move with the breeze in their faces so they can smell what is ahead, but they may move with the wind at their backs if they are more concerned about what disturbed them. Sometimes they travel crosswind for a distance, too. If whitetails or mulies are jumped going with the wind, they won't often go far in that direction. Due to variable wind conditions from day to day, deer may use different escape routes to best take advantage of their sense of smell.

Standers can avoid, or at least reduce, the chances of being winded by positioning themselves so their scent isn't blowing directly toward where deer are expected to appear and by wearing clothing designed to cover their scent. Elevated stands, where legal, are a great help in this respect.

Some of the best stands may be to either side of the line of drivers or, believe it or not, behind them rather than directly in front. Remember: Deer go where they want to on a drive, not where the hunters want them to. Standers who connect will be covering locations where jumped deer normally travel when alarmed.

In the event deer were jumped and not seen by standers, an effort should be made to find out why. A lesson can be learned from the failure of a drive if hunters are willing to take the time to do it. Most don't. An escape route a buck or doe used successfully once will be used again if they are in the same area. Snow makes the job of unraveling how deer made their getaway easier, but telltale signs can often be found under other conditions as well. It is at least worth a try. If the escape route is discovered, be sure to have a hunter watching it the next time that area is driven. It may pay off.

Snow on the ground gives hunters a slight edge when making a drive. Any deer in the area, whether feeding or bedded, will have left tracks, unless the snow fell recently. One driver should be assigned to follow the tracks with the others to either side of him or her. Drivers to the sides should try to adjust their courses according to the tracker's progress.

The best way to accomplish this is to have the tracker whistle, bark periodically, or carry a bell so others can keep track of him or her. This is a variation of a noisy drive that can be very productive. Once the deer is jumped the odds of someone's getting a shot are good, whether it is one of the standers or the drivers to the sides.

Getting Into Position

Standers should be as quiet as possible when going to their posts, as well as once there. Too much noise can alert deer to their presence and whitetails or mulies will steer clear of them just as easily as they do of noisy drivers. If standers aren't cautious, they could spook deer out of an area before a drive begins.

The chances of running into a deer on the way to a stand shouldn't be discounted, unless it is dark. I bagged my first buck on the way to a stand preceding a drive. Deer may just as easily travel by standers on their own before a drive begins, so standers should always be alert.

Try to have standers in as many strategic positions as possible. Assigning them all to positions facing the drivers just because "that's the way a normal drive operates" is a mistake. If there are enough hunters, put some on the sides and behind the drivers. When a drive is made into the wind, bucks sometimes circle back through the line of drivers and think they are home free.

On drives made with the wind at the drivers' backs most of the standers should be to the sides and behind, unless the drivers are so close together deer aren't likely to get through. If deer are able to smell drivers, it has the same effect as a noisy drive. The animals are able to tell where the hunters are and will either stay put or circle back if they can.

The rear and sides can sometimes be covered best by stillhunters. Hunters on either side of the heavy cover should move with the drivers or slightly ahead of them. Tail-end hunters should follow approximately 100 yards behind the drivers.

More often than not, drivers are started at prearranged times. Standers are given from fifteen minutes to a half hour or more to get in position, and then the drivers start. All watches should be synchronized for this purpose. Sometimes a car horn or whistle is used to signal both the beginning and end of a drive.

Instead of sitting in a vehicle or relaxing while waiting for standers to get in position, drivers should be standing on the edge of cover or just inside it until it is

Standers should always watch and listen for deer after they get in position. Deer can move by on their own before the drive begins. The hunter in this photo is about to shoot a buck that's being driven past him.

time to go—unless, of course, it is dark. If standers do move deer on their way in, drivers may get shooting before starting out. I recall one time I should have done just that instead of passing the time in the car.

There were four of us that day. I was going to be the only driver because there was snow and the wind was right. Tracks would be easy to follow and I could get any deer moving that were in the piece of cover we planned on pushing.

Just after I started I found a lone, fresh track coming out. It was big, and I felt sure a buck had made it. Those tracks were made by a deer my partners jumped when they reached their stands. The story was clear by the time I reached them. If I had been where I should have been I might have claimed an easy buck.

The standers didn't see any deer on that drive, of course. The animals had been alerted and moved out before I started in. This example also shows how important it is for standers to be as quiet as possible on their way to stands.

An important rule of drives is that standers stay put until the push is over. They should wait until they hear a prearranged signal or until someone picks them up. If any deer are taken, everyone normally lends a hand getting them out of the woods. Following up a deer that is hit and runs off and dressing animals should be postponed until the hunt is over. The same goes when drivers connect. They should mark the kill and go back for it later with other members of the group.

Dog Drives

The use of dogs to drive deer is a tactic only practiced on whitetails in North America in limited areas. Hounds are not permitted to chase mule deer during the course of a hunt.

The only states where driving with hounds is still legal are in the Southeast. Deer hunting with dogs used to be practiced in northern parts of the country, but was outlawed there about 1900. In areas of the South where dogs are still permitted to hunt deer, the cover is so thick that canines are the best means of moving whitetails out of swamps and briar patches to where hunters can get shots at them. Human drivers would pass by most deer without getting them moving in that terrain. Hounds can sniff the deer out.

Canada's province of Ontario also permits the use of dogs to drive deer.

A hunt with hounds is started by finding a fresh track crossing a road or by casting hounds in an area where they are expected to jump a deer. Either way, standers are positioned strategically in the location to be hunted before the chase begins. Standers are often positioned in a horseshoe or S-shaped pattern.

Some members of the party usually try to stay with the dogs and serve as drivers, too. They help get deer moving and steer dogs toward posted hunters when starting out looking for a fresh trail. Once a chase is over, the drivers also catch the dogs. Many hunters put radio collars on their dogs, making it faster and easier to locate and pick them up at the end of a hunt.

Dog hunting for deer is legal in parts of the southeastern U.S. and Ontario. Dogs can drive deer out of thick cover better than human drivers because they use their noses. This hound was used for deer hunting in Alabama.

Since a pack of dogs, usually numbering from three to six (some hunters use only one), often stays on the trail of one deer for some time, a chase may be stopped if they are on a doe. Some deer dogs reportedly prefer the track of a buck. Deer are easily able to stay ahead of dogs on such hunts. They are normally sneaking or trotting along 300 to 500 yards ahead of their pursuers rather than running flat out directly in front of them. The commotion created by driving dogs also moves deer that aren't being chased. For these reasons, standers must be constantly alert. A flicker of movement is often the only hint of an approaching whitetail, but it's sometimes possible to hear deer approaching, especially if there's much water around.

Beagles and basset hounds are preferred by some hunters because they move whitetails at a leisurely pace and watchers have more of a chance at a standing or slow-moving target. Others prefer bigger hounds such as black-and-tans, Walkers, or July hounds to keep deer moving at a steady pace. Purebred dogs are by no means the only types used for deer hunting. Mixed breeds are found in many packs. Dogs that only run the freshest track are preferred to those that try to follow a trail that is hours old.

Hunting deer with dogs requires as much coordination and planning as other types of drives, if not more. Hounds are not only useful for pushing deer to standers, but also for following and finding wounded whitetails that might otherwise be lost.

Some deer guides in Ontario use hounds to hunt with. Check out a list of Ontario deer guides on the internet to find those that offer dog hunts. The Ontario Ministry of Natural Resources may be able to help in locating such a guide.

Much of the dog hunting in the South is done by organized hunting clubs. The best advice for hunters who would like to try this type of hunting in that part of the country is to contact the department of natural resources in a state they want to hunt for a listing of hunting clubs. States that have permited hunting deer with dogs are Louisiana, Georgia, North Carolina, Alabama, Florida, Mississippi, and South Carolina. In many of these states hunting with hounds is only permitted in specific areas during specified times, not statewide. Always check current hunting regulations before planning a deer hunt with dogs to avoid breaking any laws.

Tracking

If you want to up your odds of scoring on a whitetail or mule deer buck by tracking him in the snow, look for the freshest tracks you can find of a buck that's preoccupied with a doe. It's well known that the rut increases the vulnerability of whitetails to hunters using other tactics. The same is true for snow tracking.

Although most of the focus of this chapter is about tracking deer in the snow, tracking is also a popular method for connecting with trophy desert mule deer in parts of Texas and Mexico where sandy soil makes it possible to track the animals for long distances. Much of the information in this chapter can also be applied to tracking deer in the sand where conditions make that possible.

When a buck is courting a hot doe, he pays less attention than he normally would, if any, to his backtrail. He's got one thing on his mind and most of his attention is focused on the doe he's after. The buck's advances also distract the doe, reducing the chances she's going to be paying as much attention as usual to what's going on around her.

I should have gotten a decent antlered whitetail while snow tracking by keying in on a buck that was with a doe during the third day of Michigan's firearms season (November 17) one year. I was hunting out of a tent camp with some friends in the heart of the Upper Peninsula's snowbelt. More than a foot of deep, fluffy snow was on the ground that morning. So much snow had come down that it coated everything.

Conditions were ideal for quietly sneaking through the deer woods. The deep snow made it impossible to move too fast, which helped me concentrate on using my eyes more than my feet. The heavy blanket of snow also had a dampening effect on noise, muffling sounds I might make with my feet, further reducing the chances of tipping off deer to my presence.

Finding the fresh tracks of a buck like this one that's preoccupied with a hot doe can increase your chances of success while snow tracking.

The deep snow, which had started falling during the early morning hours of the sixteenth, changed deer movements and it also forced me to change tactics. I had been occupying a stand overlooking a series of fresh scrapes along the edge of a swamp. Even though the snow buried the scrapes, I faithfully watched them all day on the sixteenth without seeing a single whitetail. I made up my mind to try something different if there weren't many fresh tracks by the scrapes on the morning of the seventeenth—and there weren't.

During the two-mile drive along logging roads from camp to where I parked my vehicle to go to my stand, I had noticed one area where half a dozen deer had crossed the road, heading from a large expanse of upland hardwoods toward lowland conifers. On the way back to that spot to post, I found the fresh tracks of a buck and doe crossing the road that hadn't been there a half hour earlier. The buck's tracks were twice the size of the doe's, so I knew it was a mature whitetail. Since that's what I was after, it was easy for me to decide to follow the pairs' prints.

I hadn't followed the tracks far from the road when I noticed a patch of brown on a knoll to my right that looked the color of a deer. I stared at the object for a while and didn't see any movement, so I thought it was a stump. But, as I turned my head to look away, the deer I had been looking at trotted to the right with its tail up. The deer didn't look very big.

Since the wind was in my favor, I didn't think the deer knew what I was. I thought it might be the doe that the buck was after and the buck might be nearby. I snuck forward just enough to be able to see over the knoll in the direction the deer ran and soon spotted a number of deer standing together. I stared intently, trying to make out antlers, and finally determined the whitetails were a doe and her two fawns.

Then I remembered I had seen their tracks crossing the road near where the buck and doe went across. It's not unusual to spot whitetails other than those you are following when snow tracking. Lone bucks that are looking for mates routinely check out does that are bedded or feeding and then continue on if the doe isn't receptive. So if you spot the body of a whitetail while snow tracking a buck, don't assume it's the deer you've been following. It's important to get a look at its head first.

In this case, the buck and doe I was following had gone by a knoll where the doe and fawns were bedded. After satisfying myself that no buck was with the family group, I continued following the tracks of the buck and doe. I kept moving slowly, following the tracks with my eyes as far as possible and scanning the terrain ahead and to the sides to increase my odds of spotting deer, making as little noise as possible.

The fact that I was dressed for stand hunting instead of snow tracking made it important for me to move slowly to avoid overheating besides trying to be quiet. Cold temperatures, with readings in the teens, made it easier to remain comfortable while walking slowly.

The best time to try snow tracking is after a fresh snow. It's easy to determine which tracks were made recently, and old prints are usually covered. When new snow blankets trees, it's harder for deer that are being trailed to hear and see hunters.

I hadn't followed the rutting couple far beyond the doe and fawns when I suddenly saw the rack buck I was trailing get up from a bed in a small patch of cover to my left under several large white cedars trees. I happened to see the buck through a small opening in the patch of cover, but he passed through the opening too fast for a shot. I started to bring my rifle up nonetheless, to be ready in case an opportunity for a shot presented itself.

I didn't have any trouble seeing the buck's antlers. It was obvious he had at least eight points and possibly ten. The doe got up in front of the buck and they started going away from me. If they had continued in that direction, I don't think I would have been able to get a shot. The doe, however, turned to the right and went across an opening in front of me that might have been 20 yards wide.

I knew the buck would follow her, so I covered the opening with my scope. When the running buck appeared in the scope, with the crosshairs on his shoulder, I pulled the trigger. The image of the buck, stretched out in mid-stride, with the crosshairs on his shoulder, is stuck in my brain.

It's not unusual to see deer other than the one you are tracking, so make sure to get a look at a deer's head before deciding to shoot.

The hold looked good and I felt confident I had hit the buck. I knew I would be able to recover the buck if I hit him anywhere. The buck's momentum carried him out of sight at the shot, so it was impossible for me to see if I had scored a hit. I took the time to retrieve the spent .30-06 casing from the snow and looked at my watch before proceeding forward to find out if I had indeed connected on the whitetail.

It was ten-twenty when I took the shot. I had only been tracking the pair in the snow for about an hour and I don't think I even covered a half mile.

Unfortunately, when I reached the buck's tracks, I could find no sign of a hit. There was no hair or blood. The bullet had clearly missed and I think the only way that could have happened is it was deflected. I was concentrating on the running deer so much that it would have been easy to overlook a branch or two.

I've never felt so good about missing a mature buck in my life. Although it would have been terrific to get that whitetail, the fact that I got a good shot at him while snow tracking was rewarding enough. I've tracked a number of big bucks that I never got a look at, much less a shot.

After confirming the miss, I hung back and poked along on the deer's trail, allowing them time to calm down, hoping they might soon forget about me. I got so far behind the deer, however, that they looped back across their tracks. When I crossed the other fresh tracks initially, I thought it was other deer that had gone through, but after making the loop myself, I realized it was the same deer. It was one o'clock by then, so when I came to a logging road that would eventually take me back to my vehicle, I decided to call it quits on the trail of that buck.

Background

Snow tracking used to be one of the most popular deer hunting methods in the north country such as Michigan's Upper Peninsula because snow is common during the traditional gun season, the last two weeks of November. It's not unusual to have snow on the ground for opening day. If it doesn't come by then, there's usually some of the white stuff on the ground by the second week of the season. Snow cover often coincides with deer seasons over much of the northern states and Canada.

Snow tracking isn't as popular as it once was for a number of reasons. Hunter numbers have increased at the same time as the blocks of public land where snow tracking is possible have decreased. Tracking bucks in the snow to get a shot at them defeats itself if you are constantly pushing them into other hunters (unless they are members of your party) or if the whitetails cross onto private property where you can't follow them.

The woodsmanship of deer hunters in general has also declined. Many don't want to get any further from a drivable road than necessary, much less trudge through woods for miles following the tracks of a buck that they may never see. Some hunters aren't physically capable of doing it. Others are concerned about getting lost.

The amount of time the average hunter has to pursue whitetails is probably less than it used to be, too. It takes time to learn how to distinguish buck tracks from those of does, how to determine which tracks are the best to follow, and how to interpret what a buck is about to do from his prints. This method is more demanding and tougher to master than many others, which discourages hunters who don't have much time to spend in the field.

Perseverance, physical endurance, and stealth are three of the qualities hunters who want to track deer successfully should possess. They must also feel at ease wherever deer lead them, free from worry about getting lost. A hunter preoccupied with that fear will not be able to devote the necessary concentration to the tracking technique.

The Basics

If you are interested in learning more about snow tracking so you can try it, read on. Hunting in an area where there's snow or sand is obviously necessary, which limits the practicality of this technique to the northern states and Canada where there's snow and arid areas of the southwestern U.S. and Mexico where there's sand. A chunk of land at least a square mile in size (more is much better) that you have permission to hunt is also essential. Fortunately, large blocks of state and federally owned land remain in the Upper Peninsula and in northern Wisconsin, Minnesota, Montana, and some eastern states such as Maine, New Hampshire, and Vermont. Public land is also abundant in most Canadian provinces.

To begin your introduction to snow tracking, simply find the biggest and freshest track you can and start following it. As mentioned at the beginning, it can be an advantage to follow the prints of an adult buck that's with a doe during the rut instead of a lone buck. The prints of an adult buck that's at least $3^1/_2$ years old will be obviously wider and sink deeper in the snow than those of an adult doe. The buck will usually have a longer stride (the distance between prints), too.

What Tracks Look Like

Before going any further let's discuss what deer tracks look like. Whitetail and mule deer hooves are made up of two segments or toes. There is a noticeable gap between the halves. Each half is narrower at the front than at the rear, often almost pointed. The back end of each "toe" is more rounded than the front. A pair of dew claws are a short distance above the rear of each foot on the back of the leg. Dew claws are further from hooves on hind feet than front feet.

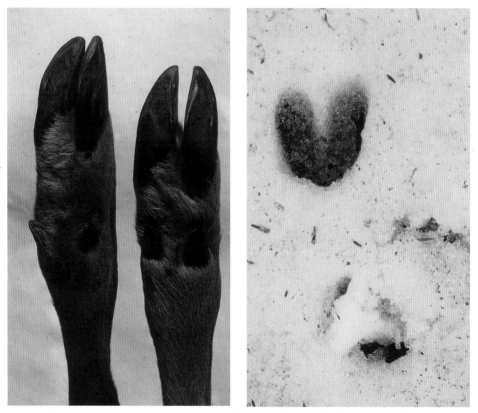

Left: This photo shows a comparison between the front foot (right) and hind foot of a buck. Note that the dew claws are larger and closer to the hooves on the front foot. The tip of a toe on the front foot has been broken off, giving any prints that foot would have left a distinctive appearance. When following a buck, look for anything unusual about his tracks that can be used to distinguish his prints from those of other deer. Right: The heart-shaped print of a walking deer. The narrower pointed or rounded end, or the bottom of the heart, is the front of the track. The deer that made the track is facing and traveling in that direction. Buck tracks like this one tend to be more rounded at the front than prints from does.

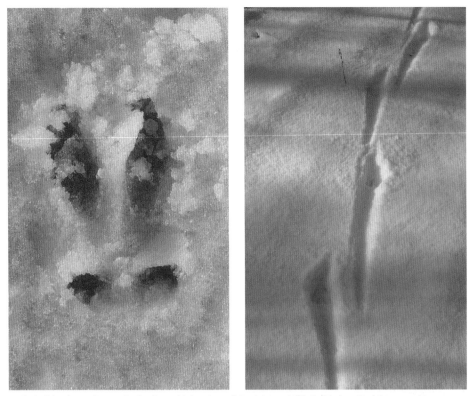

Left: A fresh running track of a deer with imprints of dew claws visible behind each of the spread toes. Right: Bucks tend to drag their feet more than does, leaving a track pattern like this in the snow when they are walking. Buck tracks are generally noticeably larger than those made by does.

On solid ground in snow that isn't more than an inch deep, dew claws seldom show. Each print of a walking deer is roughly heart-shaped, with the bottom of the "heart" (the narrow end) pointing in the direction the deer is facing or traveling. When a hoof is splayed, with each segment separate, the imprint from each toe resembles an elongated droplet of water. Dew claws are usually visible when a heavy deer walks on soft ground or in snow several inches deep, or when it runs. The running prints of deer resemble a pair of exclamation marks, with marks from the dew claws being the dots at the bottom of each exclamation mark.

Bounding deer bunch their feet together. Prints from the hind feet will be imprinted forward of the front feet of running whitetails. In the pogo-stick, bouncing gait of running mule deer, prints from feet will be in the same configuration that they are on the animal. Tracks of a walking deer will be almost in a straight line with the left and right footprints staggered on either side of center.

If you see the prints of two adult deer that are similar in size, it could be a pair of does traveling together. When one set of tracks is larger than the other, but not by much, the prints may have been made by a yearling buck and a doe or by two does, one of which is larger than the other. Prints of an adult deer with one or two sets of small tracks were made by a doe and her offspring.

The main difference I've noticed between prints made by adult bucks and does is their width at the rear. The tracks of adult does are similar in width from front to back. Big bucks leave prints that are much wider at the rear, tapering down to obviously narrower tips. The fronts of the hooves of older bucks are often more blunt and rounded than those of does from making scrapes, too. Some bucks also have a tendency to drag their feet once snow is several inches deep, leaving obvious drag marks between prints.

If you can't find the tracks of an adult buck that's traveling with a doe, go with one that's alone. He could eventually hook up with a doe. Hunters who catch up with a buck that is feeding also have an advantage as the whitetail is distracted by food. When feeding on mast crops such as acorns and beechnuts, whitetails make a lot of noise as they paw in leaves and chew the nuts, which works to the hunter's advantage.

Locating Buck Tracks

The best way to locate a buck track to follow is to drive a network of logging roads around daylight. Examine the tracks you encounter until you find the freshest prospect. How do you determine if a track is fresh? If it's snowing at the time, fresh prints will have little to no snow in them. The same is true if it stopped snowing recently. If you drive the same road at different times, as I did when I found the tracks of the buck and doe mentioned near the beginning of this chapter, and find prints the second time that weren't there before, you know they were made since you were there last.

If it hasn't snowed for a day or two, look at your old boot tracks or deer tracks that you know are a day or two old and examine them to see how details have started to fade or change in any way. You can use the appearance of those tracks to help you gauge the age of new tracks you find. If you check the same roads for tracks every day, you will know what prints are made each day.

By making a boot track in the snow next to a buck track you find, you can compare their clarity to try to determine how many hours earlier the deer walked there. If the temperature is above freezing, the snow will melt along with tracks made in it. When it's below freezing, tracks that were made an hour or more before you find them will be frozen and firm to the touch. Prints that are not yet frozen when you check them with a finger are fresh.

Even when you find the hot prints of a big buck you want to follow, don't rush off after him immediately if there's another road in the direction he's headed that he might also have crossed. Take the time to look at a map. If there's another road in the direction he's headed, examine the prints carefully for any unique characteristics that will help you identify them, then drive around to see if he crossed the next road and then the next. You can save hours of tracking and increase your chances of getting a shot by isolating the section of woods the buck is in before taking up his track.

If you are hunting a designated wilderness area where vehicles are prohibited or there are few roads, starting out on foot may be the only option for locating a fresh track to follow. You seldom have to be concerned about pushing a buck you are trailing into other hunters in these types of situations. Pushing a buck into another hunter when snow tracking on public ground can happen, however. When it does, congrat-

Feeling a deer track to see if it's frozen. If the temperature is below freezing and the compacted snow is not yet frozen, the track is fresh.

ulate the lucky hunter, if he got the whitetail, and see if the rack measures up to what you thought it would based on the deer's tracks. If the hunter missed the buck, get as much information about the deer as possible from the shooter, and then determine whether you want to continue after the whitetail. After being shot at, a lone buck will obviously be spooked and will usually run a ways before settling down again. If it's late in the day, backing off may be the best option. Bucks that are with a hot doe will remain focused on that doe and can slip up at any time.

If you are hunting with a group of hunters who prefer stand hunting, your snow tracking efforts may help them score, which is a good thing. Some hunters team up on a track, with one following the trail and a partner or two paralleling the tracker the best they can on one or both sides. Portable radios are often used to communicate between trackers and flankers. Make sure this is legal where you plan on hunting, if you want to try this.

What To Take With You

Before leaving your vehicle to follow the trail of a big buck in the snow it's important to make sure you have a few essentials with you. A compass is a must. Take a reading on which direction the deer's tracks are heading, so you know the direction you are going. When you leave the track, you can return to the road where you left your vehicle by following a compass reading in the opposite direction. Backtracking on yourself in the snow will also bring you right back to the vehicle.

A small GPS unit can be even more helpful in getting you back to your vehicle. Simply take a waypoint on your vehicle's location before heading off on the track. Make sure the unit has fresh batter-

Small GPS units like this one can be great navigational tools when snow tracking as long as batteries are fresh.

ies, and it's a good idea to carry some spares. Always carry a compass even if you have a GPS because these gadgets can malfunction and may not even work if you are under a canopy of evergreen trees.

Carry a small flashlight or two with spare batteries in case it's dark when you are finding your way out of the woods. Waterproof matches are important, too, in case you have to spend a night in the woods. Carry extra shells in case you need them to finish a deer or to signal your location to searchers, if you get hurt or lost. You will need a sharp knife to gut a deer, if your snow tracking is successful. Snack foods such as power bars, nuts, and candy are handy to carry in a pocket to give you an energy boost if you're on the trail all day.

I always wear Scent-Lok clothes when deer hunting, regardless of the method I'm using. Any scent-absorbing garments will reduce the chances of tipping white-tails off to what you are. I wear camo, with the exception of my hat, which is orange, as required by Michigan law. I prefer outer layers made of fleece, wool, or other soft fabric that is quiet and will keep me warm in potentially cold weather. I normally wear a light set of long underwear.

Knee-high rubber boots are ideal for snow tracking. Those that are uninsulated are lightweight and keep your feet dry when crossing creeks and walking through swamps. Any type of boot will work, as long as you are comfortable walking in them and the snow won't soak through them.

Short, light, fast-shouldering rifles and shotguns are ideal for snow tracking. Dedicated snow trackers often use peep sights for quick shooting. Although I'm used to using a scope and I don't consider it a disadvantage when snow tracking, the added weight is a negative. So is having snow fall off of trees and land on the optic's lenses. I carry tissues in my pocket to clean and dry scopes.

Confirming Buck Tracks

If you are unsure whether the tracks you are following were made by a buck, you shouldn't have to trail the deer far to find confirmation. Generally, bucks tend to drag their feet more than does. If the tracks lead you to a fresh antler-rubbed sapling or scrape, you're on the right trail. If the deer you are trailing intersects the tracks of other deer and follows them a short distance before leaving them or visits the beds of other whitetails, it's a buck checking out the scent of does.

And where a deer you are following puts its head down to feed from the ground, look for imprints of the tips of their antlers in the snow. Sometimes only one or two tines will touch the snow when a buck lowers his head to pick up a morsel of food, so look closely for any telltale marks in the snow. Antler or tine marks may be left in the snow near a buck's bed, too.

If the snow is deep enough, the impressions of a buck's antler beams may even be left when he puts his head down. A friend of mine from upper Michigan was walking along a heavily used deer trail one time when he found the outline of a buck's antlers that was made as it put its head down to smell the trail. Upon closer inspection, he noticed drops of urine along the trail near the antler impressions. While snow tracking bucks previously, he had observed that they frequently dribble urine along their trails. But what really caught his attention was the spread of the antlers.

If the tracks you are following lead you to a freshly rubbed sapling like this one, with bark on top of the snow (left), or a fresh scrape (right), you know you are following the prints made by a buck.

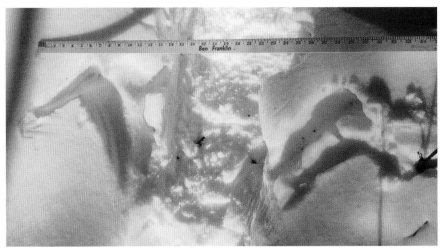

Antler impressions left in the snow by a buck with a wide rack as it put its head down to smell something in the trail it was walking on. Hunters who are following the tracks of a buck will sometimes see places where antler tines left marks in the snow where the deer was feeding or bedded. PHOTO COURTESY OF JIM BUTLER

He wasn't far from home at the time, so he went home and got a yardstick to measure the rack's outside spread and came up with $30^{1}/_{2}$ inches. The accompanying photograph shows what my friend saw. The double marks on the right side of the trail (the deer's left side) indicate either that the deer had two beams on that side or that it moved its head. Most likely, it moved its head to make the double mark. My buddy was amazed such a big buck survived since there's a lot of hunting pressure in the area he hunts. Despite his best efforts to find that deer, he never saw it.

A whitetail buck rub urinating on tarsal glands, splattering urine behind rear feet.

When a deer you are following stops to urinate, that should also be a tipoff as to whether it's a buck or doe. If it's a doe, urine will be deposited behind prints from hind feet. If it's a buck, urine will fall in front of prints from rear hooves. Mature bucks frequently urinate on their tarsal glands, splattering the liquid. When bucks rub urinate, urine will be splattered behind prints from hind feet. Does will also rub urinate on their hocks, leaving the same type of urine stains in the snow.

Pace

Rutting bucks that are alone can cover a lot of ground. It's a good idea to move at a steady pace when the buck's tracks indicate he's traveling at a steady trot. When the trail starts meandering, he's looking for food or a place to bed, so slow down and start paying more attention ahead and to the sides. Try to go as straight as possible when following a feeding deer. Look as far ahead as possible in an effort to sort out the track visually to avoid making all of the loops the deer made. It may take as long as five minutes to sort out the trail with your eyes, but it is usually worth it. Bedded deer don't think a hunter coming straight at them is as dangerous as one who is making every swing they did. A zig-zagging hunter is also more visible to a deer that is bedded.

Bucks like to bed in elevated locations with a good view. If a buck is headed for a hill or ridge, leaving the track to circle around to the side or rear might be the ticket to spotting the buck for a shot. That's how upper Michian resident Terry Weigold got a look at a trophy whitetail he was snow tracking during the December muzzleloader season. He said he picked up the big buck's tracks about eleven o'clock on December 3. The temperature was above freezing that day, so the snow was soft and quiet underfoot—perfect conditions for catching up to a deer.

Weigold commented that he knew the animal was a heavy one by the way his tracks were pressed deep into the snow. The prints were big, too.

The tracker covered about six miles of hilly terrain over a span of five hours before finally getting a look at the whitetail he was following. He stayed off to the

Terry Weigold with a trophy whitetail buck he bagged with a muzzleloader
after snow tracking it about six miles. When he saw its tracks going up a
hill, he circled the hill to get a shot at it.

side of the buck's tracks to avoid being seen and was circling to the side in an effort
to spot it where it had gone up a hill.

Weigold said this deer behaved differently from the many others he has tracked.
It ran about a mile and a half before stopping and it did the same thing two more
times. Terry explained that most bucks that are followed will run for a short distance
and then start sneaking.

He caught up to the deer after the third sprint. The whitetail was about 80 yards
away when Weigold saw it and part of its rack. He then raised the iron-sighted, .50-
caliber Thompson/Center Scout he had gotten as a gift from his wife and took careful aim.

The buck's nontypical 13-point rack proved to be bigger than Terry thought it
was. Before shooting the deer, he thought the antlers might score in the 130s. The
rack scored $162^3/8$.

Although Terry shot the trophy buck at four o'clock, his travels were far from
over. He had to locate a route to get the buck out of the woods and it was ten o'clock
that evening before he reached his destination. He returned with a snowmobile the
following day to retrieve the buck, which had a dressed weight of 207 pounds.

Bucks will often stop and wait to see if their pursuer is still following them after crossing a clearing or opening. Smart trackers who know this should circle clearings to try to get a look at the buck they are after.

When a buck starts zig-zagging down a steep ridge through thick cover, move to either side of the thick cover so you can look ahead in the direction he's headed. You might catch a glimpse of him or even get a shot. If you do see him or his tracks, and don't get a shot before he disappears, you can gain ground by cutting a corner and going directly to his tracks.

Lone bucks often bed in a position where they can watch their backtrail and have an escape plan in mind. If you jump a buck and don't get a shot, keep after him. The longer you stay with him, the greater the chances are he will eventually make a mistake.

When trailing a buck that's with a hot doe, you may see them at any time, so be alert. A doe often leads a buck on a chase before eventually letting him mount her. She often runs in circles and may even backtrack, so don't be surprised if you see deer coming back toward you when on their trail. If you see signs of chasing, listen for sounds of running deer nearby to help pinpoint their location.

Don't worry if you snap a twig or two when snow tracking. Deer frequently make the same noises. When you do snap a twig, it can be helpful to have a deer call with you and make a buck grunt or doe bleat, so any whitetails within hearing will think another deer made the noise. The buck you've been following may even come to investigate.

Keep After Him

Following the same buck during successive days can pay off if you don't get a shot at him on day one. Picking up the deer's tracks where you left them the night before is an option, but you will be further ahead if you can cut to tracks he made that morning. One time veteran snow tracker Duaine Wenzel jumped a whitetail buck from beds yards apart two days in a row. Duaine got several shots at the animal the first day when it jumped, but missed. He reloads his own rifle ammunition, but rather than take the time to pick up the brass, he hustled after the buck. He estimated he followed that animal eight miles that day without getting another crack at it.

The next morning he returned to the place where he shot at the buck to pick up his brass. Just short of the spot, the buck jumped up. Caught by surprise, Duaine didn't get a shot. He bagged the deer later that day though. As the whitetail stood up from its third bed, Wenzel nailed him.

Shots frequently have to be taken in a hurry when tracking deer. Wenzel prepares for the season by practicing throwing his rifle to his shoulder and getting on target. He uses a six-and-a-half-pound .30-06 with a 1-4X variable scope. He fires 180-grain round-nosed bullets.

Like most experienced hunters who regularly track deer, Duaine is familiar with the areas he hunts. When trailing a deer he usually knows where he is and what lies ahead. This information sometimes helps him anticipate the route a buck will take. Over the years he has noticed that different bucks in the same vicinity have a tendency to travel through the same localities when pushed.

Whitetail bucks will often return to their home territories after being tracked for miles. Duaine Wenzel once jumped the same buck from beds yards apart two days in a row. He got the buck the second day when it got up from its third bed.

The novice tracking hunter can't expect to be as skillful as an old hand at the technique right away. It takes years to develop the familiarity with the lay of the land and the animals that live on it that Duaine and others like him have developed. Regardless of whether or not hunters who track deer connect, the experience is bound to be educational. Deer give their pursuers cram courses on what they eat, the habitat they prefer, their daily habits, and how clever they can be in staying out of sight. They don't give hunters lessons willingly, of course; those who want to learn must interpret buck sign left in the snow for hours and sometimes days.

If you do score on the buck you're after, or another one you happen to stumble into, mark the location with your GPS unit, after gutting him, and head to the nearest road. If wolves or coyotes are in the area, leaving an item of clothing on the carcass should keep the scavengers away. Putting orange flagging in a tree where it's easy to see will help in relocating the carcass. Once you get back to your vehicle, you can figure out the shortest route to retrieve the deer.

Wounded Deer

All deer hunters, regardless of the hunting technique they use, should assume a whitetail or mulie they shoot at is hit. Most animals will give some indication of being struck, but not always. Deer that stagger, hunch up, kick, leap in the air, favor a leg, or break into a dead run after a shot are usually hit. Bowhunters can sometimes actually see their arrows strike deer.

If you know the deer you shot at is hit, that is usually good. A properly placed bullet or arrow will put a deer down in seconds, many times on the spot or within sight. It is the ones that are hit that make it out of sight before dropping that I will discuss here.

Try to make a mental note of where deer are standing when you shoot at them. This can be done after the animal has gone out of sight. Unless there is a good chance for another shot at a deer, it is best to stay where you shot from rather than immediately racing after a whitetail or mulie. If it is hit seriously, it may lie down just out of sight. A hunter who stumbles after a wounded animal right away sometimes reduces his or her chances of getting it.

Always try to watch a deer that has been shot at as long as possible. If it didn't show any signs of being hit at first, it may while running. Noting the course the animal follows will also make locating its trail easier.

Keep your ears open, too. A fleeing deer that is out of sight but within earshot makes a lot of noise. If the animal falls, you should be able to tell and get a fix on the approximate location.

Once a deer that may be wounded is out of sight and hearing and you have noted the spot or spots where it was when you shot, walk directly there. It is a good idea to leave a hat or coat to mark the spot where the shot was taken from, unless there is a prominent identifying feature nearby. Bowhunters should look for the arrow if unsure of a hit.

Hit or Miss?

Archers using string trackers will know if they scored a hit and be assured of finding the arrow if it missed. Gun hunters should look for blood, hair, or anything else between where they shot from and where the deer stood to determine if the bullet may have hit.

Archers who find a bloodied arrow know they scored a hit. If the search turns up a clean broadhead, the shot was a miss. A missing shaft might also mean the arrow was on target. Look for blood or hair if the arrow can't be found.

Tufts of hair or blood are sure signs of a hit. Look for these clues behind where the deer was standing, as well as at the spot. Firearms users who find a tree their slug hit before reaching a deer can almost count on a miss. It is worthwhile to check further before giving up in such a situation, though, especially if the tree or branch is close to where the deer was standing.

The location of a hit can often be determined by the color of hair or blood. Dark brown hair usually means the animal was struck in the shoulder or upper body. It will be light brown if the deer was hit in the chest or lower sides. White hair originates from legs and the belly area.

Pink, frothy blood means a dead deer—it was hit in the lungs. Dark, beet-colored blood indicates a liver or gut wound. Bright red blood usually comes from muscles or an artery. Watery blood or none at all and food particles or intestinal matter are evidence of a hit in the stomach or intestines.

If unable to determine if a deer was hit by checking the area where it was standing, move along the course it took after the shot, but try to make as little disturbance as possible. Look for blood on the ground or bushes. Archers can also keep an eye open for a broken arrow lying off to the side.

There shouldn't be any problem following a deer in snow or sand. In blankets of leaves or pine needles look for areas where leaves and turf have been kicked up by a running deer. Vegetation will be flattened and broken in fields and openings where a deer went through. Hunters who carefully watched the departure of deer they shot at should not have trouble following the animal's trail for 100 yards or more. There should be some sign of a hit discovered in that distance, but go as far as possible to be absolutely sure.

If it can be determined that a deer was hit in the lungs, there is no need to wait before following it. Enough blood should be present to easily follow the animal's trail the short distance it traveled. If it is raining or snowing there will be little choice but to follow up on a deer as soon as possible.

With a hit anywhere but in the shoulder area, it is best to wait before trying to

String trackers like the one attached to this arrow can be a major advantage to bowhunters in finding deer they shoot. They are especially helpful for archers who are colorblind.

trail a wounded deer. Don't worry if it is getting dark. As long as the weather stays clear you can go back and trail with a flashlight or lantern. Drops of blood often show up well under the illumination of a lantern.

When you are unsure how badly a deer is wounded, waiting thirty minutes to an hour is usually long enough before picking up the trail. Try to hold off longer on paunch-shot animals (at least three to six hours). Five minutes can seem like a long time when you are anxious to follow a wounded deer, so it is best to try to do something to keep yourself occupied while waiting. If hunting with a partner or two it is a good idea to go get them to help trail. It will make the job easier. If you are alone, a walk to your car or camp is a good way to kill some time.

Hunters who have access to a dog that will track deer should consider getting it. In recent years, there's been an increase in the number of states that allow the use of

leashed dogs to recover deer shot by hunters. A group of volunteers called "Deer Search" in New York State are available to assist hunters in recovering wounded deer with their specially trained dogs and similar groups may have been formed in other states. However, be sure to check local regulations before using a dog to track a wounded deer. In areas where the laws are not clear on the practice, game wardens or conservation officers may allow hunters to use a dog to follow a wounded deer as long as a dog is kept on a leash.

Before leaving the spot where the deer was hit be sure you will be able to find it again. Leave a bright-colored hat or garment there or use ribbon to mark a course to the nearest road if the area will be difficult to locate.

Try to start trailing a wounded deer from the point where it was last seen. If there is a moderate to heavy blood trail or snow, there shouldn't be any problem following the animal. Skill and painstaking care are necessary to unravel a trail with little or no blood. This is where a tracking dog can be a big advantage. The presence of scavenging birds such as ravens, magpies, and vultures will sometimes tip hunters off to the location of their kill, too.

Leashed dogs can come in handy for recovering deer that hunters shoot if there is little to no blood trail. Unleashed dogs can be put on the trail of wounded deer in parts of the south where dog hunting is legal. German Wirehaired Dachshunds, like the one shown here with volunteers from Deer Search in New York State, are a popular breed for recovering wounded deer, but a variety of breeds are used for this purpose.

Blood Trailing Tips

If you don't have a dog, scour every inch of the ground for the tiniest drops of blood and tracks left by a wounded deer. It is sometimes necessary to get down on hands and knees when searching for minute details. Wounded whitetails and mulies run more often than not, so the ground should be noticeably disturbed along the route taken.

Be sure to look at bushes and tree trunks that the deer may have brushed past. Blood will often show above ground level in these locations.

It is advisable to mark every spot where a drop of blood or track from a wounded deer is found. Plastic surveyor's tape is perfect for this purpose. White or orange ribbon, spools of string, or tissue will also work. Place markers easily on bushes or tree limbs where they can easily be seen. After several markers have been hung it is usually possible to get a general idea of the animal's direction of travel by looking back.

Try to circle ahead and to the sides when the trail is lost. It isn't unusual for deer to make abrupt changes in direction or backtrack and jump off to the side. Be alert for any deviations. If the trail is lost entirely, keep in mind that whitetails and mulies, if seriously hurt, follow a path of least resistance. They tend to go downhill rather than uphill, for instance. Additionally, wounded deer may head for nearby heavy cover or water. Injured deer that go in water may submerge themselves in a effort to hide. Others may die before making it all the way across a river or lake.

Exhaust every possibility to locate a wounded deer. Perseverance often pays off in this type of tracking, as it does when using the technique to hunt. If you don't locate the animal, it probably wasn't seriously injured. While tracking a wounded deer during hours of daylight, be ready to shoot again on the chance the animal isn't dead.

Deer hunters who are proficient with gun or bow and are conscientious about

When a blood trail is sparse, each new spot of blood should be marked with tissue, surveyor's tape, or string. A line of markers will give trackers a good idea of the deer's direction of travel and help determine where to look for more blood sign.

only taking the best shot possible can avoid unnecessary wounding. Because of variables involved in deer hunting, many of which hunters don't have control over, some wounding does occur. Few of these animals will go unrecovered if hunters follow the guidelines for tracking them given above.

For detailed coverage of this subject, refer to my book *Tracking Wounded Deer* (Smith Publications, 1996).

11

Calling Deer

Rattling antlers together to simulate a pair of bucks fighting is a popular method of calling deer, especially whitetails, to hunters for a shot. Phil Henry from Tennessee used the technique while hunting in Saskatchewan one year to take his best buck ever. But the rattling Phil did to score on his trophy whitetail is slightly different than what most other hunters do, and it worked twice for him during the same day. I call it advanced rattling.

The buck he rattled in and shot during the first morning of his November hunt was a typical 13-pointer that had a green gross score of $171^3/_8$. Since Phil wasn't going to be picked up by his guide until the end of the day, he remained in his stand and used the same tactic later in the day to rattle in a 10-pointer that would have scored between 165 and 175. He didn't shoot that one, of course, but the fact that Phil was able to repeat the results of this variation of rattling a second time verifies its effectiveness.

It's important to understand that Phil is a veteran whitetail hunter, with years of Canadian hunting under his belt. Due to his years of experience hunting big white-tails, he's excellent at judging the size of antlers on live bucks and he's taken a number of them that score in the 150s.

Most hunters rattle when no deer are in sight in the hopes of luring one or more bucks into view. What Phil did on the day he got his best buck was to wait to begin rattling until he had a rutting buck that he didn't want to shoot chasing does near his stand. He figured that tactic might make it easier to lure bigger bucks out in the open that might be hanging back in the brush, and it obviously worked.

A 150-class buck was chasing does around in front of Phil's stand that fateful morning. Not wanting to shoot a buck similar in size to others he'd taken, Phil started rattling and grunting aggressively. When the larger 13-pointer appeared on the scene, Phil didn't waste any time shooting it.

Phil Henry from Tennessee with his best whitetail buck, a 13-pointer that grossed 171³/₈, which he bagged in Saskatchewan by using an advanced rattling technique he developed. He rattled in a second buck similar in size with the same technique later in the day. PHOTO COURTESY OF PHIL HENRY

Late in the day, when an 8-pointer was chasing does around, Phil started aggressively rattling and grunting again. That's when the 10-point that would have scored between 165 and 175 appeared. Two days later, the outfitter put another hunter in that same stand to try to get the big 10-pointer. The new hunter never saw the big one, but shot the 150-class buck that Phil passed up when he rattled in the 13-pointer. The antlers on that whitetail scored 151, confirming Phil's estimate of its antler size.

Although this tactic works in Saskatchewan, it should work elsewhere, too, under the same circumstances. It's a tactic most hunters probably don't try because they are concerned about scaring away the buck that's in front of them. However, if they don't plan on shooting that deer, it shouldn't matter anyway. In

Phil Henry with a trophy whitetail he bagged in Saskatchewan prior to the 13-pointer. This one scored in the 150s.

most cases, the rattling and grunting does not scare away the buck that's chasing does nearby, according to Phil, because he's preoccupied with the does.

The Basics

Calling deer has really become popular during recent years, especially for whitetails, and that's not a surprise because this tactic can be used anywhere, at any time, to improve your chances of success in combination with just about any other deer hunting method, such as stand hunting, stillhunting, or tracking. The techniques for calling deer to you take advantage of the animals' mating instincts, curiosity, and in the case of whitetails, their social nature and territoriality.

There are two ways to bring deer to you; rattling and the use of a variety of calls. Mouth-blown and electronic calls can bring deer to hunters if the circumstances are right. Most deer calls are designed to sound like the bleats of a doe or fawn or the grunts of bucks. Although the majority of deer calls are mouth-activated, at least one made by Primos that does an excellent imitation of a doe bleat is an enclosed cannister that is simply turned upside down, minimizing the chances of making a wrong note. The cannister is small enough to fit in one hand. It's called "The Can."

Some electronic deer calls available on the market do an excellent job of imitating a variety of deer vocalizations. Where they are legal to use, they can be effective, but they are illegal for use in some states and provinces. Be sure to check local regulations before using electronic deer calls.

Rattling

The practice of rattling antlers to attract whitetail bucks originated in Texas and is commonly accepted there. It has been proven productive in other states and provinces, too, and is now widely used. Michigan resident Dave Paquette tried rattling for the first time near his home in the Upper Peninsula during the fall of 1977 and got a 10-point buck for his efforts. Five to ten minutes after Dave started twisting tines together the whitetail came trotting into view. It was opening day of the state's November firearms season. Dave had practiced rattling on three occasions during the week before the season and had brought in another buck on his last attempt.

I rattled in my first Michigan buck, a $3\frac{1}{2}$-year-old 8-pointer, in 1986. I was using a Woods Wise Rattler Bag rather than antlers. Such a bag is easier to carry than antlers and sounds almost as good as the real thing. I've rattled in many more bucks in various states and provinces since that first one, using both rattle bags and antlers. A variety of products are now available for hunters who want to try rattling, including synthetic antlers, rattle boxes, and a new product made by Knight & Hale called the Pack Rack.

When To Try It

Rattling is most effective during the first and last stages of the rut when competition among bucks to breed does is the highest, but it can work during early fall, too, when bucks are doing a lot of sparring to establish dominance. The rut usually starts in late October or early November in northern states and in December or January in the South. There may be other variations in the timing of the rut from state to state. Deer in Florida, for instance, seem to breed at all times of the year with no peak breeding period.

The onset of cool weather in the fall, coupled with shortening day length, usually triggers the rut, which can last for a month or more. Fights between bucks normally start over a doe that is ready to breed or when a buck catches a competing male in his territory. A third buck will investigate a fight out of curiosity— to join in if the squabble is in his stomping grounds or in an attempt to make off with the doe the fight might be over.

Mule deer don't establish territories like whitetails, so they aren't as responsive to rattled antlers. The technique still works on them, however. A mulie buck drawn to the sounds of a battle between two other bucks would be interested in any does that might be around or just curious.

The chances of rattling working in areas where there are a lot of does and few bucks aren't good. The same is true

When rattling, I normally use a rattling bag made by Woods Wise. The bag is easier to carry than antlers and it works well. Here I'm using a rattle bag from a ladder stand in Canada during a muzzleloader hunt.

of locations where hunter densities are high. Under this circumstance the odds favor attracting other hunters rather than deer. Large numbers of hunters are seldom a problem during archery deer seasons. Bow seasons that coincide with the rut would be the best time to try rattling in many states and provinces.

If you do see another hunter approaching during a firearms season after you have rattled, try to alert them to your presence as soon as possible by whistling or waving an orange hat or vest. I rattled in a local hunter one time when hunting in Saskatchewan. As soon as I saw him sneaking toward me, I whistled and started waving my orange hat. He waved to acknowledge my presence as soon as he saw the hat and then he moved off.

Early in the morning on a cool to cold, quiet day is the best time to rattle. Any time of the day can be productive, however. Bucks are jittery on windy days, and the sound of antlers banged together doesn't travel far then.

Antlers To Use

Either whitetail or mule deer antlers will bring in bucks when rattled. The fresher they are, the better, but an old set will do if that is all that is available. Check with a

Though they aren't territorial, mule deer bucks spend time sparring and fighting just like white-tails. Consequently, they can also be rattled in by arousing their curiosity.

taxidermist or a friend who owns plenty of antlers if you don't own any. Looking for shed antlers in the spring is a great way to collect your own rattling antlers. Synthetic rattling antlers are also available commercially. Generally, big racks are better than small ones, and the antlers should be as evenly matched as possible. Small, unmatched beams will work though.

To remove antlers from a skull, saw them off either below or above the burr. Also remove the brow tine and sharp tips of additional tines. A file can be used to smooth any ragged or rough areas. A carrying strap can be rigged for the antlers by drilling a hole through each base, putting a piece of leather or rope through them, then tying a knot in the ends of the material. If the burr is still intact at the base of antlers, which will be the case if you are using sheds, a carrying strap can simply be tied above the burr of each antler.

You might consider painting the antlers red or orange to be on the safe side, so there will be little chance of another hunter mistaking them for the real thing. To prevent antlers used for rattling from drying out, you can rub them with linseed oil or lanolin.

Positioning

The best place to try the technique is near a series of scrapes. The buck that made them isn't likely to be far away and won't take kindly to what he thinks are a pair of other bucks having it out on his doorstep.

Always try to approach a rattling location quietly. Don't slam car doors or talk if you are with another hunter. It is a good idea for two hunters to work as a team when trying to rattle in a buck. One should plan on doing the shooting and the other the rattling. The guy with the antlers should be as concealed as possible in a position next to a tree or in brush.

Also, try to select a site where an approaching buck will have some cover. They don't like to cross openings. Their tendency to avoid openings can be used to your advantage if a stand is chosen with a clearing downwind. Bucks coming to a fight will sometimes circle downwind. If there is an opening there, those that circle will have to expose themselves before they can wind you.

Mimicing A Fight

When two bucks fight they do more twisting and shoving than beating their antlers together. Keep this in mind when trying to imitate a battle. Bang the antlers together as loud as possible at first, then twist and turn them so the tines knock against each other and make as much noise as possible.

When using a set of antlers for rattling, most hunters have a tendency to hold them like they would be on a buck's head. What I think works better is to hold antlers the opposite way, so the outside curves of beams are against one another while you hold the base of each antler in a hand. Then bring the tines in contact with one another by turning your wrists inward. The chances of being poked by tines that haven't been trimmed is reduced this way.

Additional realistic sound effects can be made by pounding the antlers on the ground and raking them up and down a tree trunk or through brush, although this isn't necessary to get bucks to respond to rattling. If gravel or rocks are common in your area scrape an antler through or over them. The object is to make noise, so don't be timid about it.

The procedure can be varied any way you like. Simply try to make the sounds realistic. It is a good idea to practice

Rattling antlers to lure bucks into view is easy to do. You are trying to simulate a pair of bucks sparring or fighting, as Wisconsin big-buck expert Greg Miller is shown doing here. Any sounds of antlers making contact can work. You are at an advantage if you have seen or heard bucks fighting and know what it sounds like.

with the antlers at home to get a feel for how they should be manipulated.

Make as few movements as possible during the process of rattling antlers. If a buck shows and sees you instead of what he is expecting, he won't hang around long. You will never know he was there if he sees you before you see him.

Antlers should be rattled for as long as a two or three minutes; then take a break for two to five minutes to look around. A buck may come charging in or he may sneak. Try to be prepared for either. Curious deer will sometimes stop on the edge of cover, so look closely.

After a pause, again go through the imitation of two bucks trying to outmuscle and outmaneuver each other. If a buck doesn't respond in twenty or thirty minutes, there probably isn't one coming. Three or four series of antler clashing, ground pounding, and tree scraping should be enough in that span of time. Try not to rattle too much.

If a buck is seen approaching but looks unsure of whether he wants to come all the way, try touching the tines together lightly. A grunt or doe bleat might be enough to convince him the fight is for real, too.

When getting up to leave a calling site, do so cautiously. Look all around carefully for a deer that may have been hidden from view until then. One may decide to step in the open at the last minute.

Try rattling at locations that are at least one half mile apart. Don't expect to attract a buck at each spot. One may show at the first stand you take, or the tenth. If you choose your calling sites carefully during the peak of the rut, your odds of collecting a buck by having him come to you are good.

When stand hunting during the rut, I often call and/or rattle once or twice per hour when deer activity is slow. This helps bring deer into view that I might not otherwise see. One November day while hunting in Saskatchewan, I rattled in the same 8-pointer three different times. Each time, he came running in expecting to join the action, only to end up confused about where the other bucks were that he thought he heard. I watched him make scrapes and rub his antlers on trees in frustration before walking off. That buck provided plenty of entertainment. I didn't shoot him because his antlers were of average size and I was looking for something much bigger.

Michigan bowhunter Bruce Heslet with the full mount of a previous state record nontypical scoring 219^6/$_8$ that he called in with a Rod Benson call.

A doe bleat from a Primos adjustable call that I have around my neck helped me get this Alabama 8-point.

Calling

I've had excellent luck on whitetails with deer calls made by Knight and Hale and Primos, but these are certainly not the only companies that make quality deer calls. I've also gotten good reports about calls made by Michigan call manufacturers Rod Benson and Fred and Greg Abbas. One fall a pair of Michigan bowhunters hunting in different counties at different times used Benson's adjustable call to lure a pair of Boone and Crockett nontypicals within bow range that they arrowed. Bruce Heslet from Edwardsburg connected on a 23-pointer scoring 219⁶/₈ in Cass County that was a state record nontypical bow kill for a number of years. Mick LaFountain from Southfield nailed a 20-pointer that measured 209⁵/₈ in Livingston County.

The Abbases make a call named the "Easy Grunter." It is designed to be pinned on your shirt or coat where it is accessible to blow into without the use of hands. This comes in handy for bowhunters who have a bow and arrow in hand when trying to call in a deer they see, or who are trying to stop one for a shot when they are at full draw; gun hunters can also find this type of call valuable when preparing for a shot.

I used to just carry a grunt tube with me when deer hunting, but I now carry an adjustable model that will make buck grunts, doe bleats, and fawn calls with modifications to the reed. Such a call can be used any time during hunting season to lure whitetails to you. Both bucks and does will respond to the calls of a fawn, and doe bleats are often better for luring bucks into view than grunts, as I found out on a January hunt in Alabama with Charles Dixon one year. After trying some buck grunts from my call without success, I switched to doe bleats and it didn't take long for a beautiful 8-pointer to appear from the brush; I dropped him with a neck shot.

My brother called in another 8-pointer in Michigan toward the end of firearms season (November 27) one year with doe bleats from "The Can." He was set up near a pair of scrapes during the morning and started imitating doe bleats about an hour after daylight. It didn't take long for the buck to approach. Interestingly, the buck blew a number of times as he responded to the call. Bruce knew he was downwind from both the scrapes and where the buck was, so he was sure the buck didn't smell him. In fact, the buck was probably snorting to try to get the doe he thought he was hearing to reveal itself. Bruce remained stationary, with his rifle at the ready, until the buck eventually walked into an opening where he had a shot.

I've had my share of success imitating buck grunts with a call, too. Bucks frequently grunt when trailing or tending a receptive doe. Another buck who hears this sound frequently comes to investigate. Grunt tubes work best on bucks that are in sight but are too far for a shot or those that disappear before a shot is possible, but grunts can also bring bucks into view that might not otherwise be seen. I was bowhunting with Bill Jordan in Georgia one foggy morning. Visibility was terrible, so I grunted every fifteen minutes to try to lure deer into view; a forkhorn eventually appeared out of the fog to investigate the source of the sound.

On another Georgia hunt with Jordan, this time during rifle season, Pennsylvania outdoor writer Nick Sisley grunted in a pair of dandy bucks in a single morning with a Knight and Hale grunt tube, and bagged both of them. There was a two-buck bag limit. Both bucks had 9-point antlers, but the rack was much bigger and wider on one of them.

Deer calls are available commercially, or hunters can make their own. Some quail and predator calls available on the market work equally well on deer. I have called in several whitetail does while using a predator call. Predator calls imitate the screams of an injured rabbit, which are similar to the sounds of a fawn in distress. Alaska's sitka blacktail deer are said to be receptive to quail calls.

The simplest deer call consists of a blade of grass. Blow on it while holding it stretched between clenched thumbs. Homemade deer calls can be made from a rubber band and a couple of pieces of wood. The pieces of wood should be about four inches long and have matching narrow openings in their centers. The elastic is held taut across the opening when the wood is fitted together. The ends can be taped or bound with strong thread or string. Native Americans get the credit for devising these two deer calls.

One of the electronic whitetail calls is made by Extreme Dimension. This device can be programmed to simulate a buck fight as well as a variety of vocalizations. The speaker for this call can be set up as much as 60 feet from the hunter. For more information call 1-866-862-2825 or go to www.phantomcalls.com. Remember that electronic calls are not legal for deer hunting everywhere.

When attempting to call deer in parts of Alaska, it's important to keep in mind that grizzly or brown bears may also respond. Due to the risk involved under these circumstances, refraining from calling could be the best choice. Dean Hulce of Vulcan, Michigan, is less inclined to use a deer call on Kodiak Island in the future, due to an experience he had there during a recent hunt.

Hulce and a partner were walking along a narrow creek bottom when they jumped a sitka blacktail that quickly bounded out of the valley. Instinctively, Dean grabbed his deer call and started blowing it. Just as quickly, a deer came over the bank in response to the call and landed at their feet. Impressed with the immediate response, Dean called a couple more times.

When he heard brush break across the creek, Dean thought another deer was coming, but this time it proved to be a brown bear intent on an easy meal. As the

Nick Sisley with a pair of dandy Georgia bucks he grunted in during the same morning with the Knight and Hale grunt tube he's holding.

bruin charged toward them, Dean alerted his partner and got the bear in his scope, preparing to shoot it if it kept coming. When the second hunter realized what was happening, he fired a shot into the ground, stopping the bear in the creek a mere 15 yards away.

"I watched this giant through my scope just waiting for him to move one inch towards us," Dean wrote in an email, "as I wasn't ready to become an Alaskan statistic. After a few seconds, that seemed like two hours, the bear turned and walked away, looking over his shoulder to try to figure out what had just happened."

An experience like that is enough to turn anyone off from using a deer call. Deer hunters in western states where grizzly bears are common who are interested in doing some calling should keep the possibility of attracting a bear in mind. When deer hunting in grizzly country, especially in Alaska, it's important to hunt with at least one partner in preparation for an attack, so you can cover each other.

Calls will work any time of the day, but are most effective early and late in the day. There is more chance of a deer hearing the calls on a quiet day. Windy conditions are poor for trying to bring in deer with a call.

The same basic considerations discussed for choosing a stand for rattling apply when situating yourself to try a call. Whitetails or mule deer drawn to the sound may come on the run or sneaking. Try blowing the call at ten- to thirty-minute intervals. The technique can be varied, however.

One of the best ways to use a call is to have it handy while stillhunting. When deer are jumped and are running, a blast from a call can stop them long enough for a shot. It may even bring an animal back that has already gone out of sight, providing the buck or doe wasn't badly spooked.

A call can be used similarly while tracking or on stand. Deer that pass by without providing a shot may be lured back into view. Those that are running may be stopped by the sound of a bleat.

As with rattling, mouth-blown calls aren't likely to produce results in areas with high densities of hunters.

Fooling A Deer's Nose

M ock scrapes are one way to fool the noses of whitetail bucks. Donald "Doug" Blanchard from Twining, Michigan, employed the tactic to bag a Boone and Crockett–caliber whitetail with bow and arrow during the fall of 2009. It took three years of effort before the technique finally paid off, but Blanchard feels the work was worth it.

The 12-pointer he shot in Washtenaw County on the morning of October 27 has a gross score of 179 and nets $174^3/_8$. Doug named the deer the Volleyball Buck because it had a volleyball net tangled in one of its antlers during 2007, the first year Doug obtained trail-camera photos of it. He obtained trail-camera photos of the whitetail each of the three years he hunted it.

Doug made a mock scrape along a creek bottom in his hunting area during September of 2007, using rutting buck scent. He set up a trail camera overlooking the scrape and that's where he got his first photos of the Volleyball Buck during mid-September.

"I hunted him hard in '07," Doug said, "but I never saw him while I was hunting. I was still getting pictures of him with the trail camera at the scrape up through Thanksgiving and into December, but all of the photos were taken after dark. His movements were primarily nocturnal, so that's why I wasn't seeing him during shooting hours."

The buck's antlers had eleven points in 2007 and the rack would probably have scored in the 130s. Doug made a mock scrape in the same location in 2008 and started getting trail camera photos of the whitetail again. The deer's antlers had twelve points that year and would have scored in the 150s. The fact that some of the trail camera images were captured during hours of daylight gave Blanchard some hope of seeing the buck that year.

Donald "Doug" Blanchard with the Boone and Crockett 12-pointer he bagged with bow and arrow after hunting it for three years at a mock scrape. PHOTO COURTESY OF DONALD BLANCHARD

The Volleyballbuck, so named because of the net tangled in his antlers, in 2007. PHOTO COURTESY OF DONALD BLANCHARD

Doug did see the buck while hunting during 2008, but only once, and at a distance of 180 yards. He watched the buck breed a doe on Halloween. While shed hunting during the spring of 2009, Doug found the buck's right antler, so he knew it had made it through another hunting season.

A trail camera photo of the Volleyball buck during the fall of 2009 before Doug got him. PHOTO COURTESY OF DONALD BLANCHARD

During September of 2009, Blanchard reopened the mock scrape in the same location where he had photographed the buck in the past and his efforts were rewarded.

"Sure enough, in mid-September he took over my scrape and made it his again," Doug said. "I was getting pictures of him every day, sometimes multiple times in one day. The one thing that was different, and gave me some great expectations of getting a shot at the deer, was that almost all the photos were taken in the daytime."

"When bow season opened, I was excited to get in the woods, but, as luck would have it, I couldn't hunt on the morning of October 1 because I had to work. I hunted that evening with no luck, but did pull the card from my trail cam and discovered the buck had been under my tree stand at 8:30 that morning.

"I hunted every day I could and never got another glimpse of him until October 27. When I found out I didn't have to work that morning, I raced to my tree stand and set up. At about 7:45 A.M. I had a nice 8-pointer come through at about five yards, but I passed him up because it was the volleyball buck or none.

"At 8:00 A.M. a big doe came to the scrape then wandered off," Blanchard continued. "At 8:30 A.M. I finally saw the buck I had been waiting three years for. He came straight in facing me and did his thing at the scrape. As he started walking away, I stood up, drew my Mathews bow and released my arrow tipped with a Rage Broadhead when he was 18 yards away.

"When I saw the arrow I hit him, I thought it was low, so I started cussing myself, but I made a better shot than I thought. The buck took off running for about 25 yards and stopped. He looked back in my direction then fell over dead.

"That's when the shaking started," Doug commented. "I sat down and tried to call some of my buddies that knew about the buck I was hunting, but my hands just wouldn't work. After about 25 minutes I was able to climb down from my climbing tree stand and walk the 45 yards to my buck."

The whitetail had a dressed weight of 225 pounds and was aged at $6^{1}/_{2}$. If the buck's antlers were in the 150s during 2008, it added at least 20 inches of antler when it grew its rack in 2009. Doug's best buck prior to that fall was an 8-pointer that scored about 125. He got it from the same location as the booner.

Other Examples

Scents have also played key roles in allowing me to bag some of the deer I've taken over the years. In each case, I was able to take advantage of the deer's sense of smell to lure it into position for a shot. Essentially, I was able to fool a deer's nose into investigating scents the animal thought originated from other deer. Here are a couple of examples:

One year while hunting whitetails in Saskatchewan with guide Mike Aftanas, I used the tarsal gland from a doe he had taken to get an 8-point buck. The rut was underway and I knew bucks would be attracted to the scent of a doe, so I removed the gland from the doe and put it in a plastic bag. The next morning, I tied a string to the gland and hung it from a sapling about 50 yards from where I was posted on the ground. There were numerous scrapes and antler rubs in the area, obvious sign that plenty of bucks were around.

The purpose of the tarsal gland was not only to lure a buck to the area, but also to distract it when it arrived. A buck that had his attention focused on the scent and location of the tarsal gland would be less likely to detect my presence. The gland worked perfectly.

Around noon I heard deer running behind me. Minutes later, a dark-antlered 8-pointer appeared to my left, with his attention directed toward the hanging gland. I slowly shouldered my .30-06 and dropped that whitetail where he was standing.

After admiring the buck and tagging him, I backtracked the deer in the fresh snow that was on the ground. I discovered that the 8-point had been chasing a doe behind me. The doe was far enough

I approach a Saskatchewan 8-point that was lured into view by the tarsal gland from a doe I had hanging 50 yards from where I was posted.

Left: I put doe in heat scent in an Ohio scrape before using a climbing stand to go up a nearby tree. Right: That scrape helped me get this 6-point.

ahead of the buck that he was following her scent rather than usng his eyes. At one point, the doe made a 90-degree turn away from me. The buck over-ran the doe's trail where she turned and he smelled the hanging tarsal gland, so he came to investigate.

Another time I was hunting whitetails with a Horton crossbow in Ohio and I used a climbing tree stand to watch a fresh scrape on an old logging road. Before climbing into position, I put a few drops of Buck Stop's Doe In Heat scent in the scrape. I eventually spotted a buck about 150 yards away that was feeding farther away. I took out a deer call and made several buck grunts.

The call turned the buck toward me, but when he got close he paralleled the lane the scrape was on, staying in saplings that were too thick for a bow shot. However, when the 6-pointer got directly downwind of the scrape, he smelled the scent I put in it and went to investigate, giving me a 20-yard shot.

Hunters now have the opportunity to take advantage of and, at the same time, overcome one of the most powerful senses of whitetail and mule deer—their sense of smell—better than ever before. There are a number of ways to take advantage of the importance of scents, or the lack of them, in order to be successful. Both natural and commercially available scents can be used to attract deer to hunters, as the above examples illustrate. Odor elimination products can also be employed to reduce the chances that deer will be able to detect hunters, thereby increasing the odds of the hunters seeing and shooting whitetails and mule deer.

Natural Scents

Let's finish the discussion about scents that can be used to fool a deer's nose and then cover odor elimination for hunters. I prefer to use natural scents that I obtain directly from deer whenever possible, but when I can't do that I use scents that are commercially available. Tarsal glands removed from deer you or members of your party shoot (both bucks and does) are excellent attractants; the fresher they are, the better. Another potential source of tarsal glands during the fall is road-killed deer.

With a knife, it only takes a few minutes to remove these obvious glands from the inside of each hind leg near the knee joint.

Cut the skin around the gland and then remove skin and gland from the leg. I always carry plastic bags to put glands in, but paper bags will work in a pinch. The glands can also be wrapped in aluminum foil or put in clean, empty jars. Once glands are removed, they should be refrigerated to prevent spoilage if the weather is warm. Tarsal glands should be put in the freezer to keep them fresh if it will be days before you will get the chance to use them.

I usually freeze one gland and use the other for hunting until it starts to get ripe. Then I discard the used gland and thaw the fresh one. Tarsal glands can be used for hunting as both cover scents and attractants at any time during hunting season, but they are often most potent and likely to produce results when taken from rutting animals for use during the rut.

Stillhunters can put tarsal glands between boot laces or attach them to a short string tied to the back of boots, so they leave a scent trail. Stand hunters can also drag glands behind them on the way to their stand to leave a scent trail. Once

I prefer to use natural scents, such as tarsal glands from bucks or does taken by myself or other hunters, whenever possible. The stained tarsal gland on the hind leg of this whitetail is clearly visible.

A tarsal gland that has been removed from a hunter-killed whitetail for use in fooling the noses of other deer. A string is attached to the gland so it can be dragged behind a hunter and then hung near a stand. Tarsal glands can also be secured between boot laces to provide cover scent and serve as an attractant.

you reach your stand site you can hang the glands in a location where you hope to get a shot.

Bucks are attracted to the scent of tarsal glands from other bucks as well as those from does. Dominant bucks are especially inquisitive about the scents of strange bucks because they like to keep tabs on local competition for does. One time a cousin of mine (Craig Smith) dragged a tarsal gland from an adult buck to his stand when hunting a spot miles from where the buck he got the gland from had been. A couple of hours later, a beautiful 10-pointer came following the scent left by the gland and Craig shot it. That deer was $6^{1}/_{2}$ years old. This trick has worked a number of times over the years for Craig and his friends, but in most cases yearling bucks are the ones most likely to fall for it.

Urine collected from deer you or members of your party shoot is another type of natural scent that can be used to your advantage while hunting. Carry a clean bottle, jar, or Ziploc plastic bag with you to put the urine in. The tricky part is to remove the bladder from a bagged deer without breaking it, so the urine can be transferred to a suitable container.

Urine from a hot doe can be like gold during the rut when placed in front of your stand. However, urine collected from bucks and does that are shot can be used to attract other deer at any time during hunting season. Simply put several drops of the liquid where you want deer to stop.

Before going any further, it's important to point out that the province of Manitoba has established regulations that prohibit the use of either natural or commercially packaged deer scents. In that province, it is currently illegal for hunters to possess products "that contain urine, feces, saliva or scent glands" of a deer, elk, or moose due to concerns about disease transmission. Ontario joined Manitoba in establishing similar regulations in 2010. In Ontario synthetic scents can still be used for deer hunting. Always check current regulations before hunting to avoid breaking laws like these. Other states and provinces could follow their example in the future.

Mock Scrapes

Buck urine (both natural and store-bought) can also be used to add authenticity to mock scrapes. Mock scrapes are manmade scrapes intended to attract bucks in the area you are hunting. Whitetail bucks always make scrapes under limbs that are usually four to six feet from the ground. They paw the ground with front hooves, exposing the soil, and then urinate in the pawed ground. They also work the overhanging branch with their mouths and/or antlers.

To make a mock scrape, pick a spot where you've seen a scrape made by a buck in the past or a spot that fits the bill. The overhanging branch is a key element. Use a stick, rake, trowel, or the side of your foot to expose the soil on a patch of ground that's about a foot across. Most of the scrapes I've seen have been rectangular in shape and they vary in size. Then use a stick or shed antler to rake the bare soil as though it had been pawed by a hoof and deposit a few drops of scent.

Whitetail bucks that encounter a mock scrape will think it was made by a competing buck and check it periodically. They may add their scent to the mock scrape or make one of their own nearby. Hunters who maintain mock scrapes and set up within shooting distance may eventually get a shot at a buck drawn to it, like Doug Blanchard did.

Matt Wheeler from Coloma, Michigan, is another bowhunter who has had success using mock scrapes. He uses Moultree drippers over the mock scrapes, filling the drippers with dominant buck urine he gets from a trapper supply house. Around the first of November, he replaces the buck urine with scent of a doe in heat.

Commercial Scents

Most commercially available scents are in liquid form, but some are powders, gels, or foam. Freeze-dried tarsal glands have even been marketed by some companies. James Valley Scents in South Dakota (800-337-5873) makes top-of-the-line gels and also has liquid scents available. I've also heard good reports about "Buck Fever" synthetic liquid scents. Besides products made by these companies, I've had excellent results with scents made by Buck Stop, Wellington Outdoors (Tink's 69), and Mrs. Doe Pee.

Save the sex scents such as those labeled as buck in rut or doe in heat for use during the rut. The rut is generally from late October through November across the northern half of North America and parts of the south. In most of the southern U. S. and into Mexico, rutting activity is concentrated during December and January.

Apply sex scents to scrapes or to branches hanging over scrapes. The best buck I've collected with bow and arrow, a 120-class 8-point, was taken with the help of Mrs. Doe Pee Scent in Manitoba on November 6 one year. My guide put some of the scent in a large scrape within easy bow range of the tree stand I would be hunting from before I climbed into position.

When the buck arrived, he stood up on his hind legs three different times to work the branches above the scrape with his antlers. I waited until the whitetail stepped

Left: A Manitoba guide places a scent cannister containing Mrs. Doe Pee scent above a scrape. Note the tree stand in the background that I climbed into after taking this photo. Right: I arrowed this 8-pointer from the tree stand after he stood on his hind legs three times to work the branches where the scent was with his antlers. This is the best buck I've taken with bow and arrow.

away from the scrape and put an arrow through his lungs at 10 yards. Two days earlier a bigger 8-point had been arrowed by Mel Davis of Escanaba, Michigan, at the same scrape. That buck had his nose in a scent cannister, in fact, when the arrow hit him.

Leaving A Scent Trail

Sex scents can also be applied to drag rags or to boots to leave scent trails. Old socks work great as scent drags as well as for holding scent on boots. To use a sock to leave a scent trail, put a rock or two inside the sock, tie a rope around the top of the sock to drag it with, and then apply scent (no more than ten to fifteen drops) to the toe of the sock. Stop every 50 to 100 yards to reapply scent to the sock.

When approaching a stand site, leave the scent trail where you will want a buck to be for a shot. Don't take the scent drag directly to your stand. Either leave it on the ground or hang it from a tree where you will want to take your shot. Once you

Mel Davis from Escanaba, Michigan, with a bigger 8-pointer he arrowed from the same stand two days earlier. The buck had his nose in a scent cannister when Mel shot him.

reach the vicinity of your stand, it can be effective to leave scent trails in two or three different directions for 100 yards or so to increase the odds a buck might encounter the scent and follow it to you.

When using socks to hold scent on your boots, cut approximately the lower one-third of socks off and stretch them over the toes of your boots. Then scent can be applied to the sock. It's only necessary to put a sock on one boot, but some hunters put one on each boot. If you are stand hunting, hang the socks where you want a buck to stop for a shot.

Rags can be used in place of socks to leave scent trails. If you use a rag, fold it around a rock or two for weight and then tie a rope around the folded rag to keep the rocks inside. David Walther of AuTrain, Michigan, used a drag rag to leave a scent trail to his deer stand one afternoon, using doe in heat scent, and the effort was responsible for him getting the best buck of his life. The $8^{1}/_{2}$-year-old whitetail that followed the scent into Walther's rifle sights had a 19-point nontypical rack with three drop tines that netted $191^{2}/_{8}$. A fourth drop tine had been broken off.

Stillhunters can also leave scent trails to get bucks to follow them. If they do, they should check their back trail on a regular basis.

The Buck Stop Scent Company (800-477-2368) makes granulated scents called Buck Beads in addition to their traditional line of liquid scents. The beads are designed to release scent over a period of time in response to varying weather conditions. A line of sex scent Buck Beads can be used to leave scent trails to stand sites, too.

In addition to the sex scents, other deer scents (glandular or musk) and packaged urine can be used during pre- and post-rut periods that coincide with hunting sea-

This 8$^1/_2$-year-old buck with a huge nontypical rack was attracted to David Walther's stand by a scent trail he left with a drag rag. The 19-pointer netted 191$^2/_8$.

sons. Non-sex deer scents can be used both as a cover scent to mask human odor and an attractant. They can be applied to boots or used to leave scent trails. Whitetails and mule deer are curious about the presence of what they think is a strange deer in their area and will often investigate.

Cover Scents

A variety of cover scents and food scents are also available commercially. Common types of cover scents include fox, coyote, skunk, and raccoon urine as well as earth and evergreen aromas.

The purpose of cover scents is to reduce the chances of alarming any deer that may cross the path you took to your stand. Deer that smell human scent may change directions, run off, or blow to warn other deer of danger. If they smell what they think is the aroma of another animal that they often encounter such as a fox or raccoon, they are less likely to react.

Many deer hunters ruin good stand sites by hunting them day after day and approaching them the same way each time without using cover scents. As deer constantly encounter human scent, their use of the area usually decreases and corresponding deer sightings go down. The proper use of cover scents will reduce that problem. Varying cover scents and your approach to your stand can help, too. I also recommend having a number of stands, so you don't hunt the same spot more than two or three days in a row.

Food Scents

Some of the more popular food scents include acorn, apple, and corn. The purpose of food scents is to lure deer into view long enough for a shot. In areas where baiting is legal, deer may encounter corn or apples anywhere, so they are likely to investigate these scents. Carrying a small container of scent is certainly easier and cheaper than toting a quantity of food, especially if hunting a remote spot. Where baiting isn't legal, food scents will provide the best results in areas where the foods you are

Weapons

Crossbows are enjoying a surge of popularity for deer hunting across the United States during recent years as more states allow their use during archery seasons. For many years, Ohio was the only state that permitted the use of crossbows (horizontal bows) for deer hunting during the same seasons as vertical bows (compounds, recurves, and longbows). In most other states, crossbow use for deer hunting during archery seasons was limited to hunters who were handicapped to the point that they could no longer draw a vertical bow.

A general decline in the number of deer hunters, including those going afield with vertical bows, and an increase in deer numbers are partly responsible for the legalization of crossbows during archery seasons in the states where this has happened. Adding a new tool such as the crossbow to archery seasons is viewed as a means of increasing hunter numbers, and increasing opportunities for properly managing deer numbers and for recreation at the same time. Crossbows make it possible for some older hunters who are no longer comfortable hunting with vertical bows, even though they don't fit the official definition of being handicapped, to continue hunting. Crossbows are also easier than vertical bows for young hunters and women to master as well as for hunters who have only hunted with firearms previously.

While crossbows are viewed as a new deer management tool in the states where they have been legalized during archery seasons, information from Ohio confirms that hunters who are using them won't be more efficient at taking deer than hunters using vertical bows. Consequently, there are no concerns among wildlife biologists about crossbow use resulting in the harvest of too many deer. Crossbows are simply not as effective as some critics who are unfamiliar with them have claimed.

The states that now allow hunting with crossbows during archery deer seasons are Alabama, Arkansas, Georgia, Louisiana, Michigan, New Jersey, Ohio, Pennsylvania, South Carolina, Tennessee, Texas, Virginia, and Wyoming. A number of other

Deer hunting with crossbows is undergoing a surge in popularity as they are being legalized for general use during archery seasons in a number of states.

states allow general crossbow use during archery deer seasons for hunters who exceed a certain age. In Oklahoma, for instance, anyone who is at least sixty years old and all hunters who are handicapped can use crossbows during archery deer season. The minimum age is sixty-two in Illinois and sixty-five in Maryland and Wisconsin. In Maryland, any legal hunter can hunt deer with a crossbow during four weeks of archery season, but those who are at least sixty-five or handicapped can hunt during the entire archery season with crossbows.

Part of archery season in Kentucky is also open to general use of crossbows. Indiana currently allows all hunters to use crossbows during their late archery season, but only handicapped hunters can do so during the early season. Deer hunting with crossbows is also legal during archery seasons in the Canadian provinces of Ontario, British Columbia, and Prince Edward Island.

Be sure to check current local regulations for specific requirements and any changes. In Texas, for example, only one county does not allow deer hunting with crossbows during archery seasons. And in Michigan, for instance, crossbows are currently not legal for use during the late archery season in the Upper Peninsula only. Most states and provinces allow crossbow hunting for handicapped hunters, with a permit. Deer hunting with crossbows is bound to be liberalized in more states and provinces in the future as information generated by states that recently legalized them during archery seasons shows that these tools have a positive impact.

Many Good Choices

There is no one best rifle, shotgun, handgun, bow and arrow, or crossbow for deer hunting. There are a number of bests in each category. Carrying it one step further, there is no one best type of weaponry for deer hunting. Rifles, both modern and muzzleloaders, shotguns, handguns, vertical bows and arrows, and crossbows all have their advantages and advocates.

There are, however, some in each category that are better for some or all forms of deer hunting than others due to trajectory, recoil, weight, and killing power. For these reasons, and others, some in each class are more suited for deer hunting than others. Those are the ones we will be discussing.

One of the major reasons for the diversity of "bests" for deer hunting is that both mule deer and whitetails are easy to kill. More important than a firearm's or bow's power, within limits, is the hunter's ability to place his or her shot accurately in a vital area. A firearm or bow is often chosen to meet the individual hunter's personal needs or desires rather than for its ability to kill a deer, since many weapons can do this.

Another consideration in the line of best weapons for deer hunting is the varying types of terrain in which both mulies and whitetails are found. Firearms that are tops for deer in thick cover may be poor in open terrain, and vice versa. There are some that perform equally well under a variety of circumstances, however.

Obtaining a weapon adequate for deer hunting is probably the easiest part of the pursuit. The skills to use it properly and to be consistently in a position to shoot at deer with it are much more difficult to acquire.

Centerfire Rifles

There are a number of centerfire rifle calibers that will perform adequately for all deer hunting. They include the .243, 6 mm, .25-06, .270, .280, 7mm-08, .300 Savage, .300 magnum, 7 mm magnum, .30-06, and .308. Of those, the .270, .280, .30-06, and .308 have to be rated the best of the lot.

My personal preference in caliber for a deer rifle is the .30-06. I bought my first one because my father had one and swore by it. Actually, that was only part of the reason. Dad said a rifle in that caliber would be satisfactory for hunting any big game in North America. What I read about the ought-six bore him out, so I was convinced. The hunting I have done with that first .30-06 and the others that followed has fortified my opinion of the caliber.

A .270 is just as good as a .30-06 for deer hunting. Some, usually hunters who own them, say it is better. The additional calibers mentioned don't rank far down the list from either of these two.

Some deer hunters may scoff at the thought of light calibers such as the .243 for all-around deer rifles. I once shared the opinion, but have since altered my

Jim Haveman used a .270-caliber rifle to take this Wyoming mule deer. This is an excellent caliber for deer hunting anywhere in North America. So are the .30-06, .308, and .280.

Melissa Sterling takes aim with a youth model .243 from a blind. The .243 is also an excellent all-around deer hunting caliber. Due to its light recoil, this caliber is well suited for use by youngsters and women.

position after seeing several in action on whitetails and mule deer. Their biggest advantage is light recoil, which often results in better accuracy, when compared with calibers that pack a more noticeable wallop. The .243, for instance, is a good choice for any deer hunter, but especially for women and youngsters.

Deer hunters shouldn't worry about the old myth that light, fast bullets are useless in brush. Such a bullet won't plow through twigs and branches that are in its way and drill a deer right where the shooter was aiming—but neither will a bullet from a rifle in any of the bigger calibers mentioned. The simple fact of the matter is that no bullet designed for deer hunting has the capability of busting through brush. Wait for an open shot and a .243 will kill a whitetail or mulie as dead as a .30-06 if the bullet is placed where it should be.

What about the .30-30, .35, and .44 for deer? They are all right for hunting in areas where shots are likely to be from 50 to 100 yards maximum. Their trajectories are poor at ranges beyond that.

There are other characteristics and features of a deer rifle that are more important than caliber. Chief among these are length, weight, action, and sights. The type of terrain deer are hunted in and the most often used method of hunting them will dictate which features a hunter should consider when buying a rifle.

A stillhunter or tracker, for instance, who treads in cover where shots are less than 100 yards will want a rifle that is short, light, and fast-aiming and -shooting. One that weighs between six and seven pounds or less and has an $18^{1}/_{2}$-inch or 20-inch barrel and iron sights would be good. A peep sight is great for quick aiming.

The heavy-barreled bolt-action rifle that Joe Drake used to collect this trophy Texas whitetail is well suited for stand hunting out to long ranges.

Some who like a scope and don't mind the extra weight might want a fixed-power model or a low-power variable. The action could be lever, pump, or semiautomatic.

The deer hunter who spends a lot of time on stands or hunts country where shots average from 100 to 300 yards will want a rifle that is as accurate as possible. Weight isn't as critical here, so a rifle that weighs more than seven pounds and has a 22-inch or 24-inch barrel is okay. A telescopic sight is a must. Any type of action would do, but bolt actions are a good choice.

AR Rifles

"In recent years, AR-type rifles have become among the most popular sporting rifles sold in the United States," according to the National Shooting Sports Foundation. AR stands for Armalite, the company that developed this style rifle in the 1950s. Those letters do not stand for "assault rifle" or "automatic rifle."

These rifles come in one of the most popular deer hunting calibers (.308) and all have semi-auto actions. Many of them also come with camouflage finishes that are well suited for hunting. Modern AR-15s are modeled after and look like the M-16 service rifle that first saw combat in Vietnam.

Just like with all semi-auto guns, the trigger has to be pulled for every shot that's taken with AR style rifles. They are not automatics and they are not assault rifles, as members of the anti-gun crowd like to refer to them as. So don't be surprised if you see deer hunters carrying AR rifles. You may even want to try one out yourself.

Slings

An accessory deer hunters should seriously consider regardless of the type of gun they have or their preferred hunting method is a sling. The straps are helpful in steadying aim and for carrying a rifle over the shoulder while climbing or dragging a deer. Slings can also be used to hang a firearm on a convenient limb during a break rather than laying it on the ground. Two sources for slings are Gun Slings Direct (www.gunslingsdirect.com) and Butler Creek (www.butler-creek.com).

Bullets

Many deer hunters tend to use bullets heavier than are necessary. This is especially true in "brush country." Some hunters who frequent such cover in their search for deer incorrectly believe that the heavier the bullet they use, the greater their chances of hitting a deer on the opposite side of a thicket will be. Any bullet from a deer rifle that hits a branch or some other obstruction in its path will expand and deflect. Unless a deer is directly behind the obstruction that is hit, the slug is more likely to wound or miss the animal than kill it. Shots intentionally taken through branches with the hopes of hitting deer are unsportsmanlike as well as a waste of ammunition. If an opening large enough to get a bullet through does not exist, hunters shouldn't shoot.

Bullets over 150 grains are unnecessary for deer hunting, unless there's no other choice for the caliber you are using. Those weighing 180 or 220 grains often do not expand properly. There have been a lot of deer bagged with 180-grain bullets and larger—I have collected some myself. In many cases the projectile goes completely through the animal, inflicting less damage than a lighter bullet would. A second shot is sometimes required to finish whitetails and mulies hit with heavy bullets. The amount of shocking power a slug delivers determines its effectiveness. A bullet that opens up and expends all of its energy inside a deer gives optimum performance. When a bullet passes through a deer, some of its shocking power is lost.

Deer hunters who use .35s or .44s don't have any choice in bullet weight unless they handload. They are stuck with 200-grain and 240-grain bullets, respectively, in factory loads.

For the .243 and 6 mm, 100-grain bullets are tops. A 120-grain slug is good for the .25-06; 130 or 150 grains for the .270; 140 grains for the .280; and 150-grain slugs for the .30-30, .300, .30-06, and .308.

Generally, soft-point bullets are the best for deer hunting. Pointed soft-points are better than round-nose bullets when shooting at moderate to long ranges. Pointed bullets have less wind resistance and drop less than blunt slugs. Round-nosed bullets are best for use in rifles with tubular magazines, though.

Try not to carry cartridges, not many anyway, in pockets where they will clank together. Shell holders that fit on the belt are good for carrying rifle shells. Elastic shell holders that are designed to fit around the butts of rifles and shotguns are also available. What I do is have from two to four extra shells handy, one in each pants or coat pocket. The rest of my ammunition stays in a backpack I always carry when hunting.

Lead Controversy

Most of the commonly used centerfire rifle bullets and some shotgun slugs for deer hunting contain lead. Due to concerns about lead fragments from them allegedly remaining in the gut piles of mule and blacktail deer that are taken by hunters in California, threatening the health of condors (an endangered species), lead bullets and slugs have been banned for deer hunting in areas of California where condors live. Hunters in that state have been forced to use bullets and slugs made with other materials such as copper even though there is controversy about the validity of claims that lead fragments from hunters' bullets threaten the large scavenging birds.

More recently, efforts have begun to ban lead bullets and slugs for deer hunting on a wider scale due to alleged concern that lead fragments from them in gut piles endanger another scavenging bird—the bald eagle. It's interesting to note that bald eagles have increased enough during recent years to be removed from the threatened species list and lead bullets and slugs are used for deer hunting throughout the eagle's range. It seems counterintuitive to now claim fragments from lead bullets in gut piles from deer kills are a cause for concern after the birds have increased to the point that they are no longer considered a threatened species. In most deer country, land-based scavengers such as coyotes are far more abundant than eagles and consume most gut piles before eagles have a chance to find them.

Lead fragments in venison secured with lead-based bullets and slugs also raised health concerns for humans eating the meat. Food pantries in some states discarded venison donated by hunters to feed needy families as a result of those concerns. A study conducted by the Centers For Disease Control has since shown that lead levels in the blood of hunters who routinely consume venison secured with lead based bullets are usually lower than the levels of lead in the blood of nonhunters who don't eat venison. Even though lead has been detected in the blood of many people, those levels are low enough that they are not considered a threat; more importantly, any lead contamination in meat secured by lead bullets is so low that lead from other sources in the environment is more of a problem.

As someone who has eaten venison secured with lead based bullets for almost fifty years without any negative effects, I'm not surprised by those results. I've always discarded bloodshot meat from wound channels that may be contaminated with lead fragments as a standard practice and all hunters should do the same. Any human health risk associated with eating venison secured with lead bullets or slugs can be controlled and even eliminated in the butchering process. If someone else butchers your deer for you, remove any questionable meat from edible portions when packaging it for the freezer. In cases where the meat is already packaged, do any trimming that may be required before cooking each meal.

Muzzleloaders

Choosing a muzzleloading rifle for deer hunting is a different matter than selecting a centerfire gun. The best choices are modern inline models like those made by Knight, Thompson/Center, and Ultimate Firearms, among others, or the more tradi-

Tony Knight developed the inline muzzleloader design that is so popular today. He took the trophy Nebraska whitetail in this photograph with one of his rifles in .50 caliber on a drive.

I shot my best nontypical whitetail with a .50-caliber Knight muzzleloader in Saskatchewan. The 12-pointer had a 9-inch drop tine and a gross score of $174^4/_8$.

tional side-hammer, percussion cap style. I've had good luck with both types, but the inlines have the best performance by far. Inline muzzleloaders are more dependable, accurate, and safe—and they are also easier to clean and maintain.

One of the things that sets modern muzzleloaders apart from front-loaders with the more traditional appearance is they are designed to shoot modern rifle or pistol bullets with sabots (pronounced "say-bows"), a type of plastic patch, in addition to traditional black-powder projectiles. Saboted bullets improve accuracy and also result in cleaner kills.

Muzzleloaders like these made by Ultimate Firearms are capable of handling 300-grain powder charges and taking deer out to 300 yards. I normally load mine with 200 grains of powder.

Powerbelt bullets designed for use in muzzleloaders are an alternative to saboted bullets. Powerbelts have a gas seal on the base of each bullet that takes the place of sabots. Try both Powerbelts and saboted bullets in your rifle to find out which performs the best.

Each muzzleloader manufacturer recommends the types of sabots and bullets that perform best out of their rifles. In some cases, different sabots are used with the same bullet in the same rifles as powder charges vary. It's a good idea to follow those recommendations.

Tony Knight from Missouri came up with the original inline design for muzzleloaders and I've been fortunate enough to hunt with him on a number of occasions. Most companies who make muzzleloaders have followed Tony's lead and now make inline rifles for hunting. I've hunted whitetails with Knight rifles for many years and have never had any trouble with them, whether the weather was wet or dry.

I shot my best nontypical whitetail, a 12-pointer with a 9-inch drop tine, in Saskatchewan with a .50-caliber Knight muzzleloader at a distance of about 100 yards. The antlers on that buck grossed 174^4/8 and netted 165 under the Boone and Crockett scoring system. I was hunting with Proudfoot Creek Outfitters at the time. And I've shot plenty of other deer, both bucks and does, with Knight rifles, too.

More recently I've had the pleasure of hunting with muzzleloaders made by Ultimate Firearms and have had tremendous success with them. Bolt-action centerfire rifle barrels converted to muzzleloaders on which the ignition source is primed magnum handgun bullet casings, these rifles are capable of handling 200- and 300-grain powder charges and consistently taking deer at distances of 300 yards or more. Since I seldom hunt deer where long-range shots are possible, I routinely load my Ultimate Firearms Muzzleloader with 200 grains of powder and have taken a number of whitetails with it out to 100 yards.

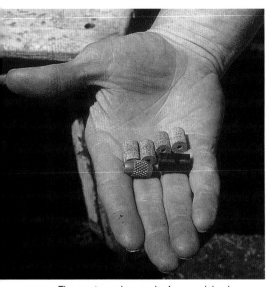

The most popular powder for muzzleloaders comes in the form of pellets that are 50 grains each, which makes it quicker and easier to load them. This is what I load my .50 muzzleloader made by Ultimate Firearms with: four Pyrdoex pellets and a saboted 300-grain lead bullet.

The most popular muzzleloader caliber for deer hunting is .50, followed by .54, but the newer .45s are catching on in popularity because they are designed for heavier loads (up to 150 grains of powder) than the norm among most muzzleloaders and are generally accurate for greater distances than traditional .50s—a major advantage in open whitetail and mule deer country. The newest inline muzzleloaders, except for those made by Ultimate Firearms, are designed for use with shotgun primers as the primary ingition source rather than percussion caps.

To make it easier for hunters to quickly load black-powder rifles with the proper charge, a number of powders used in muzzleloaders are produced in pellet form. Most pellets are 50 grains, so hunters only need to drop two pellets down the barrel for a 100-grain charge, three for 150, and four for 200. Powder pellets are also available in 30-grain sizes. However, some hunters continue to use bulk powder to measure individual charges as they have for years. Not only is it the personal preference of some hunters, claims have been made that bulk powder produces better results than the pellets. If you use bulk black powder in your muzzleloader for deer hunting, the best granulation to use is double FG (FFG).

Most deer hunters who carry muzzleloaders afield use one of two black powder substitutes that burn cleaner than black powder, leaving less residue in barrels. They are Pyrodex and Triple 7. I've had excellent results with Pyrodex, but it's a good idea to test-fire rounds with both powders on the range to see which performs best for you.

Muzzleloaders can be obtained with either single or double triggers. On models with two triggers and one barrel, only the front trigger releases the hammer. The rear one is called a set trigger. When it is pulled back it reduces the amount of finger pressure required on the front trigger to fire the rifle. Double-barreled muzzleloaders commonly have a trigger for each barrel.

Besides saboted modern and Powerbelt bullets, there are two basic types of projectiles used in muzzleloaders for hunting: bullet-shaped maxi-balls or bullets, and round balls. Thompson/Center makes a flat-based maxi-ball and hollow-point maxi-Hunter. Hornady manufactures Great Plains maxi-bullets with concave bases. Great Plains bullets are prelubricated and come in both hollow-point and solid-point versions. Maxi-balls and maxi-Hunters can be obtained prelubricated as well as unlubricated.

Round balls must be used with a patch. The conventional cloth patch must be lubricated. Cloth patches can be purchased dry or prelubricated. Some musket shooters use Crisco or Vaseline on their patches, but these preparations aren't recommended in cold weather.

The proper patch thickness to use with round balls is critical. A certain amount of pressure is required to start a properly patched ball down the barrel to ensure a tight fit. If so much pressure is necessary that the lead ball is deformed, the patch is too thick. If the ball slips in easily, it is too thin. Most sporting goods dealers who handle muzzleloaders can recommend the proper size of patch. There may be some variation from rifle to rifle, however, so if one thickness doesn't work right for you, try a different one.

No patch is required with maxi-balls or bullets. Lubricant is applied directly to the bullet, unless it is prelubricated. Whether you are applying lubricant to a maxi-ball or bullet or using one that is prelubricated, the maxi-ball or bullet is seated on top of the powder charge.

Powder Charges

A handy rule of thumb for determining a powder charge for muzzleloader hunting is to multiply your rifle caliber by two. With a .50 caliber, for instance, 100 grains of powder would be adequate. I've shot plenty of whitetails with that load out of both Knight and Thompson/Center .50-caliber front-loaders with excellent results. Powder charges of 110 grains would be about right for .54-caliber muzzleloaders.

The newer .45-caliber inlines are an exception to the powder charge rule. The Knight .45 Super Disc I hunted with for a number of years, for example, is designed to handle 150 grain loads of black powder or Pyrodex for maximum velocity and distance. However, 90-grain loads would probably work fine at distances out to 100 yards As mentioned earlier, I currently hunt with 200-grain loads of Pyrodex out of my .50-caliber muzzleloader made by Ultimate Firearms. These are the only muzzleloaders that I know of designed to handle those types of powder charges. Most muzzleloaders are not designed to handle that much powder, so do not overload them. Follow manufacturer recommendations for powder charges to avoid potentially dangerous situations.

Although inline and side-hammer muzzleloaders are the most popular for deer hunting, a third, more primitive, design called the flintlock is also used by some hunters. In fact, Pennsylvania's late season black powder deer hunt (usually from late December into January) has been limited to hunters using flintlocks since 1974. Flintlocks are only made for use with black powder. A fine granulation of black powder (FFFG) is poured into what's called the pan, located next to the hammer. The hammer strikes a piece of flint, causing a spark that ignites powder in the pan, which in turn fires the rifle. There is usually a split second delay from the time the hammer falls on a flintlock until the rifle discharges, so it's important for hunters using flintlocks to keep their sights on target longer than would be necessary for other types of muzzleloaders.

Pennsylvania also has an early muzzleloader deer season in October that was established more recently, during which both percussion cap and flintlock muzzleloaders can be used.

Saboted bullets like the one shown here that is about to be pushed down the barrel of a muzzle-loader perform best out of inline front-loaders.

Loading

Loading a muzzleloader is easy. Rest the rifle on the floor or ground with the barrel pointed upward. When using powder pellets, simply slide the desired number down the barrel. Since powder pellets are made for different calibers, be sure to use those that match the caliber of the rifle you are shooting. If using bulk powder, measure the desired amount and pour it down the barrel. Strike the barrel several times with the heel of your hand to settle the powder in the chamber.

The projectile is next: either a saboted or Powerbelt bullet, patch and ball, or a lubricated maxi. If using a cloth patch, try to be sure it is centered on the barrel and the grain of the cloth is facing the same way at each loading. Most round balls have a sprue mark, a spot of upraised lead, which should also be centered and face up.

A starter is recommended to get a ball or bullet into the bore. The bases of maxi-balls can usually be started in the muzzle with finger pressure. A starter can then be used to push the bullet a short distance down the barrel. Some hunters use the palms of their hands to start saboted bullets down the barrel. Once the ball or bullet is started down the barrel, a ramrod can be used to seat it firmly, without pounding, against the powder charge. If using pellets, stop applying pressure as soon as the saboted bullet makes contact with the powder charge. Too much pressure may break the pellets, which could result in a hang fire (delayed ignition).

Experiment with different loads to find out which one produces the most consistent results out of your rifle.

Once a satisfactory hunting load has been determined, it is a good idea to mark the ramrod at the muzzle while it is resting on a seated ball or bullet; the mark will serve as a guideline for future loads to make sure all rounds are seated at the same depth. A piece of tape or a felt-tipped pen can be used to make the mark. A mark can also be scratched in with a knife blade.

Safety Features

With muzzleloaders, as with any gun, it's important to keep safety in mind. Never use smokeless powder in a muzzleloading rifle or shoot one unless the projectile is seated against the powder. A muzzleloader can't be fired until a cap or primer is placed on the nipple or in front of the breech plug. Most states and provinces consider muzzleloaders unloaded until an ignition source is in place.

The safety features on modern muzzleloaders make it possible to have the hammer cocked and a cap or primer in place while walking or sitting. These front-loaders have regular safeties like modern guns. When the safety is engaged, it's impossible to fire the rifle.

Knight rifles have a second safety on the hammers. It's a metal sleeve that can be screwed forward and backward. When in the forward position, covering a band of red paint on the hammer, this fitting will prevent the hammer from striking any cap or primer that may be in place. It's impossible to fire the rifle until the sleeve is screwed backward, exposing the red paint on the hammer. When I'm ready to hunt, I always make sure this second safety is unengaged. Then, when a shot is offered, I only have to take off the regular safety to shoot. Some hunters who haven't followed this procedure have failed to get shots at deer because they didn't recognize why the rifle wouldn't fire until it was too late.

The hammer is the safety on most traditional side hammer rifles. The safest way to carry percussion-cap replicas while stillhunting is to have a cap on the nipple with the hammer uncocked. To put the cap on the nipple, you will have to cock the hammer, but then hold the hammer with your thumb while pulling the trigger to release the hammer, then lower it slowly. Practice lowering the hammer with your thumb without a cap or primer in place to get the hang of it. Always be sure the muzzle is pointed in a safe direction when slowly lowering the hammer on a cap in case something goes wrong.

When you see a deer you want to shoot, cock the hammer to prepare for the shot. If the opportunity for a shot does not materialize, carefully lower the hammer again until another chance presents itself. When you are done hunting for the day, don't forget to remove the cap or primer from the nipple before the rifle is cased or put away.

While hunting from a tree stand or ground blind with a replica muzzleloader, I keep the hammer cocked, but without a cap on the nipple. When a chance for a shot develops, I put a cap on the nipple. I prefer this procedure because it's safe as well as quiet. The hammer frequently makes one or more clicks when it is cocked and that noise can alert, if not spook, a deer that's close.

If a cap fits loosely on the nipple of your rifle, squeeze it to tighten the fit after it is on the nipple. Loose caps can fall off at the most inopportune moments. A tool called a decapper can come in handy to remove tight-fitting caps that are tough to remove with fingers. A knife blade can be used as a substitute decapper.

Unfired powder and balls or bullets can't be removed from side hammer and flintlock muzzleloaders at the end of the day as conveniently as a modern cartridge. Actually, they don't have to be. In most cases, a muzzleloader is considered unloaded when the cap or primer is removed. I have carried my muzzleloader with the same load in it for weeks without misfires. The rifle is always put in a case when I'm not in the woods and kept inside a cabin, tent, house, or vehicle overnight. Some muzzleloader hunters prefer to leave their rifles outside when the weather is cold so the rifles don't sweat from the change in temperature when brought inside, and that's fine.

Replica side-hammer muzzleloaders like the one being aimed by this hunter at sunset are popular among black powder hunters and are accurate.

Tony LaPratt of Coldwater, Michigan, learned the importance of preventing condensation on muzzleloaders the hard way. He had been hunting a buck with a huge nontypical rack of Boone and Crockett proportions for two years and he finally got a shot at it during December of the second year. The world-class buck followed a doe into a clearing 100 yards from where Tony was posted on a hill with an excellent view and a solid rest for his black powder rifle. He was confident the deer was his, but when he squeezed the trigger, the cap fired, but the powder didn't ignite. The whitetail looked toward the sound briefly, then ran into screening cover, never to be seen again.

LaPratt said the 100 grains of black powder he loaded the rifle with had gotten wet from condensation. He had been bringing the uncased rifle inside his house, where the temperature was much warmer than it had been outside, at the end of each day's hunt. He noticed the moisture that developed on the outside of the barrel from sweating and wiped it off, but didn't realize the same thing was happening inside the firing chamber . . . until after his chance at the big buck was gone.

One of the benefits of inline muzzleloaders is they can be unloaded fairly easily without firing them. Once the hammer, trigger mechanism, and breech plug are removed, the load can be pushed out with a ramrod. That's usually what I do at the end of a hunt when I will be traveling home by airplane.

A muzzleloader that needs cleaning or can't be stored safely between hunts should be discharged at the end of the hunting day, if possible. Be sure to shoot a muzzleloader at the end of the season. With the passage of time it can be difficult to remember whether a load was left in the gun and an accident could result. If in doubt whether a muzzleloader is loaded, use your ramrod—which should be marked—to check. Don't fire a cap to test it, unless you do so on the range.

Shotguns

Shotguns are also popular for deer hunting. In fact, in parts of North America, deer hunters are limited to either using shotguns or muzzleloaders and many choose to use shotguns. Even where rifles are legal for deer hunting, many young hunters own a shotgun for small game hunting before they obtain a centerfire rifle and that shotgun may serve them well during their first years of deer hunting. That was the case when I started deer hunting. I used the same Marlin 12-gauge pump with a modified choke barrel that I had taken many a grouse, rabbit, and squirrel with to shoot my first whitetails.

Twelve-gauge scatterguns are, by far, the most popular and effective shotguns for deer hunting. The 3- and $3^{1}/_{2}$-inch loads in 12-gauge guns offer hunters more killing power than was available from $2^{3}/_{4}$-inch shells. However, it's not necessary to use maximum shotgun loads to collect deer. Plenty of whitetails are shot every year with $2^{3}/_{4}$-inch shells containing slugs in 12-, 16- and 20-gauge loads. There are even some hunters who go afield after deer with 10-gauge guns.

Orrin Nothelfer from Freeland, Michigan is a fan of 10-gauge shotguns. He said most of the whitetails he shoots with slugs from his big gun go down for the count with one shot. However, a world-class whitetail he shot on November 29 one year required a pair of slugs from his 10-gauge to anchor it. The 11-pointer's huge rack had a net Boone and Crockett score of 174. The buck was following a doe when he shot it.

If you hunt deer with a 20-gauge, 3-inch loads are recommended to increase your odds of getting a clean kill. Although slugs are available for .410 shotguns and some deer have been taken with them, they are a poor choice for deer hunting. In fact, .410 shotguns are illegal for deer hunting in some states and provinces.

Rifled Versus Smoothbore Barrels

Rifled shotgun barrels provide the best performance for deer hunting. Saboted slugs are designed for use out of these barrels. Rifled slugs are the choice for use out of smoothbore shotgun barrels.

Mike Burger from Ann Arbor, Michigan, switched from a smoothbore barrel for his Remington 870 12-gauge to a rifled barrel for deer hunting just in time to collect a book buck with his shotgun. He sighted in the new, more accurate barrel a day or two before opening day of firearms season that year after mounting a 2X-7X Leupold scope on the gun. Mike selected Remington copper sabot slugs to hunt with.

"Those copper solids are expensive, but they're worth it," Burger said. "They're real accurate. I put five shots in a 3-inch circle at 75 yards."

On the fourth day of the season, Mike was posted during the evening when he heard a shot nearby. Instinctively, he looked in that direction when he heard the gun

The switch from a smoothbore to a rifled shotgun barrel may have been responsible for Mike Burger connecting on this book buck. He felt the rifled barrel gave him better accuracy. The 11-pointer's antlers measured 174⁷/₈.

go off. About a minute later, he saw a whitetail approaching through the woods from where the shot had been. Sunlight reflected from antlers on the deer's head, so he knew it was a buck.

Mike said the whitetail wasn't running, but it was moving at a brisk pace. He thought the deer was headed for a ravine in front of him at first, but it stayed on the far side and headed north. The buck was about 100 yards from Burger.

"At the time, I knew it was the biggest buck I ever shot at," Mike said, "but I had no idea how big he really was."

The hunter had his scope set on two power to increase his field of view.

"I picked openings in the brush that the buck was headed for and put the crosshairs on them. When he reached the opening, I was ready to shoot. When the crosshairs were on his shoulder, I touched it off.

"I shot twice. I didn't notice any reaction on the first shot. After the second shot, I didn't see or hear anything.

"We later found out both of my shots hit the buck. The first one hit the heart and the second one broke his back. When I reached the fallen buck and saw how big he was, I think I said, 'Oh my God!'"

If Mike had been using a smoothbore barrel instead of the new one with rifling, he probably would not have gotten the buck. As it was, he did well to connect with both of his shots.

"I don't think I would have had a prayer of getting that buck with a smoothbore," Mike commented. "I never had the kind of accuracy with my smoothbore barrel and rifled slugs as I did with the rifled barrel and sabots."

Burger's trophy Washtenaw County whitetail was an 11-pointer that had a net Boone and Crockett score of 174⁷/₈.

A shotgun for deer hunting should be as light as possible, within the gauge limitation. The action should be fast—either pump or semiautomatic—and doubles are all right as long as they are accurate. Many states require that shotguns for deer hunting be plugged to limit their shell capacity to three. Buckshot patterns best out

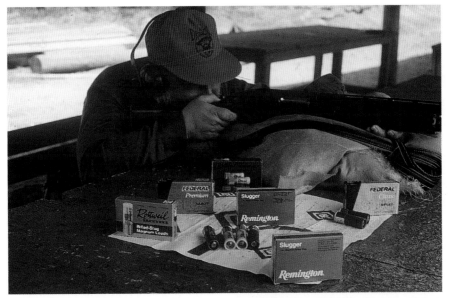

It's important to test-fire different brands of slugs through a shotgun you plan on hunting deer with to determine which one gives the best performance.

of a full-choke scattergun, but buckshot is prohibited for deer hunting in some states. Open chokes, such as modified and improved cylinder, are better for slug use.

Loads

Slugs are the best choice of ammunition for shotguns used on deer. I've found Brenneke slugs to be the most accurate out of a slug gun I hunted with, but a different brand may work better out of other guns. It's important to try various brands of slugs out of a new gun to find out which performs the best for you.

Number one buckshot is best for hunters who are required or choose to use buckshot, where legal. The larger 00, 0, and 000 sizes are second, third, and fourth choices, respectively. Buckshot is only effective at close ranges, 40 yards maximum. For longer shots, slugs should be used.

Since each buckshot pellet is capable of making a fatal wound, using loads that contain the maximum number of pellets is beneficial. Federal 12-gauge $3^1/_2$-inch shells that contain 00 buckshot, for example, have eighteen pellets, compared to fifteen in 3-inch loads and twelve in $2^3/_4$-inch magnum loads. The difference of six 00 pellets between a $2^3/_4$-inch and a $3^1/_2$-inch shell can have a dramatic impact in the field in determining whether or not a shot brings down a deer.

Handguns

Handguns present yet another category of firearm for deer hunters to choose from. Both revolvers and single-shot handguns suitable for deer hunting are available. The .454 Casull made by Freedom Arms, .480, .460, .44 magnum, and .41 magnum have proven effective for deer. Thompson/Center is a leader in the production of break-

Jim Jensen bagged his best buck, a 12-pointer netting 164⁶/₈, with a .256 magnum barrel on a Thompson/Center Contender handgun. The gun is mounted with a 1¹/₂-power scope. The Contender is designed for interchangeable barrels, many of which are great for deer hunting.

action, single-shot handguns. They make the Contender and Encore, both of which can be fitted with interchangeable barrels that are 10, 14, and 16 inches in length. Faster velocities and more energy are obtained with the same bullets from the longer barrels. Barrels for the Contender can be obtained in forty-eight different calibers, including .22 rimfire and .410 shotgun. The Encore is only designed for centerfire calibers, including those most popular for deer hunting.

Jim Jensen from Marquette, Michigan, bagged his biggest whitetail to date with a .256 magnum barrel on a Contender that was fitted with a 1¹/₂-power scope. The 12-point's nontypical antlers netted 164⁶/₈. He put a 75-grain hollow-point bullet through the buck's lungs on the evening of November 28 after it followed a doe into view.

Jensen said he shot a 9-pointer with the same barrel several years earlier. That buck was dropped instantly with a neck shot at a distance of 20 yards. He got an 8-point with a 7 x 30-caliber barrel on the same gun before that.

One of the popular Contender deer hunting calibers is the .375 JDJ. It is named for J. D. Jones of Bloomington, Ohio, who came up with that caliber. Barrels in .375 JDJ for the Contender can be obtained from him at SSK Industries.

Ken Kelly at Mag-Na-Port said the 6 x 5-caliber JDJ is one of the best Contender barrels for deer hunting because it has hardly any recoil. He added that it has plenty of punch at longer ranges, too. If it is sighted in to hit three inches high at 100 yards with 120 grain Speer bullets, it will be right on at 300 yards.

I was hunting with Larry Weishuhn in Georgia one year when he shot a 9-pointer with a .309-caliber JDJ barrel on a Contender frame. The .309 is a necked-down .444. Larry dropped the buck at 100 yards with a .150 grain bullet.

A new and improved version of the Contender (G2) was released by Thompson/Center a number of years ago. Barrels designed for use with the original Con-

Left: Larry Weishuhn loads a 150-grain bullet in his .309 JDJ–caliber handgun during a Georgia white-tail hunt. Right: Larry Weishuhn collected this Georgia buck with a .309 JDJ barrel on a single-shot Contender frame. He dropped the buck at 100 yards with a 150-grain bullet.

tender will also work on the G2. The Savage Striker is a single-shot bolt-action handgun that's available in .30-06 and 7mm-08. Remington's version of the single-shot handgun is the XP-100.

Thompson/Center also makes a muzzleloading handgun barrel for the Contender. Bob Gallup from Marquette, Michigan, has been using such a setup during his home state's muzzleloader deer season for at least a dozen years with good success.

"Hunting with a front-loading rifle wasn't exciting anymore," Bob said. "I wanted more of a challenge. That's why I switched to a handgun."

Gallup hunts with a .50-caliber front-loading handgun that has a 14-inch barrel. He loads it with 100 grains of Pyrodex powder and a saboted 250-grain .45-caliber handgun bullet. He used to load his muzzleloading handgun with 300-grain Barnes bullets, but switched to the lighter projectiles for their better ballistics.

The handgun is mounted with a $2^1/2$X-7X T/C scope. Although scoring with the sidearm can be more difficult than a rifle, Bob doesn't feel like he's at much of a disadvantage. He has the gun sighted in for 150 yards and he can still aim where he wants to hit on deer that are closer. Most of the whitetails he's shot with the Contender have been about 100 yards away.

Over the years Bob has been hunting with the black powder handgun, he's taken seven rack bucks with it. The biggest was a $3^1/2$-year-old 9-point. The other six bucks had either 6- or 8-point racks. Most of them were $2^1/2$ years old.

When it comes to centerfire revolvers, the .44 magnum has been the best of the lot because of the punch it packs, but it may soon be replaced by the newer .480 Ruger, which is supposed to have 40 percent more energy than the .44 mag. The .454 Casull, which has been around longer, but not as long as the .44, is developing a large following due to its power. The heavy recoil and loud muzzle blast from the larger-caliber handguns prevent some people from shooting them accurately. If groups from a lesser caliber such as the .41 magnum are more consistent and tighter than from the .44, it is the better choice for hunting. All of the calibers mentioned for single-shot handguns are good choices for deer hunting.

Large-caliber handguns can be tamed somewhat by having vents put in the barrels. The process is called Mag-na-porting. The vents reduce muzzle lift and dampen recoil without reducing bullet velocity or increasing noise. For more information write or call Mag-na-port International, 41302 Executive Dr., Harrison Township, MI 48045-1306 (586-469-6727). The Handgunners Hall of Fame Museum is located at Mag-na-port's headquarters.

Either soft-point or semi-jacketed hollow-point bullets are okay for deer hunting. Both Speer and Hornady make 325-grain bullets for the .480 and 320-grain loads for the .460. Corbon makes 240-, 260-, and 280-grain bullets for the .454. The .44 magnum is available in 180-, 210-, 240-, and 300-grain slugs; the .41 magnum in 170- and 210-grain; and the .375 JDJ in 220-grain bullets.

It takes more practice to master a handgun than any other type of firearm I'm acquainted with; at least it does for me. Shooters who plan on hunting deer with one should familiarize themselves with their own and the gun's limitations before going afield. Shooting should be done from a steady position—sitting, prone, or resting against or on something such as shooting sticks—whenever possible.

I own a .44 magnum Ruger Black Hawk; after I got it I practiced diligently with the iron-sighted, single-action revolver for a year with the intent of taking a whitetail with it. By the time firearms season opened, I felt confident in my ability to score on deer out to 75 yards with the handgun. However, I soon found out that shooting at targets is much different than shooting at live deer.

On the second day of the season, I missed two bucks. The first antlered whitetail that got away was a spikehorn. My .44 bullet went high when the buck stopped at about 75 yards, causing the deer to turn and come toward me. I got a second shot when the whitetail stopped again at closer range, but that round also missed.

Later in the day, a trophy buck with an 8- or 10-point rack came running by me at 35 yards. My efforts to stop the buck didn't work, so I took a few shots at the running deer, none of which connected. I know I would have gotten that buck with a rifle. It was years before I decided to try handgun hunting for whitetails again—but first I turned the .44 over to Ken Kelly at Mag-na-port for improvements that would make it better for hunting.

Besides porting the barrel and mounting a variable 2x-6x Bushnell handgun scope on the sidearm, Mag-na-port did a number of other things to transform my handgun into an effective as well as good-looking hunting gun. The 6-shooter was reblued with a teflon finish, the trigger and hammer were jeweled and polished, the muzzle crown was inverted, the forcing cone was recut to 11 degrees, and a nylon sling was added for carrying.

The changes made it possible for me to shoot the .44 magnum more accurately, as I thought they would. I practiced with the gun as much as possible, shooting it offhand as well as with a variety of rests, including shooting sticks. After lots of practice, I felt I was ready to hunt with the gun again and decided to try it out on an antlerless-only hunt in farming country designed to control deer numbers.

The hunt began on September 16 and I spent that evening in a tree stand overlooking a food plot on the edge of a cornfield. No deer appeared in the food plot, but I heard whitetails feeding in the corn around me. However, I couldn't see them.

On the morning of the seventeenth, I stillhunted along a logging road near the cornfield, hoping to intercept deer leaving the corn. Ken Kelly's father, Larry, had advised me to forget about carrying shooting sticks for handgun hunting when walking, and he ought to know because he's successfully hunted big game all over the world with revolvers. Nonetheless, the shooting sticks had worked well on the range and I decided to carry them with me "just in case."

At one point during the morning, I saw a doe walking along the lane toward me, so I quickly sat down, put the revolver on the shooting sticks, and soon found out why Larry had recommended against using the sticks. When the doe got close, she saw me and promptly went up a bank on the right side of the road. She stopped broadside for one last look before bounding away. I was unable to find the deer in the scope during my window of opportunity for a shot because I had the gun propped up too close to my eye.

Without the shooting sticks, I would have extended my arms to the proper distance for aiming and gotten on the deer quick enough to allow a shot. I guess there's nothing wrong with confirming Larry's advice through firsthand experience of my own! I saw other deer that morning, but none were in a position where a shot was possible.

On the evening of the seventeenth, I moved to a tree stand in the woods near the edge of another cornfield. There were three deer trails within easy range of the stand. The first doe I saw was about 60 yards away, but branches obscured a clear shot, so I decided to wait for something closer.

A while later, a button buck walked right under the stand. Although he was legal to shoot as an antlerless deer, I wanted to make sure I shot a doe for management purposes. I was still watching the young buck when I caught sight of movement off to the left.

An adult doe had come within 15 yards while I was distracted by the button buck. She was too close to try to shift positions in the stand for a shot, so I slowly raised the handgun and rotated it until it was pointed at the doe then moved my head to look through the scope to aim. At the shot, she dropped in her tracks and I had my first whitetail with a handgun. I bagged that doe with a 240-grain semi-jacketed hollow point.

I display my .44 magnum Ruger Handgun that was improved by Mag-na-port for deer hunting with a number of modifications while kneeling next to the doe I shot with it. This was the first deer I bagged with a handgun.

I'm impressed by the shooting ability of hunters who are consistently successful on deer with handguns—and there are plenty of examples. Mark Janousek from Olivet, Michigan, for instance, bagged a pair of rack bucks with his .44 magnum revolver one year and he had taken a number of other deer with the handgun prior to that. The year he got the double, Janousek's first buck was a respectable 8-point with a 17$\frac{1}{2}$-inch outside spread that he guessed would measure about 110. The second deer he tagged was a whopper 25-point nontypical that qualified for Boone and Crockett entry with a net score of 203$\frac{7}{8}$.

Mark got his bucks with a Dan Wesson .44 Magnum that has a 10-inch barrel and is mounted with a 2 power scope for aiming. The gun was loaded with 300-grain XTP hollow-point bullets that he loaded himself.

"I really like hunting with a handgun," Mark said. "It's more accurate than my shotgun, if I have a rest. I shoot 3$\frac{1}{2}$-inch groups at 100 yards with it, but when hunting I like to keep shots under 60 yards."

Mark said he normally hunts from a blind and frequently uses the blind's windowsill as a rest for his handgun. Due to the loud noise his gun makes when he shoots, he always carries earplugs in his pockets and puts the foam rubber plugs in his ears before taking a shot at deer. The plugs reduce the chances he will flinch in anticipation of the loud bang.

On the evening Janousek got the 25-pointer, he was hunting from a blind in a swamp. The book buck was 70 yards away when he first saw it; the whitetail was walking through water toward high ground at the edge of the swamp.

As the buck approached, Mark got excited, which is understandable under the circumstances. He fumbled around in his pockets for his earplugs and couldn't find them. Rather than spend more time looking for the plugs, he substituted a pair of .44 shells and had them sticking out of his ears when the buck stopped angling toward him at 23 paces. That's when he fired.

The first year Mark hunted with his handgun, his experience was similar to mine. He missed an 8-pointer. Although he didn't hunt with the sidearm for the next couple of years, he continued practicing with the revolver to improve his accuracy. He was obviously better prepared when he resumed hunting with it.

Many revolvers are carried in holsters. A division of Michaels of Oregon—Uncle Mike's (www.unclemikes.com)—makes handgun holsters. More holsters can be found at www.holsters4guns.com and www.gunnersalley.com, among other sources. Slings are used to carry some of the larger single-shot handguns.

If you plan on hunting with a handgun, be familiar with the regulations for transporting and carrying them in your home state as well as those you plan to travel through. Most states require handguns to be transported in a locked case in a trunk or somewhere similar where they are inaccessible to the driver. It is illegal to bring handguns into Canada.

Gun Care and Cleaning

Firearms should be cleaned on a regular basis, especially black-powder guns. The barrels of muzzleloading rifles pick up so much residue that loading them becomes difficult after they have been fired a number of times. Dirty bores aren't as much of a problem with modern rifles, shotguns, and handguns, but these guns still require care.

My dad impressed upon his two sons the importance of gun care as soon as we were old enough to hunt. After returning home from a day of hunting we had to look after our guns before anything else. If they had been fired, the barrels were cleaned inside and wiped with an oily rag on the outside. Unfired guns were simply wiped down and then put away. The procedure took a matter of minutes.

I still believe it is a good idea to look after a gun each time it is used, especially if it is wet from rain or snow. After wet days in the field, barrels should be cleaned even if the gun wasn't fired during the day. Sometimes moisture gets in at the muzzle. A good way to keep rain and snow out of the barrel of a deer gun is to put a piece of tape over the muzzle. This doesn't affect accuracy and isn't dangerous.

When deer hunting with firearms during extremely cold weather (in temperatures close to zero degrees Fahrenheit), carrying uncased guns from the cold into a warm home or camp can cause condensation (sweating) to form on metal surfaces. The moisture that is created can dampen black powder charges, causing a misfire. On centerfire guns, any moisture that remains when a gun is taken back outside will freeze and can also cause a misfire by preventing the firing pin from functioning properly. The presence of too much lubricant on gun actions can also cause them to freeze in cold weather. It is best to remove excess lubricant from gun actions before cold weather arrives.

That's what Aaron Belonga from St. Ignace, Michigan, wished he had done during a recent season. While hunting with a bolt-action .30-06 from a blind on November 16, Belonga had a big 8-pointer chasing does within 100 yards for a long time. Aaron said he made fifteen attempts to shoot the buck, but the rifle would not fire.

"I almost cried," the hunter said.

When examining the rifle after that buck got away, he found out the ejector on the bolt was frozen. Consequently, the bullets were not being seated properly in the chamber. Each time he pulled the trigger, the firing pin did not hit the bullet's primer.

On November 21, Aaron was hunting from the same blind when the same buck appeared. That time the rifle worked properly and he got the mature 8-pointer.

To prevent the formation of condensation, guns can be left outside in a locked vehicle, outbuilding, or somewhere else where they will be secure. An alternative I prefer is to always carry guns in a case when taking them from the cold to a warm environment and vice versa. Guns in cases are insulated from a rapid change in temperature, preventing condensation in most instances.

To clean the bore of a modern gun simply run a wire brush with solvent on it through, then wipe clean with a couple of patches. Try to wipe all exposed metal parts with an oily rag before putting guns away.

Front-loading barrels must be cleaned with hot water, if possible. What I usually do with side-hammer guns, after the barrel is taken off the stock and the nipple removed, is pour a pitcher of hot water down the muzzleloader barrel. That drains a lot of the black-powder residue. Then I submerge the nipple end in a bucket of hot water and work a 12-gauge shotgun-cleaning rod with a patch up and down. Once the barrel is clean I use two or three patches to dry it completely.

I soak the nipple in hot water and then wipe it off with a paper towel. I use a pointed toothpick to clean any residue out of threads. I run a fine piece of wire through the nipple hole to eliminate any particles that might block it.

To clean inline muzzleloaders, I run liberal amounts of hot water through the bore and breech ends of the barrel after the hammer, trigger mechanism, and breech plug are removed. Then I run patches through the barrel to clean and dry it. Hot water and Q-tips are also used to clean nipples, hammers, and breech plugs. A pointed toothpick or brush should be used to clean the threads of breech plugs. Breech plug threads should also be lubricated before putting them back in the rifle to make them easier to remove after the gun is fired again.

A light coating of oil goes on the exterior surfaces of the guns and their working parts. After cleaning is complete and side hammer guns are reassembled, I usually snap a couple of percussion caps to make sure the nipple and barrel are dry, if I plan on reloading them. If it will be weeks or months before I plan to use them again, I wait until just before I'm ready to load the rifles before snapping caps. With inlines, I often leave them disassembled overnight, when possible, to make sure they dry thoroughly.

When deer hunting away from home, try to remember to bring a gun cleaning kit along. The year 2003 marked the one hundredth anniversary of a popular gun cleaning solvent—Hoppe's No. 9 (www.hoppes.com). The company makes a variety of gun cleaning products and kits. Don't forget the allen or nipple wrenches that come with muzzleloaders for taking them apart and putting them back together. Otis Technology (www.otisgun.com) also has a variety of gun cleaning products.

Bows and Arrows

Now, let's consider an entirely different weapon: the bow. Unlike firearms, bows are classified by pounds of pull rather than caliber or gauge. There are a number of types of bows available today: compounds, recurves, longbows, and crossbows, with compounds being the most popular. Crossbows are being used more frequently as they are legalized in more states. A trend toward the use of longbows and recurves among archers is similar to the move toward muzzleloading firearms among gun hunters. Of the three types of vertical bows, longbows represent the earliest and simplest design. Compounds are the most recent, and the recurve falls in the middle.

Bows have come a long way. Newer models have gone beyond the realm of the simple stick and string, although the principle remains the same. Each advancement has improved the bow's efficiency for hunting. The step from straight or stick bows to recurves wasn't as dramatic as the jump from recurves to compounds, but it was still a step ahead. The curved design of the limbs on recurves resulted in shorter bows. Both wood and fiberglass eventually went into the manufacture of recurves, making them stronger and more efficient than the all-wood longbows. Some newer longbows are now also made with fiberglass and wood. While composite longbows may perform better than those of the same design made entirely from wood, recurves still have a slight edge for hunting due to their shorter lengths. With both recurves and longbows, their peak weight is reached at full draw.

On compounds, peak weight is experienced at the beginning of the draw. At full draw the archer is holding a fraction of the bow's peak weight as a result of a system of cables and pullies. The reduction can be from 35 to 85 percent. From one-half to two-thirds of the way back the reduction can be felt at the bow's

The compound bow is the most popular vertical bow. This display of the evolution of the compound is part of the Pope and Young Club museum at their headquarters Chatfield, Minnesota. Other displays include longbows and recurve bows.

"breaking point." At that point the pulleys "roll over." This feature reduces the amount of effort necessary to hold the bow at full draw, which is one of the biggest advantages of the compound over recurves. More accurate shots are usually the end result.

At one time, deer taken with compound bows with more than a 65 percent letoff on draw weight at full draw were not eligible for entry in national bowhunting records maintained by the Pope and Young Club, but due to increasing popularity of bows with letoffs greater than 65 percent, that restriction was eliminated. If battery-operated devices such as lighted sight pins are on bows when a potential book deer is bagged, however, that will disqualify an animal for Pope & Young consideration.

Arrows released from compound bows generally travel faster, have a flatter trajectory, and have more penetration power than shafts released from a recurve of comparable draw weight. Another advantage the more sophisticated compounds have over any previous type of bow is their draw weight can be more easily adjusted. Draw weights can be adjusted by 10 to 20 pounds or more.

Most compounds are fitted with two round or cam-shaped pulleys and an arrow rest in the sight window, but a number of manufacturers also make compounds with one pulley and one cam. A number of the top compound bow manufacturers are Mathews, Martin, PSE, Hoyt, Bear, Darton, Bowtech, and Parker. Some compounds, called overdraws, have the arrow rest behind the sight window rather than in it. This modification allows the use of shorter, lighter arrows than possible with conventional compounds, resulting in faster arrow speeds and flatter trajectories. Release aids are required for use with overdraw bows as well as with the new generation of super short compounds, because consistently smooth releases are a must.

Releases

In fact, a high percentage of the deer hunters who use compound bows today shoot them with releases. Releases take the place of the fingers in gripping the string or a loop attached to the string. The bow is pulled to full draw with the release and when it's time to shoot, the release's grip on the string is relaxed. Many releases are activated by squeezing a trigger, but some simply have a rope that wraps around the bow string and the grip on the rope is relaxed to send an arrow on its way.

Releases improve the consistency of arrows leaving the bow, thereby improving accuracy. Mitch Brock from Coldwater, Michigan, found out what a difference a release can make in improving bowhunting success. He had been experiencing poor success while hunting with a compound and gripping the bowstring with his fingers. Then hunting partner Don Oliver suggested that he try a string release. He bought a Winn Free Flight Release and tried it.

"In an hour's time with a release, I was shooting 100 percent better," Mitch said. "I started hitting where I was aiming consistently. It made a world of difference. With a release, I'm solid out to 40 yards, although I don't normally shoot that far when hunting."

Brock's improved accuracy with his compound bow made it possible for him to collect a world-class whitetail on Halloween evening one year near where he lives. The 16-point nontypical had a net score of $200^3/_8$. He got the trophy buck while still-

A release aid attached to a bow string. Releases help most hunters improve their bow shooting accuracy. However, these gadgets sometimes malfunction at the most inopportune times. Hunters who forget or misplace their releases are also out of luck unless they have a spare.

hunting along the edge of a bean field. He made a 28-yard shot with his 80-pound-pull Pro Line Point Blank bow. His XX75 Easton aluminum arrow was tipped with a Thunderhead 100 broadhead.

Plenty of bow releases are available on the market today. Check them out to see which type works best for you. Once you decide on a release, buy an extra, so you will have a backup in case you forget or lose the one you normally use. Releases sometimes break at the most inopportune times, too. By having an extra, you will be covered if and when this happens.

Bowhunters who use releases should equip their bow with drop-away or "pass-through" styles of arrow rests. Both types are designed to give the best arrow flight when releases are used. Finger shooters should use rests that allow the arrow to bend around the bow as it's released such as spring and flipper types.

Fingers

I still shoot a compound bow with fingers, using a spring rest, and manage to score often enough to keep me satisfied. I wear a golf glove to grip the string with, as much to keep my hand warm during cold weather as anything else. My brother Bruce holds the string of his compound bow with a finger tab. Either a shooting glove or a tab is necessary for shooting recurves and longbows.

Compounds with cam-shaped pulleys generate faster arrow speed than those with round wheels, but can be a little harder to draw because the string has to be pulled back farther before the power cams roll over. Round-wheel compounds are the smoothest and easiest to draw and that's the type I now use for hunting after using a cam bow for a number of years.

The improved accuracy that Mitch Brock realized when he switched from fingers to a release was partly responsible for him taking this Boone and Crockett buck on the edge of a bean field while still-hunting.

Although there's a trend toward short compounds for hunting, those that are at least 40 inches from axle to axle, with a brace height of 7 to 8 inches, are the easiest to master. Shorter compounds certainly have advantages for hunting, though. They are lighter and easier to handle in cramped tree stands and ground blinds as well as while walking and stalking. I recently interviewed a bowhunter who was using a PSE XForce bow that was only 28 inches in height, with a brace height of 6 inches.

Draw Weights

Hunters who get a compound bow and don't know how to tune it should have someone knowledgeable at an archery shop check it for them. A compound that is not tuned is difficult to shoot properly. While you are at it, have the draw weight checked to be sure it is accurate. The actual draw weight of a bow sometimes varies from what it is labeled as.

The limbs on most compounds are made of laminated wood and fiberglass, but some models have all-fiberglass limbs. Fiberglass limbs are not the best for hunting since fiberglass expands and contracts with changes in temperature. Ray Sischo, a former archery shop owner, explained that with fiberglass limbs "one day you might have a forty-pounder and the next a forty-two-pounder."

A compound that has a draw weight of at least 40 pounds is more than adequate for deer hunting. Linda Luna from Lennon, Michigan, has taken more than ten whitetails with a compound that has a draw weight of 28 pounds. The biggest whitetail she got with that bow was a 17-point nontypical that had a net score of $173^1/8$. That buck had a dressed weight of 200 pounds.

Compounds with draw weights up to 60-pound pull are better than 40-pound bows for deer hunting, but I wouldn't recommend that a beginning bowhunter start out at 60 pounds. Shooting a bow is more physical than firing a rifle, and by starting out with a bow that is too heavy, you may develop poor shooting habits. Muscles used in drawing a bow are seldom used for anything else; consequently, they should be developed gradually.

A compound that can be adjusted from 40 to 50 pounds or from 40 to 60 pounds is perfect for the beginning bowhunter. Lighter draw weights would be appropriate for children and some women, of course. Most states have draw-weight minimums for deer hunting. Be sure to check what those minimums are where you plan on hunting.

Recurves or longbows with 40-pound-pull draw weights and heavier are okay for deer hunting, too. One of the first whitetails I bagged with bow and arrow, a doe, was taken with a recurve that had a draw weight of 42 pounds. Recurves had a couple of advantages over compounds when the newer bows first hit the market: they were less expensive and lighter than compounds. In many cases recurves can still be purchased for less than compounds and are lighter in weight, but these considerations aren't as important as they used to be. The advantages compounds have over recurves overshadow them to some extent. The only reason many recurves have retained lower price tags than compounds is because they wouldn't sell otherwise.

As with compounds, the laminated wood-and-fiberglass recurves are superior to all-fiberglass models. Some recurves are available in takedown models. These are convenient for travel in airplanes or buses, or when packing into a remote area on horseback. Interchangeable limbs can be purchased for takedowns that vary draw weight. This feature is similar to changing weights on compounds, but it is closer to buying separate bows for each draw weight.

Recurves that are at least sixty inches long are better for deer hunting than shorter models. Recurves are usually unstrung when not in use. A bow stringer is best for this purpose, as the through-the-leg method of stringing and unstringing bows can twist bow limbs if not done properly. Compound bows remain strung, except when strings are changed.

Draw Length

Regardless of the type of bow purchased for deer hunting, be sure to get one to correspond to your draw length. An average draw length is 28 inches. Some archers only reach 26 inches, however, and others come back 30 inches or more. Draw length depends on the individual's arm length. If interested in buying your first bow for deer hunting, try to get one from a shop where personalized service is given. An alternative would be to have a knowledgeable bowhunter help you pick out a bow suited to your draw length.

One way to determine your draw length is to pull back a calibrated arrow on a compound bow to full draw. Another way is to put a yardstick on your chest and stretch your arms out along it to see how far you can reach with your hands.

Crossbows

Draw length is not a concern with crossbows. Horizontal bows are kept in a cocked position during the course of a hunt. Crossbows used for deer hunting should have at least a 150-pound pull because they are designed to shoot shorter and lighter arrows, and consequently have a shorter power stroke than vertical bows. A 150-pound-pull crossbow is comparable to a 60-pound-pull compound bow.

To cock a crossbow, a metal stirrup on the front is placed on the ground and then the shooter bends down and pulls the string back until it locks in the cocked position. Due to the high poundage of crossbows for deer hunting, cocking one manually is not the easiest thing to do. Cocking devices are available that simplify the process for youngsters, some women, and handicapped hunters.

A safety device engages when a crossbow is cocked. Then an arrow is put in place to prepare for a shot. The safety has to be disengaged before a shot can be taken. Crossbow hunters who don't get a shot at a deer by the time they are done hunting often replace their hunting arrow with one tipped with a field point and take a practice shot to uncock the bow.

I've hunted whitetails in Ohio, Kentucky, and Michigan with a crossbow and was lucky enough to bag a 6-pointer at 20 yards in Ohio. I almost collected a doe with a crossbow in Kentucky, but my arrow was deflected by a limb. On a recent crossbow hunt in Michigan, I made a nonfatal hit on a doe due to human error, proving that horizontal bows are susceptible to the same limitations as vertical bows.

Prior to the legalization of crossbows during archery seasons for all hunters in Michigan, only those who qualified for handicap permits could hunt with them. Avid Michigan bowhunter Jim Butler qualified for a crossbow permit after suffering serious injuries in a fall from a warehouse roof. The damage to his arms was serious enough to prevent him from hunting with the bows and arrows he prefers taking whitetails with—recurves and longbows. He simply couldn't pull the strings of his hunting-weight bows to full draw any longer. The alternative to using a crossbow for Butler and others like him would be not hunting at all during the state's lengthy archery season, which would be tough to take for avid bowhunters like Jim.

During his third year of hunting with a crossbow, Butler bagged a trophy 13-point nontypical on December 23. It was the highest-scoring nontypical taken in the state with a crossbow on record at the time. The antlers had a gross score of 135 and netted $127^7/_8$. The minimum for entry of nontypical bow kills in state records maintained by Commemorative Bucks of Michigan is 125.

Butler was hunting with a 150-pound-pull Horton Crossbow when he got the $5^1/_2$-year-old buck. The crossbow was so hard to cock that he had to have someone do it for him before he went in the field. And Jim didn't put an arrow in place to shoot until he was ready to hunt. The arrow was then removed from the firing position when he was done hunting.

Jim Butler was forced to switch from his recurves and longbows to a crossbow for hunting after he suffered serious injuries in a fall from a roof. There are provisions to allow handicapped hunters to hunt with crossbows during archery seasons in most states and provinces. Jim managed to take this 13-point whitetail with a crossbow. He has now recovered enough to be able to hunt with a compound bow again.

Jim was hunting from a tree stand along the edge of a rye field where as many as a hundred deer had been feeding on a daily basis when he got the buck. He squeezed the crossbow's trigger when the antlered whitetail was 20 yards away. Jim watched the deer run a short distance across a marsh before falling. He said he had seen that particular buck a number of times before, but that was the first time he was in position for a shot at it.

After years of rehabilitation, Jim is now able to hunt deer with a vertical bow again, but he's grateful he had the opportunity to participate in bow season with a crossbow during the time he was unable to shoot a vertical bow. He now carries a compound bow set at 50 pound pull when participating in archery season, but he may be able to go back to his recurves and longbows at some time.

Choosing A Crossbow

To get recommendations for the best makes of crossbows for deer hunting, I asked an expert: Brian Schupbach at Schupbachs Sporting Goods Store in Jackson, Michigan. The store handles a variety of makes and models and hears back from their customers about what works and what doesn't. As far as the best-quality crossbows, Brian said Excaliburs are at the top of the list. They are accurate and dependable. Excaliburs are one of only two makes of crossbows that can be uncocked with a string device. PSE's Tack 15 can also be let down.

A pair of quality crossbows compared—one of the narrowest and one of the widest. A Horton crossbow is the narrow one on the left and an Excalibur with recurve limbs is on the right.

Brian added, however, that it is better to shoot all crossbows than to uncock them, even those than can be uncocked, because it takes a lot of strength to uncock a crossbow without firing it. If the uncocking process is not done properly, the crossbow can be damaged. So the recommended way to uncock a crossbow is to put an arrow with a field tip on the bow and shoot it into a target or the ground. Hunters can leave crossbows cocked in a blind or tree stand for a day or two, however, without problems.

Brian commented that crossbows with recurve limbs, such as Excaliburs, are most accurate. The same feature makes them wider than other models, however, making them more cumbersome in tree stands and blinds. The design of Horton's new crossbows makes them much narrower and more compact than other makes, increasing their maneuverability in trees stands and blinds.

Schupbach ranked TenPoint crossbows as number two in terms of quality followed by Parker, Eastman, Bow Tech, and Horton. TenPoint and Parker are the only crossbow manufacturers who offer lifetime warranties. One brand of crossbow Brian doesn't recommend is Barnett because they frequently break down, requiring repairs.

Arrow Selection

Arrows are designed to match the various draw weights of bows. The proper combination of arrow and bow is important. A rifleman wouldn't think of trying to fire a .30-30 round in his .30-06. Neither should an archer consider shooting an arrow designed for a 60-pound-pull bow from his 45-pounder.

Shafts are made from a number of materials, including wood (usually cedar), aluminum, and carbon. Carbon arrows have replaced aluminum shafts as the most popular for hunting due to their uniformity and durability. Carbon arrows are also lighter than aluminum ones, usually resulting in faster speeds. Aluminum or carbon arrows can be used with any type of bow. Cedar arrows are most often used with recurves and longbows.

There's been a major increase in the number of companies offering carbon arrows to hunters in recent years. Easton sells carbons, as does Carbon Express, Gold Tip, Carbon Tech, PSE, Beman, Blackhawk Archery, and Browning—and there may be others. Refer to each company's website for specifics. Carbon shafts are slimmer than those made of aluminum, so hunters who will be switching to them may need to get new quivers or adapt the ones they already have.

Easton has an arrow selection chart for aluminum and carbon shafts that clearly shows what sizes to choose for recurve and compound bows with respect to draw weight. The weight of the broadheads you will be hunting with is also important in determining which arrows to use; this variable is also shown in Easton's chart. Most archery dealers have copies of this chart for their customers' reference. Similar charts are available for selection of carbon shafts from other companies.

Crossbow arrows can normally be purchased from the companies that sell the horizontal bows. If the company doesn't sell arrows for their bows, they can tell you who does and what type of arrow to get for the model crossbow you have.

If you are interested in having lighted nocks on your arrows to increase the visibility of arrows in flight, to help you see where they strike deer, and to make it easier to find arrows after a shot, battery operated lumenoks (www.lumenok.net) can be installed. Lighted nocks are not legal in all states and provinces, so check local regulations before installing them.

Broadheads
A variety of broadheads are available for deer hunting. The most popular type are heads on which factory-sharpened inserts are used for all cutting edges. Examples of this type of broadhead that are good choices are Thunderhead, Muzzy, Carbon Express, Tru-Fire, and Wasp. Broadhead size and weight varies from small 75-grain models up to 145 grains. The trend has been toward smaller broadheads that will fly best on carbon shafts.

The newest design of broadheads for hunting are those with expandable or open-on-impact heads. The flight of these arrows is similar to those tipped with field points. Technology has improved on these heads to the point where they are reliable for hunting. Two of the most popular expandable broadheads are Swhacker and Rage. Some of the others are made by Wasp, New Archery Products, G5, and Gold Tip.

Among fixed-blade heads that can be resharpened after use, I prefer the Nugent Blade and Zwickey models. Magnus Snuffers, Woodsman heads from 3Rivers Archery, and heads made by G5 Outdoors are also good choices. New makes and models of broadheads come out on a regular basis, so check out the selection that's available at your local archery shop or online from sporting goods retailers before making a decision about what to use. Most hunting magazines devote one issue each year to new products that hit the market. It can be a good idea to check those issues out, too, for anything that appeals to you.

Regardless of the style of broadhead you use, make sure it is sharp—sharp enough to shave the hair on your arm. Most of today's broadheads are sharp at the time of purchase, but they have to be resharpened after use. One excellent kit for sharpening broadheads is manufactured by Razor Edge Systems, 303 North 17th Ave. East, Ely, MN 55731 (800-541-1458). The same kit can be used to sharpen knife blades, too. Sharpeners are also available from Smith Abrasives, Inc. (http://smithsedge.com).

Some hunting heads perform better with one type of bow than another, so be sure to try those you intend to hunt with well ahead of the season. Arrows most often fly differently with broadheads than with field points, except expandable models, so be sure your bow is sighted in with broadheads before hunting deer. Arrows tipped with broadheads will produce the best groups when fletched with five-inch vanes or feathers with a helical twist.

Plastic fletching (vanes) have advantages for hunting arrows over feathers. Vanes aren't affected by rain and they are also quieter. If you hunt with arrows that have vanes, you must shoot them from an arrow rest. Arrows fletched with feathers can be shot accurately from either an arrow rest or a shelf because they are more forgiving—that's why they are popular among recurve and longbow shooters. Some hunters who shoot compound bows also have their arrows fletched with feathers.

A quiver will be needed to carry hunting arrows. Back, belt, and bow quivers are the three basic types for hunting. I personally prefer those that can be attached directly to the bow by clamps or screws. This way extra arrows are always at hand when needed. Whichever a bowhunter chooses, he or she should make sure the area where broadheads rest in the quiver is covered. This protects the cutting edges from getting dulled on brush and protects hunters from accidentally cutting themselves.

Bow shooters using longbows and recurve bows and some shooting compounds will also need an arm guard to protect the forearm from the occasional slap of the bowstring and to keep loose sleeves from interfering with the string.

Mastering a bow and arrow takes more time and practice than mastering firearms. Nonetheless, the effort can be well worth your while. Hunting deer with archery equipment can be more satisfying and challenging than hunting with any other type of weapon. Bow deer seasons are often longer than firearms hunts, which increases the hunter's time afield. One of the best ways to learn to shoot a bow and arrow properly is to read all you can on the subject and join a local archery club. Established shooters are always more than willing to give beginners pointers.

Bows don't normally require much attention to keep them in working order. The pulleys on compounds can be oiled occasionally, but that is about it. A light coating once a year should do the trick. Bow strings can be waxed occasionally, too. Broadheads can be protected from rust by coating them with Vaseline.

Sights

Rifles fitted with peep sights can be extremely effective for deer hunting, as Mark Remali from Calumet, Michigan, proved one year by taking a Boone and Crockett–qualifying 11-point whitetail with a Marlin lever-action .45/70 fitted with such a sight. At the same time, he discovered that it's important not to bump the sight if it's a tang-mounted folding model like his is. Many hunters who use peep sights on their rifles are stillhunters or snow trackers and they have their peep sights solidly mounted on their rifles, but Remali was stand hunting when he got his big buck.

Mark said he was confident in his ability with the peep-sighted rifle. He had practiced a lot with it out to 175 yards, shooting five-inch groups with 405-grain bullets at that distance. The only drawback with the rifle is that iron sights are more difficult to see in low light, which is when the buck appeared.

Remali was in a blind when he first saw the deer at a distance of about 100 yards.

"He came in chasing a bunch of does," Mark said. "I could not see a rack until he came into a field with snow on it. It appeared to be a big rack on a small deer.

"I was wondering if I would be able to see my front sight through the peep, so I checked. The hole on the peep sight was too small to see through in the fading light, so I unscrewed a fitting to increase the size of the sight's opening. Then I was able to see good enough to aim properly.

"I just watched the buck at first because he was busy chasing does. He eventually stopped quartering toward me. That's when I shot. He jumped and ran toward the blind. Based on his reaction, I was sure I hit him.

"He stopped at a distance of 25 to 35 yards, looking into the blind. I expected him to collapse any minute. When he didn't, I thought I might have missed, so I shot a second time. He ran a little ways and stopped.

Mark Remali with the head mount of the Boone and Crockett buck he
bagged with a peep-sighted .45/70.

"Then I shot a third time and he didn't show any reaction. It was obvious I
missed him that time. He started to walk and then fell over."

Upon examining the fallen whitetail, Mark confirmed that his first shot did
indeed connect. It's a good thing it did. After the first shot, he must have bumped the
folding peep sight and it was pulled backward, causing him to miss with the second
and third rounds.

When Mark walked up to the fallen buck, he was impressed by the size of its
antlers. The rack was so wide, the uppermost beam stuck up high above the ground.
The buck's body also looked bigger than it had when he shot it. The deer had a
dressed weight just shy of 220 pounds.

Sights are an integral part of any gun and most bows used for deer hunting. For
firearms there are two basic types of sights: iron and telescopic. Scopes are the most
widely used because of their reliability and their adaptability for many hunting situations. They have several advantages over iron sights: The target and the sights are
visible on one plane; the target is usually magnified; and scopes have the ability to
gather light under low-light conditions like those that existed when Mark Remali
scored with a peep sight. Most scope eyepieces are circular, but oblong wide-field
models are also available.

Scopes

The field of view a hunter has through a scope decreases as its magnification increases. For this reason low powers from 1X to 4X are best for close shots and finding running deer in the glass. Low-magnification scopes are also great on handguns, shotguns, and crossbows. Higher magnifications are best used for medium- to long-range shots and for looking for antlers on deer that can't be seen clearly with the naked eye.

Telescopic sights are available in either fixed-power or variable models, with a selection of reticles. Variables are the most versatile. The selection of variables includes 1.5X-4.5X, 1.5X-8X, 2X-7X, 3X-9X, and 4X-12X, but there are other options. For hunters who do a lot of stillhunting and tracking or want a scope for their shotgun, the low-power variable is tops. Stand hunters who frequent open country would be better off with the higher-magnification variables.

When hunting it is best to keep variables on the lowest power. If a deer is spotted that you want to get a better look at, crank up the power then. Try to remember to crank it back down after the higher magnification is no longer needed. I made the mistake of not doing that one time and missed a buck because of it.

While on a stand I spotted a deer about 150 yards away. I cranked the power on my scope from 3X all the way up to 9X to look at its head. It was a doe. Some time

Telescopic sights are an excellent choice for deer hunting regardless of what type of gun you plan to hunt with. Both target and aiming point are on one sight plane, the scopes improve visibility in low light situations, and they magnify the target, allowing for more precise aiming. The scope in this photo is on a shotgun and is attached with see-through mounts to allow a hunter to see iron sights for aiming if there is problem with the scope.

Most of the newer scopes like the one on this crossbow have various aiming points for different yardages. The more sophisticated scopes help hunters determine how far their target is and which aiming point to use.

later a buck came hot-footing by me no more than thirty yards away. My field of view was so small at that range with the scope still on nine power I couldn't find him in it. He was out of sight before I realized what the problem was.

Fixed-power scopes are generally less expensive than variable ones. Good choices for rifles or shotguns are 2X or 4X. The most popular handgun scopes come in 1X, 2X, 2X-6X, and 2X-8X. Crossbow scopes vary between 1X and 4X.

Crosshairs are the most popular scope reticle. The duplex or tapered variety ranks on top, followed by coarse crosshairs, and dot types. Fine crosshairs are difficult to see in low light, which makes them a poor choice for deer hunting.

The 4X scope that came with the Eastman crossbow I recently started hunting with has six crosshairs or aiming points to allow for sighting the horizontal bow in for six different yardages. The different aiming points come in handy because the short arrows propelled from crossbows do not have a flat trajectory like longer, heavier arrows released from some vertical bows with high draw weights. The point of impact of crossbow arrows varies significantly at 5-yard increments.

Many scopes now available for muzzleloaders and centerfire rifles have features similar to those of the scope on my crossbow to allow hunters to know where to aim at different distances and even to help determine how far deer are from hunters. Bushnell, for example, makes muzzleloader scopes that help hunters who use them determine where to aim out to 250 yards. Their centerfire rifle scopes allow for yardages out to 600 yards. Besides Bushnell, Nikon, Leupold, Swarovski, Pentax, Simmons, Redfield, and Weaver, among others, make quality scopes. Trijicon makes scopes that have colored reticles that are available in red, yellow, and green in addition to black.

Scope covers are helpful to have for rainy or snowy days. Butler Creek (www.butler-creek.com) makes flip-up covers for most scopes in black plastic and with see-through lenses. I prefer see-throughs, so if I see a deer suddenly and don't have time to flip the covers up I can take a quick shot with them on. Hunters should test the accuracy of their scopes both with covers on and off to see if there is a difference, if they wish to use clear types. See-through covers should be flipped up for long-range shooting.

The type of rifle or shotgun a scope is put on dictates whether it will be mounted on the side or on top. Beyond that, there are mounts that flip to the side, high mounts so iron sights can be seen under them, low mounts, and mounts that can be detached quickly. One mount is as good as another as long as it is solidly anchored and the shooter can see through the scope properly.

I use low mounts that can't be detached quickly because I have faith in the scopes on my rifles. They have never let me down. The incident mentioned earlier, when I missed a shot at a buck because my scope was on high power, was my fault, not the scope's. The only situation I've encountered where a scope would have been useless if a shot were offered is when looking directly into the sun. I always avoid putting myself in a position where aiming at a deer into the sun would be required.

I will admit that scope mounts that provide for quickly switching to using iron sights have their place. If something happened to a scope on a hunting trip rendering it temporarily or permanently useless, such a mount would prove invaluable. Fortunately, I haven't been in such a situation. On deer hunting trips away from home I sometimes carry a spare rifle.

Scope users who have flip-over or quick-detachable mounts should make sure that after using iron sights they flip the scope back or remount it the way it originally was. If it isn't aligned properly, the point of impact will be changed and the next shot taken with the scope probably won't go where it ought to. Marks of some sort can be used as guidelines to make sure the scope is always repositioned properly.

It is best to have a gunsmith or dealer mount a scope unless you have done it before. Set screws must be cinched down tight so recoil won't jar them loose. If you do the mounting yourself, use a screwdriver that fits the screws properly. Also, put some Loctite or varnish on the screw threads just before putting them in as added insurance against their loosening.

A number of years ago, one of my brothers-in-law, Bruce Dupras, bought a new rifle and scope. I advised him to have a local sport shop mount the scope. He didn't listen. Bruce went through more than a box of shells on his first trip to the range trying to sight in his rifle before he realized the scope was loose.

Red-dot sights are mounted like scopes on all types of firearms used for deer hunting. Most of them do not magnify the target, but have a red dot for an aiming point. Unlike scopes, these sights are battery operated. Aimpoint is one company that has been making this type of sight since 1975. Trijicon and Bushenll also make red-dot sights.

Iron Sights

Most rifles, shotgun barrels designed for slugs, and handguns come with iron or open sights. Hunters who can't afford a scope are stuck with them. That's not necessarily a disadvantage. Some hunters prefer open sights. In some cases, primarily during muzzleloader deer seasons in some states, scopes are prohibited.

The newer type of fiber-optic open sights are far superior to the older iron sights. The biggest disadvantage of traditional iron sights is they are often difficult to see in low-light situations. The newer fiber-optic sights help correct that shortcoming by incorporating pieces of flourescent orange and green in both front and rear sights. Hunters who use open sights and have the older style can improve their ability to aim in low light by replacing them with fiber optics.

Another disadvantage of open sights that remains unchanged with fiber optics is they are not made for long-range shooting. They perform best on deer at distances under 100 yards, although, as Mark Remali proved on the range, they can be used accurately at greater distances.

In my opinion, a receiver or peep sight is superior to the conventional rear sight for deer hunting. The eye automatically centers the front sight in the aperture for

accurate, quick sighting. Since the peep is close to the eye, it will be out of focus, as it should be; and the shooter will have only two planes to try to focus on (the front sight and target) as opposed to three points of focus when a conventional rear sight is used. Additionally, peep sights don't block parts of deer from the shooter's view as other rear sights do.

Most peep sights are mounted solidly on rifles and don't move when bumped. But folding peeps like the one Remali used are options. Those that don't move when bumped are obviously advantageous to avoid the problem like Mark encountered during followup shots on his buck.

Members of the legendary Benoit Family from Vermont, who are famous for their skill in snow tracking whitetail bucks, use peep sights on their rifles. It

Fiber-optic sights like those mounted on this shotgun are superior to the older style of iron sights and they are highly recommended for hunters who choose not to use a scope or for use when scopes are not legal.

is best to unscrew the eyepiece on peep sights and use the larger hole for hunting, especially when snow tracking, stillhunting, or conducting a drive where the odds of seeing running deer are high. If you choose to use the smaller aperture when stand hunting, there may be time to remove the fitting for a shot in low light, as Mark Remali did.

Rear sights that are standard equipment on rifles, shotguns, and handguns vary, but most are notched in the shape of a U or V. The U on some sights is squared off; others are rounded. I prefer a notch as small as possible in the round-bottomed U. Rear sights that have a triangular-shaped mark on the surface facing the shooter make it easier to find the center for aligning the front sight.

Front sights come in bead, blade, or post varieties. I like the fiber optic bead. When buying a gun with iron sights, try aiming it to see if the sight picture is satisfactory. If not, look for a different firearm or ask to have the sights changed to a style you prefer. Regardless of the other qualities a rifle, handgun, or slug-barreled shotgun may possess, its effectiveness will be minimized if the sights are less than adequate for your use.

Bow Sights

Some bowhunters don't use sights. They shoot instinctively in a fashion similar to the way a shotgunner points his gun, or they use the tip of their broadhead as a point of reference for aiming. Most archers use sights, however, as evidenced by the increasing variety of bow sights on the market. There are pins, scopes, peeps, crosshairs, rangefinders, and lighted sights.

As a gun hunter-turned-archer, I prefer a sight on my bow. It helps me to pick a spot on a deer to aim at rather than shooting at the whole animal. Sights are especially valuable for shooting at distances beyond thirty yards. Some bowhunters shoot instinctively at ranges under thirty yards, but rely on a sight for longer shots.

Due to the poor trajectory of an arrow as compared to a rifle bullet, multiple aiming points are available on most sights. A series of pins is the most common and, I think, the best for deer hunting. The pins are usually set for distances in increments of ten yards. If a bowhunter restricts his shots at deer to within thirty yards, he may only need one or two pins. Fiber-optic pins will provide the best visibility, even in low-light situations. Pendulum sights designed for use from tree stands have a single pin. The sight pin automatically swivels to adjust for the downward angle of shots at various distances.

A rear sight isn't necessary for aiming with a bow. Archers draw to the same anchor point (a corner of the mouth is commonly used) for every shot, which results in a consistent sight picture. Some bow shooters do use peep sights. These sights fit between strands on the bowstring and make more accurate shooting possible. Peeps with the largest aperture are desirable for hunting.

Nocking points are another feature on bows that allows for a consistent sight picture. Metal "stops" are clamped on the string, usually at a point from three-eighths to one-half inch above the arrow rest, to mark nocking points. Arrow nocks fit on the string directly under the nocking point. Some hunters put two nocking points on their string and put their arrows on the string between them.

Telescopic sights made for bows were primarily designed for target shooters, but can be used for hunting, where legal. They come in one, two, four, and six power. Rangefinder sights are helpful to bowhunters if they have difficulty estimating distances accurately in the field. Lighted bow sights are advantageous for seeing point-of-aim under poor light conditions, but their use is prohibited in some states. The advent of fiber optic sights for bows has reduced the need for lighted sights.

As with any other type of sight, try to choose one for your bow that you will be happy with. Test several varieties if possible.

Sighting In

Sights have to be aligned so the bullet or arrow hits where it is aimed before they will do the gun or bowhunter any good. Most iron sights are reasonably accurate as they come from the factory. Some manufacturers claim their sights are ready for use right out of the box, and that might be true, but no one should hunt with a gun until its accuracy is tested on the range.

Scopes mounted by dealers are usually bore-sighted. Nonetheless, be sure to shoot the rifle, shotgun, or handgun yourself to adjust the sights for your eyes and desired sight-in distance. Do it as far in advance of the opening of deer season as possible, especially in the case of a brand-new gun. Problems with guns and sights don't develop often, but if they do they should be recognized as soon as possible so they can be corrected.

One year a friend of mine ordered a deer-hunting rifle on which the firing pin broke after several rounds were fired. Fortunately, he got it months before the season and was able to get a rifle to hunt with to replace the faulty one.

Hunters who don't have access to a regular range to sight in their guns should select a location with an adequate backstop. Gravel pits are a good choice. State and provincial departments of natural resources or fish and game usually have certain areas designated for target practice, if a range isn't available. Targets can be pinned or taped to cardboard boxes or paper shopping bags. A few rocks put in the bottom of a shopping bag will hold it in place on windy days as well as when bullets or slugs hit the paper. I usually use a paper plate for a target. If shooting a scoped gun, a circular aiming point is colored in the center of the target with a crayon or felt-tipped pen. A heavy cross is used as an aiming point for iron sights, as the front sight will often completely cover a circle.

When shooting a gun or sight you are not familiar with, do not start out with the target far away. Twenty-five yards is far enough. If the sights are way out of whack, your bullets may hit off the paper at 100 yards. Once the gun is on target at close range it can be fine-tuned for longer ranges.

Always shoot from the steadiest position possible when sighting in a rifle. The same goes for hunting. A benchrest where the shooter can sit down and prop the gunstock on sandbags is best. Trees, vehicles, or posts are also helpful in steadying a rifle, shotgun, or handgun. Try to use something such as a firm cushion, tightly rolled sleeping bag, or sandbag to rest the gunstock on when shooting from a vehicle. The prone position with a rest is also good for accurate placement of shots. A notched cardboard or wooden box makes a good rest for shooting prone.

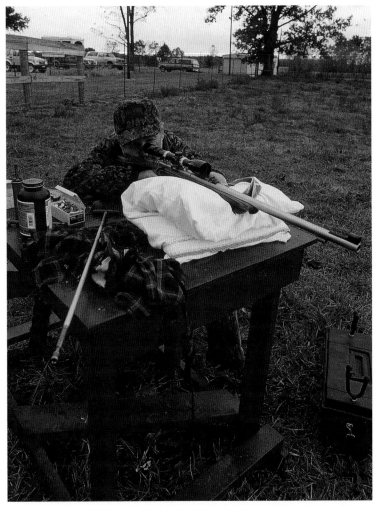

Hunters should test-fire new guns or those mounted with new sights as far in advance of hunting season as possible, as this muzzleloader hunter is doing, to make sure there are no problems. Start out at close range and use a steady rest.

If you will be using shooting sticks to steady your rifle when hunting, use them on the range, too, to make sure they work properly and to become more familiar with their use.

Slings increase accuracy from a sitting or offhand position. To get into a sling if you shoot right-handed, slip your left arm through with the rifle pointed upward and bring the strap as far back as it will go under your arm. As the rifle is lowered twist the left hand back and through the sling again. Grip the forend so the strap lies across the back of the hand. The strap should feel tight across the chest. If it is loose, pull the left hand back. When using a sling in a sitting position, your legs should be spread so your elbows can rest on your knees.

Some sort of ear protection, plugs or muffs, is invaluable for target practice.

Scope Adjustments

When sighting in a firearm, sight adjustments should be made on the basis of three-shot groups. The center of the group should be the point of correction. Telescopic sights are the easiest to sight in. The simplest way to align the crosshairs is to move them to the center of the group by turning the windage and elevation knobs. To do this, the gun must be resting solidly on sandbags, lying in a notched box, or clamped in place.

Gun and scope should remain in the same position throughout the process. First, fire three shots with the crosshairs on the bull's eye. Then check to see where the center of the group is. If magnification of the scope isn't great enough to see the center, darken the spot with a pen or crayon. Next, turn the windage and elevation knobs while looking through the glass so the crosshairs move across the target to that point.

Once the adjustments are complete, another group should be fired to test the accuracy of the new setting. If the procedure is done properly, slugs should hit close to where they are aimed.

To get consistent groups, try to squeeze the trigger on each shot. If shots are erratic, one of several things are probably happening. Either the shooter is jerking the trigger, his or her position isn't steady, or the scope is not mounted solidly. Set screws can work loose from the recoil of one or two rounds if they aren't installed properly. It sometimes helps me to get the feel of a trigger to dry-fire a gun several times before loading the firearm.

When clamping a scoped gun in position isn't possible, sight correction will have to be determined by measurements. Once a group has been fired, measure the distance from its center to the center of the target. Then scope adjustment dials can be turned an appropriate number of clicks or marks. Each calibration usually represents a shift in point of impact of an inch or less at 100 yards. How the dials are calibrated is usually specified inside dial covers, on the dials, or in the instructions that come with the scope.

Some scope adjustments are calibrated in minutes of angle. Don't let that confuse you. If each mark moves point-of-impact one minute of angle, at 100 yards the point of impact will be shifted one inch per mark. The shift will only be one-half inch at 50 yards and one-fourth inch at 25 yards.

Let's look at an example. Say the center of your group was two inches below and three inches to the left of your target at 25 yards and your scope adjustments are calibrated in minutes of angle. Each mark moves point-of-impact one inch at 100 yards, so at 25 yards the shift would be one-fourth of that, or one-fourth of an inch. To adjust the crosshairs the elevation knob would have to be turned eight clicks up (four per inch) and the windage dial twelve clicks to the right.

Adjusting Iron Sights

Iron sights are most often adjusted by moving the rear one, whether it is a peep sight or the notched variety. Many types are designed to make changes to both windage and elevation easy. Set screws often control them. Some older styles of iron sights (there are still plenty of them in use) simply made allowances for shifts in elevation. Much effort was necessary to adjust for windage by pounding them (either front or rear, right or left) with a punch made of copper, brass, or nylon, and a soft mallet. Shims of varying widths were required under one side or the other of some peep sights to change their right/left alignment.

It isn't as easy to determine exactly how far to move open sights as it is with scopes. The best approach is to shoot a group and make moderate corrections if any are necessary. If the next group is still off, the shooter should have a good idea how much to move the sights a second time to finalize adjustments.

Point of impact will shift the same direction the rear sight is moved. If the center of a group is high, for example, the rear sight must be lowered. When the group is to the right, the rear sight should be moved to the left. A change in the front sight will move point-of-impact the opposite direction. If the bead is moved left, bullets will hit farther to the right than they did before the adjustment.

Bow Sight Correction

Aligning a bow sight works the same way as adjusting the front sight of a gun. The general rule is to "follow the arrow." In other words, if your arrows are grouping to the left of center, the sight should be moved to the left. Point of impact will be moved to the right. If arrows hit high, raise the sight and the shafts will strike lower.

Bow sights can be moved accidentally or jarred out of place more easily than gun sights. I have found that it is beneficial to mark the positions of pins once they're set for desired yardages. Then if they are moved, they can be easily repositioned.

Peep sights for bows are situated on the string in a position that will allow the shooter to see through them when at full draw.

Use The Same Loads and Arrows

Always sight a gun or bow in with the same shells, load, or arrows you will be hunting with. A change in brand, bullet weight, powder charge, shaft composition, or type of broadhead will change the point of impact.

Most guns or bows only have to be sighted in once, as long as the same loads and shafts are used. Alignment of the sights should be checked every year before hunting season, however, just as a precaution. Your eyesight may have changed in the course of a year or something could have happened to the sights. If a gun is dropped or falls over when leaning in an upright position, sights could be knocked off.

Deer rifles used in brush country should be sighted in for 50 or 100 yards. Flat-shooting rifles can be sighted in for 200 to 250 yards by adjusting sights so bullets hit about an inch high at 100 yards. Shotgunners who use slugs, black-powder shooters, and handgunners may want to sight in for 50 or 100 yards. Most bowhunters prepare sights for maximum yardages from 50 to 60 yards. They will also have pins set for closer distances. Gun hunters should know where their bullets, round balls, or slugs hit at a variety of ranges, too. Ballistics tables available from ammunition manufacturers give shooters a good idea how much bullet drop to expect at distances beyond 100 yards if test-firing at those yardages isn't possible.

Patterning Shotguns

Hunters who use buckshot or slugs in a shotgun with a simple sight plane and front bead may laugh at the idea of sighting in with their loads. True, sight adjustment isn't possible, but some shotguns pattern high, low, left, or right of center. If so, the situation can be compensated for when shooting at a deer. Buckshot users will have to try their loads on paper to determine what kind of a pattern they are getting. Several types of buckshot should be test-fired at targets to see which one gives the tightest pattern.

All deer hunters should be aware that shots taken at an uphill or downhill angle are different from those taken on a level. Bullets and arrows have a tendency to hit higher than normal when shooting either up or down. Exactly how much higher depends on the circumstances. It is a good idea to try some shots uphill or downhill to get a feel for the situation.

One of the first mule deer I shot was at a steep downhill angle. The buck was bedded about 200 yards below me. To compensate for the angle, I held the crosshairs low on his shoulder and squeezed a shot off. He jumped to his feet at the shot, apparently untouched. I held lower on the second shot and could see daylight between my crosshairs and the bottom of his shoulder when I touched it off. That one broke his back!

Taking time to learn where a gun or bow will hit at various distances and under different circumstances gives deer hunters confidence that will help when a shot is offered at a whitetail or mule deer. There won't be a bull's eye or X to mark a spot to aim at, though. Hunters will have to know what point of the anatomy to try for—the spot where a hit will bring the surest, cleanest kill.

Shot Placement

Without question, the best all-around hit on a deer is in the lungs. This is because they are vital organs, they present a relatively large target, and their location is easy to determine. A deer hit in the lungs with a projectile from any of the weapons discussed in this book is not going to go far.

The lungs fill a large part of the chest cavity. On broadside to slightly angling-away shots with gun or bow, aim for a spot directly behind the front leg, in the middle of the body. Even if the shot strays one way or the other, the hit will be fatal. A bullet or arrow that enters behind the front leg will ruin no meat. Hunters who are in tree stands should aim a little above the center of the body behind the shoulder to allow for the downward trajectory of their bullet or arrow.

It's extremely important for bowhunters to aim behind the shoulder to avoid hitting the heavy shoulder blade or scapula that is directly above each front leg. The outline of that heavy bone can usually be seen under the skin on deer that are close when there's good light. A shoulder blade hit with an arrow often results in poor

On this broadside buck, aim for the X with gun or bow for a lung shot that will be behind the shoulder blade. Firearms hunters using the guns mentioned in the text who want to drop this buck on the spot can aim where the + is. The o marks the aiming point for a heart shot for bowhunters who are concerned about a deer "jumping the string." Hunters in tree stands should aim a little higher than shown here to allow for downward trajectory.

penetration and a nonfatal wound, unless you are using a heavy draw weight bow and sturdy broadheads.

If you happen to make a shoulder blade hit with an arrow, always follow up on the animal after waiting at least an hour to determine if the head penetrated enough to damage at least one lung. If there is lung damage, a deer won't go too far before bedding down. When there's a light to moderate blood trail that eventually peters out and the deer remains on its feet for more than 200 yards, the injury is probably nonfatal. By avoiding the shoulder blade, you won't have to worry about that scenario.

While shoulder shots should be avoided by bowhunters, that type of hit on deer that are broadside with a shotgun slug, rifle bullet of .270 caliber or larger, or a bullet from a .50-caliber muzzleloader will often drop deer in their tracks. These projectiles will smash through the heavy bone, take out the lungs and/or heart and possibly break the opposite shoulder as well. If you want to anchor a whitetail or mule deer on the spot, aim for the center of the shoulder, slightly above the center of the body.

A disadvantage of this type of hit is it often ruins some meat from one or both shoulders. There's bound to be lead fragments in some of the meat if a lead-based bullet or slug was used, and it's important to trim any meat contaminated with lead. The advantage is you don't have to worry about looking for the animal you shot because, chances are, it will be lying right where it was standing when you shot.

On a deer that's angling away like this one, place a shot with gun or bow in line with the opposite shoulder.

For whitetails or mule deer that are angling away at a sharp angle, the shot should be placed in the middle of the body and on a line with the opposite shoulder. In some cases, the point of aim would actually be behind the rib cage.

Gun hunters should try for the back of the neck on deer facing directly away from them, unless the hunter is in an elevated stand. From a tree, hunters should attempt to hit between a deer's shoulder blades in the middle of the back. The backbone will be broken if you are on target; the lungs are to either side. This type of shot is not recommended for bowhunters because the potential of making a non-fatal hit is high due to the presence of heavy bones.

Ground-based gun hunters can bring a deer down by hitting between the hams below the base of the tail. This shot is only recommended for long guns with good penetration power.

My brother Bruce dropped a dandy 8-point whitetail with a rear-end shot one year. Bruce missed an angling shot first, but when the buck turned straight away he was on target. His 150-grain .30-30 slug piled the deer up on the spot. The bullet ranged forward into the lungs. There wasn't a speck of meat ruined, either.

Hunters faced with shots at whitetails or mule deer angling toward them should aim for the center of the side of the chest closest to them. A bullet, slug, or arrow that enters at that point will angle across the chest cavity, damaging the lungs and possibly the heart. When a deer is facing you, aim for the base of the neck or center of the chest.

A heart shot is always fatal, but the heart is a small target compared to the lungs. The heart is lower in the chest than most hunters realize, too. There is a crease of

On a deer that's angling toward you, aim with bow or gun for the center of the side of the chest that is facing you, as shown. A hit in this location will go inside (to the left of) the shoulder blade and into the chest cavity.

skin on the back of the front leg where it joins the body that is a good aiming point for those who want to try for the heart.

The heart shot can be the best place to aim for bowhunters who are about to take a shot at a deer that is alerted. Deer that are nervous tend to drop and turn when they hear a sound such as an arrow being released. This is called jumping the string. By aiming low on the chest cavity, hunters compensate for that tendency. If a deer does start to drop when the arrow leaves the bow, you should make a lung hit. If the deer doesn't react, the arrow should slice through the heart.

Properly placed neck shots with a firearm kill immediately. The only problem here is that the strike zone is narrow. A hit to either side of the vertebrae can wound. Bowhunters should not take neck shots.

When a buck is facing you like this one, gun or bow hunters should aim at the base of the neck, marked with an X, to hit the chest cavity. Gun hunters have the option of aiming higher on the neck, too.

Intentionally aiming at the head is worse than trying for the neck. A deer's brain is small, the potential for wounding great.

Whenever taking a shot at a deer, do so from the steadiest position possible. If there is time, use a rest. Shooting sticks come in handy in open terrain and many rifles designed for long-range shooting can be equipped with bipods. At least try to shoot from a sitting position. A sling helps steady your aim.

If your sights are on, if you know where to aim, and if you can hit where you aim, you will get that whitetail or mule deer. Each of these considerations is equally important. They all must come together to make consistent kills.

Hunters should always be sure a deer that is down is dead before dropping their guard. If the whitetail or mulie shows any signs of life, shoot again. If you are close to the animal, a neck shot is best. However, if the animal is struggling to get up and the neck is in constant motion, put a second round behind the shoulder. It is better to be safe than sorry. I've heard too many accounts of supposedly dead deer getting up and running off. A dead deer's eyes will be dull, lifeless, and open. There will also be no evidence of breathing.

Cameras

Hunting deer with a camera, whether a still or video camera or both, is loads of fun and can make deer hunting a year-round pursuit. There are no seasons, bag limits, or sex restrictions when you are after deer with a camera. Camera "hunters" don't even need a license.

Camera hunting is a logical offshoot for bow or gun hunters interested in "shooting" deer year-round or individuals who are interested in hunting deer, but don't want to kill them. Besides hunting during what are normally considered the off-season months in spring, summer, and winter, cameras offer the opportunity to continue hunting in the fall after you've filled your tag or to film animals you aren't interested in shooting with a gun or bow. The use of a video camera while you are hunting with gun or bow also makes it possible to film your hunt.

Deer hunting with a camera is every bit as challenging as trying for a whitetail, blacktail, or mule deer with bow and arrow. Best results with both are obtained at close range. For this reason, the camera user often has to be a skillful hunter, at least when after wild deer. Penned, caged, or tame whitetails and mulies are fair game for deer-fancying shutterbugs and videographers, too. Hunting skill isn't normally necessary to get within range of these animals.

Even for hunters who aren't interested in "hunting" deer with cameras, the devices come in handy for preserving a permanent record of the results of your hunts, and that will also be covered in this chapter. Videos cameras will be covered first followed by a discussion of still cameras.

Selecting A Video Camera

High definition (HD) video cameras are the newest, most advanced type available for filming deer and deer hunting. If you hope to shoot professional-quality video for airing on television someday, this is the type of camera you should get. Video you shoot is digital and is recorded on a tape, memory card, or disc.

247

A whitetail buck checks out a standard-definition (SD) Canon GL2 video camera I had been filming him with. SD cameras are fine to film for personal use, but high-definition cameras are now used by most professionals to film footage for use on television.

If you are also a still photographer, some top-name camera manufacturers such as Canon and Nikon make HD video cameras that are adapted for using the lenses you may already own for their still cameras. And you can also take digital still photos with the HD video cameras by flipping a switch. In fact, most video cameras also have the option of taking still images with them. Still images can either be recorded between video clips or on a separate memory card. It's better if still images are recorded on a separate memory card rather than between video clips because the latter can make editing video clips more difficult.

"Shooting" deer with a camera in a park where they aren't hunted, like I did with this whitetail buck, doesn't require much skill, but it can be fun as well as increasing your "hunting" opportunities. PHOTO COURTESY OF LUCY LAFAIVE

If you are simply shooting video for personal use or to share with friends and family, standard definition (SD) cameras will work fine. And if you happen to capture some amazing footage with an SD camera, it can still be copied for use on a television program. Tapes are used to film with SD video cameras. Most take sixty-minute mini-DVs, but tapes vary depending upon the camera manufacturer. An excellent source for all types of videotapes is Tape Resources, 5265 Providence Rd, Suite 403, Virginia Beach, VA 23464 (800-827-3462).

Whether an HD or SD video camera, one that has a standard zoom that goes out to at least 20X is best suited for filming deer. If you plan on filming hunts, you will also want a wide-angle lens for filming video in blinds and tree stands. Wide-angle lenses aren't standard equipment on most video cameras, so it's normally necessary to purchase one separately that fits your camera. I've been filming with a Canon GL2 SD video camera since 2003; I bought a .65X wide-angle to screw on the front of the lens the camera came with, and it has worked well.

Prices of video cameras vary depending upon the size and quality you want. Choose one that best fits your needs and budget. Campbell Cameras (www.campbellcameras.com) specializes in video cameras designed for filming deer and deer hunts. They sell camouflage camera covers that fit most video cameras. Many of the cameras they sell come with camo finishes.

Video Accessories

Most video cameras are battery-operated, and the batteries are usually rechargeable. I bought a long-running battery and one similar in size as a backup. It's important to have at least one backup battery to fall back on when the one you've been using runs out of juice. Video batteries drain much faster in cold weather.

If you plan on videotaping in the rain, you will need a rain cover for your camera. This is a good investment. If a video camera gets wet, the water can ruin it.

A sturdy carrying case to keep the camera clean and dry during transport is another important accessory. I have a padded hard case for mine that protects it from damage when being bounced around, when the case falls over, or when other gear is piled on top of the case. I carry spare batteries, tapes (including a cleaning tape), and a battery charger in the case with the camera.

The heads on SD cameras get dirty periodically and unless they are cleaned, the camera will not record properly. That's where the cleaning tape comes in. I always run a cleaning tape through my camera before putting a new tape in and sometimes more often than that. Most SD cameras flash a message across the screen when the heads get too dirty, and if you don't have a cleaning tape with you, that puts an end to your filming until the heads are cleaned. For that reason, it's important to carry a cleaning tape with you when filming deer or hunts.

A sturdy tripod is another important accessory to have for filming with video cameras. When zooming in on deer at high magnification, you need a tripod to steady the camera. Without one, the footage will be shaky and hard to watch. A tripod with a fluid head is also helpful to allow you to follow a walking or running deer with the camera smoothly. Tripods also come in handy when filming hunts, either

A sturdy tripod with a fluid head is an important accessory for filming deer with a video camera. Having cooperative subjects who aren't camera shy, like this whitetail doe, is also helpful.

some one else's or your own. It's almost impossible to hold a camera steady by hand when a gun goes off nearby.

If you plan to film from tree stands that are not large enough to accommodate a tripod, camera mounts that screw into trees for steady shots are the answer. A camera mount designed for use in trees is called The Third Arm (www.the3rdarm.com). Some hunters who hunt from blinds use custom clamps to fasten cameras to windows for hands-free filming. Camera mounts can also be purchased to attach video cameras to guns or bows to film shots at game. Small, lightweight video cameras work best for this purpose. Due to bow and gun movement when shots are taken, however, video of shots from cameras mounted on guns and bows will not be of the same quality as footage from cameras solidly mounted elsewhere. To film from vehicles, window mounts for your camera can come in handy.

Read the instruction manual that comes with a video camera thoroughly before attempting to film deer with it. To better acquaint yourself with how to use the camera, practice on pets, zoo animals, family members, and friends. Then when you feel comfortable about using the camera, start filming deer. The more you do it, the better you will become.

Most people tend to concentrate on zooming in as tight as possible on deer to show what the animal looks like or what it is doing, which is great, especially if deer are doing something interesting or unusual. But wide-angle shots that show whitetails and mulies in different types of habitat are also nice to have and so are extreme closeups, if possible, of just the head, mouth, ear, tail, or legs. Try to get as much variety as possible, spending no more than ten seconds on one shot, unless something interesting is happening such as a specific behavior you want to capture.

Any of the deer hunting tactics covered in this book can be used to film the animals, but stand hunting is most effective. That's also the best hunting technique to use to film hunts. With the camera mounted on a tripod or some other solid foundation, point the camera toward where you expect to see deer after you get in position. You can see what the camera sees by viewing the opened LCD screen.

Capturing A Hunt

When a deer comes into view, turn the camera on and start filming once the animal is in the right position. If it's a deer you want to shoot, make sure the whitetail or mulie is in the frame before taking your shot. A grunt or bleat may get the deer to stop if it's moving. If they are stationary and you expect them to remain there long enough for you to take a shot, you can zoom in on them as tight as you want before pulling the trigger or releasing the arrow.

This may make the process sound easy, but it's far from it. Trying to film a kill on camera yourself adds another element to the hunt that complicates matters and can result in a missed opportunity. It's much easier if another person is available to do the filming, so the hunter can concentrate on hunting rather than trying to run a video camera at the same time as they try to shoot a deer, but that's not always possible. Don't try to film a kill if you are inexperienced or if you will be upset if a deer gets away due to efforts to film it.

I missed a huge whitetail buck in Saskatchewan during November of 2003 during my first attempt to film a kill as a result of the extra effort involved. I hunted a week or more before I saw a buck I wanted to shoot, which would have scored at least in the 160s and maybe the 170s. In the meantime, I had a ball filming the smaller bucks I passed up, including several that would have scored in the 140s and one that was in the low 150s.

When the big buck showed up and I had him on camera, a severe case of buck fever hit me. I was so intent on capturing the shot on camera that I rushed the shot, shooting before I should have, causing a miss. There's no doubt in my mind that I would have gotten that buck if I wasn't so intent on filming the shot or if the video camera wasn't there.

Although missing that buck was a disappointment, I've chalked it up to another important lesson among many that I've learned over the years during my progression as a deer hunter. Several days later, I ended up shooting a beautiful 10-pointer that grossed in the 150s

A growing number of deer hunters take video cameras with them to blinds and tree stands to film deer they pass up and to record the action of the hunt.

and I did manage to get it on camera...sort of. I bumped the end of my rifle barrel on the window of my blind as I was raising it for a shot. The buck heard the sound and took a couple of bounds before stopping. He was on the edge of the frame when I dropped him in his tracks.

I did a much better job of videotaping the kill of a 12-pointer I got in Saskatchewan during the fall of 2009. I've become better at and much more comfortable filming than during that first attempt. On other occasions, bucks have appeared so fast that I barely had time to shoot them with a rifle, much less try to film the action. That's okay by me.

Hunters interested in filming their hunts have to decide for themselves if it's okay to shoot a deer even if it's not on camera. Besides not having enough time to film a deer you want to shoot, there may be occasions when a whitetail or mulie is out of the camera's view or blocked from view by brush or trees. And light for filming often ends while it's still legal shooting time. You should decide ahead of time what you're going to do if that buck you've been waiting for arrives after camera light is gone.

Instant Replay

One advantage of capturing shots at deer on video, besides being able to share the moment with others, is documenting exactly where your bullet or arrow struck a deer so you can determine the location when you replay the tape. That information can prove helpful in recovering deer that you've shot. It can also confirm if a nonfatal hit has been made and that the deer will survive with no ill effects.

I used video I took of a whitetail doe that I shot with an arrow from a crossbow to verify I made a nonfatal hit, for example. The scope on the bow was sighted in for 20 yards and the shot I took was only 15 yards from a popup ground blind. I aimed behind the middle of the doe's shoulder when I shot. It looked like the arrow went a little high, but it still appeared to be in the kill zone. The arrow flew so fast, though, that I wasn't exactly sure where it hit.

After following a sparse blood trail for 200 yards without finding the deer, I returned to friend Dean Hulce's camp to view video of the shot on a television set. After replaying the clip a number of times and slowing it down, it was clear the arrow went through the muscle on the top of the doe's back above the chest cavity, not doing any serious damage. Then it was clear why the doe had traveled much farther than she should have if I had made a lung shot.

Field Judging Bucks

In trophy buck camps like those in Alberta, Saskatchewan, Iowa, and Kansas, shooting video of bucks you've passed up during the course of the day and viewing the footage taken by all of the hunters who have video cameras during the evening is an excellent way to learn how to field judge the antlers of bucks. Guides and experienced hunters offer their opinion on what the antlers will score to verify whether or not the hunters made the right decisions. In some cases, inexperienced hunters in camps where I've been have passed up trophy-class whitetails that they should have shot.

Alfred Kiesling from Mooresville, North Carolina is a perfect example. He was hunting with Proudfoot Outfitters in Saskatchewan one year and bagged a buck with antlers that had a gross green Boone and Crockett score of 158. He returned the following year, hoping to collect a whitetail with a bigger rack. He brought a video camera with him on the return trip and it's a good thing he did.

Since Alfred planned on being selective during his return trip, he figured he would be passing up bucks that were smaller than the one he got the previous year. He brought the video camera along to film some of the whitetails he passed up, so he could look at them in the future and share what he saw with his friends. The camera ended up serving a much more important purpose.

Like many deer hunters from the states who are used to seeing small-bodied whitetails with small to average-size antlers, Kiesling had difficulty accurately judging the antler size on big bodies of the Canada whitetails he was seeing. He, like most whitetail hunters from the U.S., simply didn't often see bucks with antlers that score more than 140 and he wasn't able to tell the difference between a 150- and a 170-class animal. But fortunately, his video camera could.

Most whitetail hunting in northern Saskatchewan where nonresidents are allowed to hunt is done from baited stands or blinds, so there's ample opportunity to videotape deer as they come and go. During the rut, most adult bucks cruise by baits looking for receptive does, but they occasionally stop to feed, too. Consequently, it's not unusual to see the same bucks on consecutive days and sometimes more than once during the course of a day.

Proudfoot puts all of their hunters in enclosed blinds where their chances of being detected by whitetails is reduced. The blinds also help keep hunters warm during the cold weather common during November. During Alfred's first day in a remote blind, the best buck he saw was a nice 10-point that he estimated would score in the 140s. Since he was concentrating on becoming familiar with his surroundings and deer movements during the first day in the blind, he didn't shoot any video.

By day two, however, he got his video camera out when the same 10-point returned a couple of different times. Kiesling held the camera by hand when zooming in on the buck, resulting in shaky footage of the whitetail, but the video still accurately captured the dimensions of the buck's antlers. When Alfred showed his video to the guides and experienced hunters in camp that evening, they had a hard time believing he had passed on the buck two days in a row. They made it clear that the antlers were much larger than the hunter thought and that he should shoot the deer, if he saw it again.

Fortunately for Kiesling, he did see the buck again the next morning and was able to collect it. The 10-pointer that he had passed up two days in a row had a gross green Boone and Crockett score of 172^6/$_8$. The deer had a live weight of 250 pounds and was 200 pounds dressed.

Alfred wasn't the only hunter who had a video camera with him in that camp. There were at least ten of us who had various makes and models of video cameras. Many video cameras are reasonably priced these days and are easy to use, making it

Hunters in deer camp watching video of bucks filmed during the day. It's a good way to learn how to judge antler size and find out if you passed up one you shouldn't have.

easier for hunters to justify using them. A professional-quality camera isn't necessary to capture good video of deer you see.

Every evening after dinner, those of us who had video footage of bucks we passed up or shot would plug our cameras into the television set to share what we saw with the rest of the hunters. Every session was entertaining as well as educational. Each member of the group was then able to benefit from what a number of people saw. The guides and experienced hunters provided their input about what they thought antlers of various bucks would score, giving the inexperienced members the benefit of their knowledge to use during the rest of their hunt.

More Examples

Kiesling wasn't the only hunter who underestimated the size of the antlers of bucks they saw while I was at that Saskatchewan camp that year. On the first day of hunting during the second week, a pair of hunters, one of whom had never shot a whitetail before, passed up typical bucks that would have scored at least in the 170s and took video of the deer. Both hunters started their day with the mindset of not shooting anything on the first day of hunting to reduce the chances of shooting one that was "too small." That strategy cost them bucks of a lifetime.

Both hunters ended up shooting much smaller bucks than they could have. It didn't make much of a difference to the inexperienced person because he still had a terrific time and was happy to collect his first whitetail ever. The more experienced hunter made another mistake on his second day of hunting, shooting a 130-class 10-point that he thought was the one he passed up the day before. Although the buck he shot was still his best ever, he was disappointed about not making the best choice he could have.

In each of those cases, other hunters were put on the stands where the bigger bucks had been filmed, but the bucks weren't seen again for the rest of the season. So trophy bucks that are filmed don't always give hunters a second chance. The fact that other bucks were shot from those stands may have had something to do with that. The noise and commotion associated with retrieving deer from those locations may have scared the larger whitetails away.

Captured On Tape

North Carolina hunter Phil Stover was also the beneficiary of the value of having a video camera on a Saskatchewan hunt. The camera operated by hunting partner Eddie Johnson played a role in Stover bagging a world-class buck. It was the third trip to the province for both hunters and they had each tagged quality bucks on previous trips, so they had their sights set high that year.

On the fourth day of their hunt, Johnson dropped a 160-class buck about 3:00 P.M. A half hour later, a much bigger buck appeared and Eddie filmed it with his video camera. Eddie wanted his partner to move to the blind where he filmed the bruiser on the chance Phil might get a shot at it. After viewing the video, that's exactly what Phil did.

Phil had his mind made up that he was going to take the buck his buddy filmed or nothing. It was easy to set such a lofty goal after seeing proof of its existence.

Phil Stover with a Saskatchewan Boone and Crockett whitetail that he got after his hunting partner, Eddie Johnson, videotaped it. PHOTO COURTESY OF EDDIE JOHNSON

And the fact that it showed up after Eddie shot his buck and didn't seem spooky was evidence enough that it could return.

Two days later, which was the last day of Phil's hunt, the big buck made another appearance and Stover didn't waste any time putting a bullet into the whitetail. The 13-pointer had a green gross score of 196^4/$_8$ as a typical. The buck's amazing brow tines were 11 and 11^5/$_8$ inches in length. Thanks to a video camera, Phil knew what he was looking for and immediately took advantage of the opportunity when it presented itself. And I'm sure that's not the last big buck that will end up with someone's tag on it after first being seen on videotape.

Cold-Weather Precautions

One of the most important precautions we learned about viewing videotape taken in cold weather is that it is essential to let video cameras return to room temperature, or at least close to it, before attempting to play the footage back. Ideally, video cameras should be in an enclosed case or backpack, but a garbage bag will work when bringing them inside from the cold. They should be left inside the unopened case, pack, or bag for at least an hour, and two or three hours is better, to allow them to warm up slowly before you attempt to play the tape. If temperatures are extremely cold, allowing a camera to warm up overnight before attempting to view deer that have been filmed is even better.

Condensation can form on the inside of video cameras as well as on the lenses when they are brought directly from the cold into a warm camp, and that moisture can ruin tapes and cameras. When outside temperatures are above freezing, it's not necessary to wait as long before viewing deer hunting video, but when temperatures are in the 30s and 40s, cameras should still be allowed to acclimate inside for a while.

Avoid Taping Over Footage

There's another problem that can be encountered when viewing video of deer filmed during the course of the day. Some hunters have rewound tapes to the point where they are shown shooting a deer for later viewing and then forgotten to advance the tape before filming the next time. The camera then tapes over the segment and it is lost. To reduce the chances of this happening, it's good to get into the habit of checking your tape to make sure you will be filming with unused tape before starting to film. Also, when you are finished filming for the day, always make sure to advance the tape to the point where you quit filming or even a little beyond, to create a blank space between each day's filming. By doing this, you will avoid taping over valuable action.

Telling The Story

If you hope to use a video camera to tell the story about your deer hunt, it's important to film as many other elements of the hunt as possible besides deer you pass up and the kill. Other wildlife you see are part of the hunt, so filming them is a good

idea, if you can. Film the blind or tree stand you hunt from and you getting in position, if possible. During slow times when no deer are in view, use your wide angle
lens to tape yourself talking about the weather and what you've seen.

You can keep a video diary of the high points of each day's hunt by talking into
the camera at the end of each day, at camp. You will also want to film the camp, both
interior and exterior views, parts of a meal, the cook, and other hunters in camp with
their deer. If you are using the services of a guide or outfitter, they are also an important part of the story. After you shoot your deer, you will also want some footage of
you walking up to it, tagging it, transporting it, weighing it, measuring it, and anything else that is part of the story. If you've shot a buck, don't forget to take some
tight shots of antlers to show them off as well as anything unusual about the deer.
The more elements of the hunt you are able to capture with your camera, the better
the story you will be able to tell with it.

Verifying Legality

Videotaping the kill of a trophy whitetail or mule deer can come in handy in another
way too—to verify the deer was taken legally. I recently read an account about a
deer hunter who bagged an exceptional buck within view of private property he did
not have permission to hunt. When the owner of the private land saw the hunter with
the big buck, he accused the hunter of killing it illegally on his property, notifying
the authorities. Fortunately, one of the hunter's friends had videotaped the kill and
the tape was used to prove the buck was taken legally where the hunter had permission to hunt.

This type of situation does not come up often, but if it happens to you, you will
want to have some proof of your innocence. Still cameras can also be used to verify
the location of a kill by taking photos where a deer died. That's a perfect lead-in to
discussing the selection of still cameras for hunting as well as for documenting the
scene of a kill.

Camera Selection

While some still cameras that were made for film remain in use, most of today's
cameras make digital images. There are many advantages digitals have over film
cameras. No film processing is involved. It's possible to view the finished product
immediately and, if you don't like it, you can take another to replace it, then delete
the unsatisfactory image. Images can be transferred directly from the camera to a
computer and the same memory card can be used over and over again, saving money
that used to be spent on film and processing.

Another important advantage available from digital cameras is that high-capacity
memory cards are available that allow you to take hundreds of images without having to stop to change film or cards. For many years when I photographed with film,
thirty-six-exposure rolls were the largest available. I've lost track of the number of
times I wished it were possible to make more than thirty-six images before having to
stop to reload. I missed plenty of action while reloading film cameras. That is less
likely to be a problem during the digital age.

Fortunately, the best digital cameras for photographing deer, in terms of design and use, are much the same as the film cameras before them. Single-lens reflex (SLR) 35-mm cameras are the best choice for photographing deer. The photographer sees exactly what he or she is shooting with a SLR 35-mm because viewing is done through the lens. It is similar to looking through a rifle scope.

Digital cameras are rated in terms of megapixels. The higher the number of megapixels the camera has, the better the quality of the images it produces. Digital cameras that have a minimum of four megapixels will produce respectable images, but those with six or eight are better. The digital camera I'm now using, with which I took many of the photos that appear in this book, has 8.4 megapixels. It's a Canon Eos 20D. Digital cameras with as much as eighteen megapixels are available now, but it probably won't take long for that to change.

Camera manufacturers Canon and Nikon are known for quality, but most cameras on the market today will take quality images. Other companies that make digital cameras include Pentax, Sony, Olympus, Kodak, Panasonic, and Fugi.

If you plan on photographing deer, make sure you have a selection of lenses available. A variety of lenses isn't as important if your main focus is photographing deer that you have bagged.

To beginning photographers, especially those familiar with pocket cameras or the photo app on cell phones, SLRs often look complicated. The various dials give them that appearance. Actually, 35s are not difficult to use. In fact, many of the new 35-mm SLR digital cameras are easy to use because most of the functions are fully automatic, but it's still important to understand how an SLR functions.

Read the owner's manual that comes with your camera thoroughly, so you understand how best to use it. Then, as recommended for practicing with video cameras, photograph pets, zoo animals, family, and friends to become comfortable with using the camera.

It's the Lenses

The feature that makes SLR cameras the best choice for hunting deer is that they can be fitted with a variety of lenses. Lenses range from wide-angles to telephotos. Wide-angle lenses make subjects look farther away and smaller than they do to the naked eye. Telephotos increase the size of subjects and make them look closer. A normal lens is the same magnification as the human eye. In other words, a subject viewed through a normal lens will appear approximately the same as it would without looking through a camera.

Normal lenses for 35-mm cameras are usually 50 mm. A 25-mm wide-angle would decrease the size of subjects by one-half. Such a lens will also make the subject look twice as far away as when viewed with a normal lens. A telephoto that is 200 mm will magnify subjects four times and make them look closer.

Cameras other than SLRs usually come with nonremoveable lenses. Some of them have low-powered telephoto lenses. Telephoto lenses are a must for obtaining satisfactory photos of deer. The most popular sizes for "shooting" deer are 135, 200, 300, and 400, but larger lenses are available, too. Lenses can be purchased that have

Telephoto lenses are a must for getting good closeups of deer with a camera. The photographer in this photo is using a 135 mm (2.5X) lens to photograph a velvet antlered whitetail buck in a park where deer are used to people.

either fixed magnifications or a range of magnifications. The latter types are called zoom lenses.

I now use a pair of zoom lenses for most of my photography. I photograph live deer most often with a 70- to 200-mm zoom and capture images of dead deer with a 24- to 70-mm zoom. Having two zoom lenses is easier than carrying four or five fixed-focal-length lenses.

As the lenses increase in magnification, their light-gathering ability usually decreases. The light-gathering ability of a lens is determined by the smallest number f-stop the diaphragm will open to. Fast lenses will have a maximum diaphragm opening of 2.8 or larger. Slow lenses may not open any farther than 5.6 or 4.5. Fast lenses can be used in situations where light conditions are poor, but the lighting has to be good where slow lenses are employed.

My two favorites in telephotos are the 135 and 300. My 135 is an f/2 lens and my 300 is an f/2.8, both of which are made by Canon. Some photographers who regularly shoot deer swear by 400s and even 600s.

Lens extenders, called doublers, can be used to double the magnification of telephotos. Doublers fit between the camera body and regular lens. Those I have used yielded poor results. Extremely good light is necessary to use lens extenders because they reduce the light-gathering ability of lenses. Best results are obtained with extenders made by your camera's manufacturer.

The weight of telephoto lenses increases in proportion to magnification. A 300 mm is generally heavier than a 200 mm, and a 400 mm is heavier than either of the others. This is an important consideration when it comes to taking photos of deer. The heavier a lens, the less likely it is that a photographer will be able to take good pictures when holding camera and lens by hand. Weight induces wobbling, which blurs pictures.

Fast shutter speeds are often enough to offset the jiggles caused by holding a camera with a telephoto by hand. It is even better to rest a camera mounted with a long lens against a tree, fence post, car, or anything else to steady it. A tripod is better yet for shooting with telephotos. Tripods enable camera deer hunters to get satisfactory shots of deer with a telephoto lens, even at the low shutter speeds that are sometimes necessary in the morning and evening when light is poor and deer are most active.

A couple of general rules that apply to shooting deer with a camera are to use a tripod whenever possible and shoot at the fastest shutter speed the available light will allow. Try to press the shutter release smoothly, too, as you would squeeze the trigger of a rifle. Punching the release will increase the chances of camera movement, which can blur pictures.

Always try to focus on the eyes of a deer before taking its picture. When using autofocus lenses, simply put the autofocus square or circle that's visible through the viewfinder on a deer's eye or eyes before tripping the shutter. The eyes are the center of attention. If they are in focus, the photo will be acceptable. And above all else, take a number of exposures of your subject, if possible. Don't be satisfied with one or two shots. Those extra exposures can make the difference between mediocre and excellent results. It only takes one good shot to make a photo session with deer worthwhile in terms of getting a "trophy." The one you didn't take may have been the best.

Most SLRs come equipped with motor drives that automatically cock the camera after each exposure. Most digital cameras also come with automatic flashes that light up the subject if there isn't enough available light to properly expose a shot.

A beginning camera hunter shouldn't expect to get top-notch results the first time out. Becoming proficient with a camera takes practice, just as proficiency with a gun or bow and arrow does. Zoos are perfect practice ranges for deer photographers. Try to take as many images as possible of a variety of subjects at a zoo before heading into the field.

Accessories

Digital cameras are battery-operated and most are rechargeable. I always have a spare with me to fall back on when the one in the camera dies. I also carry at least one spare memory card in case the one I'm using becomes full. If you expect to do a lot of shooting, having a couple of spare batteries and cards is recommended.

And it's always a good idea to download the images from your camera before going on a trip or a hunt during which you expect to do a lot of filming. Once the images are on your computer, they can be deleted from the camera, leaving maximum room for new images. You don't want to have to do what a photographer who I shared a hunt with one time did. When his memory card reached capacity in the field and he didn't have a spare, he spent precious time looking through the images on his camera and deleting those he didn't want, to make room for more.

Having at least one external hard drive attached to your computer on which your images are backed up is a good practice, too. I have two external hard drives that I back my images up on and I know photographers who have more. It's an excellent way to protect what you've collected in case there's a problem with your computer.

A camera case is another accessory that comes in handy to protect and carry your equipment. One that will hold extra lenses, batteries, and cards is ideal.

Evaluating Results

Overexposed pictures are the result of too much light on the subject. Underexposures mean there wasn't enough light. The meters and flashes on most modern cameras are so sophisticated that under- and overexposed images are not as much of a problem as they used to be. If the camera you are using consistently produces poor results, however, it should be repaired or exchanged for another.

Fuzzy or blurred photos are the result of poor focusing or camera movement caused by a too-slow shutter speed or an unsteady lens. If you use autofocus lenses, they will sometimes focus on trees, brush, blades of grass, other vegetation, or twigs that are between you and your subject. This results in images that are out of focus.

For best results, switch lenses to manual focus to photograph deer among trees or brush. Autofocus works fine most of the time when deer are photographed in the open.

Unlike hunting with gun or bow, success with a camera is subject to the user's interpretation. Deer successfully bagged with a bullet or arrow are dead. There is no in-between. Images of deer shot with a camera are imprinted on film or a memory card. The images can be distant, close up, in focus, out of focus, fuzzy, sharp, underexposed, overexposed, or a combination of these.

From my point of view, I would consider a photo of a whitetail or mule deer that is in focus, properly exposed, and reasonably close a successful shot. Anything else would be a miss. I can remember times, however, when I was happy with any image of a deer on film.

The quality of a photo isn't the only factor that determines its value to the photographer. Memories that go with it add their special appeal to exposures of deer. A image that is of poor quality may be valuable (a trophy) if it brings to mind pleasant or humorous memories of the circumstances under which the shot was obtained.

Photos of Success

Hunters who are successful in bagging a deer during the fall hunting season frequently want to get pictures of themselves with their kill. SLR 35s with a normal or wide-angle lens are fine for this use, but any type of digital camera will work.

Fully automatic 35s are the simplest cameras to use. All there is to do with these is center the subject in the viewfinder and shoot. The best deer-kill photos are the ones taken immediately after the kill, so hunters should try to carry a camera with them. The happy expression of a successful deer hunter at that time is bound to be more appealing than a forced grin later. A natural setting also adds a great deal more to such a picture than a cluttered yard, basement, or a deer-in-the-bed-of-a-pickup pose.

And if you want to document the location where a deer died, having a camera with you is a definite advantage. If you are not hunting far from your vehicle or camp, however, a camera can usually be retrieved for that purpose before a deer is moved. When bowhunting, it's not unusual to wait a half hour or more before taking up the trail of an arrowed deer, too, which can be ample time to get a camera before a downed deer is located.

Try to get in close for photos of hunters with their deer. Close-ups are often more dramatic than exposures taken from a distance that lack detail. Too much background can detract from the subject. Before taking closeups, remember to make sure the deer's tongue is in its mouth. If it's difficult to impossible to get the tongue back in the mouth due to lockjaw, cut the exposed tongue off. Wiping off excess blood will make the photo look less gruesome, too. Strategically placed leaves, guns, bows, and backpacks can also be used to cover blood.

A camera comes in handy for photographing successful members of your party. A normal or wide-angle lens is perfect for this use. Try to fill the frame with hunter and deer. The best photos are taken as soon as possible after the kill. Make sure the deer's tongue is in its mouth and as much blood as possible is removed or covered.

If you are hunting by yourself, you can take great photos of yourself with your deer if you have a camera with a self-timer and wide-angle lens and a tripod. Simply focus on the fallen deer's eye, leave room for yourself, set the timer, press the shutter, and get in place. I use slow shutter speeds to allow for maximum depth of field. The shadow of the tripod-mounted camera is intentionally showing in this photo to illustrate its use, but try to avoid shadows like this under normal circumstances. Many of the photos in this book of bucks I've bagged were taken this way.

Deer hunters who are alone when they make a kill can still get photos. Most digital cameras have self-timers. Simply set the deer up where you want it, leaving room for yourself in front of, to the side of, or behind the animal. To frame and focus the photo, use a stick with a hat on it as a dummy for yourself. If using a wide-angle lens, forget the stick with a hat on it and just allow for plenty of room where you plan to be. The camera can be set on a tripod, backpack, rock, or stump.

Focus either on the deer or hat, then get in position. Self-timers usually give the hunter at least five seconds to get into position from the time the shutter release is pushed. For best results, I use a slow shutter speed, which allows a small lens opening, and focus on the downed deer's eye. This allows enough depth of field that the hunter is usually also in focus.

Make sure no obstructions such as grass or twigs obscure any part of the deer or yourself; when wearing a hat or cap, tip the brim up so it doesn't shade your face. Take a number of exposures, varying the angle, to make sure you get the best shots possible.

16

Clothing and Equipment

One of the most miserable days of deer hunting that I've ever spent was in northern Saskatchewan during early December one year. The air temperature was a few degrees below zero Fahrenheit and the wind chill was probably close to 30 below. I dressed warm, with lots of layers. If I had taken a small portable heater to my blind with me that day, as I should have, I probably would have been reasonably comfortable. Without a heater, though, I was underdressed. Fortunately, I was hunting from an enclosed ground blind. Keeping all of the windows on the blind closed retained some of the heat my body generated. In spite of the cold air temperature, the sun also helped provide some heat.

What made matters worse was deer weren't moving. I didn't see a single whitetail that day. They were probably tucked away in some thicket doing their best to stay warm, too. The lack of deer activity allowed me to spend more time than I would have liked focusing on how cold it was. Time dragged. I was ready to call it a day by 4:00 P.M., but I had to wait until 5:30 when some one picked me up. Having to endure such extreme cold that day was enough to convince me to never do it again.

To make sure it would never happen again, I acquired two things: a Heater Body Suit and a portable propane heater. The Heater Body Suit is a heavy, one-piece suit/bag made of heavy material designed to keep hunters as warm as possible in cold weather. The portable heater does the same thing. Most outfitters provide them, but bringing one with me ensures I will have one when and if I need it.

Some of the best deer hunting I've experienced has been in snowy, cold weather when I was dressed properly for the conditions. Being miserable is both undesirable and unnecessary with the choices of clothing and equipment hunters have available to them today. If you hunt whitetails or mule deer in the northern United States or Canada during November or December it's possible for daytime temperatures to drop to zero or below, so it's important to be prepared. Your effectiveness as a deer

A portable heater like this one can be the difference between comfort and misery when temperatures are cold. Whenever you use a heater in a blind make sure it is ventilated to avoid the buildup of carbon monoxide.

hunter will be determined in part by your comfort, which is directly related to the clothes you wear. The type and amount of clothing a deer hunter wears will be dictated by the weather and the type of hunting that is to be done.

Temperatures can be warm to downright hot during early fall deer hunts, for instance. Under these conditions, it's important to dress as lightly as possible regardless of how you will be hunting. At the other extreme, during some late deer seasons, temperatures can be brutally cold. Dressing as warmly as possi-

Layering is the key to dressing properly for deer hunting, especially in cold weather, as clearly shown by this late-season muzzleloader hunter. A Heater Body Suit could be substituted for the blanket. As the weather warms or your activity level increases, layers can be taken off. The process can be reversed as the temperature drops.

ble is the name of the game under those conditions and wearing a number of layers of clothes is the key to staying warm.

Layering clothing is actually the key to dressing properly for deer hunting regardless of the weather conditions. Thanks to the quality and variety of clothing available to deer hunters today, it's easier than ever to dress for comfort. Most hunters will have to prepare for conditions somewhere in beetween the two extremes mentioned above. Since I've been lucky enough to hunt whitetails and mulies during the entire spectrum of possibilities, I think I can provide some valuable advice on how to dress for the hunt. Let's start with the warmest conditions first.

Clothing For Warm Days

Outer garments of lightweight, loose-fitting cotton or cotton blends are best for such situations since cotton is light and quiet. Camouflage clothing can be purchased with shirt and pants separate or as a one-piece suit (coveralls)—either is perfect for deer hunting. I prefer to wear long-sleeved shirts and long pants when deer hunting in warm to hot weather because the fabric reduces scent dispersal, deters biting insects, and protects the skin from being scratched by thorns, briars, and brush while afield. However, when hunting in areas where biting insects are not a problem and getting scratched isn't a concern, wearing short-sleeved shirts and shorts is an option for hunters who are hunting from blinds or tree stands and hunters who expect to see deer at long distances.

Deer hunters who try their luck where biting insects are a problem during early seasons should consider wearing outfits designed to discourage these pests. The two-piece Bug Tamer outfit made by Shannon Outdoors (www.shannonoutdoors.com) is perfect for keeping bugs at bay in warm weather. The clothing is designed to prevent bugs from biting through it, yet allow the free flow of air.

ThermaCELL (www.thermacell.com) is the latest innovation in protection from biting insects. When activated, these pocket-size units powered by butane cartridges create an area measuring 15 feet by 15 feet around them that is free of biting insects. These units are supposed to be ninety-eight percent effective and are undetectable by game. In view of the spread of West Nile Virus from mosquitoes in the United States, protecting yourself from being bitten by mosquitoes is an important safety consideration.

Controlling or limiting a deer hunter's scent is important in warm weather and the Scent-Lok Company (www.scentlok.com) makes that possible through their Savanna Series of clothing. Other companies who make scent-absorbing clothes might also have options suited for hunting when temperatures are warm to hot.

Hunters can wear lightweight fluorescent orange vests over the camouflage if hunting with firearms. A bright-colored cap or hat that is ventilated is also a good idea for warm-weather gun hunters. Camouflage hats are fine for archers, but if you buy a camo cap with a brim, it may be best to wear the hat backwards when hunting so it won't interfere with your draw.

As temperatures cool below the 70s, hunters should add another layer of cloth-ing to their outfit to maintain comfort, especially when stand hunting. A shirt and pair of pants or jeans can be worn under the camo outfit for added insulation. Many

Left: Thermacells like this one are the latest innovation in keeping biting bugs at bay during warm weather. When activated, they are supposed to provide a bug-free zone around you. Bug suits are an alternative. It is important for hunters to protect themselves from mosquitoes that carry West Nile Virus.

Right: Light cotton clothes and short-sleeved shirts like those worn by this South Carolina hunter are a good choice in warm weather. This photo was taken on August 15, which is when deer season begins in part of that state, but warm temperatures are possible into October, and sometimes later, in the south.

hunters who try to squeeze in quick evening hunts after school or work simply put camo on over casual clothes when they leave their vehicle to head for their stand. A light set of long underwear can be substituted for an inner layer.

The 45- To 65-Degree Range

Heavier outer layers are called for when temperatures are in the 45- to 65-degree range. A medium-weight coat and pants that are made of soft and quiet fabrics such as cotton, wool, or fleece are good choices. I always wear a Scent-Lok suit when deer hunting for this temperature range as well as others, but there are a variety of outer layers for hunters to choose from. Wool is an especially good choice for cold weather since it insulates even when wet. However, I only wear wool paired with long underwear because wool irritates my skin. When temperatures are in the high 40s and 50s, I normally wear a set of light- or medium-weight long underwear.

Since I hunt multiple seasons, including those for bow and arrow, I buy outer layers in camo and then add an orange vest and/or orange hat for firearms hunts. I make sure to get outer coats and pants in large enough sizes to allow for a number of layers underneath.

Since I hunt both with firearms and with bow and arrow, I normally select camo clothes for outer layers and then add an orange vest and hat for gun hunting. Hunters who only go afield with firearms may want to select brighter-colored outer layers.

Toward the upper end of this temperature range, I normally only wear a long-sleeved shirt under the coat, unless it is windy and wind chill is a factor or the temperature is supposed to plummet during the course of a day of hunting, according to the weather forecast. When it's windy or the temperature is supposed to drop into the 50s, I add a light layer of long underwear on top and bottom. That's also how I dress when daytime temperatures average in the upper 40s with light winds. I might wear a heavier shirt made of flannel rather than cotton when temperatures are in the 40s, too. I usually carry a light pair of cotton gloves with me to keep my hands warm when temperatures are at that level.

When I plan on stand hunting for most of a day or all day, I normally carry a sweatshirt or sweater in my backpack as an extra layer in case I get cold early and late in the day. That's when daytime temperatures are usually at their lowest and extra insulation might be needed.

Dressing in the above manner should be comfortable for most deer hunters whether they are stand hunting, stillhunting, stalking, or participating in drives. Everyone's body and how it functions varies, however, so my suggestions should simply serve as guidelines. The more time you spend deer hunting under varying weather conditions, the better you will know what layers work best to keep you comfortable.

Long Underwear

The layering system I use when temperatures drop below the mid-40s is primarily based on adding varying weights of long underwear. There are at least five types of long underwear: fishnet, polypropylene, capilene, silk, cotton knit, and heavy insulated. I wear capilene underwear most often. This material is similar to polypropylene. The advantage of wearing long underwear made of capilene and polypropylene is the fabrics wick moisture away from the body when you sweat, which reduces your chances of getting chilled in cold weather.

Capilene long underwear comes in three weights—light, medium, and heavy. Since I do a lot of cold-weather deer hunting, I own lots of long underwear. I have two pairs of the heaviest layers, at least six sets of medium-weight layers, and lots of light layers.

On days when temperatures will be in the low 40s to upper 30s, taking into account wind chill, and I will only be inactive for two to three hours at a time, I normally wear medium bottoms under medium-weight camo pants. On top, I wear a light layer of Capilene, a shirt of choice and a medium- to heavy-weight coat. For all-day sits, I may put on a heavy pair of pants and/or a lightweight bottom under the mediums and wear a medium top under a heavy shirt.

When temperatures range from the 20s to the low 30s and I plan on sitting, I often put on heavy- and medium- or lightweight bottoms under pants, and light- and medium-weight tops under a shirt and coat (three layers on top and bottom). A warm hat, gloves, and boots are necessary when it gets this cold, too, of course. Still-hunters, stalkers, and drivers might want to eliminate the heaviest layers of long underwear mentioned above, and they won't need a hat and boots as heavy as those necessary to stay warm when stand hunting. The same is true for snow trackers, who could probably get by with light layers of long underwear.

Colder Conditions

When the thermometer dips into the teens and single digits, I often wear three sets of long underwear, with two of those layers being the heaviest I've got. One of them is Capilene and the other is a heavy, insulated type that I've had for years. A warm hat, gloves, and boots are necessary under these conditions as well.

Because I often wear a number of layers of long underwear under coat and pants, I select outer layers that will be large enough to accomodate multiple layers. I wear heavy Scent-Lok outer layers that are designed for cold weather and at least one of the inner layers is a Scent-Lok base layer to provide maximum scent suppression. King of the Mountain (www.kingofthemountain.com) makes an excellent line of wool hunting clothes that are designed for cold-weather hunting. Raven Wear (800-387-2836), based in Alberta, Canada, also makes cold-weather hunting clothes.

When dressing for extremely cold weather, I've found that it is important to put outer layers on in an entryway, shed, or even outside to avoid overheating and starting to sweat. Another option is to turn the inside temperature of the camp or home down to reduce the chances of getting hot while putting the final layers on.

To increase the odds of staying warm when stand hunting in cold weather, some hunters wear insulated coveralls or pull a sleeping bag over themselves in their blinds. Large body suits (Heater Body Suits) that are available commercially serve the same function. Heating pads that are manufactured by a number of companies can also help cold-weather hunters stay warm. These pads can be put in boots or pants pockets, worn under hats, or wrapped in scarves to keep feet, hands, heads, and necks warm. Direct contact between the pads and skin should be avoided, however, to prevent burns.

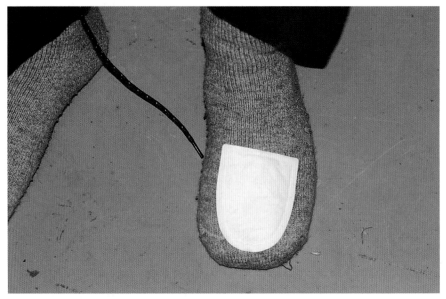

Heating pads can help keep hunters warm in cold weather. They can be placed on socks, as shown here, in gloves, in a scarf worn around the neck, or on the back of a shirt to warm the back. They should not be placed directly on the skin.

Some hunters who try their luck from enclosed blinds in cold weather rely on portable or propane heaters to keep them warm. On a recent hunt in Saskatchewan, I used a portable Coleman propane heater that I brought with me to heat my blind when the temperature was −10 degrees Fahrenheit. I would not have been able to remain comfortable while stand hunting in weather that cold for more than an hour without a heater. At least one window should always be open for ventilation when using a heater in an enclosed blind.

When selecting camouflage clothing to wear for hunting, try to select patterns that blend in best with the habitat you will be hunting. A wide selection of camo patterns are available today. Realtree, Mossy Oak, and Trebark are some of the most popular. Skyline and Natural Gear also make quality products. I've worn both Realtree and Mossy Oak camo patterns with excellent results. A line of hunting clothes designed specifically for women can be found at www.shesafari.com.

When deer hunting away from home, the rule of thumb is to bring enough clothing to stay warm in the coldest weather possible. If it is warmer than expected, some layers will go unused. That's far better than encountering cold weather and not having enough clothes to stay warm. Hunters unprepared for low thermometer readings can't put on layers they don't have.

Some deer hunters use suspenders to hold up their pants, but I prefer a belt. I usually carry a sheath knife on it, and I can use my belt to drag a deer if I forget a rope. A tracking hunter I know wears a belt from six to eight inches longer than usual so he can tuck shed layers of clothes under it when he is moving on a track.

Another type of weather deer hunters should always be prepared for is rain, unless hunting in the northern U.S. and Canada late in the season when the tempera-

Umbrellas that screw into trees to provide hunters with a portable roof on rainy days can come in handy.

ture is below freezing, where snow is the norm. A heavy-duty, two-piece rain suit has served me well over the years. The bottoms of the pant legs have zippers on the sides, so they can be pulled on over boots. The bib-type pants are held up with suspenders. The coat has a hood attached to keep hat and head dry.

To protect from rain when stand hunting from a spot on the ground or an open tree stand with no roof, I carry an umbrella designed to screw into trees to provide a portable roof. These are available through Cabela's. These umbrellas designed for hunters have kept me dry numerous times.

Footwear

Now let's move on to footwear. Tennis shoes with a light pair of socks are fine for stillhunting or stalking early in the season. Avoid wearing white tennis shoes for deer hunting. If you can find them in green, brown, gray, or black it's much better.

Bean Boots (www.llbean.com; 800-441-5713) are ideal for early fall hunting where wet ground may be encountered. Developed for use in the big woods of

Knee-high rubber boots are necessary when hunting wet ground for keeping feet dry. Rubber boots also reduce the amount of scent hunters leave where they walk. A number of companies make quality rubber boots that come with or without insulation.

Maine, these boots have rubber bottoms and leather tops. This style of boot has served me well while bowhunting at home as well as in a number of other states and provinces. Bean Boots can be obtained with and without insulation.

If thorns or cactus are present where you will be hunting, a light pair of leather boots might be a better choice. High-topped leather snake boots are availble for hunters who will be hunting where poisonous snakes are a concern. Snake-proof chaps are an option, too.

Boot Blankets like these can be worn over other boots to keep feet warm when stand hunting. Don't put them on until you are in your stand.

Rubber boots are the ticket for walking in wet terrain. Whenever I wear out a pair of waders, I cut off the heavy boot and wear these deer hunting early in the fall. There are no laces to worry about and they are durable and light. LaCrosse, Rocky, and the Muck Boot (www.muckboots.com; 877-215-6778) make quality knee-high rubber boots for walking through water. They have both uninsulated and insulated models for warm and cold weather.

Wool or cotton socks are satisfactory for use during both early and late fall. Scent-Lok makes socks that I often wear when deer hunting.

Boots with removable felt liners are the best I've found for keeping my feet warm in cold weather. I wear the leather-

Boots with removable liners like these are great for cold-weather hunting. Be sure to remove the liners at the end of the day so they can dry. Having a spare set of liners ensures you will have a dry set.

top, rubber-bottom variety. The liners absorb perspiration. LaCrosse makes some of the warmest cold-weather boots I've worn and the company has a number of models for cold-weather use. Northern Outfitters (www.northernoutfitters.com) also makes boots designed for cold weather, and they have a line of cold-weather clothing, too.

Products called Boot Blankets, available commercially, are designed to fit over the largest cold-weather boots and provide more insulation, which will help keep your feet warm. Although I've never found the need to wear these, I've hunted in Canada with some hunters who have and they've told me the blankets work in cold weather when stand hunting. Don't put Boot Blankets on until at your stand. Hot Mocs (www.hotmocs.com) are another product designed to be pulled over boots; these have a pocket for a heating pad to help keep feet warm.

I used to buy cold-weather deer hunting boots at least one size larger than my feet so I could wear extra layers of socks. The insulating properties of today's boots have improved so much that now that is no longer necessary. One pair of heavy socks keeps my feet warm in the boots I now wear. Boots made by Northern Outfitters are designed for use with a light pair of socks.

When wearing cold-weather boots with liners, be sure to remove the liners from boots at the end of a day of hunting to let them dry. An extra pair of liners can come in handy to make sure you have a dry pair from one day to the next.

When the weather is cold, rubber or leather boots are okay for deer hunting in situations where you won't be staying in one place long, such as making drives, still-hunting, or tracking. Boots of this type that are light and fit snugly will make it easier to "feel the ground" better, increasing the ability to walk quietly.

Heads and Hands

Something to cover the head is as important as warm clothes when sitting in cold weather. A lot of heat escapes via an uncovered head. I wear a Scent Lok hood most often when stand hunting for deer. If I'm hunting with a firearm or the weather is cold, I normally wear an orange baseball-type hat over the hood. When stillhunting or tracking, I prefer to wear a wool knit hat or short-billed hat but any type that you are comfortable with will do.

The Polar Wrap (www.polarwrap.com) is a hood designed for deer hunters who are afield in cold weather. The front portion of the wrap that fits over your nose and mouth has a special feature that's supposed to recycle warm air that you exhale to help keep your head and face warm. The makers of Hot Mocs also make beanies designed for use with heating pads that fit in a flap that pulls down over the back of the neck. Stormy Kromer hats come in different colors and are designed for deer hunting in cold weather. They have flaps that can be pulled down over ears for added warmth.

A flap of wool or fleece sewn to the back of a cap or hat prevents snow from falling down a deer hunter's neck when the white stuff covers trees. A piece of material can be pinned to a hat quickly and easily for hunters who aren't into sewing. Another way to keep snow from falling down your neck is to wear a scarf. Scarves protect the front and back from cold breezes as well as snow. The hood of a sweatshirt is another way to keep snow off the back of your neck when walking through snow-covered woods, but the material also covers your ears and dulls your hearing.

Hands need protection during cold weather. I wear light to heavy Scent-Lok gloves most often. They are not bulky, so I can easily handle a gun, bow, or camera with them on. I usually carry two pairs in case one gets wet. I frequently stick gloved hands in my pockets to keep them warm during long waits in cold weather. Hand warmers or muffs can come in handy, too.

Bowhunters who use a three-fingered shooting glove can keep that hand warm by cutting the middle fingers off a cotton glove for that hand. The shooting glove can be strapped on over it. I now wear a full-fingered golf glove on my shooting hand when bowhunting.

Equipment

Proper clothing; a gun, bow, or camera; ammunition or arrows; and a hunting license are the essentials for deer hunters. Before venturing into the field, however, hunters should slip a few additional items into pockets or a small pack. One item no deer hunter should be without is a compass. A GPS (Global Positioning System) unit is also a good idea when hunting in unfamiliar country, but one of these isn't as important as a compass. Don't just buy a compass and GPS; try them out to make sure they are accurate and you know how to use them. Some of the best GPS devices for hunters are made by Garmin, Lowrance, Delorme, and Magellan.

Before going into the woods, mountains, desert, swamps, or wherever you are hunting, try to take a compass reading to determine which way you are heading and which way you will have to go to get back out. It only takes a couple of seconds. With a GPS, mark your vehicle as a waypoint before leaving. Then, when you are ready to return, it will show the shortest route to get to your vehicle. GPS units are a more valuable navigational tool than a compass in that regard, as long as the unit works properly.

Always carry a compass, even when hunting areas you know well. One morning I needed mine when I least expected I would. I was hunting in familiar country, terrain I could say I knew intimately, when I got disoriented. The problem was caused by a heavy snow the night before. I simply couldn't get my bearings without my compass because many of the visual landmarks I normally used to navigate were blotted out by the snow. The snow was so heavy in the woods that day, it could have prevented a GPS from working properly.

Metal from a gun will sometimes throw a compass off. Test yours with and without a gun in your hands to see if it makes a difference. If the gun affects your compass, set it aside when taking a reading. When deer hunting, it is also a good idea to look at a map or carry one that shows all roads, power lines, railroad tracks, lakes, and streams in the area you will be hunting. If you have a GPS, the unit should have a map of the area.

When disoriented in areas that have roads or identifiable features on all sides, simply use a compass to head in one direction. A GPS will show you which direction is the shortest to reach a road. You will eventually come out to someplace familiar. If you ever become totally lost in an area where the potential for finding familiar

Some of the equipment deer hunters should carry with them when afield. Important items include a compass, knife, lighter, flashlights, gloves, rope, folding saw, deer call, space blanket, orange vest, extra clothes, and snack foods (not shown).

ground in one or more directions isn't likely because you don't have a GPS or it isn't working, the best thing to do is stop where you are and build a fire. Wandering aimlessly is a waste of energy and will only make matters worse.

To build a fire you will need matches or a lighter—other essentials every deer hunter should carry. Book matches are fine, but carry some in a waterproof case on the chance that those in a pocket get wet. Aluminum match cases are available in sporting goods stores. I use spent plastic shotgun shells to keep my matches dry. Twelve-gauge and 16-gauge cases fit together snugly. It is a good idea to include a striker in a watertight container with matches. A space blanket will help hunters who are forced to spend a night in the field to stay warm. They are small when folded and lightweight, so they are handy to carry.

If the woods are wet when you want to start a fire, use the inner bark of birch trees, small twigs that grow under dense-needled pine trees, birds' nests, or unraveled threads from a sweater, shirt, or coat for tinder. The tissues or paper towels you should have with you can also be used to start a fire. Tissues can be used in other ways, too. They come in handy if nature calls, to blow your nose, or to dry a scope or camera lens. Paper towels can be used to wipe the inside of a dressed deer carcass or to clean and dry bloody hands after the chore is done. Rubber gloves can be included in your gear if you want to keep hands clean and dry while dressing a deer; they will also reduce your chances of getting an infection or disease.

Don't forget a knife to dress a whitetail or mulie with. Either pocket or sheath models are fine, as long as they are sharp. I've carried a sheathed folding Buck Knife with me on deer hunts for many years and have lost track of the number of deer I've field dressed with it. A folding saw will come in handy for trimming branches that may be in the way around your blind or tree stand. I always carry a folding saw with me for that purpose when going up a tree for the first time with a climbing stand.

A plastic bag will be useful for holding the heart and liver from that dressed buck or doe. Eating organs from deer is not recommended in areas where chronic wasting disease is known to exist.

You should carry a flashlight to help you see before daylight or after dark. I like the two-cell models, but some hunters get by with small penlights. Lights that can be strapped to your head with an elastic band or those that clip to the brim of a hat are handy because they leave your hands free for carrying other things. Carrying two lights makes sense in case one malfunctions. Regardless of the type used, be sure it has fresh batteries. It is a good idea to carry spares, too, along with extra bulbs. If you have a flashlight reserved for use during deer season, try to remember to remove the batteries or turn one backwards after you are done hunting for the year so they won't corrode.

A length of stout rope is another item you don't want to be without. It will be useful to hang or drag a mulie or a whitetail. Thin rope or a piece of wire should be included to fasten a tag to that buck or doe. A spool of Game Tracker string or roll of surveyor's ribbon will be useful to mark your way to or from a stand, the trail of a wounded deer, or the route to take to reach a deer left in the woods overnight.

High-energy snacks such as candy, power and granola bars, raisins, and brownies should be carried while deer hunting. A Thermos of coffee, hot chocolate, bouillon, or soup can be a great pick-me-up on cold days. Also, try to pack a lunch if you plan on being in the field most of the day. If you are operating out of a car or camp, you may want to return to it for lunch. If so, a Thermos and sandwiches don't have to be carried with you, but try to make it a point to carry high-energy snack foods with you in the woods. Then you will always have them in case you don't get out of the woods when expected.

An optional item you might want to carry if hunting with gun or bow is a camera. Photos of a bagged buck, scenery, and camp scenes will bring back fond memories in future years. Make sure your camera has a built-in flash because many of the best shots on a deer hunt will be in low-light situations.

Binoculars or a spotting scope are also optional, but they can be a tremendous aid in any type of deer hunting, especially in open country. A 30-power Bushnell spotting scope I brought on a Wyoming mule deer hunt was a great help by allowing me and my partners to monitor deer in the sagebrush country from our camp when doing pre-season scouting. And I've used a compact set of 8X Nikon binoculars countless times to assess the antlers of bucks to determine if they were shooters.

Add a quality laser rangefinder to the list as well. These are invaluable for deer hunters who routinely stillhunt or spot and stalk, but I also use my lightweight Bushnell Rangefinder when stand hunting from a spot for the first time to determine the distance to various landmarks soon after getting in position. Rangefiners are especially important for hunters using archery equipment because a difference of five to ten yards in range estimation can make the difference between a hit and a miss. I carry mine in a case that fits on my belt, so it's handy when I need it.

I also carry shooting sticks when gun hunting in terrain where a long shot is possible. I've used the folding aluminum shooting sticks made by Underwood on a number of occasions with favorable results. It's amazing what a solid rest the sticks provide. I dropped an animal at 200 yards while using them. Stoney Point also makes shooting sticks and there's one called the Bog Pod (BOGgear.com).

Bowhunters may want to include a stick or tube of camouflage coloring for application to their shiny faces. A lightweight camo face mask is an alternative. If you've got a white beard like me, you will also want to cover that and a face mask works best for that. Unless you are hunting in snow country, a white beard stands out in deer woods.

A piece of thread tied on a gun, bow, or stand will serve as a constant indicator of which way the wind is blowing. The least little breeze activates it. I always have a piece of thread tied to my bow quiver. A strand can be attached to the barrel or scope of a gun, too.

Deer calls can be useful at times while hunting whitetails or mule deer. A blast on them will sometimes stop a running buck long enough for a shot. Calls can also be used to lure deer into view that you might not otherwise have seen.

Slingshots often come in handy when hunting brushy draws. Bedded deer can be tricked into showing themselves if you flip a stone into a thicket from an observation point. Some deer scents are now available in pellet form that can be dispensed with a slingshot, too.

I always have a couple of small screw-in hooks in my backpack, too, that I use to hang my bow or gun from when hunting from a tree stand if a handy limb isn't available for that purpose. Realtree makes a product called an Easy Hanger that's designed to hang bows from after being screwed into a tree. Even when hunting from the ground, I will sometimes use a screw-in hook to hang my rifle from where it will be handy instead of hanging onto it all of the time.

Small day packs or fanny packs are excellent for carrying some of the extra gear deer hunters should have with them. When hiking into a remote location in cold weather, I frequently carry a large backpack and frame to accommodate extra clothes and gear. On most deer hunting excursions, though, a medium-sized, frameless pack made of fleece is adequate. Hunters who hunt by tracking will want to travel as light as possible, fitting essentials in coat and pants pockets.

Gun and bow cases are other important items that hunters should have. Soft zippered cases are fine for transporting guns and bows in vehicles. Be sure to get padded cases large enough for the equipment you have. Scoped rifles, for example, require much wider cases than unscoped guns. And crossbows require cases specifically designed for their shape. If you will be traveling by airplane, a padded hard case is essential to protect your gun or bow and arrows during the trip. Metal cases are probably the most durable, but I've also used hard plastic cases without a problem.

Elastic shell holders that fit around the butts of rifles and shotguns can come in handy to carry extra rounds of ammunition. Cartridge carriers that can be worn on a

You will need a padded hard case to transport your rifle or bow and arrows in if you plan on flying. Gun cleaning supplies should also be included, as they are in this case. Soft gun cases are recommended for use when transporting guns in vehicles and to prevent condensation when bringing guns from warm to cold environments and vice-versa.

belt are a great way to have plenty of ammo handy without it making noise. Uncle Mike's makes a selection of both types of products.

Two-way radios and cell phones can be handy pieces of equipment to have along on a hunt, too. Radios are great for communication among hunting partners. When hunting with Bill Jordan in Georgia we used to set specific times for radio checks to compare notes on deer activity, determine how long to hunt and make sure there were no problems. Radios and cell phones really come in handy in the event of an emergency. If an accident occurs, help can be summoned quickly. When carrying a cell phone with you while hunting, however, either set it on vibrate or only turn it on when you need to use it to avoid spooking deer.

Guides

I first hunted whitetails with Proudfoot Creek Outfitters near Leoville, Saskatchewan, when the business was started in the late 1980s and I have hunted with them periodically ever since. I've taken my best typical and nontypical whitetails while hunting with them over the years, including some that are bigger than most hunters shoot in a lifetime. One of the chapters in this book has the story about the big typical that qualified for honorable mention in Boone and Crockett Records (page 116).

I'm pleased to report that I took my second-best nontypical whitetail during my 2010 hunt with Proudfoot Outfitters and I got it in far less time than it normally takes me. On the second morning of my hunt, I shot a 13-pointer that had a green gross score of $171^3/8$. I actually could have shot that buck on the first morning of my hunt, but, believe it or not, I passed him up. I had difficulty judging what the antlers would score due to a long nontypical tine growing from the base of his right antler. Basically, I underestimated what the rack would score. After looking at video I took of the buck at camp that evening, I realized my mistake, and my judgement was reinforced by the guides and other hunters.

Fortunately, I got another chance at the buck the second day and didn't waste any time taking advantage of it. On the afternoon I filled my tag, I saw another monster buck that I would have shot if I didn't already have my deer. It was an 11-pointer that would have scored at least in the 160s.

Ownership and guides at the deer camp have changed over time and I've seen them increase the operation from a farmhouse with one bathroom to a lodge that can handle at least fifteen hunters per week. The quality of the hunts in all respects is better than it's ever been and the camp is located in a great area. I wish I could say all of the deer camps I've hunted at were as good.

The Saskatchewan lodge that Proudfoot Outfitters now offers quality whitetail hunts from. When I started hunting with them, they were operating out of a farmhouse.

I learned some lessons about how to choose a guide for deer hunting the hard way. Even though I learned these lessons many years ago, they are just as appropriate today as they were then. Sharing some of the mistakes I've made in selecting guides will, hopefully, reduce the chances of others making the same mistakes.

Colorado used to have an early-season rifle hunt in high-country wilderness areas primarily for trophy mule deer bucks. The season was in August, so the bucks' antlers were still in velvet. Due to the remoteness of the terrain, coupled with my lack of experience hunting mulies at the time, I decided to hire a guide and outfitter.

It took me three years and a lot of money to find an outfitter who offered what I wanted. The first one I signed up with took as many hunters as he could fast-talk into booking with him. Consequently, his camp was overcrowded and service was lousy, but he was in a good area. I saw some good bucks and should have had one due to initiative I took on my own. I hit a nice buck and went back to camp for help tracking it, but the outfitter refused to assist.

The second year I had a guide who limited the number of hunters in his camp and was conscientious about the care of his clients; however, his approach to finding deer at that time of year wasn't adequate. I can say that now, but didn't know it at the time. The territory he hunted had a low density of deer.

Year number three, everything fell in place. I hired an outfitter who restricted the number of hunters in his camp, knew how to hunt deer extremely well, and was in a good area. The man's name is Rudy Rudibaugh of Parlin, Colorado. He operated the 711 Ranch for many years when he wasn't in the high country until his death in 2009. I hunted with Rudy for a number of years with both gun and bow and took a nice buck each time.

If I knew then what I know now, I probably never would have booked with either of the first two outfitters. The first fellow I signed up with offered the cheapest rate of any I contacted. He also guaranteed me a buck with at least four points on a side.

The saying "you get what you pay for" is as true for guides and outfitters as anything else. Good guides aren't inexpensive. When a hunter pays for a cheap hunt, that is exactly what he or she gets. I should have also questioned my bargain-priced guide's guarantee of success. A 100 percent chance of success is unheard-of, with the possible exception of hunts on hunting preserves or game farms, on any deer hunt I know of that is run on the up-and-up.

After my first experience with an outfitter, I was happy to locate one the second year who told me how many hunters would be on the hunt and leveled with me about my chances of scoring. My mistake this time was not comparing the area this guy operated in with others in the state.

Permits had to be obtained to hunt in his area. The number of permits was limited. Additionally, only bucks with four points on a side were legal. These factors indicated the territory had a limited surplus of deer. The restrictions were imposed to prevent an overharvest.

There were other locations in the state at the time that had healthier deer populations, which were also reflected by hunting regulations. No restrictions were placed on the number of hunters who could try their luck in Rudy's area, for example. And any antlered buck was legal.

The problems I encountered finding a satisfactory guide were my fault. I simply wasn't careful enough in making the selection at first. For that reason I suggest that deer hunters interested in securing a guide or outfitter try to investigate all the angles thoroughly before committing themselves. The only way the selection process can be done properly is to start looking well in advance of a hunt: from six months to a year or longer in many cases.

Locating Outfitters

Planning is a must for hunters interested in trying their luck in states such as Wyoming and Montana; first off, you have to make sure you can obtain a license. Applications have to be in well before the season and then a drawing is held to fill the quota of nonresident licenses. Hunters have to be assured of getting a license in Wyoming, Montana, and states like them before securing a guide or outfitter.

Even though a commitment can't be made to a guide or outfitter in Wyoming, for example, until the hunter knows he or she will have a license, tentative arrangements should be correlated with deciding on where to hunt because a specific region has to be indicated on the license application.

I should point out here that deciding on an area with the highest possible density of whitetails or mule deer in any given state isn't a prerequisite to enjoying a successful guided hunt, although it should be considered. Good guides can usually get their hunters into deer regardless of their abundance because they are familiar with the country and the animals' movements within it.

There are a number of ways to get the names and addresses of reputable guides and outfitters. Attending outdoor shows, especially those geared toward deer hunters, is one way of contacting potential outfitters. Many states and some provinces have annual deer shows that are usually held during January, February, and March. Some of the vendors at these shows operate hunting camps. There's no better way to determine if one of them offers what you are looking for than talking with them face-to-face. You can ask all kinds of questions about their operation, their accommodations, and the success of their guests, as well as pick up any literature they have. Most camp operators also have photos, photo albums, or videos available in their booths to give potential customers an idea of what their operation is like.

In some cases, it may be best to review an outfitter's literature before asking too many questions about the operation. By reading their literature first, you will have a better idea if they offer what you are looking for and what types of questions to ask. The literature is sure to answer some of your questions.

Deer shows like this one are great places to locate potential guides and outfitters. These shows, now held in many states, provide the opportunity to ask questions in person. They are also great places to see many of the big bucks bagged the previous fall.

Another benefit of attending deer shows is to have the chance to look at the antlers of some of the big bucks bagged in your state the previous fall and find out what counties they came from. The head mounts of numerous bucks and what the racks scored are usually on display. This is a good way to bone up on judging the size of antlers.

Some of the best deals can sometimes be found on the last day of shows. I know a couple of guys who have gotten bargains on hunting trips by waiting until the last day of shows to book trips with outfitters who are anxious to fill open spots in their camps. As I mentioned earlier, however, don't book a hunt based on price alone. Make sure your other requirements will be met before committing to a hunt. If you have unanswered questions, wait until you get satisfactory answers before making a decision.

Banquets sponsored by state and provincial hunting organizations or chapters of national organizations such as Safari Club International and Whitetails Unlimited are also great places to get deals on guided hunts. Some outfitters donate hunts to these organizations for publicity and to help them obtain operating funds through auctions. Some of these hunts go for bargain prices at auctions. If there are not many bidders on hunts you are interested in during auctions, it's possible to save lots of money by being the winning bidder.

Before bidding on a deer hunt that's being auctioned, however, try to learn as much as you can about the outfitter first. Getting a list of hunts to be auctioned beforehand, so you can do some research, is an excellent way to prepare for the auction. If the outfitter is at the banquet, make a point of talking to them and find out if any members of the organization have hunted with them. Even if you decide not to bid on a hunt at a banquet, you may learn enough about the outfitter to book a hunt with them at a later date.

Doing a search of deer hunting guides and outfitters on the internet is another great way to compile a list of potential hunting trips. If you are interested in a specific state or province, be sure to include that in your search to narrow down the number of possibilities as much as possible. Most Canadian provinces require that nonresidents use the services of an outfitter to hunt deer.

Check out the websites of outfitters you are interested in to find out as much as you can about them. Then contact those that are high on your list to get more information.

Some outfitters advertise in the classified sections of outdoor magazines such as *Outdoor Life, Deer & Deer Hunting, North American Whitetail,* and *Bowhunter.* Some are mentioned in magazine articles, too. Outdoor television shows are also great places to get the names, addresses, and phone numbers for outfitters. State and provincial departments of fish and game and tourism should be able to provide lists of outfitters or give you information about where to get lists of guides and outfitters. Some states and provinces have organizations composed of outfitters and guides. Chambers of commerce are also good contacts in Texas, for one, to get a line on deer-hunting services.

Word of mouth is another source of information on guiding outfits. Acquaintances who have gone on guided hunts can provide a name or two along with a recommendation or a word of caution.

Narrowing Down The List

After you've obtained names and addresses of operators in the area you want to hunt and you've narrowed the list down to the ones you are most interested in, give them a call or write them an introductory letter or email. If you write, make the query as brief as possible. Tell them what type of hunt you are interested in, how many people are in your group, and the weapons you plan to use. Some guides only handle bowhunters, or only those who use firearms. If you have preferred dates for a hunt, that should be included, too. Also ask for information on their rates, services, past success, and references from recent seasons (names, addresses, and telephone numbers of hunters who have used their services).

Some outfitters operate out of remote tent camps accessible by ATVs or horses, like this one in Manitoba. Some excellent deer hunting is available in these areas and camps that are set up properly are comfortable.

Some guides operate out of comfortable lodges or motels and use vehicles as the principle means of travel to and from hunting areas. Others get into backcountry on horseback or by all-terrain vehicles (ATVs) and tent out with their hunters. Drop-camp arrangements are also possible. In this situation an outfitter provides a fully equipped camp and leaves hunters on their own, then picks them up at a later date. Hunters who have a complete line of camping gear may simply want an outfitter to transport them and their gear to and from a remote campsite.

Some guides or outfitters may be eliminated by their initial response or lack thereof. The next step involves corresponding with the references mentioned by operators who reply. If one or two guides look more promising than others, check out their references first.

Check References

To increase the chances of replies from an outfitter's past hunters, try to ask for brief answers and provide a stamped, self-addressed envelope. The more convenient it is for them, the more likely they are to provide the desired information. Following is a sample letter that could be sent to references through the postal service or email.

If you don't receive replies from hunters you want input from, try calling them. Some people don't like to fill out questionnaires no matter how simple the query may be.

Dear Mr. or Ms. _____:

    I am considering a hunt with *(guide's or outfitter's name)* and was given your name as a reference. Any information you can provide about your experience with him or her as a guide or outfitter would be appreciated. Answers to the questions below will help. A return envelope is enclosed for your convenience. Thank you for your assistance.

When and where did you hunt with the person mentioned above? _____

_____

Were you successful? _____

If you weren't successful, why? _____

Size and sex of deer, if successful: _____

Other deer seen? _____

Was the guide easy to get along with? _____

Were services adequate, good or bad? _____

Which services weren't adequate, if any? _____

Did the guide seem to know what he was doing? _____

Would you hunt with this guide/outfitter again? _____

Why? _____

How many hunters were in camp besides you? _____

Do you know the names and addresses of other people who have hunted with the

guide whom I can contact? Please list: _____

_____

_____

_____

Additional Comments: _____

_____

_____

_____

                         Sincerely,
                         (Your Signature)

Making A Choice

Comments from past hunters should give you a good idea who the best guide or out-fitter is. Beware guides who hesitate to give references, unless it is their first year in business. The final selection shouldn't be made until you find out, via another letter or two and maybe a phone call, what openings they have for the upcoming season, how many hunters will be along, and what the total cost will be for the type of services they provide. Also, make sure you know exactly what equipment they will be providing and what they expect you to bring.

Don't be afraid to ask questions. You are going to be shelling out good money for a hunt. Try to make sure you will be getting what you pay for. And be sure you know what you are paying for. In many cases, guide fees do not include hunting licenses. If that's the case, find out how much licenses cost along with when and where one can be purchased, if a drawing is not involved. Some outfitters purchase licenses for hunters before their arrival, as long as they have the necessary information and the money is sent in advance.

Most outfitters require a deposit to book a hunt (usually 50 percent) and the final payment upon arrival. Some outfitters accept personal checks and credit card payment. Others don't. Be sure to find out what is acceptable ahead of time. Also make sure you get a receipt for your deposit, so you have proof of payment, and find out if it is refundable or transferrable to another year, if something comes up and you can't make the hunt.

Even though you want to make sure you get what you pay for, don't expect your guide or outfitter to be a slave. Most guides and outfitters put in long days as a rule. Being too demanding and alienating someone who can make a telling difference in the success or failure of your hunt is not a good idea. Help out with camp chores whenever possible, and don't try to tell the outfitter how to run his or her business. Providing helpful input and making suggestions at opportune moments can work in your favor though.

Special Regulations

Be sure to ask if there are any special hunting regulations you should know about. Some states require proof of completion of a hunter safety course, even if you have been hunting for years. Most require some type of hunter-orange clothing during firearm seasons. Others have stringent restrictions on the weapons that are legal.

Hunters going to Canada from the U.S. to hunt, for example, have to register their long guns with customs when entering the country, and no handguns are allowed. The process will be speeded up if you get a registration form ahead of time from your outfitter, so it can be filled out before you reach customs. There is talk about suspension of Canadian gun registration in the future, but it was still in effect during 2010.

If you are taking your child on a hunt to Canada by yourself, you must have a signed letter from your spouse that was witnessed, giving their consent for the trip. If taking a child with you that is a relative or friend, I assume you would have to have letters from both parents. There's also a minimum age for youngsters to be able to transport a gun of their own. That information would be critical before planning a trip to another country with a child.

And I understand the requirements for a Canadian citizen to transport a gun into the U.S. for hunting are even more difficult than vice versa. Taking guns into Mexico requires some planning and preparation, too.

It won't hurt to ask the guide or outfitter about what weather can be expected, too, so you will know what types of clothing to bring. Some states and provinces have special clothing requirements, so it's a good idea to ask about that as well.

A guided hunt can be one of the most pleasurable and successful you will ever go on, but it can also be the worst. The difference is often determined by the amount of screening you do before deciding on a guide or outfitter.

After the Kill

Once a deer is down, the hardest part of a hunt is normally over. At that point the successful deer hunter can turn his or her attention to care of the carcass. Proper handling from the time a whitetail, blacktail, or mule deer is dropped until the meat reaches the freezer will ensure a supply of healthful, tasty venison for months.

A supply of venison is a bonus of deer hunting that my wife, Lucy, and I always look forward to. The meat is delicious, high in protein, and better for us than domestic meats such as beef and pork. A deer on the meat pole represents an economic benefit to us. Venison meals reduce the amount of money we have to spend at the supermarket for domestic meats. In fact, most of the meat we eat is from wild game such as deer. Frankly, without venison from the deer I bag each year to carry us through the winter, our budget would be strained farther than we would like to admit.

Some hunters insist on considering the cost of firearms, bows, other equipment, and hunting expenses such as gas, guide fees, and plane fares as the price paid for venison. The dollar value per pound of venison can be high in many cases using this rationale, much higher than meats available at the butcher shop.

But I think the money I spend on deer hunting buys me the opportunity to hunt deer, nothing more. I don't have to shoot a deer to get returns on the money invested in deer hunting. I buy recreational value, a commodity that is difficult to put a price tag on. Countless times I feel I have gotten more than my money's worth on a deer hunt even though I didn't collect a deer.

Many people spend money to watch football, baseball, basketball, and hockey games for the recreational value involved in watching the teams play. The price of admission doesn't include a meal; neither should deer hunting. That is why I feel venison is a bonus of any deer hunt.

I can honestly say I haven't had any bad-tasting venison from whitetail or mule deer, regardless of the animal's age, if the carcass was cared for properly. Distasteful meat is often the result of poor handling somewhere along the way between the time it was shot and the time it was cooked. There is no excuse for this.

Tag It

One of the most important tasks that must be taken care of once a deer is down, after you've taken some time to admire and photograph it, assuming a camera is handy, is to tag it. States and provinces provide tags with hunting licenses to put on a bagged deer to validate it as a legal kill. Most deer tags require you to use a knife to cut slots for the date and sex of the kill, and, if it's a buck, there may be places to mark how many antler points it has.

Take care of that process as soon as possible and attach the tag to the carcass as required by law. If a piece of string or other type of fastener is necessary to attach the tag to the animal, try to remember to bring one with you, either in a pocket, backpack, or back tag holder, if one of those is required. Many tags are self-adhesive once backing is removed. Those can simply be wrapped around an antler or the gambrel of a hind leg.

The gambrel is a convenient place to tag does. Gambrels are on the backs of both hind legs of deer above tarsal glands where there's a triangular-shaped patch of skin between a large tendon and the leg bone. A knife can be used to cut a slit in the skin of the gambrel to tie a tag to or insert an adhesive tag through. Tags can actually be attached to any of a deer's legs, but those not inserted through a gambrel can slide off when the deer is being dragged if they are not securely attached.

Field Dressing

Once a deer is dead, it should be dressed (the viscera removed) as soon as possible. Most deer are field dressed at or near where they are killed, but in parts of the south where weather tends to be hot, bagged deer are taken out of the field intact and transported to a processing facility. They are hung there, gutted, and immediately put in a cooler to prevent spoilage. Gutting deer is delayed under these circumstances to prevent contamination of the opened carcass from bacteria and insects. The following instructions apply to whitetails and mule deer that are gutted in the field.

There is no need to "bleed" a whitetail or mule deer by cutting its throat. Most of the blood that hasn't drained out of the wound will be in the body cavity and will drain during the cleaning process. A cut in the hide on the underside of the neck is definitely not recommended if you think you may want to have your deer's head mounted.

Wear Gloves

Wearing a pair of thin rubber surgical gloves, available at most drug stores, is a good idea when gutting deer to prevent getting bacteria that can cause disease or infection on your hands. This is especially important if you have open cuts on your hands or if the weather is warm to hot, but there are advantages of using rubber gloves in cold weather, too. Gloves will protect hands from becoming bloody and prevent the necessity of washing them after gutting a deer in subfreezing temperatures, thereby making it easier to keep hands warm once the job is done.

I've gutted lots of deer with bare hands and never had a problem. However, the number of serious illnesses that deer can carry has been on the increase during recent years, so it's important to take some precautions. Rubber gloves are cheap, readily available and disposable, so there's no excuse not to use them.

Besides wearing gloves, it's usually a good idea to take coats off and roll long sleeves up past elbows before starting to gut a deer to reduce the chances sleeves will get bloody. Watches should be removed and put in a pocket for the same reason.

Removing Sex Organs

If the deer is on an incline, position the carcass so the head is uphill.

The penis and testicles on bucks can be removed before opening the body cavity. Some states require that proof of sex remain intact on a deer carcass. In that case, this step can be skipped. To remove penis and testicles, simply cut the skin around them; they can then be pulled away from the body. To start a cut in the skin around the sex organs, pinch a fold of skin between thumb and forefinger, then slice the skin. Opening the skin this way prevents unnecessary cuts in the meat.

A tube is connected to the penis at the rear. You can cut the tube where it enters the body and discard the sex organs or pull testicles and penis back with tube attached and lay them on the ground behind the carcass. The tube should then be cut and the organs discarded after the bladder is removed, which will be one of the last steps in the gutting process.

Opening The Body Cavity

To start the dressing process, make a horizontal cut in the belly area while standing over the deer, facing toward its head. This cut doesn't have to be long; about three to five inches is fine. Try to cut in the center of the belly where there is little or no hair. Keep the knife blade, which should be sharp, level when making the cut, and take it easy. Make short, slicing strokes. Do not stab a knife blade into the belly to start a cut. As obvious as this may sound to most deer hunters, I know some beginners who have done just that. The intestines or stomach may be ruptured by stabbing a knife blade into the abdominal cavity, which is not desirable.

Several layers of muscle and tissue lie beneath the skin. All have to be cut through to reach the body cavity.

After the cut is completed, insert the middle and index fingers of the left hand (if right-handed) under the skin and lift the skin up and away from the viscera. Now you can start a cut toward the head, working the knife blade between your fingers.

Cut at least as far as the sternum in the center of the rib cage. This is as far as you want to go if you're going to want a head mount of the deer. If you don't plan on doing a head mount, cut through the ribs, if possible. Most heavy-bladed knives that are sharp will cut through ribs. You can use both hands to hold the knife to cut ribs if

The most important step in the field dressing process is opening the body cavity. A horizontal cut can be made through the skin and the layers of muscle on the belly or at the base of the rib cage.

Once an initial cut has been made, use your fingers to lift the skin and guide the knife blade to open the body cavity.

Extend the cut to the sternum on deer that will be mounted. The cut can be extended through the ribs on deer that are not to be caped for mounting.

necessary. There is nothing that will rupture in the chest area. The ribs can be cut as far as the brisket.

Another way to open the body cavity is to make the initial opening just behind the rib cage. With a deer resting on its back, there is a space between skin and internal organs here. Therefore, the chances of accidentally rupturing anything are reduced.

Once an opening is cut, use the middle and index fingers to elevate the skin and guide the knife blade toward the rear. The cut can be extended farther forward by going back to the starting point and slicing ribs.

Removing Internal Organs

Now that the carcass is open, the intestines, stomach, and liver can be rolled out on the ground after the connective tissue is cut. Use your knife to cut any tissue connecting this material to the sides or back of the body. There will be a thin, muscular membrane across the body cavity in front of where the stomach was. This is the diaphragm, which separates the chest cavity from the body cavity. The diaphragm should be cut free along the ribs and back.

Although most of the intestines will be removed from the body cavity, don't try to pull the lower digestive tract free from the rear of the carcass. If you do, it will break. Leave the lower digestive tract intact. It can be pulled free later after a cut is made around the rectum or anus.

The next step is to cut the diaphragm, a thin muscle separating the body cavity from the chest cavity. It should be cut all the way around where it is attached to the cavity walls.

The heart and lungs can be removed next. They can be pulled out once the windpipe and esophagus are cut. The windpipe is all the way forward in the chest cavity and the esophagus, which carries food to the stomach, is next to it. The windpipe is circular and semirigid. If the ribs have been opened, it's easy to see and cut the windpipe and esophagus above the lungs. If the rib cage is uncut, you will have to

Then reach forward to the front of the chest cavity and cut the windpipe, which will free the heart and lungs. Be careful not to cut your hand.

Pull the lungs and heart out.

reach forward and grasp the windpipe above the lungs with a free hand. Then use a knife in the other hand to cut the windpipe and esophagus above where you are holding it. Be careful during this process to avoid cutting the hand that's on the windpipe.

After the windpipe and the esophagus have been cut, the heart and lungs can be pulled free and removed.

Remove the viscera from the body cavity, leaving the lower digestive tract attached.

Kidneys and fat may remain along the back after everything else is removed from the body cavity. These can be easily removed by pulling on them.

The Final Step

Next, cut completely around the anus so the lower end of the digestive tract and bladder can be pulled forward and discarded. This step is much easier if the pelvic arch is split open. An axe or saw works best for this, but a sturdy knife blade can be used if you exert enough pressure at the pelvic joint. Splitting the pelvis isn't necessary to remove the lower digestive tract, though.

If you don't split the pelvic arch, fat and other tissue may remain after the digestive tract is removed. It's important to pull and cut any obstructions out and discard them. The opening that is created will allow blood to drain from the body cavity and aid in cooling the meat in the hindquarters.

After the lower digestive tract and bladder are removed, the tube connecting the penis and testicles to the body can be cut, if it wasn't done earlier.

If intestinal matter or stomach contents got on any part of the meat as a result of cleaning or from wounds, cut away a thin layer of the contaminated meat to remove the source of contamination.

Draining Blood

Once cleaned out, a carcass can be elevated to help it drain and cool. It can be propped up against a stump, on bushes, or draped over a log. Most of the blood can

Cut all the way around the anus to free the lower digestive tract.

Once the lower digestive tact is freed, it can be removed, along with the sex organs, if the deer is a buck.

be drained by simply lifting the front quarters off the ground. Unless it's a small deer, two people are normally required to lift a deer to drain blood remaining in the body cavity.

If you've got a rope and there's a tree nearby with a sturdy limb, the carcass can be hung from the tree temporarily. If you've shot a buck and you plan on having the head mounted, hang the deer by its antlers. If you don't plan on mounting the head, a rope can be put around the neck for hanging. Using a stick to spread the rib cage will aid in cooling the carcass while it's hanging.

Heart, Liver and Tenderloins

Be sure to salvage the liver and heart from your deer, if they are undamaged, except in areas where CWD is a concern. Liver flukes may make the livers from some deer

Tenderloins after they have been removed. I like to eat the tenderloins from deer I shoot when they are fresh.

undesirable for consumption. Flukes, which resemble leeches, are common parasites in the livers of adult whitetails in parts of their range. These parasites often leave visible scarring on the outside of livers they infest. If no scarring is visible, the parasites can be detected by cutting into the liver. Healthy livers and hearts are great eating. If you don't want them, it probably won't be hard to find someone who does. Bring a plastic bag with you to put the organs in.

Some hunters prepare and eat the liver from a deer the same day it is bagged. I try to do the same thing with the tenderloins. They are narrow strips of tender, delicious meat on either side of the inside of the backbone. Each one is about a foot long. I usually wait until I get home to cut these delectable pieces of meat out. They can be pulled out once one end has been cut with a knife blade, if the carcass is fresh. If tenderloins are removed a day or more after a deer was shot, it may be necessary to make cuts along the sides of these pieces of meat to make it easier to get them out in one piece.

Ideally, a whitetail or mule deer should be skinned and butchered the same day it is shot. This is a must when hunting in warm weather, but isn't as critical when temperatures are from below freezing to around 40 degrees. Some hunters recommend aging deer carcasses. This is difficult to do properly, except under controlled conditions. I have found that venison tastes better when butchered as soon as possible.

Hanging A Carcass

When a deer carcass won't be processed promptly, it should be hung so it will drain and cool. It's also easier to skin a deer when it's hanging. The carcass can be hung with the head up or down. A deer that isn't drained should be suspended with the head up. If the whitetail or mule deer will be caped, hanging it with the head down is best. To remove the entire hide, the carcass can be hung either way.

A stout branch or piece of wood should be inserted through the gambrels of both hind legs to suspend a deer with its head down. Make a cut in the skin of gambrels that is large enough to allow a stick to pass through. Be careful not to cut the tendon. If metal gambrel hooks are available for hanging deer upside down, that's even better. While the deer is held in position—with the hind legs straddling a beam, pole, or limb—the stick can be passed through the gambrels so it rests on the support.

To hang a deer with the head up, a rope can be used to fasten the carcass to a support. One end of the rope should be around the deer's neck or the base of the antlers. If you plan to have the head mounted, hang a buck by its antlers. If it is hung by the neck, hairs will be broken that can't be repaired.

I sometimes hang my deer from a tree in the woods if getting it to camp or home isn't convenient right away. This isn't possible where there are no trees, of course. In such a situation, prop the body cavity open with a stick and spread the hind legs to

Gutted deer can be hung with their heads up to drain. Bucks should be hung by their antlers, if the head is to be mounted, like this trophy Saskatchewan buck hoisted by a winch on an Argo.

In warm weather, deer carcasses can be protected from insects by covering them with porous game bags. Sprinkling pepper on the meat will keep flies off of it, too.

allow as much heat as possible to escape from the carcass. The carcass should be in the shade, if possible, resting on its back. Body heat won't be able to radiate properly from a carcass lying on its side; consequently, the meat in the area that is on the ground could spoil if left for any length of time.

When leaving deer carcasses in areas where scavengers such as coyotes, wolves, bear and mountain lions live, it's a good idea to leave an item of clothing with human scent on it draped over the carcass or a branch next to it, to keep scavengers away. If the carcass is in an unfamiliar location that might be difficult to relocate, mark the spot with orange tape, a vest, or a hat and mark a trail to it. If you've got a GPS with you, you can take a waypoint at the carcass to help guide you back to it.

If human thieves are a problem in your area, you might try marking the carcass by notching the ears. Or try putting a business card, a slip of paper with your name on it, a penny, or some other identifying article in the mouth of a dead deer. If your tag is on a whitetail or mule deer, that should be proof enough who the animal belongs to. The local sheriff, game warden or conservation officer should be notified of the theft of a deer and what to look for in identifying the carcass.

If a deer must be left outside in warm weather, flies can be kept away from the meat by sprinkling pepper over the inside of the carcass and on any exposed flesh. Porous meat bags that keep insects off the carcass are even better. Flies will lay eggs on unprotected areas otherwise. When you have shot a deer in warm or hot weather where flies are a problem, it's actually better to put off dressing the carcass until it can also be skinned and butchered or put in a walk-in cooler. This should be done as soon as possible, of course, keeping the carcass in the shade until it can be processed.

Transporting A Deer

There are a number of ways to get a deer out of the woods. Probably the most commonly used method is dragging. This is the best way if there is snow on the ground or there isn't far to go on hard-packed ground. Bucks come complete with handles (antlers) for dragging. If there is a hunter for each side and there isn't far to go, this approach works fine.

A better method for dragging either bucks or does is to use a rope. The animal's front legs should be folded on top of its head then a rope should be tied around the neck and legs. The rope can be tied at an end or the middle. If the middle of the rope is secured around the deer's neck there will be two pieces, one each for a pair of draggers. If there is only one dragger, each of the two pieces of rope can be tied to opposite ends of a stick or branch to rig a makeshift harness.

Brian and Jeremy MacDonald use a plastic ice fishing sled to pull a buck out of the woods. The sleds make dragging a deer on bare ground easier.

Bucks with racks like this mule deer come with handles for dragging.

A stout stick or broom handle can serve as a grip for two people to drag a deer. Deer slide easier if their front legs are tied together on top of their heads.

When the end of a rope is tied to a deer for dragging, it can be adapted to allow two hunters to pull by tying the tag end of the rope to the middle of a sturdy stick or pole. The pole should be long enough to extend across the pullers' chests and work like a yoke. When pulling alone, a short stick can be tied to the rope to serve as a handle. This is easier on the hand than gripping the rope.

If for some reason you don't have a rope, a belt will do to drag a deer. When there's no snow on the ground, consider using a plastic icefishing sled to drag your deer. The animals slide easier when inside one. Brian and Jeremy MacDonald from Buffalo Narrows, Saskatchewan, used such a sled to drag out a 10-pointer I shot while hunting with them one year and it made the chore easier than it otherwise would have been.

If at all possible, get help to drag a deer rather than do it yourself. Hauling a hundred pounds or more of dead weight, whether on bare ground or snow, is strenuous. It is difficult enough with two people, let alone one. Make it a point to take frequent breaks when dragging a deer, even if there are two of you. There shouldn't be any rush to reach camp or the nearest road. Overexertion can quickly turn a successful hunt into a tragedy. More than one deer hunter has suffered a heart attack while trying to muscle a carcass to car or camp.

Deer shouldn't be dragged over sand or mud, if possible, nor should they be dragged for long distances. If they are, there is a good chance the meat will get soiled and bruised. Alternatives to dragging a carcass are carrying it yourself or transporting it by horseback, boat, canoe, motorcycle, snowmobile, or all-terrain vehicle (ATV) such as a four-wheeler. There are restrictions on the use of motorized vehicles in some states during firearms deer seasons. Be sure to check local regulations before using an ATV or snowmobile to retrieve a deer.

All-terrain vehicles (ATVs) such as four-wheelers and snowmobiles are great for hauling deer back to camp. Horses are frequently used to pack out deer from remote areas, too.

I have saved myself some long hauls with deer carcasses by dragging them to a nearby river and retrieving them with a canoe. Deer should be carried inside the boat or canoe whenever possible, but when there isn't enough room they can be pulled in the water. The carcass will float just below the surface. The hair on a deer's hide is hollow and will hold the carcass up. If this is attempted on a river try to go downstream, since the submerged deer creates a lot of drag. The inside of a carcass that is dragged in the water should be rinsed with clean water and wiped out thoroughly once you reach your destination. This will remove dirt and speed up drying.

I have carried a few deer on my back, and it isn't as bad as it may sound. The best way to do it is to cut the carcass in pieces, either halves or quarters. I've skinned and quartered a number of deer that were killed miles from my vehicle and carried the quarters out in a large backpack, with the meat in plastic bags or game bags. Plastic bags work fine in cold weather, but are not recommended for use in weather that is warm to hot because they will increase the chances the meat spoiling.

If a deer is small it can be carried whole, but for safety reasons this isn't recommended during firearm seasons, at least not during daylight hours. Carrying a whole deer can be done safely after dark when gun season is open and at any time during archery hunts. To be on the safe side, a brightly colored vest or garment should be attached to the carcass of a whole deer when it's being carried.

Looman's Outdoor Products in Reeseville, Wisconsin, makes a two-wheeled cart for transporting deer whole from the field. It's called the Trans-Port-RRR Big Game Cart. For more information call 920-927-3445.

It is illegal to transport a skinned or quartered deer from the field in some states, so be sure to check the regulations that apply to your hunting area before doing so.

Caping

If you are interested in having the hide tanned or the head mounted from a deer you shoot, the deer should be skinned before it is butchered. One of the biggest mistakes deer hunters make when caping a deer head that is to be mounted is not allowing for enough hide. It is better to give the taxidermist too much than not enough.

When caping a deer, it is best if the carcass is hung upside down. The skin will fall away from the carcass when it is hung this way. A deer can still be caped when hung head up as well as when the carcass is lying on the ground. The process simply takes longer.

To cape a deer, make a cut through the hide that extends completely around the body about a foot behind the front legs. The skin can then be sliced along the inside of each front leg from where they join the body to the knee. Leg cuts should intersect the cut made when field dressing the carcass. A second major cut should be made in the middle of the back, perpendicular to the one around the body. The cut should extend up the back of the neck to a point just below the base of the antlers, assuming the deer is a buck. From there a short slice can be made to the base of each antler. On antlerless deer, make the cut up the back of the neck to a point just past the ears.

With these cuts made, the hide can be separated from the body by slicing with a knife blade between the skin and muscle. The best place to start separating skin

Larry Weishuhn shows the proper way to cape a deer here. The process is easier when a deer is hanging upside down like this one is.

from flesh is on the deer's back at the intersection of the two major cuts. Once started with a knife, the skin often peels away from the carcass if you pull on it.

When you reach the front legs, skin them to the knees. The lower legs can be removed and discarded. A knife works fine to remove lower legs by cutting into knee joints. Twisting the lower leg to break the joint once an initial cut is made can make removal quicker and easier when using a knife. If a bone saw is handy, that makes removal of lower legs just as easy. Cut the leg bone just above the knee joint with the saw.

After the cape has been skinned as far as the base of the head, the head can be cut from the carcass with the cape attached. A saw is the best way to cut through the neck, but a knife can be used to sever the head from the neck at the joint. The head, with antlers attached, and cape are then ready for transport to a taxidermist. It's best to let the taxidermist skin the head and remove the antlers from the skull.

Completing The Skinning

After a deer is caped, the hide from the rear portion of the body can be removed. The only cuts necessary to complete skinning are on the insides of the hind legs. Once these are completed, the skin can be worked free on the legs and the remainder of the carcass, one side at a time.

To skin a deer that isn't to be caped, when hanging head-up, simply extend the cut that was made to dress the animal up the middle of the chest and the underside of the neck to the head. Next, make a cut in the hide all the way around the neck where the vertical incision ended. Then slice the hide up the inside of each leg from the cut running the length of the deer's body. The hide can then be slowly separated from the carcass, working on one side at a time.

To remove the entire skin from a deer hanging upside down, make the cuts along the inside of each leg to intersect the cut made to field dress the carcass. Also extend the cut made to field dress the deer to the throat. Then start separating skin from

Texas whitetails being skinned with heads hanging down. Each hind leg is skinned first and then the hide is worked free over the body. Skinning is easy on fresh carcasses. The skin can be pulled down over most of the body once flaps of hide large enough to hang onto are worked free with a knife. Note that metal gambrel hooks were used to hang these deer.

muscle with a knife blade on the hind legs, pulling the hide down as you go. When you reach the tail, the tail bone can be cut with a knife so the tail remains attached to the hide.

Once the tail bone has been cut, it's often easy to peel much of the rest of the hide away from the body with minimal cutting, especially if the carcass is fresh. When the skin has been separated from the carcass to the base of the skull, the head can be removed from the carcass with a saw or knife. You can separate the loose hide from the head, if desired, before or after the head is cut from the carcass.

The skinning process is more awkward when a carcass is on the ground rather than hanging, but it isn't difficult if done one step at a time. The operation is easy with two people working together. With a deer laying on its side, simply skin the half of the carcass that is exposed. Once that half is skinned, pull the loose hide back over the exposed flesh to protect it from dirt and flip the carcass over to skin the opposite side.

Skinning The Head

If more than a day (or a few hours if the weather is warm) will elapse from the time a cape or hide is removed from the carcass until it can be delivered to the taxidermist, salting or freezing the hide will be necessary. Before a cape is salted or frozen, it should removed from the head by completing the skinning, unless you have a freezer big enough to accommodate the head and cape or it's below freezing outside. If it's below freezing outside, head and cape should be put where they are safe from scavengers as well as from neighborhood dogs and cats.

The best way to skin the head is to invert the hide over the skull while it's resting on a workbench or table. Cut the ears off close to the skull. A dull instrument, either a spoon or a screwdriver, is best for prying the skin loose from around the base of the antlers, but the tip of a knife blade will do. A pair of pliers can also be used to pull hide from the base of the antlers, but take it easy to avoid tearing the hide. Exercise extreme care when you reach the eyes. Use a sharp knife to cut the skin flush with the eye socket. The tear duct is on the inside corner of the eye. Be sure to continue separating the skin as close to the skull as possible in this area. Caution is required in skinning the nose and lips, too.

The cape can be put in a freezer once skinning is complete and then it can be taken to a taxidermist at your convenience along with the antlers.

Salting A Cape

If the cape must be shipped to a taxidermist, the skin should be salted first to cure it. For salting, the ears must be skinned after the cape is removed from the head. Slowly and carefully invert the skin on the back of each ear over the inner cartilage until you reach the tip.

Before the completely skinned cape is salted, remove any fat or flesh that is clinging to the skin. There is usually a thick layer of meat around the lips. Try to trim as much of this as possible without damaging the skin. Lay the cape on newspapers when you are ready to apply the salt. Do the salting in a basement, garage, or outbuilding where the cape can remain undisturbed during the curing process. Ordi-

Greg Simons saws the antlers from the skull of a buck by cutting from front to back across the top of the eye sockets.

nary table salt is fine for applying to capes. Don't be stingy; pour lots of salt on and rub it in all over, with special attention to lips, nose, ears, and edges of the hide.

The salt will draw moisture out of the deer hide. Once the cape is totally dry, it is ready for shipping. Put it in a paper bag or gunny sack, then package it for shipping. Never ship a deer hide enclosed in a plastic bag.

Do not salt a cape or hide you plan to freeze. The salt will prevent freezing.

Removing Antlers

The antlers from your deer must be brought or shipped to a taxidermist along with the frozen or salted cape. Since the taxidermist won't need the skull, the antlers can be sawed from it with a large hacksaw or bone saw. Start sawing on the back of the skull so the saw blade passes just below the tops of the eye sockets and complete the cut on the bridge of the nose. When antlers are shipped, pieces of heavy cardboard should be taped to all antler tips to prevent them from breaking through the box they are in. An alternative is to put pieces of a rubber hose over each antler tine, including the ends of the beams.

Hunters who shoot a buck with a set of antlers they want to save don't have to go to the expense of having the entire head mounted. The antlers and skull plate can be mounted on a plaque with a piece of felt covering the exposed bone. Antlers mounted this way make attractive decorations. Kits are available with the necessary materials for mounting.

European Mounts

Another option is to have the entire skull, or part of it, with antlers attached, mounted on a plaque. This is called a European mount. Most taxidermists will prepare this type of mount. You can do it yourself by removing all tissue from the skull and then bleaching it.

John Benedict from Auburn Hills, Michigan, learned how to do European mounts when he was stationed in Germany with the military. That's the type of mount he's been doing of most of the deer he's bagged for years, and he's taken lots of them, including many of record-book proportions. He said he normally has the mount done within a week of when he takes a deer and the process only costs $5 to $10, not including the plaque.

Materials you will need to do the job, according to Benedict, include three knives, one of which is a long, narrow-bladed fillet knife (very sharp). Another knife

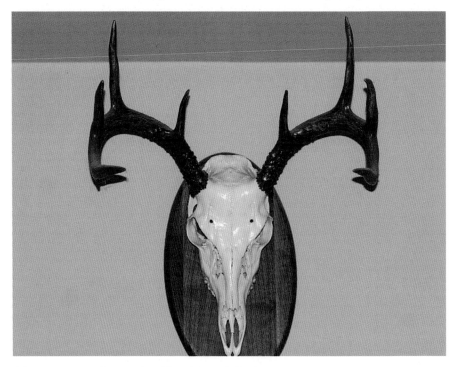

A European mount of my best bow kill, which I got in Manitoba.

should be a medium-sized one for cutting meat from the skull and the third should be a heavy, wide-bladed knife for scraping tissue from bone.

You will also need a big (ten-quart) roaster pan to boil the skull in and a camp stove to boil the skull on, if the boiling will be done outside. The kitchen stove can be used to boil skulls inside, as long as your spouse, other family members, or roommates do not object. Long-nosed pliers, a big set of tweezers, cotton balls, peroxide, and a dinner plate or platter will be required too, along with a supply of old newspapers or paper towels.

Once the deer's head has been skinned, remove as much of the meat from the skull as possible. Then the eyes, brain, and lower jaw can be removed. The fillet knife is ideal for reaching through the hole in the back of the skull where the top vertebra was attached, for removing the brain in pieces. After most of the brain has been removed, fill the brain cavity with water and swish it around before dumping it out to get rid of small bits of tissue that may remain.

After as much tissue as possible has been removed from the brain and nasal cavities, the skull and lower jaw are ready to boil. The lower jaw can be discarded if you want to do a mount without it. Bring the water to a boil in the large roasting pan, submerge the skull all the way to the base of the burr at the bottom of each antler, and low boil for thirty minutes. Adding hot water periodically may be necessary to replace what boils away. It's important to not boil skulls too long. If you do, the bones will fall apart.

The meat and tissue that remain after boiling will be relatively easy to scrape off or pull away from the bone. Be very thorough in removing every bit of material you can reach that is not bone, using knives, pliers, and tweezers. Then the skull can be bleached with 40-volume peroxide, which can be obtained from beauty salon supply stores in pint bottles.

"Be careful with this stuff (peroxide)," John cautions. "Anything it touches will turn chalk white (including your skin). It will ruin clothes, and sting if you get it on your hands. I keep a pan of clean water handy to rinse my skin off quickly in case of a spill or splatter.

"Pour some of the peroxide into a bowl and, using the tweezers, dip cotton balls into the liquid and swab the bone thoroughly. Have a catch basin of some sort (I use a platter) under the skull to collect the run-off. Continue to wet down the bone until you have covered all of the area that needs to be white—be careful not to whiten the bases of the antlers. You will notice that the peroxide acts as a cleaning agent and more tissue will come away from the bone. Use the cotton balls to clean this membrane off the skull, and have several fresh cotton balls ready to use. Although some bleaching will be evident by the time you finish, most will occur in the next few hours (sunlight will accelerate the process) as the skull dries.

"With a full skull mount, I normally push some soaked cotton balls up the nasal cavity and drop some into the brain cavity to sit overnight before I put the mount in a warm well-lighted area to dry."

Once cleaned and bleached, the lower jaw can be replaced on the skull, if you decided to save it. Full skulls can be displayed as they are without going on a plaque, if desired. Plaques for European mounts can be ordered from taxidermy supply houses.

An alternative to doing a European mount with the entire skull is removing the top part of the skull, with antlers attached, using a bone or hack saw. The brain is much easier to remove with this method and there's less of the skull to clean and bleach.

Quartering

The carcass can be quartered after the hide has been removed. It's great if the carcass is hanging. If quartering is done in the field, with the carcass on the ground, it's best to do it while the carcass is lying on the skin to keep the meat as clean as possible.

A knife is all you will need to remove front legs and shoulders, hind legs, and loins from the carcass. These pieces represent at least ninety-five percent of the meat on a deer. While lifting or pushing up on the front legs, cut between shoulder blades and ribs to remove the front quarters. Hind legs, or hams, can be removed by cutting the hip joint. You can locate this joint by moving the leg back and forth a few times to see and feel where it is.

The loins or back straps are boneless strips of meat on both sides of the back-bone along the back. On northern deer, there's normally a layer of fat covering the loins. Cut away this layer of fat, so you can see the top of the spine and the outline of the muscle on top of the back, before removing the loins. Make two cuts along the sides of each loin to remove them. With the first cut, separate the loin from the back-bone by cutting as deeply as possible next to the backbone, from the base of the neck to a point just in front of the hindquarters. The second cut will intersect the first one from the side where the loin ends at the top of the ribs. Once those cuts are made, the loins can be peeled away from the carcass from front to back, using the knife to cut any muscle that may still be attached.

After the four quarters, tenderloins, and loins have been removed from the carcass, I trim as much boneless meat that remains on the carcass as possible, primarily in the pelvic area and neck. There's very little meat on the ribs of most deer. These final pieces of meat that are removed from the carcass are great for stews and casseroles, or can be ground into burger.

If you quarter a deer carcass this way while in the field, it dramatically reduces the amount of weight you have to carry because most of the skeleton is eliminated. This procedure may be required in areas with chronic wasting disease (CWD). Scraps of meat and bones that are left in the field will be eaten by scavengers.

If the weather is warm, the meat should be put in cloth bags for transport. Cloth meat bags are available in most sporting goods stores or they can be made from old sheets and pillow cases. Plastic garbage bags work fine to put meat in when the weather is cool to cold. If you plan on carrying the head and hide of a deer where they will be visible, a bright red or orange coat or vest should be draped over them to avoid being mistaken for a live animal.

If you don't have an enclosed backpack large enough to carry a quartered deer, pack frames can be used. The meat can be tied to frames with rope. It is a good idea to distribute the load between two hunters, especially if the deer was big. Each can take half. If you are alone, two trips may be necessary to transport a large deer.

Hunters who don't care about saving their hide or cape can halve or quarter their deer with the hide intact. Skinning can be taken care of later.

Whole deer that are to be transported by vehicle can be tied on the car roof or over the trunk, or put in the trunk or in the bed of a pickup. Don't put a deer over the hood, where heat from the engine will increase the chances of spoilage. If the weather is consistently warmer than 40 degrees Fahrenheit and you will be on the road for hours, use ice to keep the meat cool by putting it in the body cavity.

The best way to transport a deer during a long drive is quartered in a large cooler with ice. Some states require that deer be transported visibly and in one piece. Here again, try to be familiar with the regulations in the state or province you are hunting.

Butchering

The meat from a deer, like the hide, should be processed as soon as possible. It may be best to care for the venison first if there is a chance of spoilage. I used to bring my skinned deer to a local butcher and he cut the carcass while I waited. Any odds and ends were ground into hamburger. At home, my wife and I packaged and labeled the venison, then put it in the freezer. We removed all hair and fat from the meat and trimmed damaged portions as we wrapped it. Now I do the butchering myself, unless pressed for time. All fat and bones are removed. The boned, trimmed venison that results takes up a minimum amount of space in the freezer and is ready to cook, once thawed. The process takes time, but proves to be worth it when we enjoy delicious meals of venison. If venison is frozen with the fat intact, the quality of the meat will deteriorate.

Butchering your own deer also saves money. Most establishments that regularly butcher deer charge high fees. For this reason, and because there is a chance of the meat from your deer being switched with or mixed with the meat from other animals, hunters should know how to cut up their deer. The procedure is simple.

A couple of sharp knives are all you will need to butcher a deer. A workbench, kitchen counter, or covered kitchen table will do to work on. Use freezer paper or aluminum foil to cover a table, not newspaper. The carcass must be quartered as discussed earlier for butchering.

I remove all meat from front legs and shoulders for use in stews, casseroles, or burger, but the shoulders can be used as roasts.

The neck can be cut next. Some hunters leave the neck intact and cook it as a roast. This is not recommended, however, in locations with CWD because there are lymph nodes in the neck. I usually trim meat from the neck for burger or stews.

Steaks and roasts are the primary cuts from the hindquarters, with the exception of the flank and shank. The flank is a thin muscle in the belly area and the shank is the lower portion of legs. Meat from these locations are best used for stews or burger.

The hindquarter is made up of three large muscles and it's possible to see the lines that separate these muscles after fat and pieces of thin muscle that are on the surface are removed. Cut each of these muscles from the bone after fat and loose pieces of meat are trimmed. Each of the large muscles from hindquarters can be cooked as roasts or sliced into steaks.

The loins can be sliced into steaks or chops. Try to trim as much sinew and fat as you can from loins first. Whether you plan on serving loins as chops or steaks, you can save time during the butchering process by freezing a meal-sized chunk of meat whole and cutting the chunk into individual chops or steaks after it's thawed for a meal.

Packaging Venison

Hair and fat should be removed from cuts before they are packaged. Use freezer paper or heavy-duty aluminum foil to wrap the meat. Some hunters seal meat in clear plastic bags such as ZipLocs and then wrap in freezer paper or foil. A felt-tipped pen can be used to write the type of meat, the cut, and the date on freezer paper. Make labels out of masking tape when venison is stored in aluminum foil.

Butchering a deer may seem like an endless task the first time it is attempted. This is only because the steps are unfamiliar. The chore will become less tedious in future attempts as you become more proficient at butchering and realize that the dividends of your labor will be delicious meals of venison. It helps to have at least two people working together on a carcass. If at all possible, have someone who has butchered a deer before show you how.

The procedure I have listed here for butchering deer is by no means the only way it can be done. Many hunters develop their own routine for reducing a carcass into the cuts they like.

Try to be conservative when discarding bloodied meat that looks like it is beyond salvage. Saltwater is great for getting blood out of meat. Cuts that look bad may be able to be saved by soaking them overnight in a saltwater solution in a refrigerator. But be sure to discard any meat that contains or is suspected of containing lead fragments from bullets or slugs.

Many hunters have beef suet or pork fat mixed with ground venison. My wife and I seldom do this because we prefer lean burger. We use ground venison in spaghetti, meatloaf, and casseroles, and it tastes great. Another option for ground venison is to have it made into sausage. Some meat-processing plants regularly make venison sausage for hunters.

Antlers

The antlers grown by bucks and some does add greatly to the appeal of deer hunting. The unique characteristics exhibited by most racks and the impressive size that some antlers attain fascinate hunters. Simply put, antlers are important to most deer hunters. They are symbolic in many ways, but primarily serve as momentos of successful hunts.

Large sets of antlers are accorded special recognition. Those that meet certain standards are listed in one or more of at least four national record books, depending on what type of weapon was used to bag the deer that grew them. The Boone and Crockett Club has the highest minimum standards for entry of deer antlers in their records. Consequently, most deer in their record books have been taken with center-fire firearms. However, deer collected with muzzleloaders or bow and arrow that meet their restrictive standards are elligible for entry. The Pope and Young Club maintains lists of record deer collected by bowhunters. The Longhunter Society keeps records for muzzleloader kills. The Buckmasters Whitetail Organization has categories for acceptance of whitetails taken with all legal weapons that meet their minimums.

The first three record-keeping organizations all use the Boone and Crockett Scoring System for measuring whitetail and mule deer antlers. This system takes into account the lengths of antler beams and tines, the circumferences of the beams at four places, and the inside spread between the beams. Symmetry from one antler to the other is important in the B&C scoring system. Differences in measurements from one beam to the other are considered deductions.

B&C recognizes two different antler configurations—typicals and nontypicals. Typical racks have primarily normal antler development, with most of the tines

183 6/8

187 6/8

245 7/8

Both mule deer and whitetails have typical and nontypical antlers. This photo shows the head mounts of two typical mulies next to the mount of a nontypical, along with their antler scores.

growing from the top of main beams. Typical tines are not forked on whitetail antlers, but they are or can be on mule deer and blacktail racks. The lengths of nontypical tines, which are those that sprout from the sides or bottoms of beams and main tines of whitetail antlers, are deductions on typical racks.

Nontypical antlers are those that have a number of nontypical tines, with their combined lengths totaling about ten inches or more. However, the hunter who bags a book deer has the final say as to whether the buck is entered as a typical or nontypical. Some antlers that would qualify as nontypicals have been entered in records as typicals. The lengths of nontypical points are added to the score of nontypical racks rather than subtracted.

The B&C minimum score for entry of typical whitetail antlers in all-time records is 170 and 160 for honorable mention. The all-time and honorable mention minimums for nontypical whitetail antlers are 195 and 185 respectively. Different minimums are in effect for the small subspecies of whitetail in the desert southwest called coues deer. The minimums for all-time and honorable mention typical coues deer racks are 110 and 100. The numbers for nontypical coues antlers are 120 and 105.

For typical mule deer racks, the minimum scores they have to achieve for all-time and honorable mention listings in B&C are 190 and 180 respectively, and the numbers for nontypical mule deer antlers are 230 and 215. Typical Columbian blacktail antlers must measure at least 135 to be considered for listing in all-time

Head mount of a typical white-tail with unbranched 10-point antlers coming straight up from the top of beams.

A nontypical whitetail buck. This rack has about 40 points.

records and a score of 125 is necessary for honorable mention. The numbers for sitka blacktails are 108 and 100.

Since it's normally more difficult to take a book deer with a bow and arrow than a firearm, the minimums for entering bow-killed bucks in Pope and Young Records are lower than those for Boone and Crockett. Typical and nontypical whitetail racks only have to measure 125 and 155 respectively to be considered, for example. The antlers of coues whitetails have minimums of 65 for typicals and 95 for nontypicals. Mule deer antler minimums for P&Y are 145 for typicals and 170 for nontypicals. Numbers for Columbian blacktail typicals and nontypicals are 90 and 125 and sitka blacktail antlers must measure 75 to qualify for entry.

Minimum antler scores for entry into Longhunter Society Records are slightly higher than those for Pope and Young. Typical and nontypical whitetail antlers must measure at least 130 and 160. Typical coues racks have to score at least 70. The minimums for typical and nontypical mule deer are 146 and 175. The numbers for Columbian and sitka blacktails are 95 and 75 respectively.

Buckmasters has their own scoring system designed to give antlers credit for all of the bone they have. There are no deductions for lack of symmetry in this measuring system. Inside spreads are also not included in Buckmasters tallies because this measurement is of space or air rather than antler. Nontypical antlers are classified as "Irregulars" by Buckmasters and there is also a "Semi-Irregular" classification, depending upon how many irregular (nontypical) points the rack has.

Antlers of whitetail bucks taken with firearms have to score a minimum of 140, using the Buckmasters system, to qualify for entry in their records. Bow kills, including those taken with crossbows, only have to measure 105 to be considered. Information about the Buckmasters Trophy Records is available at their website: www.buckmasters.com. Mike Handley is the Trophy Chairman. Questions can be addressed to him at P.O. Box 244022, Montgomery, AL 36124. To reach him by telephone dial 334-215-3337, extension 232.

Besides national big-game record-keeping organizations, many states and provinces have separate records lists for deer taken within their borders. The minimums for state and provincial records are often lower than those on a national level, but most of them use the Boone and Crockett Scoring System. Hunters who bag exceptional whitetail bucks with bow and arrow or muzzleloader could qualify for listing in at least four sets of records—state or provincial, Pope and Young or Longhunter Society, Boone and Crockett, and Buckmasters. At least three of those record-keeping systems would be available for entry of high-scoring mule deer and blacktails.

Many hunters want to shoot a deer with a record-book rack and the opportunity to do so is now better than ever, especially on the level of state and provincial records. Whitetail and mule deer wearing antlers that meet record book standards on a national level can be hard to come by because they simply are not abundant. Those that do exist usually spend their time in remote, lightly hunted terrain, in refuges, or on private property. Many of these deer may be primarily nocturnal, too.

Trophy Bucks

Numerous trophy bucks are bagged each year. The definition of "trophy buck" varies from one hunter to another. The first buck I shot was a trophy to me at the time, and it only had three points. Now it would generally take whitetail and mule deer bucks with better than average racks to qualify as trophies for me because I've taken so many bucks over the years, including some whoppers. My best typical whitetail has ten points and an inside spread of about 21 inches (see chapter 7 for the story about how I got that deer). My best mulie has nine points with a spread comparable to that of the whitetail. Both racks are better than average and I'm happy that I was fortunate enough to get them even though many larger racks have been taken.

Something unique about my best mule deer head is that the antlers are in velvet. I shot this particular buck many years ago during a special early hunt in Colorado while hunting with outfitter Rudy Rudibaugh of Parlin. Ken Asbury was my guide.

Point Counts

There are two popular methods of classifying the number of points on a set of antlers: eastern and western count. In some parts of the west the brow tines or eye guards are not considered points, and only the side with the most tines is specified. Using my mounted mule deer as an example, one antler has three points, and the other four, discounting the brow tines. My buck is a four-point by western count.

Every tine over an inch in length is considered a point by eastern count. In my opinion this system is better. It coincides with the classification used by Boone and Crockett and Pope and Young. The other method can be confusing because it doesn't give a total picture of what a rack looks like. A four-point buck by Western count can have four points on one side and two, three, or four on the other. The rack may have brow tines or it may not.

It is usually possible by eastern count to get an accurate idea how a set of antlers is proportioned. An eight-point normally has four on a side; a seven-point generally has four on one side and three on the other. Occasionally a buck will have an odd rack with two points on one side and four on the other.

Measuring Whitetail Antlers

On the chance you shoot a buck with a rack that might qualify for national, state, or provincial records, you should know how to measure the antlers to see if they will qualify. The procedure is relatively simple. All that is required to score a set of antlers is a quarter-inch, flexible steel tape for measuring (any tape would do for rough measurements) and a piece of paper and a pencil or pen to jot down numbers.

The steps in measuring whitetail or mulie antlers for record classification, regardless of the category, are similar. For any projection to be considered a point, the distance it extends upward or outward must exceed the length of its base in addition to being at least an inch long. Let's take a typical whitetail rack to start with.

Measuring the beam length of a Boone and Crockett buck by taping a cable around the outside curve in the center of the beam. Afterward, the portion of the cable that corresponds with the beam length is measured on a flat surface.

To keep track of figures in an orderly fashion, set up three vertical columns on a sheet of paper. Two are for figures obtained from each antler, and the third is for differences in measurements between the antlers. There is one measurement required for scoring that won't fit into any of the three columns: the inside spread of the main beams. It can simply be written to the side or at the bottom of the paper and added to other figures later.

The first lengths we want to measure are the main beams. These are taken from the lowest outside edge of the burr (the circular formation at the base of the antlers where they join the skull) over the outer curve of the antlers to the tip of the main beam. The tape measure should follow the center line of the antler. The best way to measure beams is to lay a cable along their length and then measure the cable. A piece of string or rope will work if a cable isn't available.

The lengths of typical tines are measured from their intersection with the main beam to the tip on the outside of the antler.

When using a tape measure to determine the lengths of the beams, it may be necessary to obtain this figure in stages since most beams are curved. A control point should be marked each time a change in direction of the tape is required. All figures should be to the nearest eighth of an inch.

Enter the measurement for the right antler in the appropriate column and the same for the left. If one beam is longer than the other, enter the difference in the third column. (See sample scoring sheet for further guidance.)

Now measure the length of each normal point on each antler. To arrive at an accurate score, the tape should extend from the nearest edge of the main beam to the tip over the outer curve of the tine. Tips of main beams are not measured as points. These are already included in the figure for the lengths of the beams.

Measurements of corresponding points on each antler are then compared and any difference is written in the appropriate location. Typically, a record whitetail buck will have from eight to fourteen normal points; however, a greater number is possible.

The next step is tallying the total length of abnormal points. These should be measured from the base, whether on the main beam or a tine, to the tip along the outside curve. On a typical whitetail head any points that jut out at odd angles from the main beam or branch from any of the tines are abnormal.

Occasionally, a point coming off the top of the beams may be considered abnormal. Let's look at an example. Say one antler has six points and its mate, seven. The extra tine is between the second and third points and is only four inches long. Point number three on the opposite antler is ten inches long.

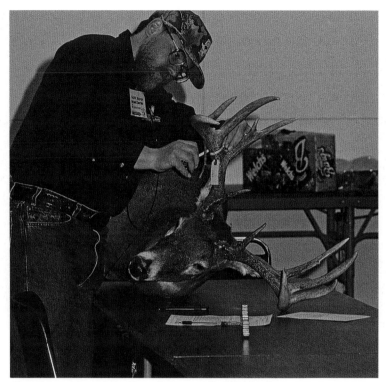

Circumferences are taken at four places on each whitetail antler.

If the four-inch tine were considered normal, it would become the third point and scored with its longer counterpart. This way six inches would be lost, and there would be no mate for the fifth point on the side with the most tines and additional inches would be lost. So consider that extra point abnormal. Only four inches would be lost that way.

Enter the figure obtained from abnormal points in column three.

Beam circumference at four points is next. The first one is gauged at the smallest point between the burr and first tine. Jockeying the tape around in that area may be necessary to locate the smallest circumference. The smallest circumference between the first and second points is considered next, followed by a similar position between second and third tines and third and fourth. In cases where the first point or brow tine is missing, the first two measurements can be taken at the smallest point between the burr and second point. On beams with four points, measure the last circumference halfway between the beam tip and the third tine.

The final measurement that affects the score of a rack is the inside spread of the antlers. This must be assessed at right angles to the center line of the skull and can be taken at the widest point between beams.

If the figure obtained is greater than the longest main beam, the difference must be entered in column three on the tally sheet. A number less than or equal to the length of the longest main beam can be written in as credit for inside spread.

The inside spread of a set of deer antlers is taken perpendicular to a line through the center of the head at the widest point, as shown.

For instance, let's say the inside spread of the antlers on the sample score sheet came out to be an even 25 inches, instead of $21^{1}/_{8}$. In that case it would be greater than the longest main beam, which was $23^{2}/_{8}$. So their difference, $1^{6}/_{8}$, would go in column three and spread credit would be $23^{2}/_{8}$.

An official scorer for Boone and Crockett or Pope and Young would jot down several additional measurements that simply indicate the conformation of the rack. They don't affect the score. These are the number of points on each antler, tip-to-tip spread, and the greatest outside spread.

Once all of the necessary measurements are determined, the final score can be totaled. To tally this figure, add all the numbers in columns one and two plus the inside spread. Then subtract the total of column three from that total.

Final score for this head is $6^{3}/_{8}$ points short of the minimum qualifying tally (170) for all-time listing of a typical whitetail in the Boone and Crockett Record Book, but it would qualify for honorable mention. This rack would easily surpass the minimum for Pope and Young (125) and the Longhunter Society (130). The antlers would also meet the minimum of 140 for Buckmasters records. The Buck-masters tally can be obtained by subtracting the inside spread from the gross score and then adding the length of abnormal points as well as deductions for symmetry ($4^{6}/_{8}$) to that total, giving the antlers a final score of 154

If a rack is close to or exceeds the appropriate minimums, it should be taken to an official scorer for verification. However, 60 days must have elapsed from the time the head was collected until it is officially measured. This allows for drying, during which time some shrinkage occurs.

Sample Score Sheet for Rough Scoring Deer Heads

EXAMPLE: TYPICAL WHITETAIL	COLUMN 1 (RIGHT ANTLER)	COLUMN 2 (LEFT ANTLER)	COLUMN 3 (DIFFERENCE)
1. Length Main Beam	$23^2/_8$	$22^7/_8$	$^5/_8$
2. Length First Point	$5^6/_8$	$5^6/_8$	—
3. Length Second Point	$7^1/_8$	$7^3/_8$	$^2/_8$
4. Length Third Point	9	$8^7/_8$	$^1/_8$
5. Length Fourth Point	$8^6/_8$	$8^5/_8$	$^1/_8$
6. Length Fifth Point			
7. Length Sixth Point			
8. Circumference between Burr and First Point	$5^3/_8$	$5^3/_8$	—
9. Circumference between First and Second Points	$4^7/_8$	$4^6/_8$	$^1/_8$
10. Circumference between Second and Third Points	5	$4^7/_8$	$^1/_8$
11. Circumference between Third and Fourth Points	$4^6/_8$	$4^7/_8$	$^1/_8$
12. Total lengths of Abnormal Points (on typical heads this figure is subtracted from score, but on nontypicals it is added)	$3^2/_8$		
Inside Spread of Antlers:	$21^1/_8$		
Total Column 1:	$73^7/_8$		
Total Column 2:		$73^3/_8$	
Spread Credits:	$21^1/_8$		
	$168^3/_8$		
Total Column 3:			$4^6/_8$
Total Score:	**$163^5/_8$**		

During early hunts in some states, deer antlers may be in velvet when collected. Pope and Young does accept antlers in velvet for their records since many bow deer seasons open before bucks have shed their velvet. Racks will have to be injected with formaldehyde or freeze-dried to preserve the velvet. Velvet must be removed from the antlers of deer for entry in other national records.

The same procedure as above can be followed for scoring a nontypical whitetail rack. However, the total length of abnormal points is added to the score rather than subtracted. The tally of the lengths of abnormal points should be listed as a plus figure along with inside spread, rather than placing it in column three as before.

Measuring Mulies

The guidelines for measuring and scoring mule deer racks is nearly the same as the procedure for whitetails, with a couple of minor exceptions. Mulies usually have fewer normal or typical points than whitetails, often four per beam, not including the beam tip.

Due to the difference in structure of mulie racks, circumferences are taken differently. As with whitetails, the first two circumferences are measured between the burr and first point and the first and second. The third one, however, is measured between the main beam and tine number three. The final circumference is assessed between the second and fourth points, always at the smallest place.

A list of official Boone and Crockett scorers in your area and other information can be obtained by writing to Boone and Crockett Club, 250 Station Dr., Missoula, MT 59801 (406-542-1888). Pope and Young information can be obtained from Glenn Hisey, Box 548, Chatfield, MN 55923 (507-867-4144), and the email address is admin@pope-young.org. For muzzleloading records, contact the National Muzzle Loading Rifle Association, P.O. Box 67, Friendship, IN 47021 (800-745-1493). The departments of natural resources and fish and game in each state might also be sources for contacting official scorers in your area.

Photos of a record-book set of antlers, front and sides, plus a nonrefundable entry fee, must be sent with official score sheets that are to be considered for record-book entry. Fair chase statements and copies of licenses must also be submitted to confirm the animal was taken legally and within the guidelines established for each organization. Copies of tags are required for muzzleloading records, too.

Antler Cycle

Although the structures that bucks grow on their heads every year are often referred to as horns, the growths are not true horns. They are antlers. Unlike antlers, horns such as those worn by sheep, pronghorn antelope and cattle are not shed, although pronghorns shed an outer sheath. Deer shed their headgear every year. Most antlered whitetails and mulies are bucks, but occasionally a doe will sprout a set. Some antlered does are bagged by deer hunters in North America every year.

Bucks normally shed their antlers during the winter, after the rut is over and testosterone levels decline. Both beams may be lost at approximately the same time, or there could be a week or more lag from the time one antler is lost until its mate drops off. The timing varies from deer to deer. All of the bucks in a given area won't lose their racks at the same time, either. The health, nutrition level, and age of individual animals makes a difference. Severity of the weather is also thought to affect the length of time deer sport their antlers.

In my home state of Michigan, bucks start dropping antlers in December, usually by the middle of the month in the Upper Peninsula and toward the end of the month in southern counties, but some antlerless bucks have been mistakenly shot for does in the Upper Peninsula as early as December 2.

Mark Eby from St. Ignace, Michigan, actually saw a trophy 12-point buck lose both of its antlers one year while bowhunting around mid-December. The whitetail was about 50 yards away when it used one of its hind legs to scratch its head and one of the antlers fell off. Then the buck put its head down as if it was going to rub a tree and the second antler fell off. Although Mark didn't get the buck, he got its antlers, retrieving them after the deer walked off.

Another year Eby found a freshly shed antler with four points on New Year's Eve near one of his late season tree stands. He hunted the stand the evening of the 30th and the antler wasn't there. It was there when he returned the following day. A search for the buck's second antler was unsuccessful.

I saw an 8-pointer lose one of its antlers on the evening of January 22 one year. I was photographing it and another buck that still had his antlers in the yard of a friend who was feeding deer during the winter. He had placed food in cardboard boxes for the deer. The 8-point was eating from one of the boxes when something spooked him, causing him to jerk his head up quickly. When the buck jerked his head up, the left antler fell off his head and into the box.

Judy Ritzenhein of Norway, Michigan, collected a trophy set of whitetail antlers in Delta County near the family deer hunting camp on the morning of December 13 one year without firing a shot. She was on her way back to camp after taking a walk when something on the ground caught her eye.

It was a whitetail antler that had recently been shed. It was the left beam and was lying with the tines pointing downward. She said there was blood on the antler base.

The base of an antler that fell off of a buck's head minutes earlier on January 22 one year when it jerked its head up suddenly.

Judy Ritzenhein of Norway, Michigan, with the shed antlers she found on December 13 one year soon after they had been dropped.

Moments later, she found the buck's right antler about 10 feet away, with the tines pointed upward.

The rack had obviously come from a big buck. There were a total of eleven tines, six on the right and five on the left. One of the points on each side angles forward from the same location on the second main tine. The bases of the beams measured five inches in circumference.

Judy's husband Jim decided to have the antlers mounted for her as a Christmas present. A local taxidermist placed them on a plaque for display.

Surprisingly, Jim found an antler that had been shed a year earlier during gun deer season, and it proved to be from the same deer. On November 20th, he was walking through some tamaracks when he tripped on the antler from the right side of a buck's head. When Judy later found the matched set, he recognized the

Don Doryk from Leoville, Saskatchewan, found this shed antler on April 26. He had been on the trail where he found the beam two days earlier and it wasn't there. Bucks that are in excellent health and not stressed by weather will hang onto their antlers longer than normal.

similarity between the one he had stumbled upon and the one from the same side she had.

The tines were shorter and the beam wasn't as long on the antler from the previous year, but the curve of the beam and the positioning of the points were the same on both antlers. The fact that Jim retrieved the antler only about 100 yards from where Judy made her find is another indication the antlers are from the same deer.

Although bucks start losing their antlers in December, a few bucks will be seen still wearing headgear as late as March, especially if they are being supplementally fed. One year after an extremely mild winter, Saskatchewan guide Don Doryk, who lives near the community of Leoville and guides for Proudfoot Creek Outfitters, found a recently shed antler with five points on April 26. In Florida, bucks' antlers are reportedly lost and grown with no pattern, due to the relative consistency of the weather.

Velvet

While the antlers are growing they are covered with what is called velvet or moss. It is true skin. All of the tissue is soft and generously supplied with blood during the development stage. If the delicate antlers are damaged or the deer itself injured while they are growing, one or both sides of the rack can become malformed. This is how some nontypical antlers result. Bucks with hormonal imbalance or permanently damaged sex organs may produce nontypical formations year after year.

Once antlers are completely developed the supply of blood to them stops and the tissue dies. An increase in hormone levels brings this about. Then the velvet is rubbed off, leaving hardened antlers.

The first week of September is prime time for mature bucks to shed the velvet from their antlers. It was September 6 when a $5^1/_2$-year-old 8-point that I had been photographing all year lost the outer covering of his new set of antlers, and he played an active role in getting rid of it.

The whitetail was in the process of shedding his velvet when I found him on the evening of the sixth after looking for him for a couple of hours. He was aggressively

rubbing his antlers on a large maple tree in a meadow. Some of the velvet was already off the antler, but the tattered, bloody pieces still hung from the rack. The exposed bone was also covered with blood.

The buck would rub his antlers vigorously for a while then stop and lick the tree like he was lapping up blood or pieces of velvet. Perhaps he was trying to regain some of the nutrients contained in the lost tissue. I've read other reports of bucks eating the velvet they shed.

After rubbing on the tree for a while, the buck went to a large rock with a smooth surface in the meadow and rubbed the tips of his antlers on it for a while. That action dulled the tips somewhat, but I don't think it did much for shedding the velvet. The buck then alternated between feeding and rubbing his antlers.

It was obvious that the strands of velvet hanging loosely from the antlers bothered the buck. The dangling tissue probably obscured his vision somewhat.

This mature 8-pointer shed the velvet covering his antlers on September 6.

There also may have been an itching sensation in his scalp or at the base of his antlers from the blood vessels that formerly supplied blood to the velvet that were being shut down.

The big 8-point's antler rubbing eventually attracted the attention of a 2-year-old 8-point and a yearling buck with spike antlers. They were curious about what the bigger buck was doing and the sight of the shredded velvet hanging from his rack. The tips of a couple of tines from the smaller 8 were showing through the velvet on his antlers, so it wouldn't be long before he lost his velvet, too.

As it got too dark to photograph the velvet shedding of the big buck with the available light, I started using a flash to get as many photos as possible of the process. The whitetail eventually crossed a road and rubbed the lower limbs of a big white cedar tree. His next target was a white birch tree and then he raked his antlers through some tall grass in an effort to get rid of more of the loose velvet still hanging from his antlers.

The buck rubbed his antlers on a number of trees and a big rock in an effort to get rid of the velvet. It took him a number of hours to shed the velvet covering his antlers.

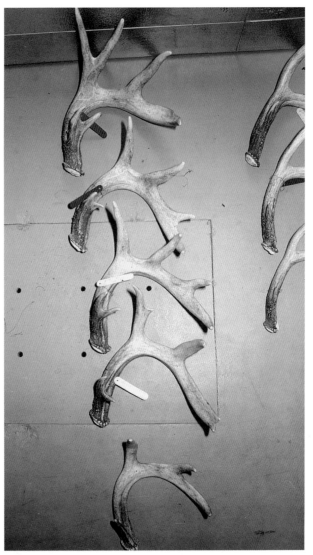

Antlers shed by the same buck from age 3$^{1}/_{2}$ through 7$^{1}/_{2}$. A genetic trait this buck showed in his antler each year from 4$^{1}/_{2}$ on was a forked brow tine. Note how the curve of each beam is the same.

By that time, it was too dark to focus the camera. I left the deer as he crossed a creek.

All of the buck's velvet was gone by the following day. The process of shedding the velvet from this buck's antlers took a matter of hours, but in some cases the antler covering is eliminated much faster.

Antler Color

Antler coloration varies from bleached white to a deep brown. My theory is that a buck living in open country where his antlers get a lot of exposure to the sun will generally have a lighter colored rack than a buck that spends most of his time in heavy cover where the sun seldom penetrates.

Some claim that antlers are stained by dried blood when the velvet is shed. Others feel that antlers derive their color from the trees they are rubbed on when polished. A combination of these factors may play a role in antler coloration.

The size rack a buck grows is dependent upon three factors: heredity (genetics), nutrition, and age. Deer that grow outstanding headgear have to be in good health, at least several years old, and genetically disposed to antler growth. Even yearling bucks can have respectable racks sporting eight or more points, provided their diet and parentage is right. Yet some bucks can be healthy and old, but sport mediocre racks because the right genes aren't there.

Antler Patterns

Interestingly enough, a buck's antlers will form in the same general pattern year after year. The number of points may increase the first couple of years, but the general shape and features of the rack will normally remain the same. However, the older a buck gets, the greater the chances his antlers will sprout nontypical points.

John Ozoga, a former whitetail researcher with the Michigan Department of Natural Resources who is currently research editor for *Deer & Deer Hunting* magazine, showed me several series of antlers shed by the same bucks over a period of years. The deer were in an enclosure and could be monitored closely. The resemblance of the racks from one year to the next for each animal was remarkable. In many cases the only change over a span of years was an increase in the circumferences of the beams. John could identify individual bucks during his observations by the shape of their racks.

Another fact the biologist learned from his studies of penned deer is that antler growth in yearling bucks can be adversely affected by an abundance of older, mature bucks. In situations where big-racked bucks were common, a percentage of the yearlings in the population grew sublegal antlers, less than three inches in length. Food wasn't a limiting factor here since the deer were on a high-nutrition diet.

For years there was speculation that bucks that grew spike antlers for their first set at $1^1/2$ years of age had inferior genetics and would have poor antler development throughout their lives. This may be true in a small number of cases, but for the most part, yearling bucks that grow spikes are part of a herd with a high percentage of adult bucks, were born late, have poor nutrition, or suffer some other type of health problem. Healthy bucks often grow respectable racks in future years. I've seen a number of spike bucks grow beautiful 8-point racks as $2^1/2$-year-olds.

Deer Management

Strictly from a management point of view, it would be better if whitetail and mule deer bucks didn't grow antlers, or if both sexes did.

An adequate harvest of antlerless deer (does and young-of-the-year bucks) is difficult to achieve in parts of North America due to the traditional stigma many deer hunters associate with shooting deer that aren't wearing antlers. If both sexes of deer did or didn't have antlers, the problem wouldn't exist.

I believe part of the reason a percentage of deer hunters resist harvesting does is due to their poor understanding of deer management. Since it will be easier to try to get hunters to understand and accept the need for shooting both bucks and does than to develop a strain of antlered does or antlerless bucks (maybe), let's get on with it.

Carrying Capacity

It would be nice if we could make deer herds continually increase by simply protecting does, but, unfortunately, that isn't how things work. Each deer range has enough browse to feed only a certain number of deer throughout the year. Available deer food is scarcest during the winter, droughts, and other periods of severe weather. So the maximum number of whitetails or mulies that can be supported in any given habitat without reducing its quality (its carrying capacity) is determined by the amount of food available to them then.

Drought, floods, and heavy snows limit the amount of food available to deer. In many cases the winter deer range is only a fraction of the size of the summer and fall ranges. Mulies and some whitetails have traditional wintering areas, which they use year after year. Their nutritional needs must be met within those limited areas.

While drought and floods are seldom predictable, winter is. The key to a healthy deer herd is maintaining its winter population at or below the carrying capacity of its

The biggest obstacle to proper deer management in much of North America is that many hunters are not willing to harvest enough antlerless deer. This not only leads to high deer numbers, it results in lop-sided sex ratios. I try to shoot at least one doe a year and I take more than that some years.

habitat. A herd that comes through the winter in good shape will produce a maximum yield of fawns. By fawning time, deer will have dispersed throughout the summer range where there is an abundance of food, enough to sustain the increased population. Before winter returns, the number of whitetail and mule deer in an area has to be trimmed to correspond with the limited food supply.

That is where hunting comes in. The purpose of the fall hunting season is to reduce the population to the level the winter range can sustain. To do this, the number of deer that were produced for the year (as close to it as possible) must be shot. Both bucks and does can and should be harvested to reach that goal.

After all, both sexes were added to the population. More of each sex than were reproduced would have to be removed from the population before there would be a net decline. Looking at it another way, some does can be shot and the herd will still increase as long as fewer are harvested than were produced for the year.

The number of births and deaths in a deer population has to balance with the food supply. Imagine a platform balanced on a central pivot like a teeter-totter. Births and deaths are on each end and food is in the center as the fulcrum. The scale may tip one way or another for a time, but will eventually return to a balance.

If a deer herd is well below the carrying capacity of its range, allowing the herd to increase is good management. This can be done by protecting does entirely for a time or harvesting a fraction of those produced each year. Does can't be protected indefinitely, though, if that route is chosen. An increasing population will reach its limit, and then must be maintained at or below that level. To do that, the annual increase of both bucks and does must be removed each year.

The annual removal of some does is essential to balance deer populations with their habitat. If fewer does are shot by hunters every year than the number produced, the herd will continue to increase until there are too many for the available food supply. Hunters who refuse to shoot does are not fulfilling the role of a deer manager like they are supposed to.

A herd at a level that is below the capacity of its habitat is preferable to one at the limit. It is like having money (surplus browse) in the bank. The closer a deer population is to the carrying capacity of its range during the leanest time of year, the lower emergency funds become. When a negative balance is reached (too many deer for the available food supply), some animals will be lost to malnutrition, disease, increased predation, road kills, and other accidents.

Overpopulation

Populations of whitetails or mulies that have gone beyond the carrying capacity of their range are the biggest problem in deer management. In order to bring them back in balance, more deer have to be removed than are produced each year. Many times it is difficult to achieve a large enough kill.

Overpopulations reduce the habitat's ability to sustain deer. More deer food is consumed than is produced. Some food sources are killed off by overuse. The number of deer the habitat will be able to support in future years will decline for each year the herd exceeds its range's carrying capacity.

If hunters are unable or unwilling to reduce a deer herd on a year-to-year basis, the health of the population suffers. In stress situations created by extremes in weather, such as winter, some of the excess whitetails or mule deer will die of malnutrition. Those in weakened condition will be easy prey for predators.

The worst side effect of an overpopulation of deer, one that few hunters are aware of, is their reduced capability to reproduce.

A biologist said it better than I can: "Reproduction is a luxury. That animal (doe deer) is geared for its own survival. If there isn't enough food, deer just won't reproduce. A doe may become pregnant, but the young will be aborted or some other means will be used to get rid of it."

In such a situation, the problem is usually too many does. A doe left to live under these circumstances can be a detriment rather than an asset. Many fawns born to weakened does will be dead at birth or die shortly afterward. Some of the young will live, but only a fraction of those that would have survived if the herd were healthy.

One of the effects of deer overpopulation is that the reproductive rate declines. Does may give birth to fawns, but they are too small to survive and die soon after birth, like the one shown here. This fawn was too weak to stand to nurse from its mother when it was born. The doe gave birth to one other fawn that was healthy. Scavengers like this raccoon soon find dead fawns and eat them.

In healthy whitetail herds adult does like this one average two fawns apiece. When too many deer are present, does average a maximum of one fawn apiece.

As odd as it may sound, more fawns will be produced by fewer does in a healthy condition than by twice as many winter-weakened females. Research has shown that on properly managed deer range 30 percent of six-month-old does will produce a fawn, 90 percent of the yearlings will fawn (some with one and others with twins), and adult does will usually produce twins.

In contrast, adult does on poor range will average from .4 to 1 fawn each. Younger does in such a situation are nonproductive.

Simply looking at birthing figures among adult does, the advantages of maintaining a balance between range and herd size become apparent. Ten healthy does can be expected to have twenty fawns. Twenty poorly nourished does will reproduce a maximum of twenty young.

Going one step farther using the same reasoning, deer hunters can harvest more whitetails and mulies annually from a properly managed herd than from one that is out of balance with its habitat, even though there are fewer animals carried through the winter in the first instance.

Sounds simple on paper doesn't it? It is, really. But how do deer managers know what the carrying capacity of habitat is, how many deer are using it, and how many of each sex should be harvested?

Estimating Population Size

In the field there is no way to account accurately for every deer. However, their numbers can be estimated with reasonable accuracy. This is done in a variety of ways. One method consists of counting groups of deer pellets on randomly chosen plots during the spring. It sounds far out and maybe a bit ridiculous at first, but think about it for a minute. When scouting for deer, one of the signs hunters look for is droppings. The frequency with which they appear provides a rough index to what extent the area is being used.

When done scientifically, the number of pellet groups in an area actually does represent the number of deer in an area. Biologists know through studies on penned deer how many times a deer defecates in a day. This information, combined with random sampling and statistical probabilities and calculations, provides a reasonably accurate estimate of populations. The entire procedure is too sophisticated to detail here, but it has proved to be one of the best ways to determine deer numbers.

There are other methods of estimating deer populations, such as marking individuals, helicopter surveys, and trail camera surveys. Each is based on sound information and involves complex mathematical calculations. The important thing to keep in mind about deer population estimates is they allow for error. Figures reflect upper and lower limits rather than a single, cut-and-dried number, even though they may be listed that way.

One method state biologists use to estimate deer populations is to count the number of pellet groups from the animals on randomly selected plots during the spring. Those numbers are plugged into a complicated formula that takes into account different variables to come up with an estimate.

As an example, the deer population of a two-square-mile wintering area near where I live was estimated. Researchers concluded that from 361 to 543 deer wintered in the yard. Another way to state the estimated population for that area is 452 plus or minus 91. The same thing is done for individual management units and entire states and provinces.

Calculating Carrying Capacity

The carrying capacity of an area is determined in a fashion similar to the way some deer-population estimates are conducted. Random plots are chosen, and the edible browse on them is cut and weighed. Mathematical computations are used to complete the survey. It is important to realize that when estimating the amount of browse that will be available in wintering areas, only the material that will be within reach of whitetails and mulies is considered. Much of the food hunters see in the fall will

This fenced exclosure erected by former Michigan DNR Forester Mike Zuidema shows how much impact local deer are having on the habitat. The only place saplings can survive in this location is where deer can't eat them. That's a clear indication that deer numbers are too high.

be covered with snow in winter or is too high for deer to reach.

Exclosures also give managers an idea how healthy the habitat is and how much impact deer are having on it. Exclosures are small plots that are fenced to keep deer out. When vegetation that grows inside the fence is compared with growth outside, the effect deer are having is easy to see. If there's little difference between the two, deer are in balance with their habitat. When plants and trees are growing inside the exclosure, but are absent outside, deer are out of balance.

Harvest Goals

Population and browse estimates are used to determine how many deer of each sex can be harvested. The number

The only saplings that could be found outside the exclosure are the size of those in front of Mike Zuidema's hands. They are eaten before they get much bigger.

of hunters expected and harvests achieved in previous years are also considered. Additional variables deer managers try to take into account are deer losses to poachers, predators, and automobiles. Another important consideration in western states is competition between livestock and deer for available food supplies.

States are usually divided into a number of different management units because of varying conditions often present within each. Harvest goals are normally determined for each unit.

It is seldom difficult to get a desired harvest of bucks. To encourage the take of antlerless deer, hunters are sometimes offered them as a bonus to the regular limit. Some areas have a two- or three-deer limit where one or two of the animals must be antlerless. "Earn A Buck" programs have been tried in some areas, too. Under this management scheme, hunters are required to shoot an antlerless deer before they can get a buck tag. Antlerless-only hunts are another option, usually held before and after regular deer seasons.

Camp or party permits that can only be filled with a doe or young-of-the-year buck are still another way that some states and provinces have attempted to increase the harvest of antlerless deer. Another option is hunter choice permits. A hunter holding one can shoot either a buck or doe. Where crop damage is a problem, farmers are issued crop damage permits that are usually only valid for antlerless deer. Additional possibilities exist and are in use.

Some years the hunt goes as expected and an appropriate number of deer are harvested. There are others, however, when not enough or too many whitetails and mule deer are bagged. Variable hunting conditions and hunter densities may make animals more, or less, vulnerable than expected. The deer range is surveyed every year to keep tabs on its status. If wintering areas are overutilized more deer will have to be removed from the population the next season through liberalized regulations.

Some or all of the deer killed each season are examined as well to determine their physical condition. Malnourished deer in the winter are a sure sign of too many animals. Biologists can determine the condition of dead deer by breaking open a bone on a hind leg and looking at the bone marrow. A healthy animal will have white, tallowy marrow from the fat contained in it. Malnourished deer will have exhausted much of the fat in bone marrow, leaving it red and gelatinous.

Underutilized wintering areas usually result in restrictive hunting regulations to allow herds on such range to increase.

Habitat Change

Habitat changes and reduction are also major considerations in deer management. Even if a herd is maintained at or below the carrying capacity of a particular range, its capacity to support as many deer as it formerly did may be reduced as the vegetative growth, usually trees, matures. Forested areas with numerous openings, both grassy and logged types, are ideal for deer. Habitat such as this will support a maximum number of deer. As trees crowd into grassy fields and they grow up out of reach of deer, the habitat's deer-supporting capability is reduced. The same thing happens when habitat is flooded or developed in some way that makes it no longer useful to deer.

Logging is one of the best ways to manage forested deer habitat. Some species of trees like aspen regenerate best when they are clearcut. A new crop of aspens sprout from the roots of the trees that were cut. Selective cutting is best for hardwood trees like maple, oak, and birch.

When habitat is lost, the whitetail or mule deer that formerly occupied it have to move to other areas or, if there isn't room elsewhere, they will be removed from the population, preferably by hunting. Remember: The birth-and-death rate of a deer population has to balance with the food supply.

Habitat that is maturing is not a lost cause in many cases. It can be brought back to maximum deer production and maintained there through manipulation or improvement. Logging is one of the best ways to keep a necessary portion of deer range consisting of woodlands productive. Controlled burns, natural fires, and planted food plots also improve living conditions for deer.

Habitat Management

When logging is utilized to improve habitat, trees should be cut every five to ten years. Obviously, this can't be done to the same group of trees that often. Most take much longer than that to mature. The practice that is used to manage forests, both for deer and timber production, involves keeping as much of the habitat in mixed-age stands of trees as possible.

In an ideal situation a percentage of the trees in an area will mature at five- to ten-year intervals. For example, consider a 40-acre stand of 40-year-old aspen. It can be cut on a forty-year cycle. A 10-acre clearcut could be made every ten years. Aspen trees are intolerant of shade and regenerate naturally when clearcut. By the time the last 10 acres were cleared, trees on the first area cut would be mature again. When done on larger acreages a continuous patchwork of openings can be maintained.

Most stands of hardwood trees (maple, oak, beech, birch) are best managed through selective cutting, where only a portion of the trees in a stand are cut at any one time. The growth rate of remaining trees is usually improved after a selective cut. Selective logging also creates openings in the canopy of varying size, allowing saplings to germinate on the forest floor and creating deer browse and a new generation of trees.

This illustrates how habitat management works. It would be great if all deer range were suitable for such a scheme. There is so much diversity, however, that individual management plans have to be developed for each range. Unfortunately, a large percentage of deer habitat across the U.S., much of which is privately owned, isn't managed at all. State and federal lands suitable for deer production are usually managed under the guidance of foresters and wildlife biologists with the U.S. Forest Service or departments of fish and game or natural resources.

Deer hunters who own land that isn't currently managed may be able to improve the habitat and realize an increase in deer on their property, which would result in better hunting. State game biologists, foresters, and county extension agents are usually available to help develop a suitable management plan. Private landowners can realize financial benefit from timber sales for habitat improvement as well as increased deer numbers.

A way to increase benefits of cutting to deer is to cut in the winter when natural browse is scarcest. Felled tree tops represent tons of nutritious natural food to whitetails and mule deer.

Management Example

But make sure you work with a reputable forester or logger when having a cutting done. My brother Bruce an I learnd that the hard way when it came to managing 40 acres we own. A number of years ago, it was obvious to us that many of the trees on our property were mature and should be cut. The thick canopy created by the large trees shaded the forest floor, eliminating most ground cover that deer feed on.

When we were contacted by a logger who was interested in cutting the trees, we discussed the options with him and were considering having him do the job. However, I told the logger I wanted to talk to other people he worked for and draft a contract for him to sign before any work was done. Despite this request, the jobber started cutting trees on our property anyway without notifying us.

Fortunately, I caught him in the act soon after he started, but he had already cut thirty to fifty trees. Needless to say, he wasn't invited back. Based on conversations I've had with foresters and other landowners since, there are plenty of unscrupulous loggers who routinely try to take advantage of landowners. I've heard stories of landowners who fared far worse than we did.

After that incident, it was obvious we needed some professional advice and I contacted consulting forester Dean Francis from Escanaba. He met with Bruce and me and drafted a management plan for our property. Due to a land stewardship assistance program that was in effect at the time, it only cost $100 to have the management plan done. This type of program may be in place in other areas and it's well worth taking advantage of.

Consulting forester Dean Francis (blue hat) handled a timber sale on 40 acres my brother and I own to maximize our income from the trees that were cut and to make sure the logging was done properly. If you handle a timber sale on your land, make sure you check the references of loggers you are considering for the job and have them sign a contract. A contract protects both parties.

When we found out that Francis would handle a timber sale for us for a percentage of the proceeds, we agreed to let him do so. We discussed which trees should be cut and which shouldn't and he took care of the rest. He determined the volume of each species of tree that was to be cut and put the sale out on bids to loggers who he knew would do a good job.

Once the highest bidder was agreed upon, Dean handled the contracts and dealt with the logger. Another major advantage of having a consulting forester handle the sale is that we received the stumpage for our trees that were going to be cut before the logger started working. The forester also monitored the job to make sure it was done properly.

The planning process took three to four years, but we felt good knowing that when the logging was done, it would be done the best way possible. The cutting was conducted during the winter so local whitetails could benefit from the food provided by the felled tree tops. We ended up with some bucks in our bank accounts and can look forward to seeing more bucks on our property.

Supplemental Feeding

Supplementally feeding deer corn, other grains, hay, alfalfa, and commercial pellets can be beneficial if done throughout the winter, so their systems can adjust to those types of foods. In fact, feeding programs of this type can increase the winter carrying capacity. If this is done, however, it is important to plan for higher antlerless harvests as well to balance the increased numbers of deer carried through the winter. Otherwise the herd will grow too fast, damaging the habitat sooner.

Emergency deer feeding programs that are started late in the winter when animals are already nutritionally stressed often do more harm than good. The digestive systems of many deer cannot handle a rapid change in diet. Deer have bacteria in their stomachs to aid in the digestive process. The type of bacteria varies, depending on the type of food that is being eaten. Deer that have been feeding on woody mate-

Supplemental feeding programs carried out all winter can increase survival of deer. Supplemental food will increase the carrying capacity of the habitat and improve the health of deer, but it is equally important to harvest more antlerless whitetails and mule deer from areas where winter feeding programs exist.

rial, for example, and are already weak, cannot adequately utilize corn given them when there is a shortage of natural food. Kernels of corn that are eaten by hungry animals lie undigested in the rumen where they ferment and form a poisonous ammonia gas that can kill the deer.

This problem does not exist when whitetails or mulies eat the felled tops of trees, their natural food. So when a food shortage occurs during the winter, it is far better to provide natural browse to the animals through cuttings rather than bringing in tons of high-energy foods most winter-weakened deer won't be able to digest.

When done properly, supplemental winter deer feeding will increase the survival and productivity of the herd. Therefore, it is extremely important, under these circumstances, to harvest as many antlerless animals as possible to offset the increase. Otherwise, deer numbers will go higher and higher and the quantity of food necessary to feed them will increase steadily, as will the food bill. While the herd is building, its winter habitat will deteriorate and its capacity to provide natural browse will reach low levels. Although the artificially-fed deer herd that has overpopulated its winter range may not need the browse, deer will eat whatever is available.

The National Park Service inherited a supplemental deer feeding situation that proved to be a problem when private property where the feeding had taken place became part of Pictured Rocks National Lake Shore in upper Michigan. The affected area is known as Beaver Basin. Deer that wintered in the basin were artificially fed for years while it was privately owned by the Michigan-Wisconsin Pipeline Company. The company spent thousands of dollars every year to sustain the whitetails during the winter.

The herd was well in excess of the carrying capacity of its range when the National Park Service acquired the land. The agency has a policy against the artificial feeding of any wildlife. Rather than halt feeding altogether, rations were reduced while a special hunt was planned to thin the herd. Some local residents opposed the hunt because they felt estimates of the herd size were too high and there was enough natural browse to sustain it in the winter. As a result, no special hunt was held and the herd died off at a rate of more than a hundred per season. This was *with* supplemental feeding. There would have been a dramatic crash had the feeding been stopped entirely.

Hundreds of deer that could have been harvested by hunters died. In the process, the habitat was damaged further. Because of this, it will take longer for that wintering area to rejuvenate to the point where a herd of any size can be maintained than it would have if hunters had removed the surplus. If the hunters who opposed the hunt had a better understanding of deer management, those animals could have been put to better use than as food for predators and scavengers.

Predation

As an offshoot of poor deer or habitat management, predators are often wrongly blamed for declines in deer populations. In Beaver Basin, for example, a number of deer were killed by coyotes and bobcats, a higher number than would have been susceptible if the herd were healthy. Winter-weakened deer that may die anyway are easy prey for predators. Loss of fawns is often attributed to predators, too. In reality, many does on poor range simply don't produce fawns that survive.

Such predators as coyotes, bobcats, wolves, and mountain lions certainly kill deer, both young and adults, from healthy populations. Their kills, however, are usually not responsible for the decline of a population any more than hunter kills are. As mentioned previously, deer managers take predation into account when setting harvest goals for hunting seasons. As long as total deer mortality is the same as or less than reproduction for any given year, the population will not decline. In my opinion, predators have as much right to deer as hunters do. They certainly earn their kills. If human hunters were as skillful as predators at getting close to deer, there would be no need for this book.

Before leaving the subject of predators, I would like to add that their populations may, at times, reach higher levels than desirable. When they overpopulate they also have an adverse impact on their food supply. For this reason, predators must be managed, too, but they don't deserve the reputation and treatment they have gotten from many deer hunters who would like to eliminate them entirely.

Management Barrier

One of the biggest barriers to blanket acceptance of deer-management decisions is getting hunters to accept the validity of population figures. They spend hours in the field and many of them see few whitetails or mule deer. This leads them to believe there are few animals around, unless they are able to see plenty of tracks, droppings, or other deer sign. The next season, when wildlife biologists say there is an overabundance of deer and more does have to be harvested, the hunters become skeptical.

There are two primary reasons for lack of acceptance of assessments of deer numbers. Some hunters spend each season, year after year, in the same area. They come to accept the territory they are familiar with as representative of their region, if not their state. Actually, there can be tremendous differences in deer densities in areas separated by fifty miles or less.

Most states and provinces are divided into management units to compensate for these differences, but it isn't always possible to accurately separate all units. Major roadways are often used as boundaries. These seldom coincide with differing deer herd considerations.

The second major reason for differing opinions on deer abundance is that many hunters give themselves too much credit and deer too little. They expect that if there are a lot of deer in the area they will see a lot, if there are only a few they will see a few. It works this way sometimes, but not usually. Both whitetails and mulies are adept at avoiding hunters. And many hunters aren't as good at sneaking through the woods or picking a stand as they think they are. I have been skunked while deer hunting enough times myself when there were plenty of deer around. I've learned to realize a hunter's limitations.

To illustrate my last point I will leave you with some facts and figures from a couple of closely monitored hunts in Michigan. One took place on a five-square-mile island in Lake Michigan—South Fox Island—during 1970. At that time the population of deer on the island was estimated to number approximately 600 animals. That meant there were about 120 deer per square mile!

The bag limit was three deer, two of which had to be antlerless. There were a total of 612 hunters who took part. They bagged 382 animals. Only 1 percent of the hunters collected three deer, 14 percent got two and 31 percent took one. A whopping 54 percent of the hunters were unsuccessful; some of them didn't even see a deer during their hunt!

The second closely monitored Michigan hunt was held inside a one-square-mile enclosure with a known population of deer. There were thirty-nine of them: seven bucks, fourteen does, and eighteen fawns. Seven experienced deer hunters hunted in the enclosure for four days. A total of eight deer were taken—three does, four fawns, and one buck. Only one of the seven bucks was sighted during the course of the hunt!

Hunts were held in the enclosure for seven years. The results each time proved that hunters are inefficient, only sighting a fraction of the population present in an area. This study was conducted in an area of limited size; on larger tracts of land hunters probably see an even smaller percentage of the actual number of deer present.

21

Quality Deer Management

Mandatory antler restrictions protect not only young bucks, they also protect bucks that are legal to shoot. Put another way, mandatory antler restrictions prevent hunters from shooting both young bucks and bucks that meet the criteria of being legal based on antler points. How is that possible?

It's simple. Under normal hunting conditions it's common for hunters to see deer that are obviously bucks, but at the same time not be able to see how many points the antlers have or how wide the antlers are due to the speed the buck is moving, how long it is in view, obstruction of the rack by brush, low light levels, or the distance involved. In many cases, these bucks have large enough antlers to be legal to shoot, but hunters are forced to hold their fire because they can't confirm it. In some cases, hunters could have bagged these bucks and would have shot them if it weren't for restrictive antler requirements.

I know it happens because I found myself in that position during the last days of a recent firearms season in Michigan's Upper Peninsula and I know I'm not alone. The weather was mild with no snow during most of gun season that year, making it difficult to determine where deer were most active. Snow finally fell on November 27. On the 28th, I took advantage of the snow cover to check out an oak ridge where I saw fresh signs of deer feeding on acorns. After scouting the area, I selected a spot to post for the last hour of daylight where I thought my chances of seeing a buck were good.

Up to that point, I had not yet seen a buck while hunting, and does were not legal targets in the area I was hunting. During the last minutes of daylight, I heard, then saw, a deer approaching. As it was walking toward me, I saw antlers. Based on the size and shape of the antlers, it looked like a 6-point. Over more than forty-five years of photographing and hunting whitetails, I've seen literally thousands of bucks with all different size antlers and I know what a 6-point rack looks like.

How many points does this buck's antlers have? Can't tell, can you? That's the same problem many whitetail hunters face every year where antler point restrictions are in effect. In some cases, a shot isn't possible anyway, but in others, deer that would be legal to shoot get away when a shot would have been possible because hunters can't tell how many points the buck has. On occasion, by the time a hunter determines a buck has enough points to shoot, it's too late to shoot. By the way, this buck has six points.

Since both of the buck tags in my pocket were restricted, however, I had to make darn sure there were at least three points on one antler. I was already 98 percent sure the antlers had three points on a side, but I had to be 100 percent sure before pulling the trigger of my Remington .30-06.

By then the buck was broadside to me and I could clearly see the beams were forked. If the antlers had a brow tine, I could pull the trigger because I already had him in the crosshairs of my scope. But, due to the angle the deer was standing and the low light, I was unable to see if either antler had a brow tine. Consequently, I had to let a buck that I'm confident was legal on my license walk away because I was unable to confirm that fact.

There is no doubt in my mind I did the right thing. I would not shoot a deer without being 100 percent sure it was legal. What happened is frustrating nonetheless. If I'd had an individual gun license in my pocket instead of a combo license, it would have been valid for a buck with at least three-inch spikes. Under those circumstances, I could have shot that buck and confirmed it had six points. More on the differences between licenses when it comes to antler restrictions will follow later.

What do mandatory antler restrictions have to do with Quality Deer Management (QDM)? In many hunters' minds, they are the same. According to my understanding of QDM, however, that reasoning is incorrect. QDM was begun as a voluntary program to give private land owners an alternative for managing whitetails. This type of management remains best suited for implementation on a voluntary basis on both private and public property.

One aspect of QDM is protecting young bucks such as fawns (6 months old) and yearlings (1.5 years old), so they reach older age classes, which contributes to a more balanced sex ratio in the herd. Doing this on a voluntary basis allows important flexibility that permits hunters who have not taken a buck before to shoot yearling bucks that may have spikes or forked antlers. This group of hunters would include young hunters, first-time hunters who are older, and some veterans who have simply been unsuccessful. Being able to experience success on a buck of any size can be important in building and maintaining interest in deer hunting.

Some overenthusiastic practitioners of QDM, usually hunters who have bagged their share of yearling bucks during their early years and no longer feel it's necessary, have developed the idea that if protecting some yearling bucks is a good idea, protecting as many of them as possible is even better. This mindset has led to mandatory antler restrictions in some areas where they are unnecessary, such as Michigan's Upper Peninsula.

Mandatory antler restrictions also reduce hunter recruitment. I spoke to a man who hunts in an area where bucks must have three antler points on one side to be legal. He told me he was excited about introducing his daughter to deer hunting. She was forced to pass up a forkhorn during her first year of hunting and never saw another buck. During her second year of hunting she saw a buck that would have been legal, but she could only see two points on the end of the beam, so she didn't shoot. After two years of deer hunting and not being able to shoot a buck, the girl is

Another drawback of antler point restrictions is they result in the harvest of the yearling bucks with the best antler development, like this one, while protecting yearlings with inferior antlers. This could result in reduced antler quality among bucks in the future.

no longer interested in deer hunting, and I know this is not the only case where this has happened.

Not all spikes and forkhorns are 1^1/$_2$ years old, either, especially in regions like upper Michigan where winters can be severe. Some bucks as much as 4^1/$_2$ years old that barely survive the previous winter grow antlers with no more than four points. DNR wildlife biologist Craig Albright from the Gladstone office did a check of the computer records of bucks brought to DNR check stations in the western UP during 2008 and discovered that a whopping 17 percent of the 2^1/$_2$-year-olds had less than three points on one antler. Six percent of 3^1/$_2$-year-old bucks failed to have three points on one antler and there were even some 4^1/$_2$-year-old bucks (3 percent) that did not have three points on an antler.

After checking his records for Marquette County in 2008, DNR wildlife biologist Terry McFadden found that 23 percent of the 2^1/$_2$-year-old bucks he examined had four points or less. In 2007, it was 10 percent.

Mandatory antler restrictions also create an elitist attitude among supporters toward hunters who shoot young bucks with small antlers. I've heard of cases where youngsters who shot spike bucks were criticized for doing so, making them feel guilty and developing in them an adverse reaction to hunting. As I understand it, the purpose of QDM is to create a herd in which all of the deer are quality animals, not just certain bucks based on antler size. No hunter should be belittled or criticized for shooting a deer he or she is happy with!

The potential for reducing the best genetics for antler development in a deer herd is also very real with mandatory antler point restrictions. Yearling bucks with the best genetics for antler development normally have six or eights point and sometimes even more. If hunters are restricted to shooting bucks with three or more points on an antler, the yearling bucks with the best antler development are targeted by hunters and often removed before they have the chance to pass on their genes. This is called high-grading. Reduced quality of antlers in future generations could result, because spikes and forks are able to reproduce.

High-grading has been confirmed on some management areas in Mississippi where the size of antlers of mature bucks actually was reduced as a result of antler point restrictions rather than increasing as expected. There's concern about the same thing happening in Arkansas. From a management perspective, it's far better that yearling bucks with six and 8-point antlers survive to breed than spikes and forks. If bucks with spikes are legal for all hunters to shoot, that's more likely to happen.

In regions like the Upper Peninsula of Michigan where winters can be severe, mandatory antler restrictions don't make sense because winter often claims bucks that hunters pass up. During tough winters, many fawns die of malnutrition and a significant number of those are button bucks. Some winters, almost an entire fawn crop is lost, making it impossible to pass up bucks that aren't there.

Adult bucks, including yearlings, are more likely to succumb to rough winters, too, because they often use up their fat reserves during the rut, and when winter comes early they don't have enough reserves to carry them through to spring. Under these circumstances, mandatory antler restrictions deprive hunters of shooting deer that are eventually lost to the population due to other causes. It's false economy to force hunters to pass up bucks that die during the winter that follows.

A ten-year study conducted in Michigan's Upper Peninsula determined that regulations allowing hunters to shoot spikes or better produced more 5½-year-old bucks than rules limiting hunters to shooting bucks with at least three points on one antler. It makes sense. The three-point rule concentrated all hunting effort on bucks with the biggest antlers.

Mandatory antler restrictions that limit hunters to shooting bucks with three or four points on an antler are supposed to result in the survival of more older-age-class bucks than when spike bucks are legal, but a ten-year study conducted on four deer management units in Michigan's Upper Peninsula from 1996 through 2005 showed the opposite was true. Spikes were legal in those management units from 1996 through 2000 and hunters were limited to shooting bucks with three points on an antler from 2001 through 2005.

Data was collected on the number of bucks of various ages that were shot by hunters during each five-year period for comparison. Results clearly showed that regulations allowing hunters to shoot spikes or better generate more bucks at least 5½ years old for hunters. A total of thirty-three bucks in that age class were registered for three of those management units from 1996 through 2000, compared to twenty-five during five years of a 3-point rule. Ten of the twenty-five older bucks that were shot under 3-point rules were taken in 2002, during the second year under those restrictions, so they survived as long as they did because of regulations allowing hunters to shoot spikes or better.

The reason bucks live longer when spikes are legal is many hunters are happy to take the more abundant yearlings and quit hunting, thereby reducing pressure on older bucks. Antler restrictions focuses all hunting pressure on rack bucks, causing many hunters to hunt longer and harder for deer with larger antlers. With increased hunting effort on older bucks, they don't live as long.

Three-point rules were renewed for one of the four DMUs (122) for another five-year period starting in 2006, while the other three went back to allowing hunters to shoot bucks with spikes or better. No bucks that were at least $5^1/2$ years old from DMU 122 were brought to DNR check stations from 2006 through 2008 after six, seven and eight years under restrictive antler regulations.

In spite of the results of that study, 3-point antler restrictions were adopted throughout the UP starting in 2008. Go figure!

Mandatory antler restrictions can make hunting regulations more complicated than they should be, too. When antler restrictions get so complicated that DNR employees don't even understand them, how can they expect most hunters to? Prior to the beginning of 2010 deer seasons in Michigan, DNR employees made errors in explaining mandatory antler restrictions to the public on two occasions that I'm aware of. The first was in a statewide news release from the Information and Education Department of the state agency.

A correction soon followed, but confusion created by the initial release would remain with some hunters. Here's the wording of the correction: "It came to my attention today that the DNRE press release issued to promote the archery season opener contained incorrect information about antler point restrictions in DMU 117 (Drummond Island). The release incorrectly said bucks with two or more points on one side could be taken with the combo regular tag in DMU 117.

"The release should have stated that bucks taken with the combo regular tag in ALL of the UP must have at least THREE points on one side. There is no separate distinction for DMU 117 when using a combo regular tag."

In fact, bow and gun deer hunters hunting on Drummond Island in 2010 who purchased an individual bow or gun deer license could shoot a buck with at least two points on an antler and those hunting on the mainland could shoot a buck with at least three-inch spikes, but they could only shoot one buck for the year. Combo deer licenses come with two buck tags, but both tags are restricted to bucks with three or four points on an antler. Deer hunters hunting under a combo license almost anywhere else in the state could shoot one buck with at least three-inch spikes.

The second instance I'm aware of during which the public was given false information involved a conservation officer who appeared on an "Ask The DNR" television program on a public broadcasting station. The officer is responsible for enforcing the laws and, therefore, should know them better than anyone else. A viewer asked about antler restrictions for combo licenses during archery and firearms seasons. The officer responded that one tag was valid for a buck with three points on one antler and the other for four points on an antler during gun season, but the tags were valid for any deer during archery season. The same antler restrictions are actually in effect during both seasons.

Besides being unnecessarily complicated, mandatory antler restrictions such as those in place in Michigan cost state natural resources agencies like the DNR money that they badly need, with little to no benefit for deer or deer hunters. Due to the fact both tags on combo licenses are restricted in the UP and individual licenses are not, many hunters choose to buy single licenses for $15. Combo licenses sell for $30.

Reduced combo license sales for one year cost the Michigan DNRE a minimum of $250,000. That comes to at least $1 million over a four-year period.

For these reasons and more, I strongly support voluntary QDM, which includes antler restrictions, but not mandatory ones. There's no question that QDM is an increasingly popular and widespread form of managing whitetails in North America. It has become so popular an organization called the Quality Deer Management Association was formed in 1991 to promote the practice.

Protecting young bucks is only one aspect of QDM, and, in my opinion, is least important, although it tends to be touted as what QDM is all about by some hunters. With the decline in the harvest of antlered bucks that results by protecting young bucks, the taking of does is emphasized by knowledgeable practitioners of QDM, to insure an adequate number of deer are taken by hunters each year to balance the herd with its habitat. To me, this is the most important part of QDM.

The Objectives

In fact, the objective of QDM is to keep deer numbers below the carrying capacity of the habitat, to ensure that both deer and their habitat will be healthy. The only way to do that is to harvest enough does.

Under such a program, the harvest of bucks and does should be equal, or at least close to it, on an annual basis because the sex ratio of fawns is evenly divided

between males and females at birth. It may even be necessary to take more does than bucks during the first years under this form of management if the population includes far more does than bucks. The end result will be a more balanced sex ratio, which is desirable in a healthy deer herd.

From 40 to 50 percent of the available does should be harvested annually under QDM, according to *Quality Deer Management: The Basics and Beyond,* by Charles Alsheimer (published by Krause Publications, 2002).

An objective of QDM is to allow more bucks to reach older age classes than would normally be possible under traditonal management practices. The

From 40 to 50 percent of the available does should be harvested annually under a QDM program to keep deer numbers below the carrying capacity of their habitat. Many hunters are either unwilling or unable to harvest that may antlerless deer.

Even though the goal of QDM is to protect young bucks, some button bucks are bound to be a part of the antlerless harvest because it is not always possible to identify buck fawns under hunting conditions. When buck fawns are taken, it is important to record them as part of the male harvest. Some states lump button bucks and does together in harvest figures as antlerless deer.

older bucks get, the more likely they are to grow large antlers. So an increase in the number of bucks that develop full-fledged racks with eight points or more is a possible additional effect of the program.

While the goal of QDM is to protect buck fawns or button bucks as well as yearling bucks, it is not always possible for hunters to differentiate antlerless bucks from does under hunting conditions. Consequently, the antlerless harvest is bound to include some button bucks. When this happens, these males should be recorded as part of the buck harvest. Some states combine antlerless bucks taken by hunters with does in their harvest figures, resulting in an inaccurate representation of how many deer of each sex were shot.

Record Keeping

Detailed data collection and record keeping are important parts of a successful QDM program. Besides the number of deer of each sex that are harvested, the ages and weights should be determined for as many animals as possible. Antler beam diameters one inch above the burrs of beams should also be recorded. Antler scores (using the Boone and Crockett scoring system) of bucks at various ages would be helpful, too, but this is optional.

Deer biologists with state and provincial agencies can provide information about optimum or desired weights of animals in various age classes in your area as well as

Record keeping is an important part of a successful QDM program. Weights, ages, and antler beam diameters should be collected from as many deer taken by hunters as possible. That data will serve as a gauge of how healthy local deer are. An adult buck is being weighed here.

what average beam diameters for yearling bucks should be. Data collected from Michigan's Drummond Island, which is 125 square miles in size and located in the St. Marys River, will serve as an example. The desired weight for button bucks from the island is 70 pounds, compared to the 62 pounds those deer averaged during the fall of 2000. Yearling bucks only averaged 103 pounds in 2000, down from 108 pounds the year before, versus the desired size of 130 pounds. The desired weight for bucks $2^1/_2$ years old and older is 150 pounds and those on the island averaged 132 pounds during 1999 and 2000. The average beam diameter of antlers among yearling bucks also declined in 2000. Antler bases of yearling bucks only averaged

The number of fawns per doe that are seen should also be recorded. In healthy whitetail populations some adult does will produce triplets like this doe did.

18.1 mm for 2000, compared to 18.9 mm during 1999. However, deer densities were not yet as bad as in 1995, when average beam diameters only measured 16.4 mm on yearling bucks. These statistics are an indication that deer numbers are too high on the island.

Recording observations of live deer in QDM areas is also beneficial. The average number of fawns per doe is valuable along with the number of adult bucks and does. The annual ratio of antlered bucks to adult does can be estimated annually based on this cumulative data. Remember that adult bucks are often more visible during the summer and breeding season than at other times of the year. Some bucks may also be nocturnal; shining counts, where and when this is legal, may help determine this. The use of trail cameras can also be valuable in providing information about deer numbers, especially nocturnal bucks.

If the management strategy is working properly, the average age of harvested bucks should increase, along with deer weights and the number of fawns per doe. If average weights of harvested deer remain the same or decline, whitetails are probably not getting enough nutrition, which normally means there are too many deer present and more does should be taken.

Habitat Improvement

One way to improve nourishment among deer on private land, besides reducing the herd, is to improve the habitat, as discussed in the previous chapter. This is another aspect of QDM available to private land owners. The QDMA (www.qdma.com) advocates, among other strategies, planting food plots to ensure deer have access to quality food at all times of the year; the organization is a great source of information about food plots.

The opportunity to manage habitat on public property is limited, however. Most state and federal agencies who manage public lands prohibit individuals from doing any habitat management on their own, even though the agencies themselves often lack the funds and manpower to do so. This disparity in the ability to improve habitat for deer on public versus private land is another reason why any mandatory antler restrictions, if and where adopted, should only apply to private lands.

Minimum Acreage

Ideally, a minimum of 1,000 contiguous acres is required to realize the benefits of QDM. However, all of the land doesn't have to be under the same ownership. Groups of neighboring property owners who each own smaller parcels have gotten together and agreed to work cooperatively to apply QDM practices. Some land owners may only have 40 acres while others have 200 or more, but they all benefit from such an agreement.

Camp NFB in Menominee County, Michigan, is an example of how QDM works. Camp members own 280 acres. They got together with the members of three adjoining camps and jointly agreed to voluntarily protect bucks with less than six points. Bucks with six points or more would be legal to shoot. Since bucks with at least three-inch spikes were legal under state regulations when the cooperative was started, their rules were more stringent and are designed to allow more yearling bucks to make it through hunting season.

Results of the voluntary program were starting to be realized after three years. During that third year under a 6-point rule, nine members of Camp NFB participated

A minimum of 1,000 acres is required to realize the benefits of QDM, but not all of the land has to be owned by one person or family. Neighboring property owners can agree to implement QDM and if enough become involved, the minimum area will be exceeded.

Buck pole at Camp NFB in Menominee County, Michigan. Members of this camp and their neighbors have agreed to adopt a six-point minimum for legal bucks and they were starting to see benefits after three years.

in gun deer season and they had eight bucks hanging by the end of the fourth day of the season. Most of the whitetails on the buck pole had at least 8 points and were a minimum of $2^1/_2$ years old. Camp members had bagged as many deer in some years prior to the adoption of the voluntary antler restrictions, but a percentage of them were always yearlings with small antlers.

Camp NFB was built in 1975, with many additions since then. The rafters and walls of the living quarters are adorned with the antlers of bucks bagged by members over the years. Many of the racks are small: these antlers from past years clearly illustrate there was a time that the hunters were content with any legal buck. The change to a minimum 6-point rule was the result of a change in attitudes brought about through years of experience and many filled tags. Wayne Kanyuh came up with the idea.

"We realized that larger bucks are going to be shot if we pass up the small ones," he said. "We finally decided we're no longer going to be content with filling up the pole with bodies. We want quality instead of quantity."

One of the camp members commented that if someone had suggested that only 6-points or better be shot when the camp opened in 1975, they would have been asked to leave.

In terms of doe harvest, Camp NFB's policy is, "If you need meat, take a doe." Although no does were taken at the camp during the firearms season of the third year under 6-point restrictions, antlerless animals are harvested during bow and muzzle-loader hunts, according to camp members. However, it is not often possible to harvest enough does during archery and muzzleloader seasons alone to properly manage whitetail populations. In fact, the biggest problem that hunters who attempt to implement a QDM program experience is removing enough does from the population to protect the habitat.

The fact that camp members have to take the time to make sure a buck has at least 6 points before shooting allows some deer to escape that might otherwise have been shot. Sometimes it's possible to tell a deer has antlers, for example, but impossible to see how many points it has. Under those circumstances, the buck usually gets away, if a Camp NFB member has it in his sights.

Menominee County is an ideal location for practicing quality deer management. Winters are normally mild, allowing good survival of whitetails. Annual antlerless quotas are normally liberal, too, which permits hunters to take enough animals to control the herd.

Traditional Deer Management

One of the major differences between QDM and traditional deer management (TDM) is in the harvest of bucks. Deer hunting regulations do not protect young bucks in most states and provinces. Button bucks routinely make up a portion of antlerless harvests and yearling bucks with spike antlers of a certain minimum length are legal to shoot.

Under this type of management, a high percentage of the antlered buck harvest in heavily hunted areas is composed of yearling bucks. This makes sense, of course, since there are normally more yearling bucks in the population than bucks of any other year class. Where most of the available yearling bucks are bagged by hunters each year, few survive to grow their second or third sets of antlers. However, this does not occur in locations that are lightly hunted or where there are large blocks of forest land or private property that enable many whitetails to escape hunters. Older bucks are well represented on such tracts of land.

Another major difference between TDM and QDM is the former is based on mandatory regulations and the latter, for the most part, is supposed to be voluntary. However, that is starting to change. There are a growing number of management units where QDM has become mandatory due to pressure from some hunters.

More On Mandatory Versus Voluntary

The purpose of protecting spikes and forkhorns, most of which are $1^1/2$-year-old bucks, is to allow many of them to live another year and grow larger antlers.

John Urbain is a former deer program leader for the Michigan Department of Natural Resources (DNR). Before he retired, his comments about protection for yearling bucks were, "I'd rather see hunters start a voluntary movement to pass up young bucks instead of making it mandatory. If you get enough support, you don't need a regulation. That way, you avoid penalizing first-time deer hunters or those who have hunted for years without shooting a buck who would be tickled to get a spikehorn.

"Several years ago, for instance, I shot a buck through the lungs and it ran out of sight," Urbain continued. "Then I heard a shot where it went that I figured was

Under traditional deer management, bucks with spike antlers like this one that
Cathy Westcott is about to tag are fair game. In most areas, there is nothing
wrong with hunters shooting spike bucks.

someone shooting at the same deer. Another hunter was standing over the buck when
I got there. He had shot it in the neck and was proud as punch.

"Come to find out, it was his first buck. He had hunted for ten or fifteen years
without getting a buck. I didn't say a word about my shot. I congratulated him and
walked away.

"Another thing I don't like about mandatory regulations that protect some
antlered bucks," the former DNR spokesman concluded, "is, if someone makes a
mistake, you're creating illegal deer that hunters can't tag."

Many western states established mandatory antler restrictions on mule deer,
according to Wisconsin DNR Deer Biologist Keith McCaffery, but they were forced
to abandon that strategy when it didn't work.

"Those states dropped mandatory antler restrictions primarily because the regulations focused (increased) mortality on mature males, virtually wiping them out, and secondarily because it resulted in unacceptable accidental-illegal kill," McCaffery said. "I would add that antler restrictions protect only the smallest antlered males and do not result in an age structure that is any more natural than without those restrictions.

"QDM espouses privatized management of deer herds; saving bucks to become older while shooting 'an adequate' number of does," McCaffery continued. "But, privatized deer management is not simple because one rarely knows deer population size on a small tract, so it is difficult to define 'an adequate doe harvest.' The natural tendency is to be conservative, with the result that most privatized herds are under-harvested, leading to growing herds and crop damage on neighboring farms.

"QDM often claims to correct alleged biological or social problems within the deer herd when no real problems have been documented," McCaffery wrote. "The only real purpose of so-called QDM efforts in Wisconsin and most of the upper Midwest is to produce older bucks and larger antlers."

McCaffery also says that protecting button bucks is not necessary to ensure an adequate number of antlered bucks. Under traditional management regulations, an average of 22 percent of the antlerless deer harvest in Wisconsin has been button bucks, according to McCaffery. That information has been gathered through mandatory deer registration.

"Prehunt antlerless composition in Wisconsin is typically 26 percent buck fawns," he wrote. "Adult bucks will be recruited in normal proportions so long as button buck harvest rates continue at or below their normal proportion in the fall herd."

Jim Hammill was a Michigan DNR District Wildlife Biologist until he retired. When I asked him about mandatory antler restrictions he said, "My son got his first deer four years ago and it was a spikehorn. I wouldn't change that for anything. He was pretty excited about getting that deer.

"Many hunters' first buck is a spikehorn. There's no reason to deprive anyone of the opportunity to shoot a yearling buck with antlers at least three inches long. Experienced deer hunters who have shot a lot of bucks, including spikes, may want to pass spikes up. That's fine, but it's their choice. It's better if it's done voluntarily.

"I think protecting spikehorns by law is the wrong way to get more older-age-class bucks in the population. There's more than one way to get there. Such a law ends up putting pressure on the animals that we should be saving—yearlings with 6 and 8-point racks. Those are the best specimens of the $1^1/_2$-year-old age class."

Scott Winterstein is a Michigan State University professor and deer researcher. One of the research projects he was involved in is an experimental antler size limit on Lake Michigan's South Fox Island. Before regulations were established protecting spikehorns on the island, antlered bucks had to have at least 6 points to be legal there. Winterstein assessed the impact of that regulation.

"My feeling is we really didn't increase the number of older-age-class bucks in the population with the 6-point limit," he said. "That criteria wasn't enough to protect all of the yearling bucks on the island. Six-point yearlings weren't unusual and we saw a couple of yearling bucks that had 8 and 9-point antlers.

"A regulation only protecting spikehorns would encompass even fewer yearlings than the 6-point rule on South Fox. It would produce some results, but I don't think it would get as good or as quick a result as a lot of people think it would. Most hunters don't have realistic expectations. And none of the hunters we've talked to wants to shoot enough does to make it work. If you restrict the buck harvest, you have to compensate for that by harvesting more does."

At first blush, mandatory protection of spikes or bucks with less than six points might seem like a good idea. Most of the hunters who support it think there's bound to be a dramatic increase in older bucks for the future if hunters are required to pass up some yearling bucks, but it doesn't work that way, especially in most of Michigan's Upper Peninsula and other areas like it, where winters can be severe. Bucks that hunters pass up often perish during the following winters, especially button bucks.

It's also important to note that the vast majority of the hunters who support mandatory protection of spikes or fork-horns are veterans, most of whom have tagged their share of spike bucks. Is it fair for them to restrict beginning hunters from shooting bucks they themselves, at one time, found to be acceptable targets? When antler restrictions are voluntary, it's easy to be flexible enough to allow lesser standards for youngsters. When regulations become mandatory, that flexibility is lost.

Although severe winters in upper Michigan routinely reduce deer numbers, every time this happens the number of bucks has bounced back on its own without the benefit of a law protecting yearling bucks. The reason bucks rebound is that enough yearlings survive hunting season to reach older age classes. The abundance of escape cover, private property, and light hunting pressure in some areas guarantee that this will happen. The elusiveness of deer helps a lot, too.

The most important factors that assure the return of bucks to upper Michigan and other northern areas like it are proper habitat management, harvesting enough does to balance the population with the habitat, and mild winters.

Mandatory protection of spikehorns like this one won't have as much impact as most hunters think it will, especially if enough does are not harvested and nothing is done to improve the habitat. Harvesting enough does is more important than protecting spikehorns.

Winter weather currently controls deer abundance and the availability of bucks in the Upper Peninsula, not hunters. Hunters who assume a change in regulations to protect spikes and other yearlings will have an impact on the availability of bucks are operating under false pretenses.

A law could be established to protect all antlered bucks in the Upper Peninsula, which would be far more beneficial if hunters are really serious about increasing the availability of bucks, but their numbers would still be low following a severe winter as long as too many deer are present. No matter how many bucks a "no spike rule" might save, a long winter with deep snow would eliminate the benefits.

A Personal Perspective

At this point, it's important to point out that I do pass up spikes myself and support voluntary protection of spikes and forks under the voluntary "Let 'em Go. Let 'em Grow" philosophy, like most wildlife professionals. I think this program, promoted by the Upper Peninsula Whitetails Association, has been a tremendous success. This voluntary program allows more yearling bucks to reach older age classes than otherwise would while not penalizing the hunters, whether novice or veteran, who are satisfied with a yearling buck.

I think it is extremely unfair to require hunters who have shot few, if any, deer to pass up an antlered buck when it's of little benefit from a deer management standpoint. However, in areas where antlered bucks are heavily exploited, resulting in few yearlings surviving due to hunting pressure, and deer management would benefit from mandatory antler restrictions, I would support the regulations under those circumstances.

Some hunters who want to see a law enacted to protect spikes where it isn't needed suggest exempting youngsters under sixteen, which helps, but it does nothing for a sixteen- or seventeen-year-old or an adult like John Urbain encountered, who may be deer hunting for the first time or who might have hunted for years with-

Mandatory QDM is destined to fail in regions that experience severe winters. Deer that hunters pass up often die during tough winters.

Voluntary programs promoted by organizations like Upper Peninsula Whitetails that encourage hunters to pass up young bucks do work and they are the best option in areas where there is a lot of public land. Under this type of program youngsters, first-time hunters, and veterans who are happy with any buck are not penalized.

out shooting a buck. Exemptions make mandatory rules complicated and open the door for abuse.

Another very important reason mentioned by biologists why protecting all spike-horns is not a good idea is they only represent a portion of yearling bucks, those with the poorest antler development. The healthiest yearling bucks with the best genetics for antler growth will have as many as eight points and some times more, with four to six points common. If any yearlings should be protected so they reach an older age class, those are the ones that should be—not spikes. Spikes that live long enough are capable of growing big antlers, but they are seldom capable of growing big racks as quickly as the yearling that had four or eight points. Spike laws have been tried in various states and one of the results has been a deterioration of antler quality rather than an improvement.

The Upper Peninsula deer population peaked during 1995 and bucks representing many age classes were present. The region had far fewer bucks in the years that followed not because some hunters shoot spikes, but because many of them died during the winters of 1995–96 and 1996–97. An estimated 200,000 deer died the first winter and 110,000 the second. The highest annual deer harvest ever achieved by hunters in the region is approximately 95,000.

Adult bucks are always more vulnerable to severe winters than does because much of their fat reserves are used during the rut. Their chances of survival are reduced when they are stressed from breeding too many does and they have to compete for limited food supplies with those same overabundant does.

The reason deer losses were so high during those winters is there were too many whitetails, because hunters did not harvest enough deer, especially does. Hunters can do far more to ensure future supplies of bucks by preventing the herd from growing too large again than by making it mandatory to protect yearling bucks. This gets back to the age-old dilemma in managing whitetails—shooting enough does. If hunters harvest enough does to balance the population with its habitat, there will be enough adult bucks available. That's quality deer management!

High Fence Management

22

Imagine a deer hunt on which many of the bucks you saw were too big to shoot. "Impossible," you say.

Not really. Although the concept is difficult for most deer hunters to grasp, such hunts have been taking place in many states and some provinces for years on properties enclosed by high fences and open to a limited number of hunters. The fences are high enough to prevent deer from entering or leaving the enclosure. The size of tracts that are surrounded by high fences so they can be managed for trophy deer hunting vary in size, but many of the larger ones encompass close to a square mile or more.

Like so many new concepts in whitetail hunting, high fence management was popularized in Texas and then spread from there. Many large parcels of hunting property are privately owned in Texas. When managing these large ranches for trophy bucks became popular and land owners realized some of the bucks they cultivated for years ended up being shot on neighboring property, the practice of fencing the deer in so they couldn't stray evolved.

High fences were also erected in response to the stocking of exotic species of big game on some ranches. These nonnative species were purchased like livestock and it made sense to prevent them from roaming onto adjoining ranches. Fencing exotics may even have been required by law.

High fence deer hunting spread from Texas to help meet the demand for trophy whitetails among hunters who were willing and able to pay top dollar for the opportunity to shoot one. Fencing a large chunk of land and managing it for mature bucks is expensive, but there were enough deer hunters who knew that and could afford to pay the market value that the practice flourished. Although the area where the deer live is fenced in, the amount of habitat within that fence is large enough on properties that are approximately a square mile or more in size that the whitetails behave as

This buck would be too big to shoot during some hunts on high-fenced properties where hunts are categorized by the size antlers a buck has. Hunts for management bucks, for instance, are often restricted to animals with racks scoring less than 125.

they would in the wild. They are certainly not tame. I can vouch for that, as can any of the hunters who have tried their luck on a high-fence ranch.

I've had experience on a number of deer hunting preserves in Michigan that were under high fence management, primarily as a guide, but also as a hunter. I worked as a guide for a number of years on what used to be called The Wildlife Place. The business included three parcels behind high fences that were each at least a square mile in size. The property has since been sold and is now called The Legends Ranch. I also guided and hunted on Deer Tracks Ranch near Kalkaska, which is 1,500 acres in size.

The deer that were on these properties when they were fenced were a public resource managed by the state Department of Natural Resources (DNR). At the time, the land owner was required to pay the state $250 for each deer that was inside the fence. DNR employees estimated how many whitetails were no longer available to the public, for compensation purposes. Once the deer were paid for, the property owners obtained game breeder's licenses from the DNR, which allow them to manage the deer and hunting on their acreage as they see fit. They set their own hunting seasons and bag limits and establish what ever regulations they want to.

Buying live wild whitetails to be enclosed behind a high fence is no longer possible in Michigan. Since 2000, land owners who want to fence their property are required to prepare a plan that provides for elimination of all wild deer from the premises as part of a permit application to construct a deerproof fence. Ideally, all of the whitetails must be flushed or driven from the property before fencing is complete. Any wild deer that remain inside such a fence after it's complete must be removed.

If the enclosed wild deer can not be captured and moved alive, they must be killed. The owners of newly fenced parcels are then required to pay the state $250 for each wild deer that is killed. Regulations for establishing high fence management opportunities varies by state and province. Some prohibit them. More on that later.

To maintain healthy deer populations behind high fences, quality food is made available to them year-round. Fields are seeded with nutritious plants and supplemental food is provided when necessary. Most bucks are allowed to reach at least $4^1/2$ or $5^1/2$ years of age, which is when many of them start producing big antlers. Emphasis is also placed on removing more does than bucks from the herds to prevent them from overpopulating and to generate a balanced sex ratio where there are close to the same number of bucks and does present.

Michigan and Wisconsin used to have the highest number of deer enclosures in the eastern half of the country. Michigan had as many as 700 and Wisconsin, 544, according to a survey done by Missouri, but those numbers are now lower. However, hunting is not allowed on all of them. Some are backyard operations for viewing and others gather byproducts from the animals to be used in commercial scents. Ohio was next in line with 286 deer enclosures.

Types Of Hunts

The Wildlife Place offered three types of deer hunts—Management, Trophy, and Alpha—based on antler size of bucks. Not all high-fence properties are managed the same in terms of hunting opportunities, but many of the best ones have similar programs, although the categories may be named differently. Management hunts were for mature bucks with usually less than eight points that scored up to 125 Boone and Crockett points. Not all mature bucks are capable of growing tremendous racks. Due to genetic limitations, some fail to grow more than six or seven points no matter how old they get and that's what this hunt was designed for.

Trophy hunts were for mature bucks with typical 8- and 9-point racks that scored between 125 and 150. Gross antler scores are normally used to determine which class a buck fits in on high-fence hunts. Since most deer hunters are not experienced enough to accurately judge what classification a set of antlers falls in, each is accompanied by a guide who determines what category the bucks fit in as they appear.

Although most bucks shot on Trophy Hunts have at least eight points, a hunter I guided one year shot a huge 7-pointer that qualified for that category. The antlers scored 144³/₈ and the deer weighed 266 pounds in the round.

Alpha hunts were for the top-of-the-line bucks with antlers that score more than 150 and usually include those with ten points or more. Only a limited number of Alpha hunts were available each year and there was often a waiting list. The best Alpha buck bagged at the Wildlife Place one year was a 10-pointer that scored 182.

Since the Alpha hunts were usually the last buck hunts for the year, timed to coincide with the peak of the rut when mature bucks are most active, it was not unusual for hunters on Management or Trophy Hunts to see Alpha bucks while afield. They were required to pass those animals up because they were too big. It was not unusual for hunters to see anywhere from one to ten or twenty bucks that were too big for them to shoot, depending upon the type of hunt they were on, during the course of a day afield. Because the proportion of bucks in the herd is so high, most hunters are able to get a buck of the caliber they are looking for under high-fence management.

Guiding

Most hunters who decide to hunt high-fence properties plan a hunt for a buck in one of the categories mentioned above, but some who can afford it make arrangements to take two or more whitetails. I once guided a fellow who shot a buck from each of the three classes during a week of hunting. Milt Vincent from Chattanooga, Tennessee was the first, and perhaps the only, person to take a grand slam (a buck in each category during one year) at The Wildlife Place. He actually got all three bucks the same day, making his hunt exceptionally successful, but we hunted several days before that, taking nothing.

Vincent wanted to concentrate on shooting an Alpha buck first and he passed up a lot of antlered whitetails before finally seeing one that fit the bill. We saw the 11-pointer soon after daylight one day and Milt made a great shot on the deer, dropping it instantly. Since it wasn't yet light enough for photographs, we remained in the enclosed blind we hunted from. Within a half hour, a perfect management buck appeared and Vincent shot it.

The 11-point weighed about 200 pounds and the antlers grossed 155. The Management buck had a bigger body, weighing about 230 pounds, but much smaller antlers that measured 117. The older buck with the larger antlers was actively involved in the rut and had lost weight chasing does.

During the afternoon, Milt and I went to another blind and we weren't there more than a half hour before a wide-antlered 8-point that fit the Trophy classification showed up and the grand slam was complete. The antlers on that buck measured about 130.

I enjoy guiding deer hunters. It's the next best thing to hunting myself. In some cases I was able to help hunters get the buck of their dreams or at least one bigger

Milt Vincent with the largest of three bucks he bagged on a high-fence property during one day of hunting. Each buck was from a different antler category.

than they had ever taken before. In every case, guiding was an opportunity to help others learn more about and appreciate whitetail behavior and how to judge the animals as well a chance to share memorable deer hunting experiences, both past and present. One of the highlights of the guiding I did at The Wildlife Place was spending time afield with baseball great Wade Boggs, who was a third baseman for the New York Yankees at the time; pitcher Jimmy Key was also on that hunt.

Boggs bagged the biggest buck during the hunt, which we were both pleased about. The deer he got was a beautiful 10-pointer that scored 168. The whitetail had a dressed weight of 195 pounds and was $4^1/_2$ or $5^1/_2$ years old. The antlers had an inside spread of $20^2/_8$ inches, both beams were around 25 inches in length, and four of the tines were around 10 inches long.

One of the highlights of the guiding I have done on properties under high fence management was to guide former New York Yankees third baseman Wade Boggs on a hunt during which he took this beautiful whitetail buck.

A Management Hunt

The only high-fence hunting I've done myself was on the 1,500-acre Deer Tracks Ranch. I was lucky enough to get the chance to hunt the property while involved in the filming of a segment for a promotional video about the place. Outdoor writer and videographer Dan Bertalan was doing the filming. Our goal was to film the shooting of a management buck. I also had permission to shoot any bucks I saw that had a debilitating injury. Due to the high number of mature bucks at Deer Tracks and other high fence properties managed for trophy whitetails, fighting is common and a number of bucks are injured each year during those fights.

There were so many quality bucks present, it took a number of days of hunting before I was able to connect on a whitetail that fit the criteria. I saw shootable bucks prior to that, but, in many cases, they weren't visible long enough or in the right place, or the lighting wasn't right to get a kill on tape. I gained new appreciation for how difficult it can be to capture the climax of a hunt on film during the time I spent at Deer Tracks.

The fact that I missed the first shot I took at a Management Deer didn't help either. But I have an excellent excuse for that miss. Unforeseen circumstances prevented me from shooting the buck I was planning on taking. Then I was distracted by a much bigger buck that was following the one I did shoot at. And because Dan wanted to film the bigger buck before I shot, the deer I shot at was farther away, with its body partially obscured from view, by the time he gave me the go-ahead.

A comedy of errors and the appearance of a trio of bucks, one right after the other, contributed to the confusion. Here's what happened. Dan and I were in one of Deer Tracks' fancy elevated log cabin blinds. The ranch owners are in the log cabin business and they incorporated their skill and experience in constructing log cabins into the construction of blinds. The blinds are roomy, comfortable, and better constructed than some deer camps I've stayed at.

The blind was overlooking a field where deer routinely fed, but on this particular day, the wind was blowing from the blind toward the food, so we left the windows closed to reduce the chances of being winded. It was a cold, quiet afternoon. When a management buck appeared and started across the field from right to left, I slowly opened one of the windows and prepared for a shot.

The padded sling on my Remington 700 .30-06 made a noise as I was positioning the rifle and the buck heard the noise, trotting across the field. But the whitetail stopped when across the field at a distance of about 100 yards, so Dan told me to take him. I had to shift positions to get the deer in my scope. When I did that, I blocked the camera's view of the buck and Dan said "Don't shoot!"

It was then that we saw a second buck following in the tracks of the first one; it was also a management deer. As I was preparing to shoot that whitetail at a distance of 40 yards, a third buck appeared and it was a real monster, so Dan asked me to hold my fire so he could film it. The last deer had a huge 11-point rack that would have easily scored in the 160s and the antlers might have grossed in the 170s.

To say that buck was distracting is putting it mildly. By the time Dan finished filming the monster, the second management buck was over 100 yards away and the lower half of its body was obscured because it had started to descend into a creek bottom. When Dan told me to shoot, I did not have my rifle firmly resting on the window sill due to concerns about my sling making more noise and spooking the second and third bucks, so I missed the buck.

We were hunting from the same blind where I missed the buck when I finally connected on a perfect management deer, and the buck I shot was almost in the same position as the one I missed. Only this time, I made sure my rifle was solidly supported and I had fewer distractions. The mature whitetail we were after was sparring with a younger buck.

Dan told me to take him when they stopped fighting and I did. A hind foot injury contributed to the lopsided rack of the management buck I shot. Research has determined that an injured buck will grow malformed antlers on the opposite side of its body from the injury. The buck's left antler was affected by the injury to its right hind foot.

A management buck I shot on Deer Tracks Ranch while filming a promotional video for the ranch.

This type of high-fence deer hunting is obviously different than what many hunters are used to, but it is available for those who would like to give it a try. Most hunters appreciate the opportunity to see quality bucks, even if they can't shoot them. Although hunts for the largest bucks can be expensive, the price of a hunt for a management buck is usually reasonable, often costing less than an out-of-state big-game hunt or a Canadian whitetail trip. And since the removal of a lot of does is required from high fence properties, the cost for a doe hunt is within the reach of most hunters.

Doe Hunts

A doe hunt on a deer ranch can be an excellent way to introduce youngsters to deer hunting. Since the age limits to hunt on deer hunting preserves are either nonexistent or more liberal than state or provincial regulations, boys and girls are often able to hunt at an earlier age on deer ranches than they otherwise would be able to. Bob Easterbrook Jr. from Madison Heights, Michigan, took advantage of that opportunity to allow his son Robbie to shoot his first deer at the age of eight. On property under state regulations, Robbie would have had to wait until he was fourteen to hunt deer with a firearm. (The minimum age for firearms hunting in Michigan has since been lowered to twelve.)

Bob outfitted his son with a rifle that fit him and made sure he could shoot it accurately. Robbie hunted with a single-shot Thompson/Center Contender rifle in .223 caliber. The rifle was loaded with 55-grain bullets.

Bob Easterbrook Jr. and his son Robbie with his first deer, which he shot when he was eight years old. At the time, Robbie would have had to wait until he was fourteen to hunt deer with a firearm on land under state regulations. Robbie shot the doe from the blind in the background.
PHOTO COURTESY OF BOB EASTERBROOK JR

Father and son hunted from an elevated blind that was roomy and comfortable. A group of antlerless deer eventually appeared and when one of the bigger ones turned broadside, giving Robbie the shot he was waiting for, he aimed where his father told him and squeezed the trigger. The boy made a perfect shot, killing the doe instantly.

Many parents such as Easterbrook, who is a hunter safety instructor, feel their children, when supervised, are capable of safely hunting deer with a gun before they are fourteen or whatever the minimum age is in their respective states or provinces.

"Robbie has always had very good hand-eye coordination, and shooting, whether with a gun or bow, seems to come natural for him," Bob said. "His prior shooting experience has been mostly with a BB gun. When I head up to our deer hunting property to get some work done, he tags along and shoots cattail heads and dragonflies. He's pretty good with the BB gun, plus I get a good chance to see how he handles a gun. Being a hunter safety instructor, he has sat in on several of my classes and I like to see what sticks.

"I've also instructed him in the shooting of a .22 rifle a couple of times. Prior to his deer hunt, he practiced with the .223 quite a bit."

Opposition

There are some drawbacks to high-fence deer management, as well as serious opposition among some individuals and organizations. A backlash of sorts is underway against big-game hunting behind high fences. South Carolina legislators passed a law in 2000 that prohibits hunting behind high fences, except at the operations that were in existence at the time the law went into effect and are registered with the state. Other states are considering similar measures.

In Montana, voters approved I-143 during November of 2000, a measure that prohibits all big-game hunting behind high fences in that state. Elk hunting on game farms was the primary target of I-143, but its provisions include deer. The Montana law prohibits the licensing of any new game ranches in the state. Those that are in existence can sell meat and antler velvet, but their permits are nontransferable. They are also prohibited from expanding their operations.

The South Carolina law represents a compromise that most people can live with. South Carolina Deer Biologist Charles Ruth said twenty-seven fenced deer hunting operations, averaging 500 acres in size, registered with the state after the law went into effect there. Hunting remains legal at the twenty-seven facilities that were grandfathered in under the law.

"This is not a property rights issue," Ruth said, "It's a hunting issue. The law didn't prohibit construction of fences on private property. It prohibits hunting behind fences constructed after the law went into effect."

"The legislation basically removed the incentive for fencing private property, unless land owners want to construct fences to exclude deer that will protect fruit trees, gardens, and other crops. At the same time, land owners who had already invested money in developing commercial deer ranches can remain in business and hunters who want to take advantage of the opportunities available at them can continue to do so.

"High fences in the state are a recent phenomenon," Ruth continued. "Most of them have been constructed since 1995. This thing kinda crept up on us. Our wildlife board took a strong position in opposition to high fence hunting during 1997, but getting a law passed is a different matter. Once our legislators found out what was going on, they didn't like it either. That's why the law was passed."

Montana's I-143 faced numerous legal challenges since it was approved by 51.4 percent of state voters in 2000, but none of them were successful, so it remains in effect. As a result, there were only about half as many game farms in the state in 2009 as in 2000, when there were ninety.

A judge wrote in his opinion in one failed attempt to overturn I-143 that, "While the effect resumption of fee killing in itself would have on the risk of disease and hybridization is negligible, the effect that resumption of fee killing (would have) on Montana's hunting heritage and fair chase hunting ethic is substantial."

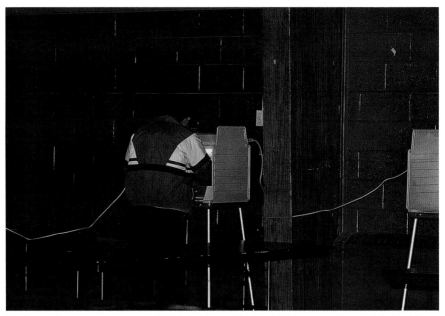

Montana voters passed a measure (I-143) during 2000 that prohibits big-game hunting behind high fences. The practice is illegal in many other states as well.

The judge also ruled, "The state has a legitimate interest in promoting fair chase hunting ethics and Montana's hunting heritage and legacy when mandated by popular vote or otherwise."

Pro-hunting groups were on both sides of the fence, so to speak, during the Montana campaign over hunting on game ranches. The initiative was supported by Montanans Against the Domestication and Commercialization of Wildlife (MADCOW).

The organization's name was chosen to plug into publicity and concern about the spread of disease among captive deer and elk. Some of the key figures who were active in MADCOW include Jim Posewitz from Helena, who is a former state game biologist who was with The Hunter's Institute (ORION) at the time, Stan Rauch, a board member of the Montana Bowhunter's Association and Gary Holmquist, chairman of the Missoula Chapter of the Rocky Mountain Elk Foundation, who also does some guiding. Anti-hunting organizations such as The Fund For Animals joined forces with MADCOW in a sense, by promoting passage of I-143 on the internet.

Passage of I-143 has had a definite impact on the income of members of Montana Alternative Livestock Producers (MALP) and they aren't happy about it. They feel the measure constitutes a taking of private property (by controlling what can be done on private land) without just compensation. In retaliation for passage of I-143, Montana ranchers closed 100,000 acres that they own to hunter access, so many hunters in that state have lost something in the debate over high-fence hunting.

Going to voters to resolve hunting issues is not normally the best way because most members of the public don't understand the subject and the implications involved with proposed changes. Voters are often swayed more by emotion and false information than facts, as referendums on bear hunting and trapping in a number of states have clearly shown. Ballot initiatives are also expensive and tough to change once they are on the books. A far better way to bring about change is by working with state agencies that manage hunting and state legislative bodies where the public has input and can impact the outcome, but don't have the final say.

Kim Kafka, who was the Vice President of MALP in 2000, would have preferred sitting at a table with members of MADCOW and the Department of Fish & Game to try to reach some common ground between the sides. The MALP representative said their organization would have been willing to work on guidelines to define criteria for high fence hunting.

Some states that allow big-game hunting behind high fences require that enclosures be a certain size before hunting is allowed, for example. In Arkansas, fenced hunting preserves must be at least 500 acres and 60 percent of the property must be comprised of forests. A Wisconsin Department of Natural Resources (DNR) spokesman said game farms there have to be at least 80 acres in size to allow hunting.

It's interesting to note that commercialization of wildlife was an issue from MADCOW's standpoint since guiding big game hunts on Montana's abundant public land for free-ranging deer and elk is big business in the state. Some people view that form of guiding as commercialization of wildlife. Apparently, commercialization of unfenced game animals is okay in the group's opinion.

Fair Chase

The issue of fair chase is one reason for the recent backlash against fenced deer hunting. The Boone & Crockett Club clearly defines hunting of whitetails or any other big game behind fences as unfair chase. All hunters who enter big game in this organization's record keeping system must sign a fair chase statement, which says, in part: "Use of any of the following methods in the taking of game shall be deemed UNFAIR CHASE and unsportsmanlike:...IV. Hunting game confined by artifical barriers, including escape-proof fenced enclosures."

The Pope and Young Club, which maintains North American big-game records for bow and arrow kills, does not accept entries from commercial fenced hunting preserves "where fees are charged for the animals harvested" either, but deer taken on fenced military property may be accepted.

Spreading Disease

But there are other issues besides fair chase that are coming to the forefront in regard to high fence hunting. The spread of disease has gotten a lot of attention lately with the identification of chronic wasting disease (CWD) and bovine tuberculosis (TB) in both captive and free-ranging deer and elk. The potential of hoof-and-mouth disease reaching North America from Europe has also surfaced.

Deer densities are often higher in fenced shooting preserves than unfenced habitat, increasing the potential for the spread of disease once it appears. And the transfer of animals among fenced deer farms is not regulated as well as it should be. Requirements that whitetails and other captive cervids (primarily elk) be tested for disease before they are shipped elsewhere exist in some states, but those regulations are sometimes ignored or circumvented through "midnight shipments." Inconsistent testing requirements and enforcement increases the probability of transmitting disease. In fact, poor control of the transfer of live deer across the borders between states, provinces, and countries makes the spread of disease inevitable.

TB is still common in Mexico, for example, and it is obvious that CWD has been spread through shipments of captive deer and elk that were infected. One of the sources of the outbreak of CWD in Wisconsin was the illegal release of captive deer, some of which were diseased, into the wild. The spread of disease among deer has certainly been increased by the popularity of captive populations. For more detailed coverage of deer diseases, refer to chapter 2.

Captive deer can and do escape from enclosures, too. If they are diseased, they can infect wild populations.

"Security of these fenced game ranches is very lax," Jim Posewitz commented. "Animals escape from them all of the time. The fencing chronically breaks, they are subject to natural disasters, and gates are often left open.

"And the state doesn't require double fencing. Captive deer and elk can still spread diseases even if they don't escape. Any single-fence operation is subject to nose-to-nose contact between animals inside and outside the fence."

The spread of TB between captive and free ranging whitetails in Michigan's northeastern Lower Peninsula, where the disease is most common, is a very real possibility through the means Posewitz suggests. However, state DNR and Department of Agriculture representatives have not done anything to address this issue yet because they claim the odds of disease transmission this way is minimal. These agencies have taken this stance in spite of the fact that one captive herd in Presque Isle County, begun when resident deer were fenced and purchased from the state, was found to have a high prevalence of the disease.

The entire herd behind that fence was eliminated. The owner of that 1,500-acre parcel has since restocked the property with whitetails that are disease-free and he voluntarily constructed a second fence around the original one to make sure the herd remains disease-free. There are bound to be other captive deer herds in that part of the state that were started with resident whitetails that have been exposed to TB. As long as single-fencing requirements remain in place, the disease can be spread between captive and free-ranging deer.

It's also important to note that baiting and supplementally feeding wild whitetails in Michigan's TB Zone is illegal, supposedly to reduce the chances of spreading the disease, but those practices are permitted behind high fences in the same part of the state.

"We don't know the level of escape of whitetails from enclosures in Wisconsin," former DNR employee Tom Solin said, "but we do know farm-raised deer escape. When captive whitetails escape, they quickly become integrated into the wild population. There's no way to identify deer that were in captivity once they are outside the fence.

"When nonnative species such as fallow deer escape from farms, we usually hear about it because they are easy to identify. I would say that we have 30 to 40 nonnative animals that escape from behind fences each year."

Nonnative animals that escape from game farms could breed with native species, producing hybrids that may be undesirable. Hybridization probably occurs on ranches where exotic and native species of deer mix on a regular basis. I once photographed a hybrid that resulted from a whitetail and sika deer.

Privatization Of Hunting

Another important high fence issue is the basis that North American wildlife management and hunting was built upon: that wildlife belongs to the public, not the person or persons who own the land that the animals live on. The responsibility to manage wildlife in the public's best interest rests with state and provincial agencies. The increase of property surrounded by game-proof fencing has begun to change that concept and some departments of natural resources adopted regulations in the past to not only make that possible, but to encourage it. More recently that trend has been reversed.

In Wisconsin, for example, land owners who fenced in their property, effectively capturing and claiming whitetails that end up inside, were able to buy them from the state for a measly $25 as late as the early 2000s. I would call that a bargain. Wisconsin was considering changes that would require property owners who enclose public deer to pay "fair market value" for them. But instead of doing that, a decision was made to make it illegal for property owners to enclose or capture publicly owned deer and buy them from the state. Under the current laws, anyone erecting a deer-proof fence in Wisconsin must make sure all deer are removed from the area to be fenced before fencing is complete.

This is because deer that are enclosed behind a fence that is too high for them to escape are, under most circumstances, no longer available to the public. That was one of the reasons that South Carolina took a stand against new high-fence hunting operations.

"Common law was a big factor in passage of our high fence regulations," Charles Ruth said. "Fish and wildlife clearly belong to the people in the state. The fences are restricting free movement of a public resource. It's not just about deer. Those fences impact all wildlife."

A quote from former President Theodore Roosevelt addresses this issue: "We do not intend that our natural resources shall be exploited by the few against the interests of the many. . . Our aim is to preserve our natural resources for the public as a whole, for the average man and the average woman who make up the body of the American people. Public rights come first and private interests second."

In some cases, commercial deer hunting preserves are suspected of stealing whitetails from the public.

"The DNR's primary concern is illegal take of whitetails from the wild by deer farms," Wisconsin's Tom Solin said. "Some operators have reportedly opened their fence temporarily and baited wild deer into the enclosure before closing the fence again."

Impact On Wildlife

Rick Campa, an associate professor at Michigan State University's Department of Fisheries and Wildlife, was involved in preparing a paper that addresses ecological concerns associated with fencing that renders some wildlife captive and excludes other wildlife from habitat behind the fence.

"One of the issues we raised is how do large enclosures impact historical wildlife movements?" Campa said. "Does the fencing alter movement or prevent access to critical habitat and/or food? Housing and commercial developments impact deer movements in a similar way. Even partial enclosures impact movements of deer.

"From an ecological standpoint, there is concern with the larger facilities. Hunting preserves that have the biggest implications are the larger ones. Where they are located is important as well as their size. Are they going to alter ecosystem evolution?"

The answers to the questions raised in the paper Campa contributed to are largely unknown. The main problem in accurately determining what effects the fences have is that there's little to no data available about wildlife movements before fencing occurred. However, it's easy to figure out what the implications are in some cases.

If a critical winter deer yard is enclosed behind a fence during the summer, for instance, that habitat is no longer available to whitetails that travel from miles away to reach it when winter arrives. Being excluded from that protective habitat could result in higher mortality among deer that no longer have access to their traditional winter range. Some of them might succumb to malnutrition, others may be more vulnerable to hunters, and predators might claim still more. An important food supply such as a stand of oak trees could impact the winter survival of whitetails that are prevented access to the acorns because of fencing.

Predators

How to handle natural predators that get inside high fences is another issue that Wisconsin has had to deal with on fenced hunting preserves because gray wolves, which have been a federally listed endangered species, were involved.

"Wolves got in two enclosures," Tom Solin said. "These fences are not predator-proof. Predators like wolves are not dummies. They realize there are more deer inside the fence than outside, so they find a way in to get at their prey. The fencing makes it easier for them to catch the deer, too.

"Wolves got in one of the larger enclosures in the state and they killed a number of deer. We have a provision that provides for losses caused by wildlife. The owners of that farm wanted to be compensated at a higher value ($200) for the deer that were killed by the wolves even though they only paid $25 for the whitetails that were inside when they put the fence up."

The state ended up paying the higher rate for the deer killed by wolves behind the fence. In both cases that wolves got in enclosures, they were live-trapped and removed, but it's sure to happen again. Other predators that can and do enter deer enclosures include coyotes, bobcats, mountain lions, and black bears.

Where It's Illegal

High fence hunting for whitetails is illegal in a number of states, such as Maine and Maryland, and it is expected to remain that way. Maine Department of Wildlife Information Representative Becky Orff said, "To us that's what is called a canned hunt and it is not permitted in Maine."

Mary Jo Scanlon of the Maryland Division of Wildlife said, "Putting up a high fence is reducing wildlife to your possession, which is against the law. I don't think that will ever happen in Maryland because there is a lot of opposition."

According to a survey done by Jeff Barringer with the Missouri Department of Conservation, other states that do not allow deer enclosures are Delaware, Massachusetts, New Jersey, Rhode Island, and Vermont. New Hampshire adopted a law similar to South Carolina's law and grandfathered in two deer hunting preserves.

Virginia's assembly passed a bill that prohibits high fencing of deer in the state, according to deer manager Matt Knox. The bill also requires the high-fence deer enclosures that are in existence to modify the fences to allow deer to come and go. Knox said he only knows of four high-fence facilities in the state where deer were hunted.

Due to the negatives associated with high fence hunting, I expect more restrictions will be established on this type of management in the future. Those restrictions will probably make significant expansion difficult. However, I do think high fence management is here to stay at some level. That's why I felt it was important to include a chapter on the subject.

Doe Decisions:
Which One Should I Shoot?

Some whitetail hunters who don't understand deer management or simply don't like to shoot does are good at coming up with excuses for not pulling the trigger or releasing an arrow when the opportunity to shoot an antlerless animal presents itself.

"There might have been a buck behind her," is one of the more common excuses. "If I had shot her, the sound might have spooked any bucks in the area. After I get 'my' buck, then I will shoot a doe."

Another version of the same line is, "If I don't get a buck by the last day of the season, then I will shoot a doe."

Something else you may have heard: "Shooting a doe is like shooting three deer. Those does are carrying next year's bucks."

And then there's the line, "I can't bring myself to shoot a doe with fawns. The little ones might not survive without their mother. I will wait for a lone doe to fill my tag."

As a result of these excuses and more, many of the hunters who use them don't end up filling their doe tags and they shirk their responsibility as deer managers. That's one of the reasons that deer numbers are too high and sex ratios are lopsided in many areas.

In the previous three chapters I've tried to make it clear that regardless of what type of deer management may exist on the property you hunt, harvesting adequate numbers of antlerless animals is essential. It's normal for hunters to wonder which does are the best to take for management purposes. This very important chapter answers that question.

I was surprised at one of the responses I received after a segment about me shooting this adult doe with an Ultimate Firearms muzzleloader during a December hunt was shown on a national outdoor television show. The person's opinion reflected a poor understanding of deer management.

Even though I was aware of how good some hunters are at making excuses that allow them to forego shooting does, and how strongly some hunters are opposed to shooting any does, I was caught by surprise by an email that I received after I appeared on a television show on the Outdoor Channel and was shown shooting a doe that had a fawn.

"I was appalled to see you shoot the mother doe with a fawn and excuse it away to ease your conscience," the email stated. "Be an ethical hunter!! There are plenty of other does without a fawn at their side."

That was the first time I had ever been faced with the issue of legally shooting a doe being labeled as unethical. Although the person who wrote the email is entitled to his or her opinion, and can decide for him- or herself which deer to shoot, it's a mistake to try to guilt other hunters into doing the same thing based on faulty reasoning. There was and is nothing unethical about shooting a doe with a fawn or fawns.

The doe I shot was taken during a December muzzleloader season on a Michigan farm in Menominee County that consistently carries too many whitetails (more than fifty per square mile) because hunters are not able to harvest enough. A friend of mine leases the hunting rights to the farm and he has an annual goal for the number of does he tries to harvest from the property. Each year, he ends up short of that goal even though he encourages clients, family, and friends to shoot as many does as possible.

When deer numbers are too high, the best way to reduce the herd and perhaps have a chance of balancing the population with the habitat is to remove as many adult does as possible. Since most adult does have fawns, it's impossible to avoid shooting does with fawns, if you are serious about any type of management. A plan that restricts hunters to shooting lone does in most parts of the country is doomed to failure since many doe fawns breed in the best habitat.

In most cases, you don't have to worry about removing too many does because adult does respond to hunting pressure as well as bucks do. When there is heavy pressure on antlerless whitetails or mule deer, adult does may even become better than bucks at avoiding hunters. That was the case on the farm where I shot the doe with a muzzleloader. By December, most adult does weren't feeding until after shooting time ended. An approaching storm front played a role in making the doe I shot move out to feed during legal shooting time.

The person who wrote the email claiming the kill was unethical was off base in assuming I could have shot a lone doe instead. The doe I shot was the only one I saw. And the day I scored was the last day I had to hunt for the season.

A herd that has a high number of does without fawns is a sign of trouble. Most often under these circumstances, the herd has surpassed the carrying capacity of the habitat for long enough that deer have started to destroy the habitat and are malnourished. Malnourished does produce small fawns that are too weak to survive or are more vulnerable to predators.

The claim that shooting a doe is removing three deer from the population (under the assumption that if the doe survives she will produce healthy twins the following year) has no merit. If the habitat is in poor shape, with too many deer already present, malnourished does average less than one healthy fawn each. By removing excess does and allowing the habitat to improve, the remaining does can and will produce at least as many fawns as survived previously and they will often be more productive. If the deer population is at or near the carrying capacity of the habitat, the only way to keep it there is to harvest does.

Hunters who advocate shooting only adult does without fawns may, in fact, be targeting deer that are potentially the most productive in the herd. Research done by John Ozoga and Lou Verme at Michigan's Cusino Wildlife Research Station indicates that adult does that have lost their fawns may, in fact, produce more fawns the following year than does that nursed fawns.

"Does that have lost their fawns are stress-free all summer," Ozoga said. "Come fall, they are in excellent shape and would conceive more fawns versus a doe that

Since most adult does have fawns in a healthy deer population and even some yearling does have fawns in the best habitat, a management plan that restricts hunters to shooting lone does is doomed to failure.

Lone does are potentially the most productive does, after avoiding the stress of rearing fawns for a year, making them good ones to pass up if hunters have a choice. Taking any doe you can, however, is a sound deer management decision.

raised twins or triplets. The doe that raised fawns would be in worse physical condition, if the habitat is not good."

I suspect the reason the person who considered it unethical for me to shoot a doe with a fawn was concerned about the welfare of the fawn. This person, like many others, thinks the young whitetail's survival is tied to that of its mother. That simply isn't true. In fact, button bucks may fare better if they are orphaned.

Fawns are weaned and capable of taking care of themselves before the first hunting season begins. Fawns start eating solids when they are between two and three weeks old, while they are still dependent on their mother's milk. The older fawns get, the more vegetation they eat. At the same time, the amount of milk they consume gradually decreases.

By the time fawns are two months old, they are capable of surviving on their own, but they will continue to nurse as long as their mother lets them. That's why it's not unusual to see a fawn attempting to suckle from a doe in September or even October. Whether or not fawns remain with their mother during fall and winter months, some of the youngsters are preyed upon by predators and others succumb to accidents, including collisons with vehicles.

Even when a doe and her fawns don't become separated, their time together as a family lasts less than a year. A doe separates from the fawns she had the previous year before giving birth again. Buck fawns normally disperse from their mother's home range, some times traveling long distances before settling down. Doe fawns may settle in a portion of their mother's territory.

There's evidence that button bucks that are orphaned have a better chance of survival than those that aren't, according to Ohio wildlife research biologist Michael Tonkovich.

"There are studies that have documented higher survival rates among orphaned button bucks as compared to those who spent their first year with mom," Tonkovich wrote in an email. "As you know, nearly 80 percent of bucks will disperse from their home range. While we don't fully understand the mechanism(s) behind this, there is some evidence that maternal aggression plays a significant role in many cases. If a button is orphaned, chances are good that he will not disperse, and as result, his chances of surviving his first year go up tremendously."

Like me, the concept of a hunter considering it unethical to shoot a doe with fawns was new to Tonkovich.

"In my years as a biologist with the Ohio Division of Wildlife, I can honestly say I've never met such a hunter. If I do, I'll tell them this: In a well-managed herd, most fawns should be weaned (or capable of surviving without mother's milk) before most bow seasons pick up steam and certainly before the firearms season, where most of the harvest still occurs."

Pennsylvania Game Commision Deer Management Section Supervisor Dr. Christopher Rosenberry had similar comments: "Biologically speaking, a six-month-old fawn is capable of surviving without the adult doe, if the doe is taken during the hunting seasons. That is why hunting seasons are scheduled when they are. The digestive tract of a fawn is able to make the switch from milk and vegetation to just vegetation by 60 days. So, biologically speaking, there is nothing that would be

Studies have found that button bucks that are orphaned have a better chance of survival because they don't disperse from their mother's home range, which can be a dangerous undertaking.

a concern if a hunter takes a doe that has fawns. There is nothing biologically unethical about this situation."

"Which doe should I shoot?" is a legitimate question that many whitetail hunters who understand and are willing to fulfil their role as deer managers face. Based on the discussion presented here, it should be clear that shooting does with fawns is not unethical. In fact, shooting does that have button bucks may increase the survival of those bucks. Beyond that, it's still up to each hunter to decide for themselves if they are willing to do so.

I asked a number of wildlife biologists what does they thought should be targeted by hunters. Some said the largest animals, to avoid mistakenly shooting button bucks. Others said $1^1/_2$-year-old yearlings that are not yet producing fawns. But I think the best answer is, "The ones that you can."

The bottom line is that too few does of all types are taken by hunters from most areas. By being too specific about what age or size doe you are willing to shoot, you lower your chances of seeing the right one, especially if your hunting time is limited. Taking the does you have a chance at when you have the opportunity, regardless of their status, best serves your role as a deer manager.

As Ohio's Michael Tonkovich put it, "I tell folks to shoot deer as they present themselves. In the course of the discussion, I will make mention of the facts that you can't shoot all the mature does due to their wariness, and size and age aren't always one in the same, but focus primarily on the fact that the most practical means for someone to study their herd—and its response to harvest and habitat manipulation— is through a harvest sample. By harvesting deer as they present themselves, you're assured a representative sample of the population and a solid basis upon which to formulate future management decisions."

24

Learning From Penned Deer

I will never forget the first time I heard a buck grunt while following a hot doe. I was watching a group of penned deer in a city park during the rut. They were close enough that I could hear the one-note, guttural sounds the buck made as he followed the doe.

Due to my fascination with whitetails, I spent as much time as possible at the deer pen watching the animals when I wasn't in school, working, or hunting. The enclosure was only about a ten-minute drive from where I live, so it was convenient to go there when I had a little free time. I didn't realize it at the time, but what I learned by watching and listening to those penned deer made me a better hunter.

Knowing what a buck tending a doe sounds like, for example, made it possible for me to tag a buck not long after first hearing the sound from that captive deer. I was posted in a spot with a lot of buck sign when I heard the unmistakable sound of a buck grunting. Recognizing the sound, I realized a buck was close and got my rifle up, preparing for a possible shot.

Seconds later, a doe went by. She was soon followed by the antlered whitetail and I dropped him on the spot with a well-placed shot. There's a chance I might have gotten that buck anyway, even if I didn't know what a grunting whitetail sounded like, but then again, I might not have. Being mentally and physically prepared for a shot when the buck stepped into view gave me an important edge. If I had waited until I saw the buck before shouldering my rifle, it might have been too late; I was hunting in thick cover and the deer could have passed my window of opportunity before I could take advantage of it.

Most hunters need every advantage they can get when their hunting time is limited. One of the ways to learn about whitetails is to take advantage of opportunities to watch captive animals. It's possible to watch penned deer for hours at a time and get valuable insights into their behavior. While you are hunting, most whitetails are

The first whitetail buck I heard grunt as it followed a doe was in a city-owned deer pen. I learned to recognize the sound from that exposure and applied it to my hunting.

only seen for seconds. When you observe them for longer periods of time, you still only see bits and pieces of behavior that it can take years to fit together for a clear picture of what the animals are all about.

You can learn more about whitetail behavior from watching penned deer for a day than you can during years of hunting, especially during the rut. Captive whitetails are also perfect subjects for testing deer's reactions to products such as deer calls. Few deer calls were available when I started deer hunting, but I tried some of them on whitetails that were in pens to find out if they worked and which sounds were responded to most often.

It would be years before grunt tubes would find their way on the market, but when they did, penned deer played a role in their development. David Hale and Harold Knight were among the first call manufacturers who came out with a quality grunt tube. They told me that they maintained a herd of penned deer of their own for study purposes. They heard bucks among the herd grunting when following and tending does like I had and played around until they could duplicate the sound with a call.

They heard their captive whitetails making other vocalizations, too, which they managed to reproduce as well. Doe and fawn bleats are among those calls that hunters can now mimic thanks to call manufacturers being able to hear those sounds from penned deer. I have also heard deer vocalizations while hunting and I know other hunters have, too, but, in most cases, those sounds are heard less frequently and with less clarity than under controlled conditions.

Most of today's deer calls, like the one this hunter is using from a tree stand, were developed after manufacturers listened to the vocalizations of captive deer.

What Researchers Say

Researchers were probably among the first to use captive whitetails and mule deer to learn intimate details about them for management purposes. Thanks to research on penned deer, we know more about the animals and their management today than otherwise would be possible. Although a lot of emphasis in research has been on the animals' biology and physiology, all aspects of their life history, nutrition, and behavior have been studied. Hunters can follow the lead of researchers and educate themselves about whitetails by watching captive deer.

John Ozoga, who is Research Editor for *Deer & Deer Hunting Magazine* and studied captive whitetails for more than thirty years as an employee of the Michigan Department of Natural Resources, agrees. He said studying penned deer definitely helped his hunting because he didn't know much about whitetails when he started research.

"Watching penned deer made me more appreciative of the rut in our environment," Ozoga said, "when it started and when it ended. It was obvious that is the time when a hunter's chances of seeing a buck are best because they are so active during that period in their life cycle.

"Our studies have shown that does are also more active during the rut. Once estrus approaches, they become more active, whether it's day or night. When a hot doe is active during the daytime, some bucks are bound to be, too, increasing the chances of hunters seeing them.

"Watching penned deer has also given me an appreciation for deer activity at various times of the day. I've noticed that there's peak activity in midday and realize there's value in staying out there then when I'm hunting.

"Something hunters should always be alert to is any time you see a doe running for no apparent reason, a buck might be responsible. It's an avoidance factor. Bucks frequently check does before the females are ready to breed and the does want nothing to do with a buck until it's time to breed. That's why they run away from them."

Researchers have learned a lot about deer by observing and studying captive animals. Hunters can do the same thing, when and where possible.

Penned deer probably had a lot to do with the development of deer scents that are now commonly used by hunters. They played a direct role in that regard on at least one hunt. While going to college, Doug Leitch worked part-time at the Cusino Wildlife Research Station where Ozoga did his research. While Leitch was there, he noticed that bucks were frequently attracted to spots where does that were coming into estrus had urinated.

One day near the beginning of Michigan's firearm season, Leitch collected the soil where a hot doe had urinated. He then deposited the urine-soaked soil in a scrape by his deer blind. The scent eventually attracted the biggest buck Doug had seen at the time. He estimated its antlers would have scored in the 160s, if not the 170s. Unfortunately, that whitetail got away.

Captive deer are now routinely used to collect urine, which is the main ingredient in bottled scents sold to hunters.

Karl Miller who was with the University of Georgia when I spoke to him, has done a lot of research on scent marking among whitetails, using penned animals.

Captive deer can also be credited for aiding in the development of many of the scents used today, like the one being applied to a scrape by Brent Hunt in this photo. Most scents are also collected from penned deer.

He's comparing his captive deer studies with research done in the wild due to concerns that he may not have been getting as accurate a picture of the activity under controlled conditions as he once thought. Nonetheless, he agrees that watching penned deer can be beneficial to hunters.

"Watching captive deer gives you a neat perspective for the animal that you don't often get in the wild," Miller said. "Most hunters don't see deer for very long when they are in the field. It's tough to learn much about deer behavior and how they react to their environment under those circumstances.

"By observing penned deer you get a feel for the animal itself. How it moves and how they behave. The more you know about their movements and behavior, the more hunters can use it to their advantage.

"You can walk up on a whitetail, if you watch its behavior, for example. If it has its head down feeding, they flick their tail before lifting their head to look around. When sneaking up on a deer, all you have to do is watch for that tail flick as a signal to stop moving before it raises its head.

"If you see a deer that has its ears focused behind it, it has heard something in that direction that it's interested in. Perhaps it heard another deer approaching and is trying to keep track of its progress. By knowing what this behavior means, whitetails can tip hunters off to the presence of other deer or other animals that are in the area."

Miller also commented that by becoming more knowledgeable about whitetails by watching penned animals, hunters can evaluate what they hear from other hunters, read in books and magazines, and see on videos, and separate the "garbage" from the "good stuff."

Harry Jacobson did a lot of research on penned deer when he was with Mississippi State University. He later retired from that position and started doing private consulting in Texas. Like the other researchers, he said that his experience studying penned deer helped him become a better deer hunter.

"By watching captive deer, you learn the stereotypic behavior of the animal," Jacobson said. "When you see an animal in the wild, that experience can help you better determine what it might or might not do. By knowing the alert postures of the animal, you can translate that knowledge into being able to determine if he or she is about to take off.

"If you see a pair of bucks that encounter one another, you can tell which is dominant by watching their postures and actions. The dominant animal will raise the hair on its neck and back (piloerection) and assume an aggressive posture. A subordinate buck will exhibit a submissive posture."

Echoing some of Miller's comments, Jacobson added that a single whitetail can tip hunters off to the presence of another animal that's out of sight by its posture and behavior. He commented that his experience with penned deer has made him a better stalk hunter. Since he primarily hunts with bow and arrow, that experience is vital in allowing him to spot whitetails and stalk to within bow range.

Other Lessons

There are a number of ways I've benefited as a hunter by observing penned deer, when I have the chance, besides learning about their vocalizations. I've become better at spotting whitetails in their natural environment, for instance, as well as at picking out antlers on the heads of bucks and judging the size of those antlers. I've also become more attuned to whitetail activity patterns at various times of the year and how weather effects their movements.

Whitetails blend in with their environment in enclosures containing natural habitat in the same way they do in the wild. They are toughest to see when they are standing motionless or bedded. By looking for hard-to-see whitetails behind fences, I've trained myself to pick out parts of their anatomy such as an ear, nose, antler, tail, leg, or horizontal line along the belly or back that will give away their location. In many cases, a slight movement such as an ear flick, head shake, or swish of a tail has been enough to give away a deer's whereabouts.

Once I spot a deer, I try to get a look at its head to determine if it has antlers. If I identify antlers, I then try to estimate how many points there are and the size of the rack. All of this "practice" has paid off for me many times while hunting.

Under hunting conditions, you may only have a matter of seconds to see a whitetail, determine its sex and whether it's a legal target, decide if you want to take the animal, and make the shot. It doesn't always happen that fast, but it does often enough that the hunter who can assess the situation as quickly as possible has a definite advantage. The use of telescopic sights and binoculars as aids can certainly help hunters determine what they are looking at, but they won't often give you more time than you otherwise would have to take advantage of a situation that develops suddenly.

By developing familiarity with the differences in appearance between bucks and does and how they move from watching penned deer, I can often tell a buck from a doe before I confirm the presence or absence of antlers. Mature bucks exhibit a rocking-chair motion when they trot, for example. The shape, size, and features of the faces, heads, and necks of bucks are often different from those of does, too.

Even though I often feel I know the sex of a deer I'm looking at or hearing before I can tell whether or not it has antlers, I never make a decision about shooting a whitetail until I know positively whether or not it has antlers. Here are several reasons why. The heads and bodies of bucks tend to be bigger than those of does, but I've seen some awful big does that have fooled me as well as other hunters. The hair on the top of the head of mature bucks tends to become a reddish-brown color during the rut from forehead glands, but I've seen does with skull caps of a similar color. And when I hear a deer grunting, I know it's a buck, but I've seen and heard antlerless button bucks doing this in addition to antlered bucks.

Weather impacts penned deer in much the same way that it does those in the wild. Their activity patterns are usually affected by the same factors. Consequently, both groups of whitetails normally feed at close to the same times and are inactive at the same times. An approaching storm front or cold front can change that pattern. By becoming familiar with the activity patterns of penned deer in your area and learning how weather might affect them, you can often determine the best times to hunt and when your time might be better spent doing something else.

Watching penned deer can make you a better hunter during the times that you do hunt. I know it has helped me, John Ozoga, Karl Miller, Harry Jacobson, Harold Knight, and David Hale, among many others.

25

Bonus Seasons

I take advantage of bonus deer seasons whenever I get the chance. These hunts not only provide the opportunity to spend more time deer hunting, they offer another chance to get venison for the freezer. Bonus seasons are often offered in areas that are normally difficult to impossible to access during the course of regular deer seasons, such as military installations, remote wilderness areas, and islands. Urban archery hunts that are designed to reduce deer numbers, along with corresponding collisions between cars and deer, during which emphasis is put on harvesting antlerless animals, are another example. Bonus antlerless-only hunts are sometimes held on a regional or statewide basis to reduce deer numbers, too.

Some of the most memorable bonus hunts I've been on were for mule deer in the Colorado Rockies when early-season firearms hunts were held for trophy bucks in select wilderness areas. I took some of my best mulie bucks during those hunts, including one year when my brother Bruce was hunting with me. Bucks were often still in bachelor groups during late August and early September when these hunts were held, and I managed to get a buck from a bachelor group that year.

All I could see was a group of bobbing antlers heading toward my brother and me. Seven mule deer bucks were taking their time, feeding as they came. A pair of the mulies had antlers that were obviously bigger than the rest. The one in the lead looked like he had the best rack, so I riveted my attention on him.

When the lead animal was 150 yards out and still coming, I put the crosshairs on his shoulder, uncertain about waiting any longer to take him. Bruce's reassuring words were what I needed: "Let him come. Take your time."

When the buck was between 100 and 125 yards away he turned to our right and was broadside. I figured that was the closest he would get. The buck jumped straight in the air when my 150-grain .30-06 bullet connected; then he took off running. A second hit put him down for keeps. The mule deer's rack had five points on a side.

Early-season hunts like those on which I took the biggest of seven mulie bucks sometimes provide the opportunity to bag bucks in velvet. David Miles is shown with a velvet-antlered whitetail buck he bagged in South Carolina on August 15 one year. Portions of that state open for deer hunting on that date. Deer are also more abundant and less wary during early hunts than they will be during later seasons.

Another time when I was hunting whitetails with an iron-sighted muzzleloader, a pair of young bucks worked toward me across an opening that had recently been logged. One had spikes, and the second had forked antlers. When the forkhorn was still about 80 yards away it looked like he winded me, so I decided to try a shot.

I aimed for his shoulder and touched the trigger on my .50-caliber Thompson/Center Hawken. The breeze whisked the smoke from the shot away quickly enough for me to see the buck bounding away with its tail wagging—a sure sign of a miss.

Something happened next that I probably will never experience again. Three magnificent bucks, each with a rack carrying at least eight points, appeared one after the other from a lane to my left and trotted by me only 35 yards away as I stood there with an empty rifle! They continued by me into a swamp. I simply stood there and watched them disappear, almost not believing what I saw.

There wasn't enough time to reload the muzzleloader. Even if there had been, I couldn't have shot anyway. I felt sure my round ball had missed the buck I shot at because of the way he acted, but I couldn't be positive until I checked. When I did follow up on the forkhorn, I confirmed that my shot did indeed miss its mark. If I had only waited, I might have seen one of the bigger bucks at a closer distance. Oh well, that's part of deer hunting!

Both of these exceptional deer hunting experiences took place during bonus seasons. They were special hunts designed to increase the harvest of an underutilized segment of the deer population or to increase recreational opportunities for deer hunters.

I collected the mule deer during late August when the buck's antlers were still in velvet. At the time, the early season centerfire rifle hunt was only held in certain high-country wilderness areas that were often inaccessible to hunters because of snow during the state's regular deer season. As a result, bucks that resided in those mountainous retreats were underharvested. An early firearms season provided better utilization of these deer and an excellent opportunity for hunters to collect trophy bucks. Now, most of Colorado's early hunts are limited to bows and arrows and muzzleloaders.

The unusual concentration of whitetail bucks crossed my path on a December hunt in Michigan after the close of the regular firearms season. The late season was established to give muzzleloading deer hunters a bonus opportunity to collect a buck or doe, if they were unsuccessful in filling their regular-season tags. The annual bag limit was one deer when the late season bonus hunt was started, but multiple deer can now be taken per year in the state. All unfilled firearms licenses remain valid during the muzzleloader hunt. The added time afield is a boon to hunters and does not adversely affect the deer herd. In fact, late seasons help in managing the state's deer herd because more does than bucks are now harvested during black powder season.

The best time to hunt deer is whenever you can, but bonus hunts such as those I've described often provide a better opportunity to see whitetails or mule deer and bag one than regular seasons do. Sometimes pre- or post-season hunts simply offer deer hunters additional time to fill one license, but it all depends on the circumstances. Other times deer taken during bonus seasons won't affect hunters' regular-season bag limits.

Island Hunts

This is usually true in cases where an area has an overpopulation problem or when an extra incentive is required to get hunters to participate. An example of such a situation is Michigan's South Fox Island, which is in Lake Michigan off of Charlevoix. Because it is remote (20-odd miles out in the lake), it was difficult to attract enough hunters there every year to harvest enough deer to prevent overbrowsing of the habitat when statewide seasons and bag limits applied. So special regulations were established for the island, providing for separate bag limits and seasons. Deer tagged there with bow or rifle don't count on a hunter's regular license and firearms hunts are held there that begin earlier than those on the mainland.

Similar opportunities are available on other Great Lakes islands and there are probably bonus deer hunts on islands in the oceans as well.

Jim Haveman hangs a doe he bagged with bow and arrow on Lake Michigan's South Fox Island. The deer did not count against his bag limit on the mainland. Bonus hunts are common on islands.

Become A Multiple-Season Hunter

A change in weapons may be all that is necessary to take advantage of bonus deer hunting seasons in many cases. As I've already mentioned, switching from a center-fire rifle to a muzzleloader will give hunters added time afield throughout North America, not just in Michigan. Many states now offer muzzleloader deer hunts either before or after regular firearms seasons. Hunting with bow and arrow in addition to firearms often opens the door to additional deer hunting opportunities. Most

Taking up bowhunting can really expand the amount of time available to you for hunting deer. Instead of hunting during one season, you can spend time afield during two or more season.

states have separate seasons for archers and firearms hunters. Archery hunts usually precede firearms seasons, but, in many cases, additional bow hunts are held afterward, providing two opportunities to hunt with archery equipment. Some states restrict deer hunters to taking one deer per year, but it may still be possible to participate in more than one season before scoring, so be sure to check local regulations. The pleasant weather common during bow seasons adds additional appeal to bowhunting for deer.

My only regret about bowhunting for deer is that I didn't start sooner. The first years I hunted deer were with firearms exclusively. Then I started bowhunting. I wasn't as successful in bagging deer with a bow as I had been with a rifle, at least at the outset. More important though, I saw more deer than I had ever seen before, had plenty of opportunities to score, and learned a lot more about deer. In the long run, I

Wes Cook with his trophy Saskatchewan bow buck bagged during gun season.

became a better firearms hunter because of what I learned while bowhunting and a better bowhunter because of my experience hunting whitetails and mule deer with rifles and shotguns.

Another advantage of deer hunting with bow and arrow is that's the only way whiteails and mule deer can be hunted in some areas, such as cities and suburbs. Deer hunting with firearms has been banned in a growing number of urban and suburban locations where the discharge of firearms is considered unsafe. Many of these areas have deer populations that have to be managed somehow and bowhunting is usually the answer. Many bowhunting-only destinations contain plenty of big bucks as well as lots of other deer.

Bowhunting During Gun Seasons

Hunters who prefer to use archery equipment during firearms hunts can do so in most states and provinces as long as they are properly licensed and they wear the amount of orange required by law during that particular season—but be sure to check local regulations to be sure that is the case. I bowhunted for whitetails in Manitoba one time when a muzzleloader season for residents only was also open and had to wear orange. During a recent gun hunt in Saskatchewan, Wes Cook from Montgomery, Alabama, decided to bowhunt and he was required to wear the same colors of clothing as those of us who carried rifles.

Cook ended up arrowing a big buck I passed up three days in a row that had 5 x 3 antlers with no brow tines. When I learned Wes was interested in the buck I was passing up, I changed stands so he could try for him, and he got the whitetail on his second day of hunting. The buck had a dressed weight of 206 pounds and the antlers had a gross score of 140.

Early Hunts

Early-fall bonus seasons are often rewarding because deer densities are at the highest levels possible. In addition, whitetails or mulies that haven't been hunted since the previous fall won't be as wary as they often are during regular seasons. It is not unusual to see bachelor groups of both whitetail and mule deer bucks traveling together during early seasons.

The only drawback to some early deer hunts is they are sometimes held in remote areas with rough terrain, which makes the territory hard to reach and the hunt a physical challenge. However, on the Colorado wilderness hunt mentioned at the beginning of this chapter, we rode horses to and from the hunting area, which made access easier than it would have been on foot. I was hunting between 10,000 and 12,000 feet above sea level in the Rocky Mountains when I downed that 10-point mule deer. The going was tough, but the beauty of the surroundings at that time of year made the hunt worthwhile. The weather was pleasant for the most part on the mountain hunt, although temperatures commonly fell below freezing at night. Rain was an almost everyday occurrence, too, and snow fell occasionally.

Late Hunts

The weather during late-season deer hunts can be downright miserable, but this factor increases the vulnerability of whitetails and mule deer to hunters. Hunters who dress properly and prepare their guns and bows for these conditions can overcome the weather. Thermometer readings were below zero on the day during muzzleloader season when I saw five bucks in a matter of seconds, as I described earlier in this chapter. Temperatures were the same throughout the hunt. All of those deer were feeding on the tops of trees that had been felled by loggers.

Cold weather had the deer moving and feeding. Bucks were feeding especially heavily during this period. The rut was over, and they were trying to regain some of the weight lost during their preoccupation with breeding activities.

Bucks may still be in bachelor groups during early seasons. These six mule deer bucks were together in September.

Deer in larger numbers are sometimes more accessible to hunters during post-season hunts, too. Mule deer characteristically move to lower elevations with the approach of winter. Some whitetails also move to wintering areas, or "yards." This movement concentrates large numbers of deer in smaller areas than they occupied earlier in the fall and can make the animals easier to find.

Late hunts are a great time to collect big bucks. Deepening snow usually forces them out of inaccessible haunts and into areas where hunters have more chance to see them. Even though deer may be concentrated and feeding more during late seasons, they can be difficult to bag. The animals are often extremely wary because of earlier hunts.

Antlerless Hunts

To aid in better managing deer herds throughout North America, antlerless-only bonus hunts are becoming increasingly popular. These are held both before and after regular seasons to help reduce populations in areas where there are too many deer. In some cases, multiple tags are available. These hunts provide an excellent opportunity to collect meat for the freezer.

Bonus deer seasons that are held on a statewide basis are usually open to an unlimited number of hunters. The number of participants is normally regulated by a permit system when special deer hunts are held in limited areas. Permits are often allocated during a random drawing from the selection of applicants or on a first-come-first-served basis. Special deer hunts held on military bases and state game areas are examples of limited-participation bonus seasons controlled by permits.

Youth Hunts

Youth deer hunts are one of the newest types of bonus deer hunts being held across North America. Michigan established a weekend youth deer hunt during 2000 that quickly caught on and has become a tradition. The hunt is held on a weekend during late September before regular seasons begin and is limited to youngsters between the ages of ten and sixteen; they must be accompanied by a nonhunting adult mentor that is at least eighteen years old. Youngsters that are ten and eleven years old are restricted to hunting with archery equipment and those that are at least twelve can try their luck with firearms. The first day of the hunt in 2000, appropriately enough, coincided with National Hunting and Fishing Day.

The purpose of this bonus season is to foster the introduction of youngsters to deer hunting. It not only provides some kids their first chance to hunt deer, it generates an added opportunity to hunt for boys and girls who have already begun hunting. Because adults can't hunt, they can focus all of their attention on making the experience as positive as possible for youngsters. Deer herds are at their highest during the hunt, and the animals are often more visible, spending more time in the open than they will later in the fall, which inceases the odds that young hunters will at least see deer. The weather is normally warmer, too, increasing the comfort level for participants.

Sixteen-year-old Nicholas Hulce from Norway, Michigan took part in the state's first youth deer season and he enjoyed an outstanding day of deer hunting in Menominee County with his father Dean on the first day of the hunt. During morning and evening hunts, the Hulces saw a total of ninety-seven deer, thirty-seven of which were bucks. Nicholas ended up shooting the biggest buck they saw for the day, a $3^1/_2$-year-old 9-pointer.

He shot the deer at a distance of 300 yards with a .30-06, although it took him two shots to connect. His rifle was sighted in for 200 yards with 150 grain bullets, but he aimed higher than he had to on his first shot, shooting over the top of the buck's back. When he lowered his sights on the second shot, he connected.

I've had the opportunity to participate in youth deer hunts as a mentor a number of times, taking a niece and a cousin hunting. Those hunts are mentioned elsewhere in this book. It was a pleasure sharing time afield and joys of the hunt with the youngsters in each case. Any state or province that doesn't currently have a youth deer hunt should consider establishing one. Boys and girls are the future of deer hunting and their participation should be encouraged and rewarded.

Many states and provinces now have special youth deer hunts. The number of states and provinces that provide youth hunting opportunities increases every year. Local sportsmen's clubs often have programs in place to take youngsters hunting who might not otherwise have the opportunity to go. State and provincial departments of natural resources and fish and game usually know which groups have such mentoring programs.

Handicap Hunts

Special bonus deer hunts are also available to handicapped and terminally ill hunters through Safari Club International (SCI), the Buckmasters American Deer Foundation (BADF) and the Outdoor Dream Foundation (www.outdoordream.org), among others. The Make-A-Wish Foundation grants the dying wishes of terminally ill youngsters, including, in the past, those who wanted to go on hunts. Due to pressure from anti-hunting organizations that protested the granting of wishes involving hunting, the foundation stopped doing hunts. Safari Club stepped up to the plate when the Make-A-Wish Foundation became selective about the wishes they granted, to make sure youngsters whose dying wish involved hunting could be accomodated. The organization began their Safari Wish Program.

I volunteered my services as a guide during a Safari Wish Hunt held at Deer Tracks Ranch of Fife Lake, Michigan, during October one year. Deer Tracks is a 1,500-acre fenced hunting preserve that is owned and operated by Dave Tuxbury. Four young men who have faced life-threatening or debilitating illness participated in the hunt. I guided sixteen-year-old Matt Taylor from Davison.

Another Davison resident and SCI member, Tim Pifher, sponsored Matt for the hunt and loaned him his scoped Winchester .30-06 to use. He also spent time with the boy on the range to make sure he knew how to handle the rifle safely and shoot it properly. Matt had never hunted before, but he was excited about the opportunity to give it a try.

And it didn't take long for Taylor to join the ranks of successful deer hunters. He was the first member of the group to score on the first afternoon of hunting. He made a perfect shot on a big-bodied 7-pointer that weighed 205 pounds in the round. The other three participants ended up getting beautiful bucks, too.

BADF began their "Life Hunts" to also grant the hunting wishes of terminally ill youngsters. Five youngsters who were either seriously ill or severely handicapped, along with members of their families, took part in Life Hunts at the 2002 Buckmasters Classic at Sedgefields Plantation in Alabama. A number of celebrities, including comedian Jeff Foxworthy and NASCAR driver Ward Burton, were on hand to lend their support to the program. A total of forty-one children took part in BADF's Life Hunts during the 2001–2002 season. The BADF hosted thirty-five Life Hunts during the 2009–2010 season. By the end of that season, the organization had hosted 424 Life Hunts since 1994.

Since 1993, BADF has been at the forefront of a program promoting deer hunting among handicapped hunters as well as making it possible for many of these individuals to participate in hunts. By the end of the 2009–10 season, the organization had assisted 3,088 disabled hunters across the country by providing special equipment and hunts designed to meet their specific needs. BADF was involved with assisting ninety disabled hunters during the 2009–10 season. I've covered a number of these hunts hosted by Smoky Lake Wilderness near Phelps, Wisconsin, and an upper Michigan chapter of BADF and the participants are always thrilled to be able to take part in an activity some of them thought would never be possible for them.

I guided sixteen-year-old Matt Taylor from Davison, Michigan, on a Safari Wish Hunt sponsored by a Michigan chapter of Safari Club International and Deer Tracks Ranch. This was Matt's first hunt ever and he took a dandy 7-pointer. Matt is shown with Tim Pifher, the SCI member who sponsored him.

If you know of a possible candidate for the Safari Wish or Life Hunts programs, contact someone from a chapter of SCI or BADF nearest you. Information about various state chapters of SCI can be found at www.safariclub.org. David Sullivan is presently the Disabled Services Director for BADF and his telephone number is 205-366-8415.

Many states and provinces have special provisions to better enable handicapped or disabled deer hunters to participate in the activity and some may have special seasons for handicapped hunters. Permits can usually be obtained to use crossbows during archery seasons or to shoot from vehicles with firearms or crossbows. Check with regulating agencies in your state or province to get specifics.

An advantage of bonus deer seasons, whether early or late, is light hunting pressure, even in situations where participation is not limited. While the odds of seeing other hunters are low during special hunts, the chances of getting a look at deer may be better than any other time of the year. At the very least, these seasons provide extra hunting time. What more could a deer hunter ask for?

Passing It On

Helping a youngster fill a tag during a youth deer hunt is a good feeling. The occasion takes on even more significance when there's the opportunity to help break in a special firearm at the same time.

The fall of 2006 was the first year fourteen-year-old Derek Smith from Marquette, Michigan, could legally hunt whitetails. Since then, the minimum age for deer hunting with firearms among youngsters has been reduced to twelve in the state. To commemorate Derek's "coming of age," his father, Craig, had given him as a birthday gift a special-production Remington .30-06 to commemorate the hundredth anniversary of the caliber. The 2006 youth deer hunt would be Derek's first opportunity to use the new rifle.

Craig had planned on taking his son hunting during the youth hunt, but he couldn't get the days off of work, so he asked me if I would take him, which I gladly agreed to do. Craig's father, George, (an uncle of mine) played an important role in introducing me to deer hunting. Likewise, I helped pass the tradition on to Craig (though George did a great job of that himself).

Although this would be Derek's first firearms hunt in which he was licensed to shoot a whitetail, he had spent lots of time in a deer blind with his father during gun season. He had also done some bow deer hunting, but 2006 marked a new phase in his development as a hunter. Even though Derek had a combo license that would make it legal for him to shoot any antlered buck with spikes at least three inches long, his father encouraged him to hold out for a buck with at least 4 points on one side. One of the tags was restricted to a buck with that type of antlers.

The reason Craig wanted his son to be selective was he felt there was an excellent chance of him getting a crack at a buck that was at least $2^1/_2$ years old. He also knew that Derek would have plenty of time to hunt during the regular firearms season. If he didn't get a buck big enough for his restricted tag during the youth hunt, he could settle for a smaller one during November, if he wanted to.

The plan was to hunt deer-rich Menominee County to increase Derek's chances of seeing whitetails during the short two-day season. Craig owns 80 acres in the county that's mostly swampland. Plenty of bucks have been bagged by family and friends on that property over the years.

A nearby farmer has also allowed Craig and his son to hunt his agricultural land for a small fee. Derek would hunt from a blind on the family property during the morning and on the farmland during the evening. We brought a portable ground blind with us to hunt farm fields from.

Dan Kirschner, a friend from Powers, Michigan, allowed us to stay at his hunting camp during the youth hunt. We arrived there on the evening of September 22 to be ready for the first day of hunting the next morning. Craig had already helped Derek sight in his new rifle.

Day 1

Opening morning was warm and humid, with fog. Derek saw a buck soon after getting in position in a blind in the swamp, and he could have shot it, but he passed it up because he didn't think it was big enough. He thought it only had six points.

During the afternoon, we moved to a large alfalfa field that the farmer had given us permission to hunt. Craig and Derek had seen some big bucks in that area in the past. We were in the process of setting up the ground blind under a huge oak tree on the edge of the field when we spotted some animals 500 to 600 yards away at the far end of the huge field.

Derek got his binoculars first to see what they were and he thought it was a pack of four coyotes. Then I got my binoculars for a better look and could tell right away that they were wolves, not coyotes. One of the four was injured and had a bad case of mange. It was limping badly, favoring its right hind leg. The fact that it had no hair on its tail made it obvious that it had mange. The three healthy animals would move ahead and then wait for the injured one to catch up.

When the wolves disappeared in the woods at the end of the field, I remembered that I had a predator call with me. I immediately dug it out and used it to try to bring the predators closer to us, so I could photograph them. However, we didn't see them again.

We climbed in the ground blind about four o'clock for the evening vigil. I brought a Bushnell range finder with me, so if we saw a buck Derek wanted to shoot, we would be able to determine how far away it was. We ranged the distance to various landmarks ahead of time, so we would know approximately how far away deer were when they appeared.

All we saw were does and fawns that evening, and not that many of them. It was windy and it started raining about seven o'clock, then picked up in intensity before dark. It was pouring by the time we got back to camp. The weather probably reduced deer activity.

Day Two

It was still raining the next morning, so we waited until it stopped before resuming the hunt. Deer were active after the rain stopped, and we saw a number of them on the drive to Craig's property, including a pair of rack bucks. One of those bucks was on the edge of a cut cornfield owned by the farmer who had given us permission to hunt.

We only saw does and fawns in the swamp during the morning of the twenty-fourth. The temperature had dropped and it was still windy. The wind was a problem in the alfalfa field that we sat on the evening before, so we checked with the farmer about moving to the cut cornfield where we saw the buck in the morning and got his okay.

The cut cornfield was surrounded by woods, protecting it from the wind, and most of the field wasn't visible from the road, making it an ideal place for bucks to feed. I had a good feeling about that spot when we climbed into the repositioned ground blind at four-thirty. Like we had the evening before, we used the range finder to determine the distance to various landmarks. Derek said it was 217 yards to the far left corner of the field.

The first animals to enter the field to feed were a trio of raccoons that came in from the far left corner. The coons weren't in the field long when they started running for the woods. We knew something scared them and thought it might be an approaching deer.

Sure enough—when the coons went out of sight, we saw an adult deer bound into the woods, with its tail up. The deer and coons scared each other.

I figured the deer would soon determine what had scared it and return to the field. About fifteen minutes later, a spikehorn appeared on the left edge of the cut corn and walked out into it. The spike worked its way down the field toward us at a fairly steady pace. A small button buck then entered the field from our right and the spike approached it to check it out.

Both deer spent a lot of time feeding within 30 yards of the blind. In fact, they were so close that we were concerned about spooking them. I was pleased that they didn't seem concerned about the presence of the blind. The camouflaged material obviously blended in with its surroundings.

I had brought a video camera with me to record Derek's hunt and managed to get some good video of the spike. Those deer gradually moved further away.

Two more antlered bucks entered the field from the far left corner, a few minutes apart, around six-thirty. Derek thought the first one was a 6-point, but I could only see big forks. That one stayed toward the far end of the field. The next buck to appear was a 3- or 4-point.

The field proved to be the great spot to see bucks that I thought it would be; the biggest one yet made an appearance a few minutes after the others, also from the far left corner. Derek said that was the one he was going to shoot as he saw its head moving through the tall grass toward the field. Its right beam had four obvious points on it and the left antler looked like a long spike. Since Derek wanted to use his restricted tag, this one fit the bill.

Derek Smith with the 7-point he bagged during a youth deer hunt with a commemorative Remington .30-06 he got as a gift from his father.

I told Derek to let the deer work its way into the field and closer to us before taking a shot. I also wanted to get it on video for a while before he attempted to shoot it.

The boy slowly and quietly put the rifle barrel out of the blind and rested it on the aluminum bar that went along the bottom of the front window. The buck he wanted was between the spikehorn and forkhorn when he turned broadside, giving Derek a good shot. We had discussed aiming high on the shoulder and that's what he did.

The bigger buck was just about to touch antlers with the spikehorn when Derek shot, dropping the whitetail on the spot. Derek automatically worked the bolt of his commemorative Remington Model 700 and I told him to keep the buck covered in case it got up, but it never did. Based on how far we knew it was to the back of the field, we guessed the buck was about 175 yards away when Derek shot, but it proved to be closer than we thought when I checked it with the range finder. The buck had only been 128 yards away.

The whitetail proved to be a 7-pointer. The left antler that looked like a long spike had two more points near the base, one of which was a brow tine. I managed to get the kill on tape as well as other aspects of the hunt. It was 6:45 P.M. when Derek bagged his first buck with his new rifle.

Hopefully, there will be many more bucks in Derek's future as a hunter with that rifle. As a matter of fact, he managed to shoot a second buck with the rifle on his father's property on the opening day of gun season. It was an 8-pointer. And he's taken more bucks since then.

Mentoring

Passing on the tradition of deer hunting is more important than ever before, as many peoples' lives become more urbanized, reducing contact with and understanding of the outdoors. If those of us who already understand, benefit from, and participate in the activity aren't willing to share the joys of hunting with others such as friends and family, many of those individuals are less likely to be exposed to hunting. Any person's life will become richer from the experience as they take part in and learn to understand the predator/prey relationship that has been going on in the natural world for eons. They will learn how to secure food for the table, and if they continue to hunt, they will benefit from the physical exercise associated with hunting and the stress-reducing benefits of being outdoors, which can help keep them healthy.

I was fortunate enough to have been born into a hunting family. My father was a hunter and so was his brother George. My mother's brother, Leonard Yelle, was also a hunter. My father and uncles passed the hunting tradition on to me and my brother Bruce. We spent more time deer hunting with Uncle George than with anyone else, so he played the most important role in our evolution as deer hunters, which is something I remain grateful for.

Most hunters get their start the same way I was introduced to hunting: through family members. Mothers, fathers, aunts, uncles, husbands, wives, and cousins most often pass the tradition on to future generations of their families. That's a great way to keep the tradition alive.

Those who are not lucky enough to be born in a hunting family but would like to try it should make friends with someone who hunts and then ask to join them in the field. Joining a local sportsman's organization is a good way to meet hunters and potential hunting partners. Boys can learn about shooting, both with firearms and bow and arrow, by joining the Boy Scouts of America. I was a Boy Scout and the experiences I had as a scout helped foster my interest in the outdoors. Rock star and celebrity hunter Ted Nugent started a Kamp For Kids in 1989 (www.tednugent.com/about/involvement/kamp/) to help introduce both boys and girls to the joys of the outdoors and hunting. In 2010, the program is going stronger than ever.

Special programs designed to introduce women to the outdoors and hunting are sponsored by natural resource and fish and game agencies of most states. It's called "Becoming An Outdoors Woman" in many states, but may be called something else in others. Check out the website for your state to find out more.

Melissa

One of the most satisfying experiences I've had with mentoring a youngster into deer hunting involved one of my nieces, Melissa. If I hadn't introduced her to hunting, I don't think she would have had the chance to experience what the outdoors has to offer in that regard. I will never forget the day she got her first buck. It was during another two-day youth hunt like the one in which Derek got the 7-pointer from a ground blind with his commemorative rifle.

Not many whitetails in the midwest are taken by stalking, but that's how Melissa got her first buck. My niece and I were in a blind on one end of a large hay field, hoping a buck would come within 100 yards for a shot. A spikehorn with short spikes did appear within that distance, but Melissa wanted something bigger.

A while later, a larger buck that she was interested in walked out at the far end of the field a good 350 yards away. I knew it was too far for her to risk a shot with her single-shot .243. The only way to get within range was to stalk closer and we pulled it off.

It was a great day for both of us. What's even more amazing than the stalk we made to get that deer is the fact that Melissa is a deer hunter at all. Melissa's mother (one of my wife's sisters) was an anti-hunter at one time. When Melissa was growing up, I was concerned that her mother would influence her opinion of hunting and might even prohibit her from taking part in the activity.

Fortunately, the time I spent with both Melissa and her mother was more important. Over the years, they both got subtle exposure to what deer hunting is all about from me. Melissa's mother also got to know other hunters who influenced her opinion of the activity. Even as a baby, Melissa was fascinated with the head mounts of some of the bucks I had taken, which are hanging on the walls of my home. She liked to touch them and frequently asked questions about the animals.

I spend more time hunting deer with a camera than gun or bow and I took Melissa with me to photograph whitetails whenever I could when she was old enough to follow me through the woods. It was while on one of those excursions that Melissa announced to my wife and I that she was going to go deer hunting with me when she was old enough. The matter-of-factness of her statement took us both by surprise. I took her seriously and, from that day on, planned for the day she would join me in the deer woods with a rifle.

As it turned out, Melissa had more of an influence on her mother in regard to her interest in deer hunting. And by the time Melissa was ready to become a hunter, her mother had a much more realistic picture of what hunting was all about than when I met her. My sister-in-law was no longer an anti-hunter and she wasn't going to stand in Melissa's way of trying something she was interested in.

Getting Started

Before Melissa would be eligible to hunt deer or any other species of game in Michigan, she had to complete a hunter safety course. Similar courses are required for youngsters in most states and provinces. I made sure she was enrolled in a class near her home and attended the sessions with her. Fourteen was the minimum age to hunt whitetails with firearms in Michigan at the time, but as mentioned previously, that age has since been lowered to twelve.

Besides what Melissa learned about hunting in the safety class, I gave her copies of an earlier edition of this book as well as other books I've written about deer hunting, to provide her with specific information about what to expect. I'm sure that helped prepare her for deer hunting.

As Melissa's first year of deer hunting neared, I borrowed a scoped .243 for her to hunt with and took her to the range to practice with it. She shot well and I was hoping Melissa could collect her first whitetail during the youth hunt that year.

The weather was mild and there were lots of deer on the Menominee County farm where we hunted on Saturday and Sunday as guests of friend Dean Hulce. Unfortunately, it rained most of one day and the bucks we saw were too far for a shot. The only deer that was close enough for a shot was a doe and Melissa didn't have an antlerless permit.

Her First Deer

It was toward the end of firearms season when I got the chance to take Melissa deer hunting again. The closure of school for the day due to a snowstorm in the northern Upper Peninsula on November 27 proved to be the perfect opportunity for my niece to bag her first whitetail. More than a foot of snow closed all of the schools in Marquette County.

Although the snow was terrible for school attendance, it was great for deer hunting. The storm provided the first significant accumulation of the white stuff across the Upper Peninsula during firearms season that year and I figured deer would be moving when the storm subsided. Whitetails were more active than they had been for most of the season when the snow started on the evening of the twenty-sixth.

We waited until midday to give snowplows time to clear the highways and then drove south out of the snow belt. Our destination was Menominee County, where only a few inches of snow had fallen. We hunted a baited stand on my cousin Craig's property.

I took the time to purchase an antlerless permit for Melissa on the way there, so we would be prepared in case we saw a doe. Craig had seen a number of yearling bucks from the blind we would be occupying, in addition to antlerless deer. I had shot a 9-pointer at the spot the year before.

It was 3:30 P.M. by the time we got in position. About a half hour later, I saw the legs of a deer approaching from the right and Melissa got ready in case there was an opportunity for a shot. The deer proved to be an adult doe that was very cautious.

The deer eventually moved into a shooting lane and my niece asked if she should shoot it. I told her it was up to her. I didn't want to encourage her to do something

Melissa Sterling with her first deer, a doe.

she might later regret. I knew that if we waited, there was a good chance we might see a buck. However, there was certainly nothing wrong with taking a doe. My first whitetail had been a doe.

Before Melissa could make up her mind, the doe moved across the opening into thick cover. A while later, the deer retraced its steps back into the open lane. The doe couldn't seem to make up its mind about which way it wanted to go.

Melissa had made it clear during the drive south that she wanted to shoot a buck. In fact, she said she wanted a 10-pointer (who doesn't). Even though this was her first year of deer hunting, however, and she only had a few days of experience under her belt, she knew that there were no guarantees about getting a buck.

The doe hung around long enough that Melissa finally decided to take the whitetail. She waited for a broadside shot and aimed carefully before squeezing the trigger. The deer bolted at the shot, but I saw it flinch from the hit and it ran with its tail down. I was confident of a solid hit and Melissa also said she felt good about the shot.

We found the doe piled up 60 yards away. I spotted the carcass first about 15 feet ahead of us and then pointed it out to Melissa.

"Is it dead?" she asked and I told her it was.

As we walked closer to inspect the animal she commented, "Now I'm sad."

I told her that was normal and there was nothing wrong with feeling that way. She then asked if she could pet it and I told her she could. As she petted the deer's head and neck she said, "I'm sorry," to the animal.

We leaned our rifles against a tree after taking bullets out of the chambers and I gave my niece a hug, congratulating her at the same time telling her that she did a great job. I told her the doe didn't suffer, that the deer was dead within seconds due to the great shot Melissa made. That seemed to help make her feel better about taking the life of the deer.

The 100-grain bullet from the .243 had connected on the doe's heart and lungs. The whitetail proved to be $3^1/2$ years old.

Her First Buck

Illness caused Melissa to miss the youth hunt the following year and she failed to fill a tag during the gun season. She was anxious to get her first buck during her third year as a deer hunter. We were the guests of Dean Hulce at his Menominee County camp during the youth hunt again that year.

By then Melissa had her own rifle. Her parents had given her a youth-model single-shot New England Firearms .243 mounted with a 3x-9x Bushnell scope as a gift the previous year. She was shooting 100-grain Remington shells.

We hunted a food plot from a ground blind Saturday afternoon and evening. It rained most of the day, reducing deer activity, but when the rain stopped before dark, there was a flurry of whitetail activity. Melissa ended up seeing about ten whitetails, including a pair of spikes, but she decided to wait for a bigger buck.

Antlerless deer and turkeys provided the only action on Sunday morning. On Sunday evening, Melissa changed locations to the large hay field. We saw the spike buck soon after getting in position, and then a bigger buck appeared about 350 yards away near a point of woods. With binoculars, we could tell it had a rack with at least six points.

"I want that one," Melissa said as soon as she got a good look at it through the glasses. "Can we get that one?"

I told her we could try to sneak closer to the deer for a shot and if we were successful in getting within 100 yards, she would have an excellent chance of getting the whitetail. The problem was we had to cross a narrow finger of the field without being seen to get into the woods and then we had to maneuver through the woods toward the feeding buck without spooking any other deer. Fortunately, the buck was facing away from us as he fed.

We managed to make it across the field by moving when the buck had his head down and crouching low to the ground when he lifted his head. Once we got into the woods, we were out of the deer's sight, but we had to be as quiet as possible. A brisk breeze helped cover any noise we made.

Melissa successfully stalked and shot her first buck, an 8-pointer, during a youth deer hunt.

Luck was on our side and we managed to sneak to within 75 yards of the buck. Melissa rested her rifle on a tree limb and dropped the deer in his tracks. We were both pleased on discovering that the buck's antlers had eight points. It was a 2½ year old deer.

As a novice whitetail hunter, Melissa didn't realize how much of an accomplishment it was to successfully stalk that buck. It was a real thrill for me to be a part of the hunt on which she got her first buck in such a challenging way.

Sportsmanship, Safety, and Hunting Ethics

Ethics, sportsmanship, and safety have always been important in deer hunting, and will continue to be. However, the impact these qualities may have on the future of hunting is now more far-reaching than ever before. They will not only be determining factors for the quality of each individual's hunting experience, but also for who, if anyone, will hunt.

There are people who don't understand or approve of hunting. They not only don't hunt, but many of them don't want anyone to do so. These individuals are organized in an effort to stop, or at the very least restrict, hunting. Examples of unethical, unsportsmanlike, and unsafe behavior provide them with ammunition that can be used against hunters and hunting. Any and every incident that may portray hunting or hunters in a bad light is seized and amplified, sometimes distorted.

False Portrayals

A television special on hunting labeled as a documentary and called "The Guns of Autumn" is a perfect example of this technique. It was aired in September 1975. Many, if not all, of the sequences in the show were atypical of hunting as most of us know it. Some of the scenes and sound effects were allegedly changed, according to hunters who took part in the filming. Anyone not familiar with hunting could have easily accepted "The Guns of Autumn" as a fair representation of hunting and formed opinions against the practice. Conservation and hunting organizations filed a number of lawsuits against CBS over the show. Some were won and others were lost.

A similar case, arising from a television program entitled "Say Goodbye," developed in the early 1970s. Alaska sportsmen were involved in this lawsuit. Film of a polar bear tagging project was changed to make it appear that hunters illegally killed a sow with cubs from a helicopter. The case was settled out of court in favor of hunters, according to lawyer John Hendrickson of Anchorage, who represented sportsmen in the case.

Our Image

If there weren't any instances of behavior or actions that were derogatory to hunting, antihunters wouldn't have gotten as much attention as they have. Unfortunately, unethical and unsportsmanlike hunters do exist. In a way, the antihunting movement has been beneficial in focusing attention on undesirable hunters and hunting practices. Once they are identified, something can be done about them. If we as hunters fail to correct any problems that exist, there may come a time when none of us will be able to hunt. To clean house, so to speak, it will be necessary to insist that unethical and unsportsmanlike hunters be kept out of the field.

There was a time when each hunter was held accountable for only his or her actions. That is no longer the case. Every action of any deer hunter reflects on all deer hunters. How I represent myself as a hunter in the field, and anywhere else for that matter, affects you as a deer hunter, and your conduct, likewise, will affect me. For this reason, each deer hunter has a responsibility to all other deer hunters to behave in an ethical, sportsmanlike, and safe manner.

Common Sense

What qualities does it take to be an ethical hunter, a safe hunter, a sportsman? Are the qualifications tough to meet?

The guidelines are so simple, such common-sense things, that every hunter should easily be able to meet them. Before discussing them I want to point out something that should be obvious: All three qualities—ethics, sportsmanship, and safety—are interrelated, although they are not necessarily the same. It is difficult to possess one without the others, though it can be done. Generally, an ethical hunter is a safe hunter, and a safe hunter is usually a sportsman, and so on.

My dictionary defines ethics as the "basic principles of right action." A sportsman is described as "one who abides by a code of fair play." Some people label anyone who hunts a sportsman. To my way of thinking that is the way it should be, but at this time I would consider it a misuse of the word. Safety is "the state or condition of freedom from danger or risk."

The way I read the definitions, sportsmanship is determined by following the rules and regulations of hunting, which in most cases are laws. An ethical hunter does what is right in a hunting situation even though he or she may not be specifically bound by law to do so. It isn't always possible, however, to draw a line between the two.

The three aspects of deer hunting addressed by this chapter are interrelated and it is not difficult to achieve them. In fact, it's easy. Just follow local game laws and common sense.

Consider this example. While still-hunting on my first mule deer hunt I spotted a huge-bodied deer no more than fifty yards away, with its head hidden behind an evergreen tree. Only bucks were legal. The shoulder area of the animal was visible, so I could have shot the deer. In all probability, due to the animal's size, it was a buck.

I didn't shoot, though. In fact, I didn't even consider it. I waited until the deer, which indeed was a huge-racked buck, showed himself before attempting a shot. As it happened, the mulie finally detected my presence and came in the open on the bounce. I missed.

When I told my story to the other hunters in camp one of them said, "Why didn't you shoot him when you had an easy shot? If it had been a doe, no one would have known the difference." That man, whom I wouldn't have been sharing a camp with if there had been a choice, was wrong. I would have known the difference if I shot a deer without identifying the sex and it turned out to be a doe.

Anyway, if I had shot that buck when I first saw him, even though I didn't know it was a buck at the time, I wouldn't have broken the law. Shooting before I saw antlers would have been wrong, however, because the possibility of breaking the law existed. So was what the other hunter suggested unsportsman-like or unethical? In my opinion it was both.

I can thank my father as the first among many who instilled attitudes in me becoming of a sportsman and ethical hunter.

There are times when, according to the definitions, ethical and sportsmanlike behavior can be separated. Suppose a wounded deer comes by your stand. You have a moral and ethical obligation to finish that animal if possible, although you may not be required by law to do so.

The same considerations apply if the hunter who wounded the buck or doe comes on its track. You killed the deer; you can tag it. But at least offering the white-tail or mulie to the person who drew first blood would be the right thing to do, depending upon the severity of the wound. Whether you had already tagged the animal before the other hunter arrived would also have a bearing on the situation.

Ethical Responsibility

Deer hunters have an ethical responsibility to their quarry to use an adequate weapon and projectile that can be handled efficiently; try for a clean, killing shot; expend every effort possible to trail and finish a wounded animal; and clean and care for the meat properly.

One year my brother and I helped another party of hunters track a whitetail one of its members wounded. It proved to be a two-day effort to kill the doe. I dropped the deer, but relinquished it to the other hunters, as we planned to do from the start.

Hunters also have an ethical obligation to each other and to hunting to pick up litter left by others; to avoid unnecessary public display of dead deer; to understand deer management practices; and to avoid unnecessary conversation about the kill, dwelling instead on the many other aspects of deer hunting such as sights, sounds, and feelings that are seen, heard, and experienced during days in the field.

I think it is extremely important that hunters be more conscious of what they say about hunting and to whom they say it. I have heard tales from well-intentioned hunters that almost turned my stomach. Imagine how a nonhunter (not necessarily an antihunter) would take such accounts. Unnecessarily gory stories from hunters themselves may easily convert a nonhunter to an anti-hunter.

Deer hunters have an ethical responsibility to the animals they hunt by doing everything possible to ensure a clean kill and then to expend every effort possible to finish a wounded deer as quickly as possible.

Ethics Can Be Personal

Everyone's ethics don't have to be the same. In fact, they differ among many hunters based on where the hunters spent most of their time hunting and the hunting traditions there, and there's nothing wrong with that. Most deer hunters may consider hunting with hounds unethical because the practice is illegal in many places, but for those hunters who grew up deer hunting with dogs in the southeastern United States or Ontario, it's part of their tradition and it's perfectly acceptable. The same thing applies to deer hunting with bait. It is legal in some states and provinces, but is illegal in others. Some hunters think baiting is unethical and others think it's no different than hunting any other food source.

Each view is actually correct, given the associated background and life experiences. It's natural for a hunter who spent their lifetime hunting in a state where dogging deer or baiting are illegal to consider these practices unethical. By the same token, it makes sense that hunters who grew up where those methods are legal and acceptable would consider them ethical, though that's not always the case. The bottom line is that it's important to understand and accept that personal ethics vary. In those circumstances, it's best to agree to disagree.

Is Hunting A Sport?

Something I have done a lot of thinking about is the classification of hunting as a sport. In the truest sense of the word I don't think hunting is a sport, but rather a sporting endeavor or pursuit. A sport is usually thought of as a match or contest between two willing teams or players that provides recreation. There is no doubt that hunting provides plenty of recreation. Take the word willing out and hunting fits the rest of the definition, too.

"Willing" is the key word, though, at least from the antihunters' point of view. Deer certainly don't participate in a hunt willingly. Calling hunting a sport can be and has been criticized for that reason.

No one can argue that hunting as it is practiced today is not a sporting endeavor. Regulations are largely designed to give deer more of an advantage than they already have over hunters by restricting the time and manner in which a hunter can harvest them. Many hunters handicap themselves further by using bows and arrows, muzzleloaders, and handguns in their pursuit of deer. My line of reasoning here may be classified as nit-picking by some people, but I think it has merit.

To be sportsmen or -women, deer hunters should hunt only during prescribed hours, not take more whitetails or mule deer than specified by law, not shoot deer of a protected sex, not shoot protected species of wildlife, ask permission before hunting private land, not litter (spent cartridges are litter), and make sure of their targets before shooting—which leads us to the subject of safety.

Safety

As I mentioned earlier, sportsmen and women are usually safe hunters. Most hunting accidents are caused by gun or bowhunters who are acting in an unsportsmanlike manner by ignoring regulations. Carelessness also enters the picture in many instances.

I remember reading an account in which carelessness and breaking a game law proved to be a deadly combination on a deer hunt. A pair of hunters were working through some heavy cover when one of them spotted a grouse in a tree. Grouse season was closed, high powered rifles shouldn't be shot in the air at any time, and the fellow didn't know where his partner was. He shot anyway. The bullet killed his companion.

This is only one example of many. Another illegal activity that often results in hunters ending up on the wrong end of their guns is carrying them loaded either in a vehicle or in camp. Leaning a loaded firearm against a tree or building or on a car is asking for trouble, too. Poor gun handling also accounts for its share of woundings and deaths. Shooting down a road, resting the barrel of a gun on an occupied boot, and disregard for the direction the muzzle of a gun is pointing can have serious consequences.

Treat Guns As Though Always Loaded

A firearm should always be treated as if it is loaded. Whenever you pick one up, check to see that the chamber is empty; don't take someone's word for it. After a day in the field, make sure all shells are removed from magazine and chamber. Work the action over and over again, then look or feel in the head of the chamber and magazine to make sure no unejected shells remain.

Don't remove only the cartridges you thought you put in. Sometimes, somehow, there happens to be one more than there was supposed to be.

I will never forget an experience that taught me a lesson in this respect. When returning to my car after hunting I used to remove the number of shells I knew I put in, then point the firearm at the ground, away from the vehicle or anyone with me, and pull the trigger so the gun wouldn't be stored in a cocked position. One evening when I did that, my gun discharged. There was no real harm done, except the unexpected shot scared me. That lesson taught me to check and double-check to make sure all ammunition is ejected.

To illustrate that my experience wasn't a freak occurrence, a similar incident that happened to a friend of mine is worth mentioning. On his way home from deer hunt-

Always treat firearms as though they are loaded and keep them pointed in a safe direction.

Always use a rope to raise and lower gun or bow from a tree stand. Never have a shell in the chamber when doing so.

ing, my friend was stopped by a conservation officer who asked to see his gun. He assured the officer the rifle was unloaded, which he was sure of, but when the warden worked the action a cartridge came out.

Never point a gun or an arrow in the direction of people or buildings. Always know where your hunting partners are. If there is a chance they are in the line of fire of a deer, don't shoot. No whitetail or mule deer is worth the possible injury or death of a person.

Horseplay and guns don't mix. Neither do alcohol and hunting. In fact, hunting while being intoxicated is illegal in many parts of North America and severe penalties are possible for those guilty of doing so. Always try to make sure there are no obstructions in the barrel of a gun, only use the proper ammunition, always keep the safety on until ready to shoot, and never shoot at a flat, hard surface or at water.

If crossing a fence or some other obstruction pass the rifle, shotgun, or bow over or under first; break the action or unload a gun if you have to carry it. Use a rope to lift and lower unloaded firearms and bows to and from tree stands. I've lost track of the number of instances I've heard or read about involving deer hunters who have been seriously injured or killed by their own guns when they discharged as they were being raised or lowered from a tree stand. Many hunters obviously do not comprehend how dangerous that process can be, but they should understand that a firearm that does not have a bullet or shell in the chamber, or a cap or primer on the nipple in the case of a muzzleloader, cannot fire.

One of the cases I know of in which a rifle discharged when it was lowered to the ground from a tree stand was especially tragic because it involved a boy who should not have had a firearm in his possession in the first place. He was hunting during a youth deer hunt that restricted kids his age to using archery equipment. He was supposed to have a nonhunting adult at least eighteen years old with him, but he was alone. The fact that laws were broken was bad enough, but carelessness is what cost the boy his life.

He left a bullet in the chamber of the rifle he was using as he lowered it toward the ground. The rifle barrel was pointed upward as the gun was lowered. Twigs or branches apparently disengaged the safety and then hit the trigger as the rifle descended, with the bullet striking the boy. If the boy had been hunting legally, there's no way this accident could have happened.

Use A Fall Restraint Device

Always use a safety belt or harness when in a tree stand to prevent accidental falls. Harnesses are a far better choice than belts or straps because they will hold you in an upright position in the event of a fall. I've worn a Seat-O-The-Pants harness for years and have found them simple to use and comfortable. If you wear a safety belt, make sure it's secured under your arms rather than around your waist.

This is such a commonsense precaution, yet too many hunters fail to take it and some of them end up paying for it with their lives. Those who aren't killed usually end up with serious injuries. Every year deer hunters are injured or killed in falls from tree stands because they failed to wear a fall restraint device.

It is equally important to use a safety belt when putting up and taking down hang-on tree stands. Safety belts should be used when climbing in and out of tree stands whenever possible, too.

Be Sure Of Your Target

Above all else, be sure of your target. Seeing a movement or a color, or hearing a sound is not enough to warrant a shot. Do not shoot until you are absolutely positive your target is a legal deer. Also, as a point of safety, firearms hunters should try to avoid wearing brown, gray, or white garments that might increase their chances of being mistaken for a deer. Many states now require gun hunters to wear fluorescent orange in varying amounts, which has significantly reduced mistaken-identity acci-

Always wear a fall restraint device when hunting from a tree stand. A harness like the one worn by Craig Smith in this photo is better than a safety belt, but a belt is better than nothing. A safety belt is also recommended when climbing in and out of a tree stand.

dents. It is a good idea to wear garments of this material even if it is not mandatory. When walking to and from hunting locations in the dark, always use a flashlight.

One other point: Just because a deer hunter happens to be carrying a gun in the woods doesn't mean it must be fired. Shooting at tin cans and various other inanimate targets will only spook deer the other way. Target practice should be done on the range.

Bowhunters must be extremely careful with broadheads. If they are as sharp as they should be, they are capable of causing injury at any time, not just when released from a bow. Keep heads in covered quivers until ready for use. Never shoot a broadhead up in the air.

Hunter Safety Courses

Many states now require young hunters to pass safety courses before they can obtain licenses. This is an excellent way to make sure future generations of hunters will be adequately versed in safe hunting practices. When young hunters are starting out is the best time to get them thinking of safety.

My father saw to it that my brother and I completed a hunter's safety course before we got our first hunting licenses. He also emphasized safety when in the field with us. From my experience I can appreciate the value of early introduction in gun and bow safety.

Choose Partners Wisely

Each deer hunter should not only strive to be ethical, safe, and a sportsman, but he or she should also expect the same from hunting companions. This becomes especially important for safety. It is a proven fact that the vast majority of hunting accidents involve members of the same party.

One of the best ways to become acquainted with sportsmen in your area is to join a sportsmen's club. Another benefit of membership is that most clubs have facilities for target practice. Membership in sportsmen's clubs on the local, state, and national levels is also a great way to promote proper hunting practices and get the hunter's story to nonhunters.

Participating in National Hunting and Fishing Day, which is now an annual observance during late September, is one of the best ways to do this. There are ways to tell your story on a continuing basis, too. One club in California, for instance, collects outdoor magazines from its members for distribution in school libraries, doctors' offices, and other key locations where they are sure to be read. Another way to reach people is through club-sponsored slide shows and lectures at schools or meetings of civic organizations. Deer and deer hunting are popular topics, and many groups are interested in learning more about both.

A sportsmen's club near where I live makes sure everyone entering and leaving the city gets a reminder about safety and sportsmanship in hunting. There is a sign along the highway that carries a message on each side. One side reads, "Stretch Your Story, Not Your Bag Limit," and the other, "Recognize Your Game First, Then Shoot." They are simple reminders, but passing motorists think about them. Drawing attention to these qualities is sure to help the image of the club as well as hunters in general.

Foster A Positive Image

Sportsmen's groups should also be constantly vigilant for newspaper articles or letters to the editor that make hunters look bad. Try to respond to them in a sensible manner in a letter to the editor. If facts have been twisted, do your best to straighten them out. Most people read their local newspaper, so this is an excellent way to reach nonhunters.

Clubs can display their disapproval of the shooting of protected animals or birds by offering rewards for information leading to the conviction of guilty parties. This helps the legitimate hunters' image.

One winter some poachers using bows and arrows got into a local deer pen that was part of a small zoo, killing three of the animals. Our archery club immediately reacted by offering a reward to help in locating the culprits. We let everyone know our disapproval through radio broadcasts and letters in the local paper. The criminals were not apprehended, but at least the public was made aware that serious bowhunters weren't going to take the blame for such actions.

Illegal hunting is probably one of deer hunting's biggest black eyes. Estimates in some states put the illegal deer kill as high as or higher than the annual legal kill. Always try to be on the watch for poaching or other infractions of game laws and report any incidents to local officials. Most states have toll-free numbers hunters can call to report violators. Under many programs of this type, tipsters turn in poachers anonymously and can claim a reward by using an identifying number.

Proper Attitude

Before concluding this chapter I would like to point out that a hunter's attitude toward hunting and the quarry probably has the most bearing on whether or not he or she will be ethical and exhibit sportsmanship.

Hunters who view hunting primarily as killing, for example, and feel they must get a deer at all costs, can't be ethical or sportsmanlike. They often must break game laws to attain their goal. These individuals miss out on the true benefits of hunting.

Hunting's primary benefit is recreational: simply to be in the outdoors; to relax in space unconfined by walls and buildings; to see, hear, experience, and learn about the many aspects of nature. Learning about and respecting deer is a major part of deer hunting; shooting a deer is of secondary importance. Nonetheless, all of us want to be successful in our attempts to bag a deer, even though the odds are against most of us. Realizing all of this is part of the attitude that breeds ethics and sportsmanship. You try your hardest against the odds, savor every moment afield, and hunger for every clue that will tell you something about a particular whitetail or mulie, or about deer in general so that you might see one, might kill one.

Yet if the season comes to a close and you haven't scored, you still feel satisfied that you tried your best and can accept hunting for what it is: hours, days, months, and years of looking, learning, waiting, searching, and hoping—not killing. It is enough to whet a true deer hunter's appetite for the next season.

Hunter safety classes are mandatory for youngsters and first-time hunters in most states and provinces, which is a good thing. This reduces the chances of accidents when they start hunting.

Choose your hunting partners wisely. It can have a bearing on your safety. Hunting with partners who are unsportsmanlike, unsafe, or unethical can detract from the experience.

Success without Success

Features of my surroundings were losing their distinctness as the light faded at the end of a day of deer hunting. This time it was more than the end of a day, however: It was the end of a season, and I hadn't gotten a deer.

Actually, my attempts to bag a deer had spanned three seasons: There had been a regular firearms hunt, the special muzzleloader season, and a period for bow and arrow. These were the final minutes of that last season. My chances of getting a deer for the year faded with the light.

I climbed down from my tree stand and walked to a nearby road to wait for my partner to pick me up. I would be lying if I said I wasn't disappointed. I was. After all, anticipation of connecting with a deer was one of the primary motivating forces responsible for getting me in the woods in the first place. There was more behind my being in the outdoors day after day, though.

The disappointment wasn't solely because I didn't get a deer. The fact that I wouldn't get another opportunity to hunt deer with gun or bow until the next fall was as much, if not more, a part of the feeling. Reflecting on the past two months of deer hunting while waiting for my ride, I realized my lengthy season had been successful even though I didn't tag a deer. A variety of experiences helped make it so.

One of the experiences was when a white weasel came by my stand on the second day of the regular firearms hunt. The weasel was wearing its winter coat of white, and it stood out in sharp contrast to its surroundings, since there wasn't any snow on the ground.

The streamlined predator thoroughly investigated a brush pile next to me, then started away after finding no prey. A squeak from my lips that imitated the sound a small mammal might make stopped the weasel in its tracks. After staring in bewilderment into the brush pile, it dove back in for another look around.

This white weasel added success for me to a day of deer hunting.

Then a red squirrel got into the act. It apparently saw the off-colored animal and came to investigate.

The squirrel made a couple of passes at the weasel as it came out of the brush pile for the second time. Oddly enough, the predator dodged the advances of the squirrel rather than attacking. Maybe it was still confused about the source of the squeak. At any rate, I let the weasel continue on its way that time, chuckling to myself as it went.

I have found that deer hunting is more than hours spent in the field with the sole intent of getting a shot at a whitetail or mulie. Deer hunting is a total immersion in the outdoors. From my point of view, any experience that makes the hunter feel more a part of the outdoors has to be considered a success. Seeing and shooting deer can be part of that success, but they don't have to be.

Success is the sum of all the experiences on a deer hunt that make the hunter's days afield worthwhile, the little and big things that make time in the outdoors richer. Hearing, seeing, and interacting with all forms of wildlife, such as the weasel I mentioned, are part of the success of a deer hunt, to me.

Year of the Predator

And I'm not alone in that regard. Many hunters feel the same, including my friend Jim Butler, who had some amazing encounters with a number of predators one fall while hunting and scouting for deer. On Christmas Eve, the rural Upper Michigan resident gave a coyote an unexpected Christmas present by saving its life. If it hadn't been for Butler, the predator would not have survived to see Christmas. Jim, who lives in Iron County near Crystal Falls, did not spare the coyote's life willingly, of course. His mere presence in the woods that day worked in the predator's favor.

Butler thinks he has too many coyotes on his property. He said he often hears the animals howling from several different locations while hunting during the fall. If it were up to him, he probably would have liked to have seen the coyote dead, but the circumstances were out of his hands.

Besides plenty of coyotes, some wolves also spend time on Jim's farm. He said he sees the tracks of what he thinks are four wolves that pass through the area every few days. Wolves and coyotes don't get along. The larger predators try to kill their competition whenever they get the chance.

The Butlers were having a family gathering on the afternoon of Christmas Eve, so Jim didn't plan on hunting that day. He's an avid deer hunter who spends as much time as possible bowhunting, but he also spends time afield with a rifle and muzzleloader during the respective seasons. Some fresh snow had fallen, so Butler decided to take a walk through an area he often hunts to see where the deer were moving.

Jim left the house at noon and he didn't bother taking a gun or bow and arrow with him because he wasn't planning on being gone long. He was walking on a deer trail when he saw two animals running, with one chasing the other. He thought they were deer at first, but as they got closer, he could tell it was a wolf chasing a coyote.

The wolf ended up chasing the coyote down the same deer trail Jim was walking on. When he realized they didn't know he was there and weren't going to stop, he reacted instinctively by quickly moving off to the side of the trail, waving his arms above his head and hollering as loud has he could. The coyote ran right by Jim close enough that he said he could have spit on it.

The wolf was only 13 to 15 feet behind the coyote. The wolf came to a screeching halt about 30 feet from Jim when it realized he was a person, then turned and left. The coyote was obviously more afraid of the wolf than a human. Jim said the coyote was probably glad to see him.

Butler added that he had found the remains of a coyote in one of his fields earlier in the year and he's sure a wolf or wolves killed that one. Based on the tracks in the snow, Jim said the wolf had been chasing the coyote for a long time, and probably would have caught it, if he hadn't shown up. As a result of his holiday jaunt, the hunter had an interesting story to share with his family over dinner.

That was actually only one of a number of unusual encounters that Jim had with predators that fall. He referred to it as "the year of the predator" due to the series of exciting episodes he had with coyotes, wolves, black bears, and bobcats. The opening day of bow deer season (October 1) is a prime example.

Jim had close encounters with a coyote and black bear that day. It was too windy to get in a tree stand, so Butler sat against a tree on the ground near a food plot containing rye and clover. At one point, he turned and looked behind him and saw a coyote in high grass a matter of feet away. Jim said both of their eyes got big from the surprise of seeing each other so close. After realizing it was too close to a person, the coyote took off.

Jim said he thinks the coyote was stalking him. He commented that it probably saw some movement of an arm or his head along the trunk of the tree he was sitting against and it snuck closer, thinking the movement was made by possible prey. Then, when Jim turned around, the coyote recognized him as a person.

Not long after the coyote disappeared, a 200-pound black bear came out of the same patch of cover the coyote disappeared in and began to feed in the food plot. The bear fed right up to Jim and walked by him about 5 feet away, not knowing he was there.

"If I would have had a bear tag, I could have easily gotten that bear with my bow," Butler said.

About a week after seeing the coyote and bear, Jim was hunting from the ground in a swamp in a different area and he saw an animal coming toward him. He thought it was a coyote at first. He could see the predator was carrying an animal in its mouth. As the predator got closer, Jim could tell it was a bobcat, not a coyote. He could also tell the animal it was carrying was blocking its vision.

Consequently, the cat was almost on top of Jim before it realized something wasn't right. He said the cat dropped the animal it was holding in its mouth and nervously stomped a front foot as deer often do when trying to get a hunter to move. Jim froze, but the cat eventually could tell it was in potential danger and took off, leaving its prey behind.

Jim said the cat had been carrying a muskrat. He thought it was a female carrying food back to kittens.

Better Than Bagging A Buck

Although Iron River, Michigan, attorney Steve Polich didn't bag a whitetail on opening day of bow deer season one year, he went home with a far more exciting and unique experience to talk about than most bowhunters did that day. He got the rare opportunity to witness the strategies of two of the Upper Peninsula's top predators—a wolf and a black bear—in their efforts to secure an injured doe.

Who came out on top? You might be surprised by the answer.

Polich set out to hunt from a tree stand on the east side of a food plot on a large chunk of private land during the afternoon of October 1. As he approached the food plot on foot around two-thirty, he noticed four deer were already feeding in the opening planted with clover. He could tell two of the deer were small bucks and he didn't want to spook them, so he remained where he was, hoping they would soon finish feeding and return to nearby woods.

The third deer was obscured by brush and the fourth was a doe. Polich said she was looking intently at him and he was sure she could see him. He was surprised she wasn't leaving the field, but he later got a better idea of why her behavior wasn't normal.

The other deer eventually moved off, so Steve kept watching the doe. After about ten minutes, the doe turned and Steve could see the gash on her flank, with body parts hanging out of a large hole. The bowhunter's initial reaction was that someone had wounded the deer, but, upon looking more closely with his binoculars, he figured the wound was too large to have been caused by an arrow.

After a long wait, the doe left the food plot and bedded in a berry patch nearby, allowing Steve to climb into his tree stand around three o'clock. The injured white-tail was 125 to 150 yards away. The doe didn't remain bedded for long, according to Polich. It kept getting up, moving a short distance, and lying down again.

"In the meantime, various deer were coming and going from the food plot," Steve said. "Her presence made them nervous. I had an inclination to shoot the doe, but I didn't want to mess up my first day of bowhunting. I decided to wait until late in the day to take care of her since I normally leave my tree stand before it's too dark to shoot anyway.

"At one point, there were ten to twelve deer on the food plot," Polich continued. "By then, the injured doe had moved to a second berry patch. All of a sudden, the deer in the opening were all alert to something. The next thing I see is a wolf.

"The wolf was coming to where the doe laid down. Deer in the food plot were wired, just watching him. The deer finally ran and the wolf ran, too, going 30 yards, running right past the berry patch the doe was in.

"After things calmed down, the wolf went back to the doe's scent trail and resumed following it. When the wolf got five yards from the berry patch, the doe charged him and he ran away. That really surprised me. I thought the more than 100-pound wolf would have grabbed the deer and finished her off.

"The wolf simply meandered off, going up a nearby ridge and out of sight. It just made no sense, based on what I thought I knew about wolves. Then I thought he might go get a couple of friends and come back.

"About 20 minutes from dark, all of the deer in the food plot got alert again," Steve said. "I thought wolves were coming back. The deer bolted and within a few minutes, here comes a black bear in the 300-pound range. I've shot bears between 150 and 500 pounds, so I'm familiar with judging their size.

"He looked like he was coming in to eat clover in the food plot. Then he got downwind of the injured doe and turned into the wind. He didn't change pace. He continued moving at a casual gait like you often see bears walking through the forest.

"The bear homed right in on the doe. When he was almost to her, she started to get up and, with lightning speed, he grabbed her by the neck and flipped her around. The bear was making a growling sound and the deer was screaming. Then there was a crunch like if you took a dry one inch piece of maple and hit it against a tree. Then the doe was silent.

"I thought the bear was going to rip her apart and eat her right there," Polich continued, "but he emerged from the berry patch, dragging the doe between his legs, with her neck in his mouth, and went back across the food plot and off the way he came from. It looked awkward the way he was dragging the deer, but he was not having a problem doing it.

The experience of watching a black bear kill and carry off a doe was exciting for one bowhunter who considered it better than bagging a buck.

"I was amazed with the ease and speed with which the bear handled this. It was all over in 15 to 20 seconds. Witnessing what I did that evening was an amazing experience. When I got home, my son asked me if I got anything. I told him, 'I got a much better experience than shooting something.'"

It's a matter of speculation what was responsible for the doe's original injuries. Maybe a wolf such as the one Steve saw had caught the doe and she managed to get away. She also might have injured herself while running through the woods, as whitetails sometimes do. However the wildlife drama started, the lucky deer hunter was able to witness the final acts of a show that seldom has an audience, and he was glad he did.

Other Things

There are other things, too, such as witnessing a beautiful sunrise or being so enchanted with the stillness of the forest you hesitate to interrupt it by moving. Many of the experiences that add to the success of a hunt are difficult to share with others. They can't be brought home like a deer. Even fellow hunters may find it hard to appreciate the singular value of your particular moments in the field.

Experiences that add to the success of a hunt are not always individual things. Good companionship and sharing the good fortune of another member of the party who tagged a deer are also part of it. The afternoon I saw the white weasel, my brother dropped a buck. His success made my day more successful.

If downing a deer were necessary for every hunter to have a successful hunt, the number of those going afield after deer each year would decline. Instead, their ranks have increased dramatically since I started deer hunting. Only a small percentage of those who go afield score. The remainder find something compelling about deer hunting other than the kill that brings them back year after year. Most hunters enjoy a hunt without bagging a deer: success without success.

Success without success is one of the easiest things to achieve on a deer hunt. No one can tell hunters how to do it; it just happens. Consistently being successful in collecting a whitetail or mule deer, on the other hand, is one of the most difficult aspects of deer hunting. That is why this book and others like it devote most of their content to the know-how involved in getting close enough to deer to shoot them, rather than the peripheral joys of deer hunting.

I think such lopsided treatment tends to emphasize the kill rather than the hunt and its sidelights, no matter how unintentional this highlighting is. But the trees, plants, shrubs, insects, birds, reptiles, amphibians, and mammals other than deer are just as much a part of the deer hunter's world as whitetails and mulies.

As I mentioned in previous chapters, killing a deer should be considered a bonus of the hunt. If it is viewed as a necessary part, only a fraction of hunters will be truly successful.

Seeing that white weasel and sharing in my brother's kill were only a couple of highlights of that year I didn't get a deer. One extremely successful day during the muzzleloading season I saw no less than thirty-three deer. Every last one of them was bald—no antlers. Only antlered bucks were legal during the hunt, but it was nice to look over that many animals. The frequent sightings kept up my hopes of eventually seeing a buck.

A comical show put on by a ruffed grouse that day also made it a little more successful. All the trees were coated with ice from freezing drizzle. The bird landed in a maple tree near me to pick at buds. It was slipping and sliding as it tried to maintain a grip on the icy branches. From its actions the grouse looked intoxicated.

The more I thought about the days I hunted deer as I waited for my ride on that last day of hunting, the more I realized how successful they had been. I smiled as I remembered an antler I found in December. I was hunting with bow and arrow then. There were three of us, and I was making a drive toward my friends Bill and Kirwin when I spotted an antler in the snow. It had four points. The beam had been shed recently; there was still blood on the base.

I tucked the shed antler in my pocket and when I reached my partners I tried to convince them I got a shot at a buck and my arrow knocked the antler off. But I have a hard time keeping a straight face when trying to fool someone, and they knew I was pulling their legs.

Two days later, Kirwin arrowed a beautiful buck that had shed one antler. It wasn't the same animal that dropped the antler I found, though. The beam remaining on the deer's head was much larger than the one I picked up. The deer was killed miles from where we had been before, too. Kirwin's success and finding that shed antler contributed to my successful year of deer hunting.

Sharing in the success of other members of your hunting party is a big part of deer hunting. My brother bagged a buck the year I didn't score, making my own season more successful.

My reminiscing was interrupted by approaching headlights that I knew would be my partner. "Maybe Bill got one," I thought. But I knew it didn't matter. The collective seasons had been successful even though I didn't get a deer. Bill would feel the same way if he hadn't scored.

INDEX